Wages of Crime

Wages of Crime

*Black Markets, Illegal Finance,
and the Underworld Economy*

R. T. Naylor

CORNELL UNIVERSITY PRESS
ITHACA AND LONDON

First published 2002 by Cornell University Press

Printed in the United States of America

Library of Congress Cataloging-in-Publication Data

Naylor, R.T., 1945–
  Wages of crime : black markets, illegal finance, and the underworld economy / R.T. Naylor.
     p. cm.
  Includes bibliographical references and index.
  ISBN 0-8014-3949-3 (cloth : alk. paper)
     1. Crime—Economic aspects.   2. Organized crime—Economic aspects.
3. Informal sector (Economics).   4. Black market.   5. Money laundering.   I. Title.
  HV6791 .N34 2002
  338.4'3364—dc21

                              2001005580

Cornell University Press strives to use environmentally responsible suppliers and materials to the fullest extent possible in the publishing of its books. Such materials include vegetable-based, low-VOC inks and acid-free papers that are recycled, totally chlorine-free, or partly composed of nonwood fibers. For further information, visit our website at www.cornellpress.cornell.edu.

Cloth printing   10 9 8 7 6 5 4 3 2 1

Contents

Acknowledgments

Over the years, as the various chapters of this book were written and rewritten, I have incurred an enormous number of debts—to colleagues, students, law enforcement and justice personnel, professional journalists, and others who must remain anonymous. Only a few can be acknowledged properly here. Thanks in particular to Peter Andreas, Margaret Beare, Alan Block, Jack Blum, Petrus van Duyne, Brenda Grantland, Dave Kaplan, Mike Klare, Mike Levi, Peter Lupsha, Bill Marsden, Willard Myers, Ethan Nadelman, Nikos Passas, Peter Reuter, Paul Saint-Denis, Francisco Thoumi, and Phil Williams. Thanks, too, to Deane Taylor for help in preparing the manuscript, and to my editor, Roger Haydon. Thanks as well to the John D. and Catherine T. MacArthur Foundation of Chicago and the Social Sciences and Humanities Research Council of Canada for financial support. And thanks to the many other persons who played a role, sometimes inadvertent, occasionally even unwilling, in the creation of each of the chapters in this book.

Chapter 1 began as a seminar talk to a group of senior Canadian government functionaries from the ministries of justice and foreign affairs, with the then-director of the Canadian Security Intelligence Service sitting alone in a corner (as a good spook, he was determined to remain inconspicuous; hence he was the only person in the room without a name tag). The argument developed further into a background paper for presentation to a round table initiated by the Justice Department and Solicitor General's office, in a futile attempt to stop the police lobby in Canada from persuading politicians to mimic dangerous legislative initiatives in the United States. Alas, in subsequent years, each time an election was called, the politicians caved in a little further. The material first appeared in print in "From Cold War to Crime War: The Search for a New 'National Security' Threat," *Transnational Organized Crime* 1, no. 4 (winter 1995); and in "Mafias, Myths and Markets: The Theory and Practice of Enterprise Crime," in the same journal, vol. 3, no. 3 (1997). The two have been united, revised, and considerably updated here, although the core message remains the same.

Chapter 2 began as lectures in a course titled "The Underground Economy" at McGill University. I developed it further into a series of talks to peace and arms control groups in North America. It was first published as "The Insurgent Economy: Black Market Operations of Guerrilla Groups," *Crime, Law, and Social Change* 20 (1993). It was polished further in "The Rise of the Modern Arms Black Market and the Fall of Supply Side Control" in *Society under Siege: Crime, Violence, and Illegal Weapons,* ed. Virginia Gamba (Halfway House, South Africa, 1998). For this volume the argument has been extensively revised and updated, with the context and conclusions completely revamped and the political message made clearer.

Chapter 3 grew out of similar roots. It was presented to audiences ranging from the Committee on International Security Studies of the American Academy of Arts and Sciences in Boston in 1996 to the KPMG International Forensic Accounting Conference in San Francisco in 1998. The ideas first materialized in print as "The Structure and Operation of the Modern Arms Black Market," in *Lethal Commerce: The Global Trade in Small Arms and Light Weapons,* ed. Jeffrey Boutwell, Michael Klare, and Laura Reed (Cambridge, Mass., 1995), and in "Loose Cannons: Covert Commerce and Underground Finance in the Modern Arms Black Market," *Crime, Law, and Social Change* 22 (1995). A shortened but clarified and updated version appeared as "Gunsmoke and Mirrors: Financing the Illegal Trade," in *Running Guns: The Global Black Market in Small Arms,* ed. Lora Lumpe (London, 2000). Arms control groups too often substitute anguish for analysis and push two central messages, both of which are wrong. One is that the real problem in the world is "light" rather than "heavy" arms—a division that no longer makes much military, technological, or commercial sense. The second is the conviction, which a glance at history should dispel, that the answer to proliferation lies in tighter supply-side controls. Not only does tighter supply-side control never work in the long run, but in societies whose citizens have no effective voice, a frequent result of international arms control efforts is to reinforce the power of illegitimate regimes. Gunrunners may be greedy and unsavory, but like undertakers and divorce lawyers, they are sometimes necessary.

Chapter 4 has a more varied history. It too began as course lectures on the topics of the underground economy and economic crime; it then went on the road as a series of talks to forensic accounting firms, law enforcement gatherings, and criminology conferences. Some of the material first appeared in print as chapter 1 in a United Nations report from the Office for Drug Control and Crime Prevention—Jack Blum, Michael Levi, Thomas Naylor, and Phil Williams, *Financial Havens, Banking Secrecy, and Money Laundering* (Vienna, 1998). As the UN report was being drafted by that office, it became clear there were serious disagreements, at least on my part, about some of the conclusions that were being drawn. The report was scheduled to be presented to the UN General Assembly in June 1998. As I feared, the report became ammunition for declaring a global money-laundering crisis and calling for changes in legislation that would radically increase law enforcement's power to prosecute as well as shift the burden of proof from the government's prosecutor to the defendant.[1]

The UN report had other aftereffects. Shortly after it was published, the phone in my university office rang. On the other end was a Canadian Crown prosecutor eager to recruit me as an expert witness in a money-laundering case. I told him I would be glad to do so if he was prepared for me to tell the court that money laundering is an artificial and contrived offense that has no place in the statute books of a civilized country. We concluded with an agreement that he would call me after the trial and we could exchange views in more detail. I am still waiting.

The UN report also led to an invitation to address a conference staged by the Royal Canadian Mounted Police to celebrate their success in prodding the Canadian government into a sweeping new anti-money-laundering law. However, after the invitation was issued, a little police intelligence work into the suspect's background led to a prompt disinvitation. When one of the co-authors of the UN report, invited in my place, arrived at the event, he was presented with a newspaper article in which I had denounced the new legislation, and he was asked if he would dedicate part of his public remarks to repudiating it. As he chuckled to me later that night over the second bottle of wine, it was an honor he respectfully declined. The current chapter 4 uses roughly the same analytical framework as the UN work, but it is transformed in content and tone and considerably fleshed out in detail.

Chapter 5 has a similar history but with slightly different audiences. It developed as well from confidential discussions with participants in the gold and jewelry business. This business truly represents beauty and the beast—dazzling if useless objets d'art are produced and marketed in an ambiance from which all the required information for a veritable encyclopedia of crime could easily be distilled. Material related to this chapter was first published as "The Underworld of Gold," *Crime, Law, and Social Change* 25 (1996). The material has been revised and updated for inclusion in this volume.

Chapter 6 began with a talk in Miami in 1989 at an event that billed itself as the world's first money-laundering conference. Perhaps the high point of enlightenment for the assembled cops and spooks, bankers and lawyers, was the keynote speech by the then attorney general of the United States in which he explained that a cornflakes box stuffed with green-backs weighs fully 18 pounds. No one made the obvious rejoinder—that a politician stuffed with self-importance probably weighs closer to 180. The material in this chapter developed further through the usual rounds of academic, professional, and law enforcement gatherings in North America and Europe. During the course of this development, two things became clear.

One was that the numbers being bandied about—supposedly to show the extent of the problem of criminal money flows—were essentially fraudulent. This was brought home dramatically in 1990 when I was invited to address an upscale conference on drug trafficking in Florence. Senior law enforcement figures denounced the menace of organized crime and cited the views of "experts" as proof that their fears were well founded. Also present was one of the UN officials responsible for creating the infamous estimate that the world drug trade generated an annual turnover of $500 billion. I diplomatically suggested to him that to get such a number, he and his colleagues must have not only included the value of every donkey owned by every campesino in the Andes but priced those donkeys as if they cost as much as a pickup truck. His response was to huff away. But he returned a while later, perhaps mellowed by cocktails, to suggest that although there were problems with the number, it was great for catching public attention.[2]

The second thing that became obvious during these peregrinations was the authoritarian self-righteousness of proponents of the new follow-the-money fad in crime control policy. A senior officer of the U.S. Financial Crimes Center (FinCEN) to whom I made the mistake of expressing skepticism told me that their new proceeds-of-crime approach was the long-sought magic bullet of crime control. Anyone who opposed it was, in his book, a sympathizer of the world's terrorists and drug dealers. Later he mellowed enough to chortle that opposing anti-money-laundering laws was like being against motherhood. At that point, I must admit, cloning started to look pretty good.

The result of my growing skepticism was a series of analyses of the logic, or lack thereof, and evidence, or want thereof, that underlie this veritable revolution in law enforcement. The first, "Follow-the-Money Methods of Crime Control," was published on its web site by the Nathanson Centre for the Study of Organized Crime and Corruption at York University in Toronto; the second, "Washout: A Critique of Follow-the-Money Methods in Crime Control Policy," appeared in *Crime, Law, and Social Change* 32 (1999); and a third, focusing more on the legal history, will appear as "Licensed to Loot?" in a forthcoming issue of *Social Justice*. The version published here includes elements from these three earlier articles along with a summary of the argument found in "From Underworld to Underground: Economic Crime, Informal Sector Business, and the Public Policy Response," *Crime, Law, and Social Change* 24 (1996), which laid out less lethal remedies attempted elsewhere in the world. Alas, in much the same way that poisonous chemical products of the Western pharmaceutical industry are swamping traditional cures based on local ecologies, so too the alternate strategies for dealing with illicit money are being swept away in a tide of Americanization.

Wages of Crime

Introduction

President George W. Bush does not believe in the greenhouse effect, shrugs off acid rain, and cannot see any hole in the ozone layer no matter how hard he squints. But he does agree with major law enforcement agencies that the sky is falling. The main thing knocking out the supports is a global tidal wave of crime and the torrents of dirty money that flow along with it.

Politicians, press, and police alike rush to tell the public that great crime "cartels" are hell-bent on world conquest. Worse, their acts of economic insurgency have increasingly coalesced with acts of political insurgency, as terrorists (usually with sinister-sounding Arabic names) become criminals to raise money, and criminals (usually with slippery-sounding Latino names) become terrorists to intimidate the forces of law and order. Together they feed at the trough of a burgeoning worldwide criminal economy that emerged, first, in the area of drug trafficking and has since diversified into everything from smuggling endangered species to peddling fake designer watches, from looting pension funds to defrauding insurance companies. The resulting mega-profits are then stuffed into secret bank accounts in offshore financial havens, from which they will periodically reappear to be used either to seize control of Fortune 500 companies or to purchase weapons of mass destruction with which to threaten the foundations of Judeo-Christian civilization.[1] And how to stop it all? The best way, insist the forces of order, is to conduct search and destroy operations against the dirty money that forms both the motive (profit) and the means (working capital) of the epidemic of crime sweeping through this increasingly globalized economy.

This firm conviction has been used by governments to help justify a string of remarkable legislative and political initiatives ranging from civil asset seizure and criminalization of association at home, to beating up on helpless island states and sending military advisors to burn down Andean peasants' huts ("cocaine labs") abroad. Particularly in the United States, although now spreading to other countries, this conviction has led to reversal of the burden of proof at trial, to the undermining of due process, and to the smearing of citizens with the taint of criminality while denying them the right to a criminal trial that might test the truth of the accusations. It has given some governments new tools to harass political opposition groups—some that are armed and dangerous, others that are merely inconvenient—by attacking their funding on the grounds that it represents the "proceeds of crime" or the means to finance "terrorism." It has also revolutionized the way financial institutions deal with their clients. In place of the old presumption of a confidential relationship between institution and client has come a different confidential relationship—one between institution and police—in which the activities of the client are monitored. Private-sector institutions and their managers themselves face criminal sanction for failure to do so, while software companies peddle fancy programs to help scrutinize customers' transactions. ("You don't finance international terrorists, drug cartels or organized criminals. Or do you?" warns the glossy advertisement of one such company.)[2] All this is rationalized by a supposed state of emergency, the case for which rests on a series of assumptions lacking logical or factual basis.

One of these assumptions is the very idea that great crime cartels are goose-stepping across the world stage. Apart from the patent misuse of the term "cartel," apart from the fact that there cannot be grand, transnational strategic alliances binding criminal groups unless there actually exist coherent, centrally controlled groups to be bound by them (something else assumed rather than proven), there is actually nothing new about criminals creating tactical combinations across borders for particular deals. Take, for example, the infamous French Connection, star of two box-office successes (or three, counting the Peter Sellers version, *Revenge of the Pink Panther*). In its time, the 1960s, the French Connection was supposedly the greatest heroin-trafficking conspiracy of the postwar era.

The linchpin was the so-called Union Corse (Corsican Alliance or Association). From its home in Marseilles, where theft, prostitution, and gambling were the principal activities, the Union Corse spread throughout the French empire and across the Mediterranean during the early decades of the twentieth century, smuggling gold and cigarettes and trafficking in counterfeit currency before establishing a presence in the heroin business.[3] In this respect it was supposedly the prototype of the modern transnational "organized crime" group. As with the Union Corse, so with a host of others, from the Sicilian Mafia (a term that properly refers to behavior, not to an organization) to Chinese triads to the modern bugaboo, the Russian *maffya*. This last, of course, is ideally designed to strike fear into hearts and minds preconditioned by Hollywood thrillers and Cold War propaganda.

There actually are similarities between the "organizations" of then and now, but they are the opposite of the popular stereotypes. Like its modern counterparts, the Union Corse was not a criminal organization so much as a loose fraternity of like-minded souls who freely formed alliances and partnerships and just as freely dissolved them. Far from exclusive to émigré Corsicans, the Union Corse welcomed as equal "members" men of Armenian, Turkish, and Lebanese origin plus any French thief, counterfeiter, or pimp who might prove useful for a particular job. In no way did the Union Corse "control" the underworld of Marseilles, or that of any other place. Corsican gangsters did their business as individuals or in small impromptu groups and not exclusively with each other. Indeed, it was their very lack of corporate structure that made them ideally placed to participate in a criminal marketplace in which quick response and ease of regrouping after successful police strikes were precisely what was needed for survival and success, then and now.

Furthermore, the French Connection heroin route, far from monolithic, consisted of a set of autonomous transactions that followed different and uncoordinated routes to New York, the final market of choice, with breakaway competitors (never countered with violence) a common occurrence. And the market structure involved a series of short-run tactical alliances, usually without direct contact among the elements, between Anatolian farmers who grew opium, Istanbul-based brokers who traded morphine, Sicilian cigarette smugglers who diversified to run morphine around the Mediterranean, French underworld chemists who operated heroin refineries, Corsican mobsters who moved final product across the Atlantic, and, for a time, Italo-American gangsters who distributed adulterated smack in the northeastern United States.[4]

In fact, back then there was a much greater need for crime to be "organized" than now. Illegal markets were small and isolated. However large the sums of money derived or however frequent the operations, the black markets and the entrepreneurs who ran them were segregated from the mainstream of economic society and from each other. But what has emerged today is a set of interrelated, mutually supporting black markets (still usually thin and imperfect) within which there exists a mix of individual entrepreneurs along with "firms" large and small, all engaged in essentially arms-length commercial exchanges. No longer isolated, these black markets are institutionally embedded in the legal economy. Few ships carry only contraband goods; it is probably impossible to find a bank that does nothing but launder illegal money; and virtually any underground entrepreneur with hopes of a durable commercial existence ensures that his or her illegal acts are embedded in a matrix of legitimate transactions. This integration, along with the evident tendency of legal businesses today to use ever-shadier methods, has allowed those isolated black markets that once had operated on the fringes of legitimate society to give way to a continuum within society that is colored in various shades of gray.[5]

A second assumption is that something called "globalization" and the accompanying spread of modern communications and transportation technology have been a godsend to international crime "cartels," which can use the technology to commit more and worse crimes while secreting the spoils (and themselves when necessary) in faraway places. The beauty of globalization is that, much as with organized crime, everyone can agree about its enormous impact because no one knows what it really is. Does it mean more international trade? No doubt there is much more today. But world trade as a percentage of Gross Domestic Product (GDP) is about the same now as it was before World War I. Does globalization mean more international financial flows? In fact, the ratio of financial flows to GDP is lower now, and the ratio for foreign direct investment no higher. Does it refer to propagation of financial shocks? In the late 1920s a bank crash in Austria set off a global liquidity crisis that helped tip the world into a massive Depression, whereas in 1997 a huge meltdown of financial markets in Asia easily coexisted with four more years of the greatest bull market in history; while the economy of North America and, only marginally less, that of Western Europe continued an unprecedented surge.

Perhaps globalization refers not to simple economic indicators but to broader political ones? Perhaps it refers to the melting away of states and of archaic political boundaries and their commercial-financial regulations in the face of the triumphant ascent of the efficient and liberating free-market mechanism (according to proponents) or of the power of money-grubbing corporations (according to opponents)? The only problem with this theory is that there is no sign of a post-Communist withering away of the state, just of some states, while others continually increase their share of world wealth and power, just as they have been doing for ages. If globalization refers to the propensity of the rich to get richer and the powerful to get more powerful, while the opposite happens to the poor and the weak, it can hardly be seen as a revolutionary new phenomenon. Nor is it immediately obvious what effect such a development is supposed to have on crime, or law enforcement, across borders.

At best globalization seems simply a modern term for a process that began at least as far back as the time of Marco Polo, if not before; it is the process by which information about trade and financial opportunities spreads across national and regional frontiers, and goods and money soon follow. If this is the case, then citing globalization as a criminogenic factor is the same as saying that over time, criminal entrepreneurs, like legitimate business people, expand their geopolitical horizons to conform to the opportunities resulting from greater ease of long-distance communication and travel. This might be true, but it is not very helpful. Furthermore, although it is certainly true that there is more economic crime across borders today, there is also much more legal business, and absolutely no proof that the ratio of illegal to legal business is increasing. Indeed, to the extent that exchanges are becoming liberalized and flows more transparent, the opportunities for crime across borders may well be shrinking relative to total economic transactions.

There is a corollary insistence that developments in communications technology combined with much greater ease in crossing national borders have had an unprecedented impact in hastening and broadening the range over which economic transactions, legal and illegal, occur. In this case, the statement is not only unhelpful, it may be simply wrong.

Obviously modern communications and transportation technology can have a major effect on economic exchanges (illegal as well as legal). Still, the fact that people use fancy technology simply means that it is available, not that it is necessary. (Witness the number of people walking the streets alone, head inclined to one side and hand against their ear, babbling apparently to themselves.) Furthermore, even to the extent that modern electronic communications, along with mass-based, cheap, and rapid international transport of goods and people, are genuinely important today, their impact is very likely no greater and arguably much smaller than was the impact of the railway, steamship, and telegraph in the first half of the nineteenth century. For that matter, their impact probably pales in comparison to that of the automobile, passenger plane, telephone, and radio in the early decades of the twentieth century.

This is not to say that electronic technology is unimportant. Techniques exist to disguise the origins of electronic messages, route them through obscure channels, and facilitate multiple iterations of formerly time-intensive actions. But techniques to do most of these things existed in a paper-and-electrical world, even if doing them was a little more difficult. Today a popular buzz phrase is "computer-assisted crime." There are even police units dedicated to it. Because a computer can be used in some way in committing virtually every criminal offense except perhaps purse snatching, this phrase is as revealing as "pen-and-paper assisted crime" would have been a couple of technical generations back.

It is true that electronic technologies have become important in counterfeiting checks, credit cards, and currency. But they represent simply the latest stage in an on-going struggle between issuers of financial instruments and would-be fraudsters that dates back to the onset of modern credit mechanisms. Furthermore, although the alarmist scenario speaks of technology as increasing the opportunities for crime groups to wreak havoc, technological change has tended to democratize the commission of crimes by rendering large organizations uncompetitive if not entirely irrelevant (counterfeiting and business fraud are obvious examples). Although technology may facilitate credit card fraud, it has largely (although not yet totally) eliminated traffic in stolen and counterfeit securities, the overwhelming share of which now have only a virtual existence. At the same time, given the alacrity with which the state has used new technologies for information and surveillance, it can be argued that they contribute more to detection and resolution than to commission of crimes.

Similarly, all the hype over today's international mobility must be taken with a grain of salt, if not the entire shaker. The passport is actually a fairly recent phenomenon; before World War I, people expected that if they had the means and could avoid being robbed, they could pass frontiers at will. Those who utter platitudes about today's borderless world should try to cross the United States–Mexico frontier during a trade dispute or drug alert.[6] The frequently cited example of the European Union is remarkable precisely because it is so exceptional. In any event, the real issue is not a (nonexistent) borderless world or the (genuine) growing ease of international travel, but the ability to enforce domestic law elsewhere in the world—scarcely a new problem. What kept Ronald Biggs safe from the U.K. authorities for thirty-five years, until his voluntary decision to return home, was hardly his ability to hide. His presence in Brazil was so open that tourists paid to have dinner and drinks with the last Great Train Robber. His resistance to arrest was far from proof of the ability of clever operators to stay aloof from justice in a world without frontiers; in fact, what protected him was a sensible local law of the most old-fashioned sort, one that prohibits the extradition of fathers of Brazilian children.

A third assumption is that the sums generated by international criminals are sufficient to threaten the very foundations of the world economic order. The world drug trade was pegged over a decade ago at $500 billion per annum, with the United States alone accounting for $100–125 billion of it.[7] Such startling figures about mega-billions of dirty dollars seemed to be confirmed by televised U.S. congressional hearings with hooded witnesses who, after privately striking deals for sentence reductions, went on to publicly dazzle their audience with tales of loading cash by the baleful into cargo planes en route to Panama, the Bahamas, and the like.[8] This conviction perhaps reached its apogee in the United States when the mass media reported, with a straight face, that the Colombian narco-baron, the late Pablo Escobar, had earned so much from U.S. cocaine sales that he once had $400 million stuck in the basement of a house—which flooded, ruining the cash before he could get it to safety abroad. For that story to be true Escobar would have had to have had an organization remarkably adept at moving huge amounts of cocaine one way but utterly incompetent in moving cash back the other; the basement would have had to have flooded just enough to ruin the paper but not enough to lift the house from its foundations or to pour through the neighborhood and alert the police; and either the money was largely counterfeit or the community water supply unusually corrosive, because genuine U.S. notes require months of nonstop soaking in ordinary tap water to succumb to any serious damage.

Added to the presumably enormous take from drugs are the supposed mega-proceeds of a host of other rackets—old ones such as the flesh trade and new ones such as the traffic in endangered species, stalwarts such as rum-running and newcomers such as nuclear materials smuggling, vintage businesses such as loan-sharking and innovative ones such as running international boiler rooms. Police intelligence units, academic crime experts, and high-price-tag research institutes compete to churn out big numbers reputedly representing the amount of ill-gotten gains. Probably the apex came in 1996 with the construction of a world Gross Criminal Product of $1.1 trillion. What is never revealed along with such numbers is the methodology used to construct them.

Take the example of cocaine revenues. Indeed, take what should be a relatively simple task within the cocaine economy—that of using supply-side data to find the total value of drug exports from a producing country. This task requires the following:[9]

1. An estimate of acreage. Although this sounds easy, it is complicated by the fact that coca plants are often mixed up with other types and the practice of mapping plants by heat signature remains as much an art as a science.
2. A figure representing the average drug content of each plant. This is highly variable, depending on the age of the plant, the frequency with which leaves are picked, and the delay before processing starts.
3. Assumptions about the quality of both the chemists and the chemical inputs. This boils down to pure guesswork.

4. A hunch about cost of transportation, security, bribes, and so forth. The only hard data come from the occasional bust; these data then have to be extrapolated to the market as a whole.
5. Deductions for the amount of seizures. On the surface this seems straightforward. But apart from the propensity of police to hype the size of a catch, the data should be adjusted realistically for the percentage of seizures that make their way back onto the market.
6. Accurate numbers for export prices. In fact, in imperfect, segmented markets, export prices vary greatly from time to time and even from shipment to shipment.

Each of these items in isolation is difficult to compute, and the results are of dubious validity. Then they have to be cobbled together. The final tally is duly reported in official documents. It then is recycled sufficiently in the press and in political speeches that the tally takes on an air of received knowledge, when in fact it is based on vague assumptions and pure guesses along with the fond hope that all of the errors are random and will somehow cancel each other out.

The reality is that no one has a clue how much illegal money is earned or saved or laundered or moved around the world, or how it is distributed among a host of malefactors. Nor is there much effort to understand the underlying structure of the criminal markets out of which these great sums are supposedly generated. Not least, the whole exercise ignores the critical fact that crime is a moral not a financial problem. Yet phony numbers are routinely trotted out to justify powerful legal and political initiatives and to frighten the public into acquiescence.[10]

Yet a fourth assumption is that the torrents of dirty money have a powerful effect in corrupting institutions and therefore weakening the political immune system of the societies being infected. Although this is a problem at home—threatening the moral integrity of manufacturers of MX missiles and Marlboro cigarettes—it is supposedly even worse in poorer countries, where defenses are weaker and the countries have much less experience in fighting back.

Of course, corruption can be, and is, a serious problem in some places at some times and in a few places at all times—particularly when it hits the top levels of the political apparatus. However, much petty corruption can be written off as a symptom of failure to adequately pay civil servants—perhaps because the International Monetary Fund, in the name of efficiency, has forced the country to slash public expenditures. Or it can be accepted as a second-best means of keeping a creaking bureaucratic apparatus at least partially functional. Nor does anyone in the West care one iota if someone in a poor country has to grease a local palm for a vendor's license or an exit visa. Massive, high-level corruption is supposedly much different, particularly if it impacts the operations of transnational corporations.

But much of such corruption supposedly rampant in developing countries had previously been encouraged by major Western powers, or at least by their intelligence services, to build up slush funds by which their Third World allies could pay for weapons, stage a countercoup, and or just keep the national wealth out of the hands of a successor regime that might use it in ways hostile to Western interests. Furthermore, it was regarded as useful to have corrupt heads of state—it was always possible to use the threat of exposure to keep them in line. To this day, it is usually only when such a head of state has outlived his apparent political usefulness, begun to shake down Western companies that have well-placed friends back home, or become so greedy as to threaten his country's ability to repay debts to Western banks that a political corruption scandal is likely to break. And even then it has a selective political agenda.

The current anticorruption campaign is driven, first and foremost, by transnational corporations worried that their competitors will gain an edge and not wanting to themselves shell out in bribes what they evade in taxes. They, and their ideological allies in the major donor institutions, also find the Crusade against Corruption a handy way to knock down barriers to their operations posed by state regulations or local differences in property and commercial law. They are joined by the leaders of new regimes, who seize on the alleged corruption of their predecessors to purge the civil service of their supporters and prepare space for patronage appointments of their own cronies. These new leaders, too, find it expedient to blame economic problems not on any dismantling of protection and social security demanded by their participation in the supposed new world order but on the corruption of the old regime.

In any event, the real corruption problem takes much more subtle forms than the payment of easily traceable bribes. And it is much more serious in the so-called advanced industrial countries than in the poorer ones. In the United States, for example, it takes the form of regulatory agencies captive of the industries they supposedly regulate, of a revolving door relationship through which top personnel routinely come and go, and the ability of the powerful, directly through campaign contributions and lobbying and indirectly through molding public opinion, to shape the regulatory environment and to influence the degree of enthusiasm with which it is enforced. By comparison, a few bribes, even substantial ones, seem inconsequential.

Fortunately, there is an alternative to this tale of great crime cartels dripping filthy lucre, spreading corruption and moral decay, while eyeing the world as their oyster, just waiting to be shucked and swallowed in a gulp. Unfortunately, it is not nearly as media-genic.

That alternate view suggests that the great majority of what is conventionally defined as crime is the province of small-time losers; if they really possessed the kind of initiative routinely imputed to them, they would have long ago realized that the serious money lies not in peddling dime bags of dope but in rigging defense contracts.[11] That view further suggests that the real threat to economic morality comes from seemingly legitimate business types intent on seeing how far they can bend the rules before they have to pay politicians to rewrite them.

It also suggests that the notion of a global alliance of criminals and insurgents is, at best, an exaggeration. And it is often laced with selective bigotry. After the 1993 bombing of the World Trade Center, for example, everyone was quick to blame the broad and multifaceted phenomenon of "Islamic fundamentalism," rather than just a collection of bent fanatics. But, after the bombing of a federal building in Oklahoma, no one took the occasion to denounce "Christian fundamentalism," a term that captures the faith of millions of decent Americans, just because some American right-wing militia groups espouse a deviant variety of it. Nor does anyone suggest that the frequent armed robberies staged by these militia groups are the work of "pistol-packing Protestants." At worst, this purported crimo-terrorist nexus is just a cover for foreign intervention and a technique to permit repressive and illegitimate governments to stomp out opposition by merging political dissent with economic criminality and attempting to impose foreign-concocted military solutions on acute domestic sociopolitical problems. Nor is this merely a Western disorder. As in Colombia, so in Chechnya.

It suggests, too, that although there are torrents of funny money floating around the globe, most of it comes from tax and exchange control evasion, particularly in developing countries. For that kind of loot, Western countries and their banks roll out the red carpet, even though the loss of money from fiscal offenses does far more damage to the socioeconomic fabric of developing countries than the laundering of drug money does to that of the major industrialized ones.[12]

It further suggests that contemporary crime control initiatives, including the anti-money-laundering drive now so much in vogue, share a common and fundamental error: they attempt to impose supply-side solutions on demand-driven problems.

The prevailing police mind-set (cops and robbers, crooks and victims) developed in the context of a battle against predatory crimes (robbery, fraud, counterfeiting, and so forth). It was then transplanted into a world of market-based crime, with little regard for the enormous differences. With predatory offenses, wealth is transferred from one person to another by use of force or fraud. There is a broad social consensus that the acts are wrong. The victim usually initiates the enquiry. And, resources permitting, most offenses are subject to some sort of investigation, even if the results leave the victim disappointed. However, market-based offenses involve mutually agreeable exchanges in which there is value offered for money. The social consensus against them is much weaker, if it exists at all. Because there are no victims to complain, the police take the initiative. Particularly in vice offenses, the number of "perpetrators" is so large that investigations are necessarily selective. People end up charged less because of the offense, which is commonplace, and more because of who they are, that is, because the police decided to go after a particular individual. The selection might be based on the person's relative importance in the criminal scene or on that person's frequency of recidivism. Alternatively, it might be based on personal, ethnic, or political animosity. The result is the same: cynicism on the part of the population and arbitrary, perhaps capricious behavior on the part of the police.

Not surprisingly, never in history has there been a black market defeated from the supply side. From Prohibition to prostitution, from gambling to recreational drugs, the story is the same. Supply-side controls act, much like price supports in agriculture, to encourage production and increase profits. At best a few intermediaries get knocked out of business. But as long as demand persists, the market is served more or less as before. In the meantime, failure to "win the war" becomes a pretext for increasing police budgets, expanding law enforcement powers, and pouring more money into the voracious maw of the prison-industrial complex.[13]

CHAPTER I

Mafias, Myths, and Markets

A new specter is haunting the West, the specter of "a Worldwide Mafia International, the first in history."[1] Thus, U.S. Senator John Kerry insists that today "Organized crime is the new communism, the new monolithic threat." East has allegedly met West in summits of the G-6 of criminal underworlds, with representatives of the United States, Italy, Colombia, Japan, Hong Kong, and Russia in attendance. The main item on the summit agenda is how to carve up the globe so that great transnational crime cartels can better exploit its wealth for their nefarious ends.

This phenomenon of "organized crime" is allegedly a much greater threat to the moral and economic foundations of Western civilization than is random street crime. Rather than a bunch of thugs who engage in episodic depredations as mood and opportunity strike, the perpetrators are sophisticated criminals in large groups who plot complex and lucrative crimes on a continuous basis at the expense of an unsuspecting, polite society. To be sure, such groups are not new. But for a long time the damage that traditional criminal organizations (the Italian Mafia, Chinese triads, Colombian cocaine cartels, and so forth) could do was limited by the fact that their activities were largely confined to their host milieus. In the last couple of decades, however, they have imitated orthodox business and globalized their reach in what is breathlessly touted as "the most massive and insidious criminal assault in history."[2] In the process, old crime organizations have been joined by upstart groups of many different ethnicities, although the most dangerous are surely the dastardly Russkis. In effect, the drug-fueled crime syndicates of the West have marched East and met with new criminal *nomenklatura* heading West, a development especially menacing given the number of ex-KGB types found in the ranks of the Russian mob. Even more frightening, these national groups have begun to develop international strategic alliances that are so dripping with wealth as to threaten the integrity of entire national economies as well as the international financial system itself.

Such alarming developments call for a strong response. After all, according to the deputy director of Britain's National Crime Intelligence Service, "there is little point in collectively having won the Cold War, when you are going to lose the war to another tyranny." Countries under siege must create new weapons. These include shifts in legal codes to eliminate some of the constraints imposed by traditional rights to due process, freedom of association, and especially financial privacy. They include new methods to search out and seize the "proceeds of crime." They include particularly severe punishments for crimes committed by organized (as distinct from disorganized?) criminals, even to the point of making membership in such groups a crime per se. Certainly not least, an adequate response requires the realization that what was formerly a criminological challenge has become a national security threat. Therefore, as a U.S. assistant secretary of state sagely observed, "law enforcement is the emerging U.S. foreign policy."[3]

Some, perhaps all, of these new methods of responding to organized crime's international march might well be justified if the major crime threat facing the modern world really took the form of great criminal cartels hell bent on global conquest. However, before the rest of the world follows the lead of the United States in making international kidnapping a legitimate means of getting the accused in front of the courts, in granting national intelligence agencies (desperate for a rationale for a continued Cold War–sized scale of existence) an expanded mandate to snoop at home and connive abroad, or in converting police forces into global bounty-hunting organizations, it might be best to ask if such a viewpoint necessarily represents the reality of the modern criminal marketplace.

Organized Crime, Disorganized Definitions

The first obstacle to understanding "organized crime" is figuring out what it is supposed to be.[4] Presumably there must be something to distinguish "organized" criminality if any special effort is to be directed against it.[5] On the other hand, by never agreeing on a definition, police and prosecutors secure a big advantage—no one can prove they are wrong in their assessment of the threat or accuse them of being delinquent in their actions against it.

Still, law enforcement has never lacked for definitional efforts. Some are simplistic, some are self-serving, some are preposterous. As far back as 1965, a conference of U.S. law enforcement agents came up with this gem:

Organized crime is the product of a self-perpetuating criminal conspiracy to wring exorbitant profits from our society by any means—fair and foul, legal and illegal. Despite personnel changes, the conspiratorial entity continues. It is a malignant parasite which fattens on human weakness. It survives on fear and corruption. By one or another means, it obtains a high degree of immunity from law. It is totalitarian in its organization.

Yet stripped of hysteria, this is probably the most comprehensive definition possible. It suggests (with some reading between the purple lines) that an organized crime group possesses the following characteristics.

Organized crime groups specialize in a type of offense that is different from that of ordinary criminals. Common criminality is mostly associated with predatory crimes—burglary, armed robbery, ransom kidnapping, and the like—acts that involve forcible or fraudulent redistribution of wealth, are episodic in nature, and require little long-term supporting infrastructure. By contrast, organized crime is associated more with market-based offenses—the production and distribution of illegal goods and services to willing consumers. These would include peddling recreational drugs, running illegal gambling operations, controlling sex for sale, and so forth.

To maintain a constant flow of product onto the market, organized crime needs a structure, much like any business. It must have a means of replacing personnel, and it must have a clear chain of command. However, most predatory crimes also require some organization. If two burglars decide to assault a third-story window, they must be sufficiently organized to buy a ladder, but it would take a big leap to claim this as proof of organized rather than ordinary criminality.[6] And not all underground entrepreneurs who peddle dope or kiddy porn belong to hierarchical and durable organizations. What makes organized crime different is that its participants organize not just to participate in the market for criminal goods and services but also to dominate that market.[7]

To achieve a substantial degree of control over a territory, a market, or an industry, organized crime employs violence and / or corruption. Of course many other crimes involve acts (or the threat) of violence—armed robbery, for example. The objective of organized criminal violence, though, is not to facilitate a one-time involuntary transfer of wealth but to enhance the group's position in the ongoing marketplace. If violence permits organized crime to drive away competitors, corruption allows it to undermine the regulatory apparatus. In both cases the purpose is to achieve monopoly power, which in turn has a higher rationale.

Organized crime, by taking control of the choicest rackets, achieves higher rates of return than does ordinary criminality. During Prohibition the racket of choice was booze. During the 1930s the action shifted to schemes such as labor racketeering. During World War II the growth sector was black market trafficking in rationed commodities, especially gasoline. In the 1950s gambling, along with loan-sharking to support it, seemed to top the list. By the late 1960s, apparently the main source of wealth had become drugs, which has reputedly continued into the present. Enormous though the sums generated appear to be, the real harm done by organized crime comes not from selling inherently illegal goods and services but from the way the profits are subsequently invested.

Organized crime uses its wealth, and its propensity for violence and corruption, to penetrate the legal economy, taking over businesses to acquire yet more criminal profit. Unlike the situation in which organized crime sells banned goods and services to willing customers, here there seems a clear victim. Money extorted through commercial crimes such as racketeering in and embezzlement from legitimate industries ultimately comes from the pockets of the population at large. Furthermore, with the penetration of organized crime into the legal economy, the nature of corruption becomes much more insidious. It is no longer a matter of paying off one policeman to ignore a local heroin deal; it becomes a matter of corrupting municipal and state politics to secure benefits such as garbage disposal contracts and liquor licenses. Indeed, it could go even further. Bribing a beat cop suffices to cover for an illegal gambling den, but "lobbying" for a change in gambling laws might require campaign support (cash and votes) for national politicians.

These five characteristics—specialization in market-based crimes, hierarchical and durable structure, use of violence and corruption to achieve monopoly power, high rates of return, and penetration of the legal economy—seem to be what organized crime is supposed to be all about. They also have conditioned the response.

There were certainly efforts in the early part of the twentieth century to deal with what today might be called organized crime activities. Indeed, legend has it that Prohibition after World War I was the true incubator of modern organized crime. In response, Treasury agents, when not otherwise occupied with things like running sting operations against doctors who insisted on treating heroin addicts as patients rather than criminals, did chase prominent bootleggers.[8] But it was after World War II, and especially after two or three decades of mounting public concern, that more modern forms of organized crime control came into being.

The effective date in the United States was probably 1970, when the federal government launched a threefold attack. The Bank Secrecy Act was designed to help trace criminal assets by forcing financial institutions to report cash transactions; the Continuing Criminal Enterprises Act imposed special penalties on big-time drug dealers; and the Racketeer Influenced and Corrupt Organizations (RICO) statute aimed to drive organized crime figures out of legitimate businesses they had taken over. RICO was at that point the star of the triumvirate. It permitted the prosecution to take two or more isolated offenses, which seem fairly trivial by themselves, and combine them in a broad conspiracy case. It created much stronger penalties if such a pattern of racketeering could be demonstrated. It muddied the traditional separation of civil and criminal procedures by allowing civil suits, brought by the government or by private parties, to strip mobsters of the businesses they controlled and to impose on them treble damages. Not least, whereas with most criminal law the presumption is for strict interpretation, the RICO statute was designed to apply widely and be interpreted liberally.[9]

RICO was strong stuff. As its advocates freely admitted, it would have been much more difficult (perhaps impossible) to win public and political acceptance had it not been for the sensational revelations of Joseph Valachi, a Genovese Family soldier heralded as the first "made member" of the Mafia to break ranks and turn informant. His testimony in various trials and before Congress is credited with putting an end to skepticism about the existence of a formal, hierarchical Mafia at the core of the U.S. crime problem.[10]

Although prosecutors initially were slow to use RICO, by the time of the 1980s drug war, it had become an important part of the arsenal. Perhaps its most important use came with the 1986 indictment of the so-called Medellín cartel of Colombian drug lords.[11] The indictment defined the enemy as "an international criminal narcotics enterprise based in Medellín, Colombia" which enabled major cocaine organizations to "pool resources, including raw materials, clandestine cocaine conversion laboratories, aircraft, vessels, transportation facilities, distribution networks, and cocaine to facilitate international narcotics trafficking." The indictment charged that the cartel not only provided facilities for members to plot strategy but it also "maintained inventory," controlled corrupt officials of foreign governments, and carried out murders to "protect its business operations and enforce its mandates."

Using RICO, the prosecution not only could pin any number of crimes on the cartel in a single court proceeding, but it could convene a maxitrial, which generated the most public exposure possible—confirming in the public's mind an image of the Medellín cartel, and with it, organized crime, an image the press had already been enthusiastically promoting. Yet by the time of the great cartel case, the glory days of RICO were over.

RICO had been part of a "targeting-up" strategy; the government's theory was that instead of wasting time on street punks, the objective should be to nail and jail mob bosses. But because RICO had failed to make any discernible dent in the U.S. vice-rackets problem, by the mid-1980s the theory had changed: the most effective way to neutralize the cartels was through anti-money-laundering regulations that would hamper the infiltration of criminal money into the legitimate economy and through forfeiture laws to facilitate the seizure of assets. These laws supposedly would strike directly at the upper echelons of crime groups whose bosses kept their distance from the street action but stayed very close to their money.[12]

Yet despite these initiatives, in the United States and across the Western world, new criminal organizations seem to spring up like poisonous mushrooms after a rain. The worst are inevitably of alien origin—after the Italians and the Colombians have come the Mexicans, Chinese, Nigerians, and, more recently, the Russians. What is more, the threat seems to be progressively worsening as criminal organizations ranging from Colombian cartels to the Sicilian Mafia to powerful Russian groups begin coordinating their efforts. Together they seem capable of thwarting criminal justice, corrupting legal markets, threatening national prosperity, and undermining national security.

If this is true, it may no longer suffice to merely block and reverse the penetration of organized crime into the legal economy or to strip groups of their operating capital. What may be necessary is to address the problem at the third, and most fundamental level—to suspend the right of free association in order to make membership in such organizations a crime per se.

That is one conclusion. It has a terrifying logic. However, there is another possible inference from the evidence. It might just be possible that targeting up through RICO failed to make much impact on the criminal marketplace not just because criminal organizations were so nefariously adaptable but because they were of so little importance to that marketplace. Similarly, it is possible that anti-money-laundering and asset seizure laws have failed to stop the criminal onslaught not because criminals are so adroit at hiding the proceeds of crime but because there simply are not such great pools of capital in their hands. In other words, there is a possibility that the entire escalation has been based on a profound misreading of the nature and functioning of the criminal marketplace and the role of "organized crime" within it.

Whose Business Is It?

If any element is central to a definition of what makes organized crime different from ordinary street crime it is the fact that participants in organized crime groups supposedly commit different kinds of crimes, which in turn have different kinds of logistical requirements. Ordinary street crime is conducted against unwilling targets on an episodic, grab-and-run basis. But market-based crimes that serve the forbidden consumption desires of complicit members of polite society require that the criminal entrepreneur provide a steady supply of product. Therefore criminals are supposed to run "enterprises" whose actions approximate legal business firms: they face market opportunities, run up costs, and incur risks while seeking to maximize profit. That is the theory. On closer scrutiny, things look a little different.[13]

One problem with this kind of definition is the use of something called profit maximization to explain behavior. Even with a strictly legal firm, this is a gross oversimplification. If a legitimate firm were really only a single-minded profit-maximizer, there would be no reason for it to remain legitimate—yet only a small percentage of entrepreneurs and corporations cross the line. The same applies with additional force to a criminal "firm." Certainly profit is an important part of the calculation. But many other motivations can be at work—ego enhancement, the thrill of the game, the search for prestige among peers, or, not to be underestimated, simple survival. After all, a legal firm exists in a political and legal milieu designed to help it grow and prosper, subject to certain constraints on permitted behavior, whereas an illegal firm is constantly confronted with regulators seeking to close it down and toss the principals into jail. Therefore even if the predominant objective of the legal firm were profit maximization, or some approximation of it, the corresponding objective for the illegal "firm" would be risk minimization—which means it is problematic whether it should be considered a firm at all.

To increase profit, a legal firm seeks to reduce the layers of intermediation that separate supplier from ultimate customer. In that way profits formerly earned outside the firm can be captured inside it—which, in fact, is the main reason firms exist. But the illegal "firm," to reduce risk, seeks to increase layers of intermediation, to ensure extra levels of insulation between the entrepreneur and the regulatory authorities. Therefore, whereas a legal firm seeks to increase the amount of activity conducted inside itself, the optimum strategy for an illegal one is the opposite: safety is best served by an increase in the number of transactions between independent actors outside the firm, the very antithesis of growth.

To service its market, a legal firm must maximize the flow of (certain kinds of) information to would-be clients, advertising the availability of goods or services. An illegal firm must be extremely cautious about the kind of information it permits to circulate, and among whom. It may attract business away from competitors; on the other hand, it may, in a potentially violent marketplace, attract those very competitors. And it will always attract the regulators.

A legal firm can collect objective data on which to base market decisions. For an illegal one there really is no market per se for its goods and services; rather, there is a set of submarkets, segmented by information constraints, regulatory barriers, social and cultural divisions, and, not least, fear.

A legal firm beyond the smallest size usually has an existence distinct from that of any particular set of manager-owners, who can change dramatically without necessarily affecting operations. An illegal enterprise and the illegal entrepreneur in charge of it are identical. All decisions are personalized, and any changes in personnel can produce erratic changes in operations, compromising its marketplace stability.

To the extent that growth is contingent upon financing, a legal firm has access to the formal capital market. Indeed, the bigger the firm, the easier the terms of access—creating a positive feedback loop that, in the absence of other constraints, might lead to monopolization. On the other hand, an illegal firm has minimal, if any, access to the legal capital market; it must rely on underground financing, which is available, if at all, on harsher terms. Furthermore, even if adequate financing were available for the illegal firm, growth increases visibility and attracts additional scrutiny.

When a legal firm turns to the external capital market, perhaps by floating stock, legal devices exist to ensure that management retains control even as ownership is diluted. The underworld firm has no such assurance. More underworld partners waters down control and likely produces squabbling over division of the spoils, because there are no objective standards by which to determine appropriate returns. The alternative is loan sharks, whose help is short term on stiff terms, which increases the danger of loss of control (or worse) for the underground entrepreneur should he fail to repay on time.

Enterprises can also grow through reinvested profits. For a legal entrepreneur, profits are an opportunity for capital accumulation, but for an illegal one, they are more likely an opportunity to enhance prestige among peers through extravagant living and acts of generosity.

This attitude is reinforced by the difference in time horizon. Usually a legal firm works on the premise that it will be around for a long, perhaps indefinite time, even if the time horizon of any particular set of executives is shorter. On the other hand, an illegal enterprise has a time horizon equal to that of the illegal entrepreneur. Thus, with its time horizon short to begin with, the illegal enterprise is always in danger of being abruptly terminated, reinforcing its tendency to take a grab-and-run attitude toward market exploitation.

The spatial horizon is also quite different. Usually a legal firm has ambitions to expand and has access to communications technology and legal infrastructure that will ensure reasonable control over considerable distance. Except under extraordinary conditions, however, an illegal firm has an opposite reaction; its main concern is to retain control of its immediate turf, because expansion into alien territory holds obvious dangers.

A legal firm is free to take its product to its buyers, be they in the neighborhood or around the world. It is more mobile than the set of customers it serves. But with an illegal firm, the reverse is likely true. It is identified with a particular territorial base, whereas its customers are much freer to shift their purchasing power elsewhere.

Any firm's costs are usually divided into those that are fixed and those that vary with the length of the production run. For a legal firm, capital costs are largely fixed, whereas labor costs are, for the most part, variable. But for an illegal firm, labor costs are more like payments for loyalty or silence than for productive services. The illegal firm has to pay them no matter what the state of its business.

For a legal firm, it is easy to define property rights, and there is an objective dispute-settlement mechanism to ease relations with suppliers, competitors, and customers. Costs for using that mechanism are incurred on a one-time, tax-deductible basis. For an illegal firm, property rights are determined not by law but by tradition or force. To the extent that a dispute-settlement mechanism exists, it is a subjective mechanism and usually the domain of the more powerful criminal elements in the immediate area. Using it can easily lead to at least partial loss of control, along with partial loss of the flow of revenue.

All of this suggests that the facile analogy between legal and illegal firms is at best a serious oversimplification, at worst simply wrong. In illegal markets that are highly segmented, decisions are personalized, information flows constricted, capital supplies short term and unreliable, objective price data lacking, and the time horizons (indeed, the very existence) of enterprises coterminous with those of the entrepreneurs. The operating rule is to reduce risk by downsizing—by multiplying layers of intermediation and therefore reducing direct control over the various stages in the production or distribution chain. This rule applies because regulators go after the biggest first, either to bust them or, sometimes, to collect a form of underground taxation, which will also limit the firm's growth and profitability. All this suggests an ever-greater degree of decentralization and an ever-increasing pool of competitors. It also suggests that most fears of great crime cartels that control markets for illegal goods and services are pure fantasy.[14]

All in the Family?

This picture of small, competitive, and vulnerable criminal enterprises is in stark contrast to the common view of great hierarchically structured organizations intent on dominating the criminal marketplace through a central command structure that passes detailed instructions from the top down and receives a return flow of payments from the bottom up before redistributing part in wages and salaries. However, this "Godfather" view of the criminal marketplace is based on a triple fallacy: it equates the criminal firm with the criminal industry; it equates the criminal industry with the organized crime group; and it equates an association of criminals with a criminal association.[15]

The basis of the stereotype was the presumed structure of an Italo-American Mafia "family." Yet when the actual operations of Mafia-style crime families were examined by the few independent investigators able to get inside, what emerged was far from a conspiracy to dominate the marketplace for criminal goods and services. The crime family (or similar structure with other ethnic groups) was not a business organization at all. Rather, it functioned as an underground government under whose auspices members had wide license to engage in business as individuals or in small partnerships, sometimes with other crime family members or associates, sometimes with outsiders. The activity might be illegal; it might be a combination of illegal and legal; it might even be entirely legal, without affecting membership in the organized crime group.

The reason is simple. Contrary to the ideological fulmination of free-market economists, business needs government, and where government does not exist, it will be invented. This dictum also applies in the underworld, where parallel governments perform several functions.[16]

The first, most important role of such a parallel government is to define property rights and regulate disputes among enterprises that by definition cannot use conventional means. The very fact that criminal business is competitive and potentially violent makes a parallel regulatory agency important. The crime family structure serves as an alternative to violence in resolving conflicts, and if in the final analysis violence is deemed necessary, the underground government functions to keep it limited and selective.

A parallel government's second function is to conduct "foreign relations." The crime boss might oversee the flow of election funds and vote-rigging operations on behalf of politicians or supervise the bribing of regulators.

A third task might be to operate a social security fund. The crime family could assume responsibility for legal costs incurred by members or take care of dependents of those killed or jailed in the line of business or duty.

A fourth chore is to act sometimes as a lender of last resort. Because criminals usually cannot tap the legal capital market, they might borrow from the crime family, more specifically, the boss. This parallels the situation in the legitimate economy, where the job of providing start-up capital to those without sufficient assets to pledge as commercial collateral is sometimes performed by government-run small business development banks.

In short, as a parallel government, the crime family (or similar device) provides the infrastructure whose benefits members cannot obtain from regular (legal) channels. But given that infrastructure, the actual conduct of criminal enterprises is left to individuals, alone or in partnership with crime family members or with outsiders.

The Bruno Family of south Philadelphia, for example, had by all appearances a hierarchical structure intended nominally to serve as a vehicle for "regulating" members' businesses. In practice, regulation amounted to little more than asking members to respect a code of ethics that prohibited prostitution, drugs, kidnapping, or counterfeiting because of the bad publicity or the law enforcement heat such activities engendered. The edicts were ignored frequently and with impunity. Meanwhile, individual members were free to conduct their own businesses, which were a mix of legal and illegal activities structured as ad hoc partnerships with other members, associates, or outsiders, without restriction. Furthermore, the Philadelphia underworld had ample independent coalitions and partnerships that coexisted peacefully with the Bruno Family. Until a change of regime in 1980, the hierarchy made no effort to use violence to extort from other underworld businesses, and there was little evidence of it even to defend the rackets, mainly loan-sharking and gambling, run by crime family members. Much the same has been observed of other Italo-American crime families—the most organized of U.S. "organized crime" groups and the ones on whose structure and behavior the popular (and police) stereotype has been based.

The relative detachment of the crime family from the actual conduct of rackets is confirmed by following the money trail. If there really were central control, those at the top of the power ladder would collect all earnings and then redistribute back down to subordinates. In practice there are two distinct ways in which money flows upward. Individual members may be in business with the boss and have to remit a share of the profits to him or his designated cutouts. This practice is the result of a particular partnership; it is not a centralized business arrangement. Also, in some cases, members are expected to contribute to a central treasury. This fund, however, does not represent the boss's personal wealth; instead, it is more in the nature of a trust fund held and administered on behalf of the group, and its contents depend on the willingness and ability of the members to contribute. Indeed, in their role as head of such an underground government, mob bosses could well sympathize with their straight counterparts. They administer governments with little or no enforcement power, whose "laws" are ignored whenever it is financially convenient to do so, and whose subjects are not only armed and dangerous but prone to cheating on their taxes.

When funds that do make it up the ladder are returned to members, the money comes not as salary payments for services rendered to a centralized criminal enterprise but as social security disbursements. No less an expert than Joseph Bonanno, boss of the New York crime family that bore his name, put it simply. "Family membership," he insisted, "does not entitle one to a monetary stipend." The advantage of membership, he stressed, was that "it simply places the family member in a society of friends who can help each other through a network of connections."[17] It was, in short, more a Rotary Club than a Standard Oil of crime.

On balance, no better evidence exists that the crime family and the criminal enterprises run by its members are distinct than the fact, revealed in one study of the actual functioning of an organized crime family, that the income and wealth of family members show no clear relationship to their position in the structure. In fact, in the study there were ordinary members who were richer than some of the bosses.[18]

Yet the conventional image of organized crime is not entirely the figment of law enforcement imagination. There clearly was something that set Italo-American organized crime groups apart from others and for a time assured them an exceptional position in the criminal marketplace. The answer, though, lies not in formal organizational structure. That notion began with a simple but fundamental error: U.S. law enforcement took a term—Mafia—which in Italy referred not to a group but to a form of behavior (selling protection and connection) by a type of individual (an "entrepreneur of violence" rather than a violent entrepreneur), and transmogrified it into an organization. It compounded the error by making *omertà* an oath of allegiance among a criminal fraternity when in fact it is a concept endemic to Sicilian society as a whole with its profound distrust of outsiders.[19]

Thus the key to Italo-American criminal business lay not in an organizational structure but in a social matrix in which kinship links based on both blood and marriage were reinforced by fictive "family" relations through "godparenting."[20] Actual business relations could be based on kinship and extended family, on fictive family, on individual friendship, or on formal (although unwritten) contract.[21] As the real or contrived kinship relations melted in the face of acculturation at the same time that their traditional rackets went into decline, the U.S. Mafia became marginal to the crime scene; nature, not law enforcement, took the real toll. By the time the FBI trumpeted its most-recent "final victory" over the mob bosses, the "Mafia" was already a shadow of its former self.[22]

The fate of the Bruno Family is instructive. When the old boss was murdered in 1980, an upstart attempted to remodel the family. New members were chosen not on the basis of their criminal talent but on their willingness to serve directly the new boss's moneymaking operations. The live-and-let-live policy toward other underworld actors was changed in an attempt to extort from whoever was unable to resist, and there was an effort to force all made members to pay tribute to the boss from their own earnings. The result was a rising tide of internal violence and a series of murders that culminated with several members defecting to the authorities. The man who would be capo ended up in jail and his crime family in chaos. His error appears to have been that he started to believe the mass-media and police stereotype.[23]

If it is true that mob businesses are essentially independent and individualistic, and that the family, if it exists at all, is a combination of government and forum for exchanging tips and contacts, how could the popular stereotype have persisted for so long? There were certainly many countersigns. But there were also the famed Joseph Valachi revelations, which confirmed to the authorities what they wanted to believe, turned the crime hunt into a television extravaganza, and prepared the public for the RICO statute.[24] Yet ironically, when Valachi's own testimony is subjected to a detached reading, away from the glare of the cameras, it presents a totally different picture.

> VALACHI: "You don't get any salary, Senator."
> SENATOR: "Well, you get a cut then."
> VALACHI: "You get nothing, only what you earn for yourself."[25]

As Valachi described it, the only serious commercial advantage to Mafia membership was that it gave each member some assurance that the others would not cheat him, although they were free to scam anyone else. Even the family's governance role was distinctly limited: members did favors of a military nature for the boss, and he in turn provided them with some protection for running their rackets.

> SENATOR: Now what he [Vito Genovese] got out of them, your actions and those of other members of the family, was to kill off or otherwise deal with people who were bothering him; is that right?
> VALACHI: Anybody bothering him, naturally he has the soldiers.
> SENATOR: That is the function of the family?
> VALACHI: Right.
> SENATOR: That is mutual protection?
> VALACHI: Right.
> SENATOR: Through strong arm methods by you and by other soldiers?
> VALACHI: Right.
> SENATOR: That is the total of it
> VALACHI: Right.
> SENATOR: Otherwise, everybody operates by himself. They may take partners but that is their option.
> VALACHI: Right.[26]

Yet it was from this kind of testimony that both the image of the centralized criminal conspiracy to dominate the marketplace for illegal goods and services and the RICO statute were born.

These fundamental errors of logic and interpretation—equating an association of criminals with a criminal association, confounding the criminal firm and the criminal industry, and attempting to convert a military or fraternal hierarchy (an extremely simplistic one) into a business structure—have been replicated with respect to many other groups.[27] Chinese triads, for example, contrary to a plethora of books bearing lurid titles such as *Dragons of Crime,* are not hierarchically controlled; some members are strictly legitimate businessmen; traditional ceremonies have no criminal function; and members freely engage in business with nonmembers. Although membership provides contacts and an exchange of favors, these are useful but hardly essential for criminal activity. Even payments to leaders take the form of voluntary gifts on important ceremonial occasions rather than profit shares on the "godfather" model.[28]

However, police analysts of "organized crime," along with their mass-media cheerleaders, rarely let facts stand between them and a good story.[29]

In the Medellín cartel RICO case of 1986, prosecutors collected a number of separate incidents involving cocaine trafficking—one had to do with smuggling product into the United States; another was a CIA-inspired tale that the Sandinista government of Nicaragua was providing transshipment facilities; another grew out of a major seizure of precursor chemicals; yet another involved the murder a former drug pilot who had turned state's evidence—and tossed them together into a mishmash that was then sold to the public as the first full dissection of how the "cartel" operated.[30] As two *Miami Herald* reporters gushed, "The finished document brought a new organized crime phenomenon to the American consciousness."[31] That, of course, was the intent all along.[32]

One thing conspicuously absent from the indictment was a definition of the term "cartel." A cartel is a conspiracy in restraint of trade, an illegal clique to restrict quantity, divide up the market, and push up prices. Yet the actual characteristics of the cocaine business were and remain quite unpropitious for the exercise of monopoly power.

Consider the input–output structure. At the bottom are the *campesinos* who grow coca as part of the traditional peasant economy, as they have for centuries. They number in the tens of thousands, scattered over a huge area. Next come coca-paste manufacturers, still in the thousands, mainly well-to-do peasants or local merchants throughout the Andes who are close to the points of production of the leaf. Next come coca-base manufacturers, who are sometimes the same people who make the paste, and sometimes the same people who refine the base into cocaine. Then there are scores of refiners spread not just through inaccessible parts of Colombia but across Peru, Bolivia, Ecuador, Venezuela, Brazil, and Mexico. The lower levels of production are handled by far too many participants to organize into a cartel, and the upper stages are too geographically dispersed.

Next comes marketing. Sometimes manufacturers move their product themselves and sell to distributors inside the target market; sometimes they sell to professional smugglers. The entrepreneurs who handle the actual transportation are sometimes employees of the exporters or of the smugglers, sometimes independent agents contracting on a fee-for-service basis, and sometimes freelance owner-operators. In almost all cases the cocaine, on arrival in the country of final destination, is resold to wholesalers. Those wholesalers deal with regional distributors, who sell the product to dealers, who in turn may resell to several further levels of intermediaries before the product reaches the customer.

At no stage is there a concerted effort to monopolize the business, and far from an integrated organization, cocaine trafficking proceeds through a complex of arms-length commercial transactions. To claim, as the U.S. prosecutors did in their RICO indictment, that the big Colombian drug lords finance the growing of coca leaf is akin to stating that someone finances diary farming by buying an ice-cream cone.

The reality is that the Medellín "cartel," even at peak, never attempted to control the price of cocaine by restricting supply. Instead, as an underground government, it represented a cooperative effort by dozens of independent producers to use violence to achieve specific ends vis-à-vis political opponents and to reduce it vis-à-vis each other. On occasion the largest cocaine barons would issue joint declarations, the most famous of which was a denunciation of some of their peers for selling *bazuko* (a mixture of poor-quality cocaine base and marijuana) inside Colombia. In so doing, what they represented was not a cartel but a *gremio*, a trade association, standard in Colombian business, set up to engage in political lobbying and to maintain the industry's public image.

On the economic front there were some instances of cooperation. Larger producers would occasionally front a shipment for a smaller one; sometimes ad hoc groups would buy shares in large loads. There was some cooperation in moving individually produced product to individually controlled marketing outlets abroad when transportation was available whose capacity exceeded the needs of any one producer. None of this adds up to a conspiracy to dominate a market. Even the fact that some producers briefly ran an informal mutual insurance company to reduce losses from seizures hardly makes for a cartel: virtually all businesses take out insurance, and Medellín "cartel" members could scarcely ask Lloyd's to underwrite their risks.[33]

Thus, the reality is that far from being run as a top–down conspiracy, the Colombian cocaine business was (and is) conducted using much the same sort of business relations as those that characterized the U.S. Mafia. Boundaries are fluid, the characters change, and their links show the same confusion of kinship relationships, formal and informal partnerships, and arms-length commercial exchanges. Despite tactical cooperation at the political level (financing electoral campaigns or running death squads, for example), there was (is) no effort to restrict product quantity to control price. Indeed, throughout the so-called Medellín cartel's existence, the trend of prices was down, and inside the target market, conditions were a free-for-all.

Just as with the Mafia and its rackets, more accurate information about the Colombian cocaine traffic was available—but it said politically inconvenient things. The Medellín cartel had its equivalent of Joseph Valachi, a star informant whose actual testimony stated the opposite of what the authorities and the press imputed to it. When Max Mermelstein (supposedly the most senior "cartel executive" to become a government informant and a key witness in the RICO case) testified before Congress, he insisted that all members of the cartel maintained their own marketing branches in the United States (thus precluding any effort to control price by manipulating quantity). Even the social security aspects of cartel operations were remarkably limited. When asked further about how the cartel protected its officers, Mermelstein replied that arrested members pick their own lawyers and that "everybody is also responsible for paying for their own."[34]

Immediately after the death of Pablo Escobar, the reputed capo de tutti capi of the Medellín cartel, the U.S. Drug Enforcement Administration (DEA) began insisting that even worse enemies were lurking in the Colombian jungles. It shifted the spotlight to the Cali cartel, immediately imputing to it responsibility for 80 percent of the world's cocaine, the figure formerly blamed on the Medellín cartel. This example of rising to a market opportunity is so remarkable that it should be studied at business schools around the world. Said the DEA, "The [Cali] cartel is the best and brightest of the modern underworld: professional, intelligent, efficient, imaginative and nearly impenetrable. . . . No criminal organization rivals them today or perhaps any time in history." *Time* magazine chipped in with the usual multinational, multidivisional corporation analogy, claiming that

> The Cali families are conservative managers, much like other big corporate heads. In the home office sit the chief executive officer and his senior vice presidents for acquisition, sales, finance and enforcement. The logistics of importing, storing and delivering the product to wholesalers are handled by dozens of overseas branches, or cells, overseen by the home office through daily, often hourly phone calls.

This is remarkable intelligence about an organization the DEA claimed was "nearly impenetrable." The only thing missing was a list of their golf club memberships.

About the only person to protest this nonsense was Gilberto Rodriguez-Orejuela, the supposed boss of the supposed cartel. While offering to surrender, and making no secret of the nature of his principal business, he scoffed: "You think one person . . . can control all the cocaine being sent from Cali?" He went on to state, "The Cali cartel . . . [is] a figment of the

DEA's imagination. . . . There are lots of groups, but there is no cartel. The police know that. So does the DEA. But they prefer to invent one monolithic enemy."[35]

Then, after the (remarkably easy) defeat of the Cali group, came a never-ending succession of Mexican "cartels," each seemingly more fearful than the previous.

Why the persistence of the stereotype in the face of the evidence? There is apparently a comfortable symbiosis of objectives between law enforcement and the mass media. The first institution shows a propensity to hype the target both to enhance self-esteem and to coax more power and money from governments. The second needs to cater to a public in search of vicarious thrills. A coldly calculating cartel uniting stone killers and Harvard MBAs is excellent for selling copy; a jumble of crude, uncoordinated, and trigger-happy wheeler-dealers, some of whom are wired up on their own product, is much less so.

The Culture of Violence and Corruption

Organized crime supposedly differs from ordinary criminality in its propensity to use corruption and violence to achieve its ends. Clearly, organized crime by any definition has no monopoly on bribery; that offense is common in white-collar crime as well. Violence too is by no means exclusive to organized crime. Therefore, if organized crime is in some way exceptional, it must deploy corruption and violence in a different way; after all, police keep telling the world that the hold of organized crime continues to tighten, yet violent crimes in North America and western Europe continue to drop, as they have for about thirty years.

To be effective in raising the rate of return of a particular firm or group of firms, corruption must be used selectively. Corruption run amok is less a payment for a specific service than a general license fee paid by everyone to operate. This is why "organized crime" groups might attempt to centralize the corruption function in the hands of the boss and to target payments not to individual police officers but to senior officials of the police and the municipal administration. But the power of traditional organized crime to influence the U.S. regulatory apparatus has been in sharp decline since the 1960s. There are still instances of police officers, civic officials, and politicians accepting payoffs, but these are much more episodic than in the past.[36] Even where systemic, corruption—unless it increases monopoly power—has nothing to differentiate it from bribery by ordinary criminals, or for that matter, by legitimate business people.

Similarly, there is a logical expectation that acts or threats of violence used by organized crime are not random and gratuitous; rather, they are selective and directed to some specific end. At least in North America, the targets of acts of violence are not regulators or the general public but other participants in the criminal marketplace. Even then the perpetrator must be careful. Violence brings unwanted attention from the regulators, which is especially inconvenient to criminals engaged in on-going market enterprises rather than episodic predatory ones. Violence can impose direct business costs by interrupting the flow of transactions. (That is precisely why trust and kinship are so much more important to assure that contracts are respected.) If criminal markets were truly monopolized, the costs of violence (or corruption) would merely be passed on to the consumers of illegal goods and services. To the extent that those markets are competitive, the costs have to be swallowed by the criminal firm.

Furthermore, there are many possible uses for violence aside from monopolization. It might be used, when other measures fail, to enforce discipline within a criminal firm or to assure that contractual obligations incurred by outsiders are met. If so, there is nothing in the act itself, or the motivation, to distinguish it from the type of violence used by ordinary criminals who might find themselves in the same position. Indeed, the fact that individual members of organized crime groups might require some sort of permission to carry out such acts suggests that criminals associated with "organized crime" might be less inclined to violence than are "unorganized" ones in the same kinds of businesses.[37] But this does not necessarily enhance market power and therefore raise the rate of return by driving out competitors. It might merely change the identity and affiliation of those competing within a certain area.

Cashing In

Another alleged characteristic of organized crime—that its activities generate an inordinately high rate of return—is questionable in both theory and practice.

A legal firm faces three major constraints on its profit rate—increased competition attracted by its own exceptional performance, public opprobrium (i.e., the charge of profiteering), and ultimately, regulatory sanction. On this front, it would seem, the illegal firm has an advantage. But in reality the illegal firm faces all of these constraints and more: there are few barriers to deter competitors, customer loyalty is minimal, and regulators usually target the largest and most profitable first. The result is that contrary to the stereotype, profits in most criminal industries are widely distributed among many. And for individual underworld entrepreneurs, not only are earnings likely to be relatively modest but there will probably be constant demands that they be shared among an array of hangers-on.

At first glance it would also seem that the legal firm suffers a disadvantage to the extent that part of its revenue is paid in taxes. However, illegal enterprises have to pay their own form of taxes—tribute payments to a local crime boss or bribery payments to regulators.

To be sure, the criminal entrepreneur might have other advantages— an ability to use violence or its threat to enforce contracts, intimidate customers, cheat suppliers, and scare off regulators. But the reality is that there are serious limits as to where and how often those actions can be taken. When they occur, they are as much a sign of the weakness of the criminal entrepreneur as a mark of success.

Not surprisingly, every close investigation of the actual returns to criminal enterprises shows that the overwhelming majority are not only small, unstable, and highly competitive but that they collect only modest and irregular earnings.[38] Raised against the facts is the power of abiding myth.

No better example exists than that of the fabled wealth of Meyer Lansky. In 1967 a *Miami Herald* reporter estimated Lansky's fortune at $300 million. The legendary Lansky, basking in public glory, said nothing to disabuse the public. For three decades the $300 million figure was repeated without serious dissent. Yet after Lansky's death, when his family opened the archives, so to speak, the largest value that could safely be put on his net wealth at peak was $3 million—comfortable, although scarcely the stuff of which legends could be fashioned.[39]

Nor is this puffery merely the domain of over-enthusiastic reporters. In a 1985 study for the U.S. Presidential Commission on Organized Crime, Wharton Econometrics claimed that then–Gambino Family boss John Gotti was hauling in $300 million per year at a time when his own tax returns reported an annual salary of about $36,000 from his job as a salesman for a plumbing supply company. True, Gotti held, through various front men, secret stakes in a number of ventures, including bars, a discotheque, a motel, a Chinese restaurant, and a school bus service. But that was hardly the investment portfolio of the chief executive of a General Motors of crime. His portfolio also contained some middle-class real estate and one modest speedboat. But it did not include a chateau in the south of France or a yacht that slept forty.[40]

The bias toward large numbers reflects the fundamental presumption that organized crime operates collectively as a business rather than as a para-political association. If decisions are made not with respect to small and individual enterprises but with regard to the marketplace as a whole, it stands to reason that such decisions require substantial amounts of operating capital and generate equally substantial amounts of profit. By the same kind of circular reasoning, the greater the threat to the integrity of legal markets the mob is assumed to pose, the greater the amount of seed money criminals logically must have at their disposal to finance a move into legitimate enterprises.

In the 1950s and 1960s, this seed money was assumed to come from illegal gambling. This was a notion given official approval by a congressional committee when it claimed in 1951 that illegal gambling was yielding the mob annual revenues of about $20 billion. Researchers for the committee later revealed the scientific basis for the estimate. They took the $12 billion figure casually suggested by the California Crime Commission and the $30 billion figure offered by a city of Chicago "expert" and, in their own words, "picked twenty billion as a balance between the two." It was certainly a frightening number, equal to some 6 percent of the then-current U.S. GNP.[41]

By the 1980s, the search for seed money had moved from gambling to drugs and from the United States to the entire world. The result during the 1980s and early 1990s was the $500 billion estimate of annual turnover in the worldwide illegal drugs business; of that amount, the United States was supposed to have accounted for at least $100 billion. The $500 billion figure was the result of "research" attempted by the United Nations agency responsible for coordinating the global assault on drug trafficking—when the boss was desperate for a quick number before a press conference. Thereafter the figure was cited often in the mass media. It achieved new dignity when no less an authority than *Fortune* magazine repeated it.[42] With that accolade, the figure was quoted with approval by the U.S. Senate Judiciary Committee. Yet when one of the senior UN officers involved in the original estimate was queried skeptically about its accuracy, he replied that whatever its scientific failings, $500 billion was a useful figure for capturing public attention.[43]

He was quite correct. Both the world total of $500 billion and the U.S. market's share of $100 billion were widely reported. On the other hand, an independent Rand Commission study that suggested the actual U.S. drug market figure might be as low as $20 billion was pointedly ignored.

Even if it were true that such great sums do pass through the world drug trade accounts, that scenario does not automatically translate into a fearsome attack on the world economic order by criminal robber barons rolling in cash. To begin with, the sums cited are usually for gross expenditures. But how much people spend on drugs is not the same thing as how much criminals earn from supplying them.

Furthermore, the fact that there is a constant flow of drugs onto the market does not mean that the drug-trade equivalent of Microsoft puts them there. A host of small traffickers engaged in episodic transactions might assure more market stability than one large firm whose operations could easily be interrupted by the criminological equivalent of an antitrust suit. Hence even the total net earnings (a term that applies to the market as a whole) is useless as an indicator of criminal financial power unless and until distribution of that profit among participants is taken explicitly into account.

Finally, assuming that the figures for total drug expenditure are fairly close to the popular estimates, it is necessary to ask why. Large expenditures are the result of either large quantities or high prices. It is unlikely that quantities are rising because the total user population of North America appears stagnant or falling. If gross expenditures remain high, it is because prices are high, for which there are three possible reasons. One is price-fixing cartels—which simply do not exist. The second is the high cost of production—which is scarcely the case, because the raw materials from which the big three recreational drugs are fashioned are prolific weeds, and the transformation process, even with heroin, is hardly expensive. The third is enforcement. Prices are high precisely because enforcement has made the business risky. But if drug prices are high, and therefore the sums flowing through drug markets are large, because enforcement has been successful, it is strange logic to point to the enormous value of the annual drug trade as evidence of lack of capacity to enforce and therefore of the need for drastic new enforcement tools.

In reality, enforcement has two effects. It drives up the total value of the drugs being traded by pushing up the price, therefore imposing a higher financial burden on users. Also, it forces traffickers to increase the layers of intermediation, and thus the resulting profits must be distributed over large numbers of participants. It is hard to see what more could be expected or desired from law enforcement than this.

The Hostile Takeover

When the organized crime threat first came to be taken seriously in the 1950s and 1960s, the main worry was not just that criminals might accumulate large amounts of wealth by catering to illegal desires. Rather, it was the prospect that this wealth could be used as seed money for criminal infiltration of legal business. Part of this concern may have been deliberately contrived: it was difficult to get the public upset about illegal gambling but easy to sew fears about a hostile takeover of major sectors of the legitimate economy by Cosa Nostra Inc. Part of the concern, however, was certainly genuine. At the time, evidence indicated that criminals had infiltrated such sectors as construction, entertainment, waste disposal, and garment manufacturing—sometimes directly, sometimes through control of unions. The more recent possibility that drug wealth might be similarly used, but on a much greater scale, has rekindled those concerns.

The debate, however, fails to distinguish criminal assets, which are the means to commit more crimes, from criminally earned assets, which are the results of those crimes—an important distinction because the second is not automatically or inevitably recycled back in the form of the first. Nor, for that matter, is there a clear differentiation between criminally earned assets and assets earned by criminals, a category that could include those assets resulting from the profits of perfectly legitimate ventures. The fact that a convicted criminal owns a business hardly suffices to make that business a criminal enterprise.[44]

Take the example of the superstar informant Joseph Valachi. A prototype of the petty gangster working alone to seize whatever opportunity for a quick buck came along, Valachi graduated from thief to loan shark, with a brief incursion into the numbers racket and, during World War II, peddling stolen ration coupons. It is true that loan-sharking led to his partial takeover of a restaurant when its owner, a gambling addict, defaulted. But the restaurant, like a later venture in the garment trade, was legitimate, and it was acquired because he needed the steady income. Later, in his garment business, the only criminal acts were committed by his strictly legitimate partner, who stole the money that had been withheld from employees' wages to cover social security taxes; as a result, the federal government seized their machinery and put the firm out of business. In a delicious irony, it was the dishonesty of his legitimate business partner, and the consequent loss of legal income, that prompted Valachi to enter into the drug ventures that led to his arrest and, according to no less an authority than Rudolph Giuliani, to the passage of the RICO statute.[45]

Leaving aside the issue of under what circumstances and how often criminally earned assets are actually used to corrupt legal markets—an empirical question to which the answer seems to be "rarely"—there are three more fundamental considerations.

The first is whether in fact there are huge amounts of criminal wealth waiting to penetrate the legal economy. This is more than a matter of absolute numbers. For if criminal earnings, however large in aggregate amount, are relatively well distributed over many entrepreneurs, there seems little danger of wholesale and directed takeovers that could fundamentally transform legitimate business sectors. Rather, if they were to move into operating businesses, as opposed to making passive investments, criminals would replicate in the legal economy the structure that prevails in the illegal one—many small and competitive firms.

The second is whether major and expanding sectors of the legal economy are vulnerable to takeover. The historical pattern has been that criminal (and criminalizing) investments occurred in sectors typified by small, backward firms in which technology was primitive and the labor force unskilled and uneducated—sectors long in decline. Moreover, far from a business venture being taken over by criminals, the usual pattern has been that some mobster took an official position in which he supervised collection of extortion payments, leaving management of the business itself to people who actually knew how to do it. Furthermore, the main tool of takeover was either collecting on illegal debts (something rendered less likely by the advent of consumer credit and the existence of small business development banks) or deploying captive unions (something rendered less likely by federal action against the most important of those unions and the general decline of organized labor).

The third is whether the initiative in bringing career criminals into legitimate businesses necessarily comes from criminals. The main problem today may not be criminals taking over and subverting legal business so much as legal business using criminal methods and therefore sometimes contracting with career criminals for particular jobs to achieve profit targets.[46] Indeed, there is something artificial in the distinction between a career criminal (who is usually part time) and an otherwise legitimate entrepreneur gone (temporarily?) bad.

Furthermore, is there really much of a difference in operational methods between, for example, mob-run waste disposal firms and garbage industry giants whose shares are traded on the New York Stock Exchange? The first achieved notoriety for price-fixing, bribery, bootlegging fuel, and midnight dumping—until replaced by the second, which quickly achieved notoriety for price-fixing, bribery, bootlegging fuel, and midnight dumping.[47]

If there is such little difference in results, the real problem is probably not organized crime but a general degradation of business ethics, a development that requires a more profound explanation than that it originated as a plot among aging Italian godfathers. Indeed, their role may be fairly derivative; many of the most notorious criminal entrepreneurs involved in trafficking in gold, arms, and drugs got their start smuggling cigarettes on behalf and with the active collaboration of the Anglo-

American tobacco cartel.[48] And if it is true that much of the initiative comes from the legal participants, the main target of crime control should be golf-club-wielding executives of brand-name corporations rather than pistol-packing mobsters with Hollywood-inspired nicknames.

That, of course, flies squarely in the face of the popular stereotype about transnational conspiracies invigorated by the boundless opportunities of a (supposedly) borderless world and by the infusion of new blood from the old Soviet Union.

The Russians Are Coming! The Russians Are Coming!

Vital to the international criminal conspiracy theory is the notion that a new organized crime threat is coming from Russia, that it is directly linked to the residual apparatus of the old Communist state, and that it apparently applies the Leninist principle of democratic centralism sufficiently well to control the activities of approximately six thousand recognized criminal groups. From where did this new Red Menace suddenly spring?

Certainly economic crime was well entrenched in the old Soviet Union, and it went through a number of distinct phases that affected the broader society in different ways.[49] First, during the period that the Soviet Union's central planning apparatus was functioning well and the political system commanded a fair degree of loyalty, criminal activity tended to be symbiotic with the regime. Planned output goals put forth by governmental officials frequently exceeded the capacity of the resources allocated to achieve those goals, yet the political and economic advancement of managers and apparatchiks required that those goals be met or surpassed. Therefore they would turn to the black market to acquire the extra resources required. Because the role of the black market was to grease the legal economy, providing some flexibility for managers to meet their goals, it was tolerated by the political authorities as the price of assuring that the planning system operated efficiently.

At this stage, which lasted into the early post-Stalin period, self-aggrandizing enterprise crime of the Western type was rare, in part because there was little social acceptance of it. In fact, the communist ideology, if not the regime itself, had emerged from World War II with much more internal social legitimacy than Western Cold War ideologues would admit. Moreover, there was relatively little incentive to commit economic crime. Access to the good life in an environment of scarcity and tight rationing depended on political power, not on income. It was almost impossible to manage large sums of illegal money: banks were monitored closely, there were no private businesses through which it could be laundered, and hordes of cash might rot before it could be converted safely into rationed consumer goods. And the disincentives were strong: whereas political dissidents were subjected to internal exile, committed to psychiatric hospitals, or sometimes sent to the Gulag, economic dissidents were shot.[50]

Beginning sometime in the 1960s, economic crime entered a more parasitical phase that reflected two structural changes. One was the rise of a new generation of leaders who lacked the ideological commitment of the veterans of the Bolshevik Revolution. The second was the failure of the consumer goods sector to replicate the success of the planning model in producing capital goods and military hardware; as a result, output continually lagged projections at a time of sharply rising expectations among the general population. Activity in the so-called second economy therefore shifted from trafficking in productive resources to meet state-set goals into misappropriating allocated resources to manufacture basic consumer goods for black market distribution, with the off-the-books proceeds going to the individuals who ran the operation. Along with this came a growing appetite for a lifestyle that the system itself could never support. Illegally obtained money was lavished on imported luxury goods that were either smuggled in or diverted to the black market from elite stores.

Initially, political tolerance at this parasitical stage reflected the corruption of individual functionaries plus the general hope that popular discontent could be reduced if a supply of basic goods not available in adequate quantities through the planning mechanism could be found on the black market. During the 1970s and into the 1980s, the motives for official tolerance became more complex. Although never admitted publicly, the second economy came to be seen as a means of sopping up some of the theoretically nonexistent unemployment and of channeling into commerce the energies of ethnic minorities left out of a mainly Slav-dominated power structure. It was this, the late parasitical stage, that was the incubator of the Soviet "mafia," a phrase the Soviet population picked up from watching old American gangster movies.

In the old Soviet Union the term "mafia" (or maffya) was used to refer not to broad criminal conspiracies but to occupationally specific corruption. There was a fishing mafia and a fruit and vegetable mafia, both of which diverted goods away from state outlets onto the lucrative black market. There was a hotel mafia, which refused to book rooms, even in mostly empty establishments, unless additional payments were made. There was a transportation mafia that did likewise with airlines and trains. And so forth. Individual acts of corruption soon gave way to systemic fraud, with state functionaries covering up and sometimes participating.

But there was no ruling commission of any sort to coordinate operations either then or in the predatory stage that followed.

By the beginning of the 1980s, perhaps a little earlier, economic crime shifted to a predatory mode, eroding the foundations of the system and ultimately helping to precipitate its downfall. During the 1980s, while Cold War propagandists in the West were still busy peddling the stereotype of a Stalinist totalitarian state, Soviet central authority was routinely defied; the planning mechanism was subverted by deliberately falsified information, sometimes on a massive scale;[51] and regional power brokers forged alliances with mafia bosses in which they exchanged political support for muscle and money in a combined assault on the central government's authority. While in the United States Republican ideologues thundered on about the Evil Empire, Mikhail Gorbachev was speaking publicly about large areas of the Soviet Union being outside central control.

It was an era, too, when criminality of a Western type became widespread. Drug trafficking exploded after the war in Afghanistan. In a remarkable remake of the U.S. experience of the 1920s, a well meaning but clumsily executed anti-vodka campaign shifted bootlegging from a cottage industry to a large-scale racket. This campaign managed to undermine state finances, promote the massive looting of sugar supplies, and feed the coffers of big-time crime while doing nothing to reduce alcohol addiction among the population. And during perestroika, along with the liberalization and decentralization of legitimate business operations came the spread of extortion rackets.

Thus the most important form of economic crime was no longer symbiotic with the central planning system, nor, for that matter, was it even parasitic on the system. Although residuals of those relationships certainly existed, the real action was in activities that were economically corrosive and allied with an upstart class of political aspirants from the republics and regions in a wholesale assault on the central authority. The dominant form of economic crime had shifted from bolstering the planning apparatus—the core of the central power structure in a multinational state—to, first, subverting the state, and then to helping the emergent anti-Soviet political class overthrow the state, leaving political chaos and ethnic warfare in its wake.

In short, the spread of economic crime destroyed any remaining viability of the planning system from three sides: it diverted resources away from the formal economy; it undermined the central power necessary to make the system work; and it warped social values away from collectivism and toward individualism. Crime thus brought the spirit of capitalism to a morally, politically, and financially bankrupt USSR and turned the predators loose first within the Soviet Union and then across Europe and North America. Some came as individuals, some as gangs; none, however, represented a massive international criminal conspiracy hell-bent on world conquest.

Fighting Back!

Crime is a serious social problem. But as to whether the contemporary world is being subjected to "the most massive and insidious criminal assault in history," it is a pity one cannot go back in history and ask the opinion of those on the receiving end when the Spanish conquistadors plundered the Americas, or when the British Empire sacked India, kidnapped millions from Africa into chattel slavery, or addicted massive numbers of Chinese to opium. Nor is there any proof that the current threat is sufficient or of such virulence to justify some of the emergency measures advocated in many countries, and in the United States most prominently.

To begin with, it is by no means clear that the most pressing crime problem facing the West is actually organized crime, whatever that may mean. Nor even whether it is instigated by career criminals, who can be differentiated from the rest of society by socioethnic roots or an antisocial and predatory psychology. Rather the real problems may be twofold. One is the spread (if indeed it really is spreading) of business crimes, for which, so-called organized crime groups can be assigned little responsibility. The owner-manager of a cash-based retail business who conducts seemingly normal trade might, for example, start the slide down the slippery slope by selling for cash to evade excise and sales taxes, or by skimming from the till to evade income taxes. Going a little further, he or she might pad the payroll to inflate costs in order to cheat creditors or partners—or the long-suffering tax collectors. At some point this ill-fated owner-manager might spend the cash on illegal gambling or drugs, have to borrow from a loan shark to replace the lost operating capital, and then skim more cash to repay the loan shark. Desperate for cash flow, the owner-manager might connive with others in the same market area to fix prices; or perhaps the owner might accept cash from someone who wants to use the location to run a numbers racket. Down even further, he or she might purchase smuggled cigarettes, pirated videocassettes, or stolen jewelry for resale; sell customers' credit card numbers to the operator of an internet porn site; pay someone to torch an adjoining building to claim the insurance; or hire some bikers to break the legs of union organizers. At what point does that individual cross the line from legitimate businessperson gone astray to career criminal? More important, should it matter?

The second area in which criminal activity may pose an increasing threat is at the lower end of the income scale. This activity usually involves a range of offenses from petty theft to welfare fraud, and it results from a mixture of desperation, expectations inflated beyond means, and general deterioration of social attitudes; these, in turn, reflect not the machinations of evil aliens running organized crime cartels but a growing maldistribution of wealth, deterioration of working conditions, and shrinkage of the traditional social safety net.

Moreover, even in those fields in which organized crime might play a role, it certainly has no monopoly. And the offenses that supposedly necessitate organization are precisely those that are consensual, which often calls into question whether they should be crimes at all.

Traditionally, the sanction of being charged—and convicted—of a crime was a powerful deterrent because it targeted a special subset of actions that the public at large accepted as being particularly odious. In the case of economically motivated offenses, the proscribed actions were largely predatory, and they involved the involuntary transfer of wealth through force or fraud where the harm was clear. Under those circumstances, labeling someone a criminal was by itself the most important part of the punishment—fines and imprisonment were secondary; they were as much atonement as punishment. However, the more the criminal sanction is used to forbid conduct involving personal moral choices, the more it loses its bite. The public at large ceases to view the criminal act with opprobrium. Therefore, to maintain any capacity to deter, the secondary part of the sanction must be greatly escalated, perhaps out of all proportion to the public's perception of the severity of the actual offense.[52]

Even if society persists in criminalizing personal moral choices, the resulting market-based offenses are radically different from traditional predatory ones in that they have a supply side and a demand side. This has both moral and practical consequences.

In moral terms, there is nothing inherent in the offense that makes the two sides of the market distinguishable. For a market to operate there must be willing suppliers, but there must also be willing customers. The suggestion is sometimes made that legitimate citizens who shop in illegal markets are unaware of the nasty stuff behind the supply. This is tantamount to suggesting that the rash of Hollywood thrillers, in which heroes and villains compete to coat the streets with blood and gore, all accompanied by a sound track of grunts, shrieks, and explosions, has served to reduce demand for illegal goods and services. The opposite is more likely true; if anything, the public has an exaggerated picture of the blood and gore involved, and that probably adds to the thrill of buying the product. Another common suggestion is that customers are in some way victims. That also does not hold. Unless it can be established that a drug user, for example, was forcibly held down and injected not once, not twice, but often enough to create a heroin addiction, it must be assumed the user is just as much a consensual participant in the criminal marketplace as anyone on the supply side. To the extent that it is ever possible to portray drug users as victims, the question must be asked: Victims of what and who? Does the responsibility for the drug habits of dwellers of blighted inner cities, for example, rest with the suppliers, or with the industries that have fled elsewhere to seek cheap and nonunionized labor, or with the political authorities who have slashed education and welfare spending and basically abandoned those areas to their fate?

In practical terms, although supply-side control may work for predatory offenses, it is rare, perhaps impossible, to find a black market successfully tamed by an attack from the supply side. Individuals may be punished, but as long as the culture of demand persists, the market continues to function as before. Yet the entire thrust of organized crime control to date—whether through RICO-type statutes, anti-money-laundering and asset-seizure initiatives, or criminalization of association—has been on the supply side of the market equation.

Furthermore, even if it were true that part of the current threat takes the form of powerful criminal syndicates marching across the globe, no one has ever proven that existing laws and methods, if properly used, are inadequate to the task. In all the hype about the presumed threat of organized crime, no one seems to have asked whether part of the (alleged) failure of the legal and police infrastructure to cope with it has more to do with incompetent prosecutors and ignorant or misinformed police officers than with a lack of harsh new laws.

Not least, although perhaps there are forms of crime sufficiently international to require some sort of political response, when law enforcement and foreign policy are confounded, all too often the first gets twisted to serve the independently derived needs of the second, which themselves may not pass objective scrutiny.

Thus, the U.S. drug war in the Andes has never had much to do with drugs but with countering leftist insurgents, although the distinction is glossed over by exaggerated claims that the insurgents control cocaine trafficking. And the invasion of Panama, which led to the devastation of slum neighborhoods and the death of hundreds of innocent civilians in order to capture one renegade CIA agent, was justified as the World's

Biggest Drug Bust—taking to its logical absurdity the notion of police action by a military eager to meet a growing post–Cold War threat to the Pentagon budget. Interestingly, and disturbingly, this confounding of crime prevention with foreign policy concerns is far from new. In the 1950s, two right-wing U.S. senators were vying with each other to see who could best capture the media spotlight to help in securing their party's presidential nomination. One of them, Estes Kefauver, chose as his vehicle the menace of the Italo-American Mafia; the other, Joseph McCarthy, seized upon the International Communist Conspiracy, and then, to further advance his public fame and political fortune at the expense of his rival, insisted that the Italo-American Mafia was itself merely an arm of international Communism.

Indeed, this confusion of foreign policy and crime control can be a two-way street, used by law enforcement to its own purposes as readily as by politicians. When William Gately, the U.S. Customs special agent who led Operation Casablanca, a much-publicized drug-money sting operation against a series of Mexican banks, stood before a 1998 meeting at the U.S. Justice Department's National Drug Intelligence Center, he explained his operating philosophy. Americans, he insisted, should never forget how Pancho Villa crossed the border with his bands of desperados to loot and burn U.S. towns. The United States, Gately insisted to a rapturous crowd of law enforcement honchos missing only their six shooters and ten-gallon hats, has to go back across the border and kick butt. Emerging U.S. foreign policy indeed.

CHAPTER 2

The Insurgent Economy
Black Market Operations
of Guerrilla Groups

Today's archetypical terrorist no longer crouches in a moldy basement, its cracked windows draped with black cloth, humming the "Internationale" as he wires a windup alarm clock to a box of stolen dynamite. Instead, he boots up his laptop to check if the latest tax-deductible donations received by his U.S.-based "charitable" organization have been deposited in his Swiss bank account. Then he mutters a soft *allahu akbar* while dialing up FedEx to arrange delivery to the nearest synagogue of a load of anthrax bacilli recently purchased from an ex–KGB officer.

Such a stereotype has led alarmed governments to pass draconian laws against fund-raising by "terrorist" organizations. Countries as varied as Israel and Great Britain have passed legislation targeting "terrorist funds" for search and seizure as part of their counterinsurgency campaigns in occupied Palestine and Northern Ireland, respectively. Financial sanctions, formerly reserved for pariah states, are being applied to insurgent groups to cut off their sources of black market earnings. And a division of the United Nations Office for Drug Control and Crime Prevention has been created to study the phenomenon of insurgent financing on the implicit assumption that crime and insurgency, if not identical, are closely related, at least in their financial aspects.

Furthermore, egged on by the U.S. State Department, many countries have signed the International Convention on the Suppression of the Financing of Terrorism. Signatories pledge to criminalize not only fund-raising by groups they designate as foreign terrorist organizations but the act of knowingly donating to them as well. The convention requires further that these countries empower their law enforcement authorities to freeze and seize money that *could* be used for terrorist purposes.

Leave aside the obvious problem that "terrorist group" is a nonsensi-cal term: terrorism is a political tool, not an objective, and it is used with at least as great facility by governments as by insurgent groups opposing them. The central question then becomes whether crime and insurgency are really coalescing into a long-term strategic alliance (as distinct from the occasional tactical combination) within the ambit of a growing world-wide black market economy. If so, are both amenable to the same forms of control, specifically an attack on their financial foundations? To an-swer such questions requires an in-depth look at what insurgent groups, regardless of ideology, actually do, which in turn demands a look back into late-twentieth-century history as well as a glance forward into the near future.

Contention, Expansion, and Control

A world of difference exists between the motives of insurgent versus crimi-nal groups. Criminals commit economic crimes to make money. The buck, so to speak, stops there. But to an insurgent group, money is merely a tool—one that is necessary but not sufficient to achieve the group's goals. Like the formally constituted governments they challenge, insurgent groups have political programs, even if sometimes simplistic; they have control over armed forces, even if sometimes makeshift; and they directly compete with the state for territory, population, and resources. An in-surgent group, unlike a criminal one, but like the government it combats, undertakes a wide range of expenditures on everything from warfare to welfare, while striving to prevent financial corruption among militants and to overcome fiscal resistance from the general population.

Expenditure obligations depend on both the scale and the form of a guerrilla struggle. In the earliest stages of an insurgency, a guerrilla group operates in (to use the terminology of El Salvador's old Farabundo Martí para la Liberación Nacional, or FMLN) zones of contention. Here the rebel organization engages mainly in hit-and-run operations—assassinations and kidnappings of officials or raids on police and mili-tary barracks—to politically discredit the government. In this stage, beyond which urban guerrilla groups rarely advance, expenditure re-quirements are overwhelmingly military and relatively small.

As a guerrilla group matures, it becomes more deeply entrenched in a particular geographic area, known as a zone of expansion. In such a zone, the strategy switches to classic low-intensity warfare: the main targets cease to be political symbols; instead, they are economic structures. The objective is not yet the capture of territory. Rather it is the destruction of basic infrastructure and the disruption of industry and commerce to cause investment to shrink, capital to flee, formal production to fall, and un-employment and inflation to rise.[1]

Following such principles, the National Union for the Total Indepen-dence of Angola (UNITA) guerrilla movement for twenty-five years has made the Angolan economy its principal target. UNITA has destroyed wheat and manioc crops destined for local consumption, it has driven the government out of diamond-mining areas and attacked coffee plantations to undermine the country's foreign exchange earnings, and it regularly sabotages the railway and road network to disrupt commerce.[2]

Similarly, Peru's Sendero Luminoso, before the capture and jailing of its leadership, targeted mines, the main (legal) source of the country's for-eign exchange, through direct attacks and politically inspired strikes. It bombed factories and kidnapped executives of transnational corporations to provoke capital flight. And it blew up power lines both to hurt the for-mal economy and to deliver, at little risk, a massive demonstration of the government's impotence.[3]

So too in nearby Colombia, where over the last fifteen years rebels have bombed the oil pipelines more than a thousand times and kidnapped hun-dreds of oil company executives and workers, causing investment to dry up and costing the government heavily in lost export revenues and royalties.[4] Those same Colombian guerrillas make electricity towers a prime target—to publicize their opposition to privatization and to raise the cost of electricity by driving up repair bills.[5]

Indeed, it is sometimes possible to strike more directly. For example, in 2001, rebels in North Acheh shook the financial foundations of the In-donesian government by seizing control of a huge Exxon-Mobil gas fa-cility that had paid the government $2 billion in taxes and royalties. The seizure sent the company's main customers (South Korea and Japan) scrambling for alternate sources of supply and forced the Indonesian gov-ernment, formerly intent on reconciliation, to shift the struggle against separatism from the political to the military front, precisely what both the rebels and the military wanted.[6]

This kind of tactic can be remarkably cost-effective. Thus, in Papua–New Guinea, after years of fruitless agitation for autonomy, the Bougainville Revolutionary Army turned its attention to the world's largest copper mine. After two decades of operation, the mine had grown to more than four miles in circumference, had piled up millions of tons of tailings, and had poisoned the island's largest river with toxic metals. Almost the entire work force of the mine was imported, along with the soldiers to protect it. Although the mine paid the Papua–New Guinea government a billion dollars in taxes and royalties, Bougainville itself got perhaps $20 million. In 1992, using bows and arrows, spears, and stolen shotguns, the rebels, who demanded a referendum on independence and $11.5 billion in compensation, shut the mine. The Papua–New Guinea government in desperation turned security and counterinsurgency over to a private mercenary force made up mainly of former South African commandos which precipitated a major scandal without reopening the mine.[7]

Nor does the target have to be a physical resource. Campaigns by groups as varied as the Uruguayan Tupamaros in the 1960s to the Basque-separatist Euskadi ta Azkatasuna (ETA) today aim to disrupt the tourist trade by kidnappings, bombings, and assassinations in hopes of denying the government a major source of foreign exchange.[8] Years before the Afghan Taliban earned so much opprobrium by blowing up the huge Buddhist statutes in Bamian, the Egyptian Gamaat al Islamiya threatened to destroy the pyramids and other pharaonic monuments; if successful, they would have struck a blow for their vision of Islamic purity as well as against the government's tourist revenues.[9]

As an insurgency succeeds in eroding the formal economy, either by direct action or as the result of government countermeasures, the population comes to depend increasingly on the informal economy for survival. This trend reinforces the success of guerrilla tactics in several ways. It further discredits the government among those sectors of the population most prone to accept the guerrilla movement's message; it shrinks the fiscal resources available to the government; and it expands the relative size of the black markets from which guerrilla movements draw material support. Needless to say, the more unbalanced the existing distribution of income and the larger the percentage of the population already scraping by within the informal economy, the more the burden of a meltdown can be made to fall on the government and its wealthier supporters.

In this second stage, financial sustenance is of growing importance. Military expenditures escalate as the size and firepower of military units increase along with the frequency and scale of operations. At this stage, the social service component of the guerrilla group's budget also becomes significant. Funds are needed to care for the dependents of its militants and potential supporters—because a true insurgent movement, as distinct from one engaged purely in political adventurism, must displace at least partially the social services provided by the government under challenge. This reinforces the guerrilla group's popular appeal while diminishing that of the government.

Finally, as a guerrilla movement becomes more secure, it creates zones of control, which are economically useful for stabilizing the funding base.[10] This is one reason why Colombian guerrilla groups have insisted, as part of the terms of a ceasefire, that the government cede to them de jure control of a tract approximately the size of Switzerland. Zones of control are also politically useful in that they confer greater legitimacy (along with international visibility) on the guerrilla movement. This was the motivation behind the Afghan mujahideen's waste of equipment and manpower in the late 1980s in an effort to seize the city of Jalalabad and declare it the capital of "free Afghanistan." Zones of control, too, are important militarily. They can form, as they did for the Eritrean People's Liberation Front, the base from which to shift from guerrilla warfare to a full-fledged insurrection capable of ousting the formal government.

In this third stage, with the guerrilla movement firmly implanted on a piece of territory from which the state is effectively excluded, the group may need, on top of its normal expenses, funds to upgrade its arsenal to defend its gains. To these obligations are added those of providing social services to the general population of the zone of control and building the infrastructure necessary for the development of an economy parallel to (and, increasingly, instead of) the official one.

Thus, Peru's Sendero Luminoso, after it had taken over an area and chased out or killed officials of the old regime, would abolish markets and impose planting quotas to establish a new, cooperative rural society. In the cities, among the urban poor, it would organize the social services and infrastructure (soup kitchens, electricity, water, and so forth) the government did not or could not provide.

Similarly, the New People's Army (NPA) in the poorest rural areas of the Philippines implemented land reform: it expropriated big landlords and redistributed their agricultural equipment and livestock, while it forced smaller landlords to cut rents and compelled merchants to raise the prices they paid to farmers. It also attempted to replace capitalist principles with a cooperative parallel economy whose marketing links stretched into the cities, where products of the parallel economy were sold in informal markets.[11]

Even the Bougainville rebels did likewise, although not from choice. Papua–New Guinea blockaded the island, forcing the population to improvise (for example, by using coconut oil for lubrication and converting old washing machines into electric generators) and to smuggle essentials from sympathetic kinfolk in the Solomon Islands.[12]

Much the same held true in portions of Kampuchea run by the Khmer Rouge and in the Jaffna Peninsula of Sri Lanka before the Liberation

Tigers of Tamil Eelam were evicted. It holds true today in UNITA-controlled parts of Angola and in Nepal, where Maoist guerrillas run about a third of the country, while the rest is in crisis caused by the flight of Indian businesses, the collapse of tourism, and a tax strike by local merchants.[13]

In creating a parallel political economy, however, probably no group has matched the Lebanese Forces during the 1980s. It was not only the most powerful and best organized of Lebanon's myriad militias, para-militaries, and guerrilla groups, but in its enclave (embracing East Beirut and the area to the northeast) it reproduced most of the functions of the formal state. Its armed forces were outfitted with sophisticated equipment. It ran a police and intelligence force. It provided social services: housing for Christian refugees from elsewhere in Lebanon; food subsidies; fuel distribution; an information apparatus of newspapers and magazines, radio and television services; and a transportation system, including both a ferry service to Cyprus and an airstrip to partly replace the official one under the control of a rival force.[14]

At each stage, as it moves from contention to expansion to control, a group's obligations rise, while the nature of those obligations shifts increasingly from current to capital expenditures. To meet these additional needs, the group can rely on contributions from outside sponsors, or it can tap the resources of the host economy. Although these sources are not necessarily exclusive, each poses distinct advantages and disadvantages, and each calls for distinct tactics.

Underground Politics and Covert Foreign Aid

A guerilla group's private supporters abroad might be motivated by ideological solidarity—as were those on the impressive list of right-wing lobby groups, Christian fundamentalists, and paramilitary thrill-seekers who stepped forward to aid the Nicaraguan Contras after the U.S. Congress cut off official aid in 1982.[15] The UNITA guerrilla movement in Angola fared similarly. Indeed, UNITA even had the backing of a U.S. tax-exempt foundation that sold special commemorative silver and gold coins to precious-metal enthusiasts and right-wing monetary cranks, with the proceeds going variously to UNITA, the Mozambique National Resistance (RENAMO), and the Contras.[16]

Or supporters can be motivated more by religious or ethnic solidarity. In the early stages of its post-1969 campaign against the British, the Provisional Irish Republican Army's main source of income was contributions raised among Irish Americans, who were collectively much larger than the population of Ireland itself.[17]

Sometimes outside sponsorship trespasses into clear illegality. Irish money, nominally for humanitarian aid and therefore tax deductible by U.S. contributors, was diverted into black market arms purchases. Indeed, the Provos were probably the most successful, with the possible exception of Zionist groups, in using charitable foundations as a source of funding for military action.

Not only may donations be diverted into arms expenditures, but the solicitation process may be close to extortion. The Secret Army for the Liberation of Armenia (ASALA) shakes down Armenians across Europe to fund arms purchases. Other émigré communities have had similar experiences—with the Turkish Grey Wolves in Germany, the Kurdish Workers' Party (PKK) in France, Croatian rightist groups in North America during the Balkan wars, the Sikhs in Vancouver during the Khalistan insurrection, and the Kosovo Liberation Army (UCK) in Germany and Switzerland.[18]

Granted, with many insurgencies in developing countries, the exile population is too poor to give much direct financial aid. Nonetheless, opportunities exist. In the 1970s, one of the most important sources of support for the emerging Eritrean Liberation Front was members of the diaspora, 250,000 strong, who were encouraged to contribute 10 percent of their annual income through a charitable organization, the Eritrean Relief Association.[19] More recently both Tamil and Somali exiles have been accused of pulling off welfare fraud in their countries of exile (especially in Canada, with its more generous welfare services than those of the United States) to finance military operations back home. But how large the total is, how much is really organized as opposed to individually initiated, and how much of the fuss is really a cover for colored-immigrant bashing remain unclear.[20] The confusion is all the greater given that some of these accusations originate from besieged governments; that of Sri Lanka claimed in 1996 that only 10 percent of Tamils in Canada were genuine refugees and that the rest were simply there to raise money to fund terrorism back home.[21]

In a more benign fashion, some guerrilla groups—such as El Salvador's FMLN and the Philippines' NPA—have quietly influenced aid flows into their respective countries from nongovernmental agencies abroad, steering the funds into projects that fit the guerrilla group's own development program. Indeed, sometimes there is nothing very quiet about it: in Japan, nongovernmental organizations openly proclaimed their support for the NPA during fund-raising appeals; in Germany, others did the same for the FMNL. Such a strategy permits a guerrilla group not only to score a propaganda coup but also to channel more of its limited budget into military operations.

Alternatively, the guerrilla group can rely on public sponsors. Sometimes this might be inadvertent. Start-up matériel for the Khmer Rouge, while the group was still a marginal political force in the 1960s, came from the massive black market in U.S. goods intended as aid for the South Vietnamese regime. Similarly, part of the logistical needs of various Somali militia groups were met in the early 1990s by hijacking emergency food aid and diverting it to Kenya to be bartered for weapons and for the popular local narcotic qat.[22] SWAPO, the South West African People's Organization, would deliberately inflate the number of refugees in camps under its de facto supervision and thereby increase the amount of international aid it could divert.[23]

Sometimes donors are complicit, at least tacitly. One reason that the United States in the 1980s seemed relatively complacent about the Khmer Rouge's theft of supplies from refugee camps for Cambodians in Thailand was that the operation permitted the United States to support the notorious group without risk of public opprobrium. Sometimes, diversion might be a condition for the aid itself: the Sudan People's Liberation Army or its factions charge the international relief agencies fees to deliver assistance to the starving masses in whose name they fight, and then they use the aid agencies' trucks and aircraft for their own purposes.

For the guerrilla group there are two great advantages to assistance from a foreign government. One is the likelihood that the funds will be supplied regularly as long as the guerrilla movement conducts operations that fulfill the political objectives of the sponsor. The second is that outside aid can solve one of the main logistical problems insurgent forces face, namely, the supply of sophisticated arms.

In the early stages of an insurgency, local arms supplies may suffice. They might be manufactured. The FMLN, in its zones of control, established a string of underground factories that made crude weapons. Or the arms might be stolen. One of the boldest actions of the Uruguayan Tupamaros during their peak in the early 1970s saw them donning naval uniforms, marching into a training school, and looting it of arms and ammunition.[24]

There is also the local black market, supplied by underpaid and disgruntled soldiers. The more weapons the United States poured into the hands of the Philippine army, the greater the firepower of various Moro separatist groups in Mindanao. And in the 1980s, while the U.S. government denounced a mythical arms pipeline from Nicaragua to the El Salvadoran rebels, both Salvadoran and Guatemalan officers, along with Nicaraguan Contra leaders, topped up their offshore retirement savings plans by selling U.S.–supplied military hardware to the FMLN.

At some point, however, most successful guerrilla insurgencies find that local arms supplies are no longer adequate, because of a lack of either quantity or sophistication. Then the advantages of an outside sponsor become evident.

Thus, by the end of 1986, when the USSR announced its intention to pull out of Afghanistan, the United States and its allies had already provided the Afghan mujahideen rebels with some $3 billion in military aid, and hundreds of millions more had gone to the refugee population in Pakistan for humanitarian assistance. It was the largest insurgent-support operation in history, and analysts have calculated that the amount spent would have been sufficient to equip a field force of 200,000–300,000 men with sophisticated weaponry.[25]

At least, that was the theory. The reality was a little different. From one end of the supply chain to the other, diversion was the rule. Arms suppliers inflated invoices and pilfered cargo before loading. The CIA reputedly lifted weapons to support other insurgencies, such as those in Nicaragua and Angola, which Congress had banned from receiving official U.S. aid. On disembarkation at the port of Karachi, Pakistani military intelligence, which officially ran the aid operation, helped itself to a share, partly for its own use and partly for sales on the black market. The residual was handed over to Afghan resistance groups, not according to their military worth but in proportion to their political influence. And their political leaders sold off some into the black market. A similar traffic characterized the humanitarian aid. The result was that not only did international aid organizations have to scour the bazaars to buy back the diverted food, clothing, tents, and medicine, but some Afghan rebel chiefs used the proceeds from taxing opium to buy weapons already paid for on their behalf by the United States and Saudi Arabia. In the final analysis, somewhere between 60 and 85 percent of the aid flow was diverted, and not onto just the local but also the international arms black market, from which all manner of guerrilla groups and bandit gangs were able to draw their logistical requirements.[26]

Granted, relying on external sponsors has the advantage of guaranteed supplies of arms and regular flows of money, but there are evident disadvantages. If the source is revealed, aid from foreign governments makes the recipient appear to be a tool of outsiders. Worse, external aid comes with strings attached. To minimize those constraints, many guerrilla groups who receive outside aid make sure that they have alternate and supplementary sources of money. And to avoid those constraints altogether, others rely only on what can be raised through their own underground operations.

Bankers, Bagmen, and Bandits

If guerrilla groups act like nascent governments when they spend money, they act more like maturing criminals when they raise it. Whether insurgent or criminal, a group's choice of fund-raising technique depends on its relationship to the broader society and its relative strength vis-à-vis the enforcement arm of the state.[27]

When criminals are confined to a limited territory or linked to each other by only loose associations—as in urban street gangs, for instance— their criminal activities are essentially predatory. Vulnerable to the law enforcement apparatus, they concentrate on activities that minimize the length of their exposure and produce quick, usually one-time-only returns. Hijacking, bank robbery, and ransom kidnapping nicely fit the bill.

At a more advanced stage, criminal activity might pass from the predatory to the parasitical. Thus, with better supporting infrastructure, criminals engage in activities such as protection rackets, insurance scams, counterfeiting, bankruptcy frauds, and so forth, which impose an on-going drain on the formal economy in favor of the criminal one.

At the most sophisticated, the actions of criminals move from being parasitic off polite society to being symbiotic with it. In the symbiotic phase, territorial reach might easily extend to the national level or beyond, and the central focus of criminal enterprise becomes the provision of goods and services to polite society. This may take the form of illegal consumer goods—recreational drugs, sex for sale, illegal gambling, and the like. It may take the form of supplying to otherwise legitimate corporations a range of services—from security (including union busting) to illegal waste disposal—that those corporations cannot be seen supplying themselves.[28]

Similarly, when a guerrilla group exists in a state of geographic or political insecurity in the face of determined opposition from the state (in zones of contention), it may finance itself by predatory activities such as armed robberies and ransom kidnappings.

Subsequently, when the guerrilla group has better access to the resources of the territory in which it operates (in zones of expansion), and when, by the same token, the state is weaker and unable to provide adequate protection to the more-well-to-do population, fund-raising activities shift to the parasitical mode, particularly to extortion or "revolutionary taxation." There may also be a voluntary component, and in this regard some differences exist between insurgencies of the left and right. With the former, the sympathetic population is usually too poor to give much. Hence the main target is usually the wealthier elements, whose contributions are rarely, if ever, voluntary. However, even right-wing insurgencies sometimes target the well-to-do for a shakedown. Whereas the returns from predatory activities such as robbery or kidnapping are episodic, parasitical activities are more likely to yield a steadier income at much less risk.

Finally, when the guerrilla group has largely or completely secured control of territory, and marginalized, if not eliminated, the formal presence of the state (in zones of control), it shifts to symbiotic forms of fundraising. The key difference may not be the actual action that raises money so much as the way in which that action is conducted. "Taxation" might evolve from simply calling on a businessperson to extort money at gunpoint into having officials of the movement regularly contact businesses in the zone of control to negotiate the amount due in exchange for bona fide services rendered. At this point the analogy between criminal and guerrilla economic activity needs serious qualification.

In the symbiotic phase, criminals become an integral, functional part of the society off which they formerly had preyed. Rather than their income and wealth being a direct deduction from those of legitimate, formal society, the income and wealth of both increase (even though formal measures such as Gross Domestic Product might not measure it) because the criminal sector supplies goods and services that, for a variety of reasons, formal society's legitimate enterprises cannot be seen as providing.

By contrast, guerrilla groups that oppose the status quo do not set out to make their activities symbiotic with those of formal society but to create parallel economies from whose benefits the state and its supporters are excluded. Thus, when a guerrilla group has secured control of territory, it can act as a surrogate state, promoting certain economic activities in exchange for a share of the income. The most important sources will be taxation of commerce, exploitation of natural resources, and imposition of user fees for services. Just as the state in the official sectors of the economy relies on a mixture of public acceptance of its legitimacy and public fear of penalties to assure that taxes are paid, so too in the unofficial sector the guerrilla group's revenues depend on its establishing in the public mind some balance between the perceived legitimacy of its objectives and its perceived capacity to enforce its will.

In this case the economic development of the controlled area and the economic well-being of the population depend on the guerrilla group's provision of security and infrastructure. But any growth of income and wealth in the guerrilla-controlled area represents a deduction from the economic resources available to, and therefore the political-military power exercised by, the state against which the guerrilla group is working. Indeed, that separation can be formalized by the guerrilla group issuing its own currency and banning that of the state it opposes, a tactic employed by Liberia's National Patriotic Liberation Front or Kampuchea's Khmer Rouge, for example.

There is an important distinction here between guerrilla groups that operate in opposition to the state and paramilitary groups that operate to reinforce the state by conducting operations the state cannot itself be caught performing. Such official tolerance or covert encouragement differentiates, for example, Colombian paramilitary units organized by the army and the drug barons from antistate guerrilla forces. The objective of the paramilitary groups is to use the resources of the black market, particularly the drug trade, to defend the status quo in the face of the guerrilla challenge, and taking the occasion to knock off peasant or union leaders, nosy journalists, or opposition judges en route. The objective of the guerrillas is to build a parallel economic system to support political opposition, and they have no moral or ideological objection to financing those activities by taxing the drug trade.

Hence, in their most sophisticated stage, the activities of antistate guerrillas are indeed symbiotic, but symbiotic with the unofficial, underground, or parallel economy rather than with the official one. The greater the relative growth of the unofficial economy, the smaller is the percentage of the official economy available to the state to sustain its legal functions.

An important conclusion follows. Mature criminality is compatible with the continued existence of the formal state and can even be employed to defend it; mature insurgency threatens the overthrow of that formal state and, by definition, cannot comfortably coexist with it. This distinction was neatly summed up in South Vietnam in the 1950s when the government ceded control of the Saigon-Cholon vice rackets to the Binh Xuyen gang of river pirates in exchange for their keeping the city free of Communist guerrilla activity.[29]

Granted, a guerrilla organization that uses international black markets to finance its activities may form mutually profitable relations with international criminals. This is the case surrounding the narcotics trafficking out of Burma, for example, where insurgent groups of the left, right, and simply ethnocentric all trade freely with Hong Kong– and

Bangkok-based dealers. With these international criminals, the guerrilla group has no territorial or political dispute; their relations are purely opportunistic.

Granted, too, in the early stages of an insurgency, a guerilla group may cooperate with domestic and local criminal organizations on the basis of their shared status as social outcasts and their shared immediate objectives.[30] In Italy in the 1970s, urban guerrilla groups engaged in joint operations with different gangs—robbing banks, holding up payrolls, stealing paintings, and engaging in ransom kidnapping. At one point the Unity of Communist Combat group was even reputed (although never proven) to have joined members of the Calabrian 'Ndrangheta in a raid on a Club Med that netted $2 million worth of cash and jewels and three hundred foreign passports. But paramilitaries of the right joined these criminal groups in joint operations with greater frequency, often with the Italian intelligence services as go-between.[31]

However, there are many instances in which these supposed alliances turned out to be fictional. Argentinean criminal kidnappers used to claim to be guerrillas because guerrilla groups, with better infrastructure, could hold victims longer and therefore could command a higher ransom. In Ireland some bank robberies by criminals were followed by their claims that the IRA was responsible to throw the police off the scent. In the Philippines, businessmen frequently faced extortion demands from criminals (including army and police officers) claiming to be tax collectors for the New People's Army.[32]

Even in the short term, however, the two groups have different objectives: the criminal group seeks a smooth getaway and post-operational secrecy, whereas the guerrilla group revels in noisy confrontations with the state and brags about its prowess in the aftermath. Furthermore, whatever short-term alliances of convenience may occasionally emerge between well-entrenched criminals and anti-regime guerrillas, in the long run the two groups usually end up on opposite sides of the barricades, and inevitably so if the guerrilla group's ideology is anticapitalist. For the guerrilla group, the underground economy and the treasures it yields are tools that will enable the group to carry out a political agenda; for the criminal organization, the riches of the black market are an end in themselves. The Brazilian guerrilla theorist Carlos Marighella pointed out in his manual on revolutionary tactics that for the public to be able to differentiate a left-wing guerrilla's bank robbery from that of either a criminal or a right-wing revolutionary, it was necessary for the guerrilla to avoid misguided violence or taking money or personal property from customers of the bank. At the same time, he advised, the guerrilla should propagandize by handing out leaflets explaining the purpose of the raid or by writing slogans on the wall before leaving.[33]

It was good advice, although it is unclear who followed it. Despite claims by national security services that the manual was widely read in Latin America and Europe, the reality is that Willy Sutton's memoirs had a much wider circulation.

Of course the lure of quick wealth can on occasion cause a guerrilla organization, or at least some of its militants, to degenerate into simple criminality. When the Red Army Faction (or Baader-Meinhof gang) in Germany started scoring big returns from bank robberies, it attracted a new type of recruit more interested in easy money than difficult revolutions. The options were starkly drawn after the end of the 1950 Huk rebellion in the Philippines, when some elements took to the hills to engage in social banditry, redistributing stolen wealth among poor peasants, while others settled down near U.S. military bases to collect rake-offs from the gambling and prostitution rackets and to sell themselves to local bosses as strikebreakers and security guards.[34]

The danger of criminalization of motive is particularly acute when individual militants are allowed to run their own enterprises or rackets in exchange for kicking back a certain sum to the group as a whole. The Provisional IRA had a reputation for tight discipline, and its gunmen were reputed to turn over to the organization everything they collected (on pain of execution if they were caught holding back). By contrast, members of the Ulster Defence Association (UDA), once the IRA's main paramilitary antagonist, used to display their commitment to the Protestant ethic by routinely grabbing 70–80 percent of the take for themselves. These antics produced so much dissension that by the end of the 1980s the group was close to collapse and had to be reorganized with a new, "clean" leadership.[35]

Predators and Patriots

Predatory acts, whether they are performed by guerrillas or ordinary criminals, are a category that covers a wide range of crimes—from armed robbery to ransom kidnapping to certain types of business frauds. Some are simple, others highly idiosyncratic.

At its most primitive, fund-raising can take the form of straightforward looting. Indeed, the opportunity to join the fun can be a powerful lure to potential recruits. When the Sudan People's Liberation Army (SPLA) stages a raid on a southern Sudanese town populated by people other than Dinkas who form the SPLA backbone, its ranks are often swollen by those who have not the slightest sympathy with the guerrilla's political objectives.

At the other end of the complexity scale, maritime fraud was, for reasons peculiar to Lebanon's political and physical geography, a specialty of some of its guerrilla groups, who took advantage of the disintegration of state authority to seize small Lebanese ports. The guerrillas arranged with Greek or Cypriot shipowners that cargos officially bound for the Orient via the Suez Canal would be secretly unloaded at one of the ports controlled by the guerrillas. The cargo would then be sold locally or mixed with the transit traffic to the Persian Gulf. The ship, if old, would be scuttled. If new, the ship would be reported lost at sea—although after one or more name changes, it might return to active service. In the meantime, the shipowner collected both a percentage from sale of the cargo and the insurance money on his "lost" ship, while possibly still operating the ship under another name elsewhere in the world.[36]

Some guerrilla groups have participated in counterfeiting their antagonist's currency both as a means of fund-raising and as an instrument of economic warfare. This tactic dates back at least as far as the heyday of the Internal Macedonian Revolutionary Organization, founded in 1895 to battle Greece and Turkey. It used counterfeiting, along with robbery, kidnapping, and extortion, to supplement the funds and arms provided by sympathizers in the Bulgarian army.[37] Counterfeiting also figured in the toolkit of the Cristeros, a Catholic fundamentalist group fighting Mexico's efforts in the 1920s to exorcise the power of the Church and seize its property.[38] In the 1930s, Serbian revolutionaries led by a Greek Orthodox priest planned to use counterfeit U.S. currency to finance a coup.[39]

If it is merely a form of fund-raising, counterfeiting must be kept secret, thus sacrificing political for financial gains. An apparent foray by IRA members into using counterfeit U.S. dollars to pay travel expenses ended ignominiously in 1987 with the seizure of $2 million in phony bills and an arrest.[40] Only briefly more successful was an Australian-based counterfeiting operation run by Tamil Tiger sympathizers, who passed on phony airline tickets, fake traveler's checks, and counterfeit cash to the Australian public, until busted by the Australian federal police in 1991.[41]

More successful was the $20 million in counterfeit Afghan government currency given by the CIA to the mujahideen. Here the immediate objective was purchase of supplies, with discrediting of the government merely icing on the cake if and when use of the counterfeit funds was revealed.[42] On the other side of the world, members of radical right-wing groups in the United States, such as the Posse Comitatus, have counterfeited U.S. currency (whose legality they refuse to recognize) both to finance insurgency training and to disrupt the enemy economy. Other U.S. militia groups have passed more arcane instruments, such as money orders and so-called comptroller warrants, although sometimes the objective seems more to scam fellow citizens than to undermine the government.[43]

Clearly it requires special circumstances for a guerrilla group to engage in maritime fraud. And historically, most insurgent counterfeiting operations have involved hiring underworld specialists, although today's electronic technology may have eliminated that need. However, there are two traditional criminal rackets open to virtually all insurgent groups regardless of geographic location or technical capacity. Bank robbery and ransom kidnapping have provided almost the entire operating budget of urban guerrilla groups such as the Italian Red Brigades and funds from these sorts of operations allowed the Salvadorian FMNL guerrillas to shift from hit-and-run tactics to full-scale insurgency. They have figured prominently among the fund-raising tools of every group from the Tamil Tigers to the ETA Basque nationalist movement.

In his how-to manual, Brazilian guerrilla theorist Carlos Marighella not only explained the difference between guerrilla and criminal bank robbery, but he explicitly recommended bank robbery as the first stage of revolutionary action. Indeed, decades before that manual was written, the Zionist group Irgun Zvai Leumi in Palestine supplemented money and weapons sent over by American mobsters with the proceeds of armed robbery—of banks, trains, payroll offices, and diamond dealers. The group's rival, the Lohamei Herut Israel, did likewise. On the other hand, the more respectable Haganah eschewed such brutal tactics—a British army raid on the Great Synagogue in Tel Aviv turned up counterfeiting equipment plus £50,000 worth of forged British government bearer bonds.[44] Many other groups followed suit. From its inception, the Tamil Eelam Liberation Army (bitter rivals of the Tigers) specialized in robberies: its first major guerrilla operation was to loot $600,000 worth of cash, gold, and diamonds from a Colombo bank.[45]

Nor are some of these political heists minor in scope or size. The Argentinean Ejercito de Revolución Popular (ERP) in 1972 achieved the distinction of committing the country's largest-ever bank robbery when it relieved a state-owned institution of all the cash in the vault. And a world record was set in Beirut in 1976. Of the eleven banks in the financial district looted by various factions, the worst hit was the British Bank of the Middle East. From it, Saiqa, a pro-Syrian Palestinian faction, withdrew $4.5 million in cash and traveler's checks in addition to grabbing from the safety deposit boxes somewhere between $20 million and $60 million in cash, bearer bonds, gold, and jewelry.[46]

Robbing financial institutions of hard cash has advantages over loot-ing supplies directly from stores and warehouses. Cash is more flexible. And a major holdup can be a propaganda coup, provided it does not lead to public backlash. (For that reason, Sikh separatists in the Punjab took care to pick on banks owned by the Indian government.)[47] The stolen money can also be represented as the property of the "financial class," especially because depositors (as distinct from holders of safety deposit boxes) rarely, if ever, lose anything directly in a bank robbery. During a major bank job conducted by the Baader-Meinhof gang, one of the guerrillas menacingly advised the patrons, "Keep quiet and nothing will happen to you." Then he added reassuringly, "After all, it's not your money."[48]

The proceeds of a bank robbery can take the form not just of cash but of politically damaging information. When, in 1969, the Uruguayan gov-ernment responded to a bank employees' strike by securing a military de-cree that ordered them back to work, it simultaneously created a network of inside informants whom the Tupamaros guerrillas were able to use to pull off a spectacular series of robberies. One of these robberies yielded not only cash and negotiable securities but documents and bank account records that, once published, implicated twenty-two prominent citizens, including a serving cabinet minister, in tax fraud, illegal currency specu-lation, and exchange-control evasion.[49]

By contrast, ransom kidnapping was for a long time strictly a criminal enterprise. If a guerrilla group did kidnap someone, it was generally for political purposes—to make a propaganda statement or to secure the re-lease of prisoners. However, by the end of the 1960s, the situation had changed. In the wake of Che Guevara's defeat in rural Bolivia and the general trend toward urbanization of developing countries, guerrilla war-fare also became more urbanized. The result was easier access to tempt-ing targets. In addition, the logistical needs of some of the more ambi-tious groups were rising. And there was growing public resentment across much of the developing world of the activities of both indigenous eco-nomic elites and transnational corporations. Together these factors pre-cipitated, in the early 1970s, a wave of ransom kidnappings, particularly in Latin America, with wealthy landlords, businessmen, and transnational corporation executives as the prime targets.

The advantages were many. Well-to-do individuals (at least in the early days) were easier targets than were banks with guards, safes, and alarms. Ransom too could be tailored to fit the guerrilla movement's logistical and political needs. A ransom could be demanded in the form of food and medicine for the poor, a settlement of labor disputes that included wage hikes or reinstatement of discharged workers, or simply cash. And the cash could be in local currency or, especially with ransoms for foreign corporate executives, hard currency, which was particularly useful when dealing with the international arms black market.

Argentina seems to have pioneered modern political kidnapping.[50] The pattern was set in 1971 when the ERP nabbed the British head of the local Swift Company plant and freed him on payment of $62,500 in food for the poor. That marked the beginning of a kidnapping campaign of such dimensions that by the mid-1970s, the ERP bragged about its war chest (including the proceeds of bank heists) of $30 million. The ERP's apparent success attracted other Argentinean groups to the business.

Guerrilla groups discovered that kidnapping had fringe benefits in the form of political gains. For example, kidnapping business executives, especially ones from foreign corporations, might precipitate destabilizing capital flight. Kidnapping a wealthy businessman or rentier created even better anticapitalist propaganda than hitting a bank; the guerrilla group was able to personalize the message rather than rely on vague slogans about the "financial class." Kidnapping an executive from another region of the same country permitted a separatist group to highlight the problem of exploitation of local resources by outsiders. Kidnapping a foreign executive had the further advantage of telling the public that the guerrilla group was fighting imperialism.

Thus, Argentina's Montoñeros set a new world record when the Born family, owners of one of the world's largest grain-dealing firms, paid the ransom on their kidnapped sons. The price was $60 million in "bail" plus "fines for exchange irregularities" paid to the Montoñeros as "representatives of the national interest." In addition, the Borns had to distribute $1.2 million in goods to the poor as punishment for "hoarding and creating shortages." Finally, they were required to place in their factories busts of Juan and Eva Peron, in whose name the Montoñeros claimed to be fighting.[51]

By the onset of the 1980s, however, political ransom kidnapping was on the wane in Latin America—except in Colombia. Although firms specializing in corporate security were quick to claim credit, the real reasons had more to do with changes on both the political and financial fronts. In the context of the 1980s, transnational corporations were no longer popular bêtes noirs. During the great debt crisis and its attendant economic depression, that role had been usurped by international bankers who were unreachable in their New York, London, and Tokyo headquarters. And some Latin American guerrilla groups had found more reliable sources of funding. Elsewhere in the world, however, ransom kidnapping remained very much a part of the guerrilla group's kit of revolutionary fund-raising tools.

In the 1980s much attention was focused on a few factions in Lebanon that engaged in high-profile, usually low-return, kidnappings of foreigners. Remarkably little attention was paid to Iraqi Kurdistan, where, in 1981, guerrillas initiated a series of abductions of foreign skilled workers and professionals in the oil business. The abductions were seen as a handy way to recycle back to the Kurdish population part of the oil wealth that was being extracted from Kurdistan wells and at the same time to publicize the Kurdish cause and embarrass the Iraqi regime. The captives were smuggled across the Iraq–Iran border and placed in the custody of the Iranian Pasdaran (Revolutionary Guards) until the ransom in cash or medical equipment was met, with the Pasdaran taking a cut.[52]

Farther east, in Afghanistan, Pakistan, and India, where ransom kidnapping used to be only a criminal activity, the increased availability of arms, the wealth of the drug trade, and mounting political tensions resulting partly from the Afghan war and partly from ethnic separatists added a distinctly political dimension to the business. Indeed, by the end of the 1980s, parts of the subcontinent boasted a veritable wholesale market. Victims would be sold by captors, sometimes for as little as 5 percent of the ultimate ransom, to other groups better positioned to wait until the final price reached an acceptable level.[53] Kidnapping had the further advantage of allowing guerrilla groups to fine-tune their message. Take, for example, a series of kidnappings that occurred during the 1990s in Assam, a state in northeastern India. Assam produces over half of that country's tea crop, which is an important source of foreign exchange, on plantations largely owned by transnational corporations, virtually all of whose executives are foreigners or come from elsewhere in India. Hence, the United Liberation Front of Assam (ULFA) targeted for kidnapping executives of foreign-owned tea plantations.[54]

Although kidnapping as a tool for guerrilla fund-raising has its attractions, there are powerful disincentives—only one being the use of better security measures by the corporations to protect executives. More importantly, although in the heyday of anticapitalist and anti-imperialist agitation, political points could be scored with a well-targeted kidnap, the event could also produce a public relations disaster. That was the experience of the IRA when a series of kidnappings culminated in a botched attempt to ransom a valuable racehorse and a disastrous effort to collect from the employers of a business executive; the executive died of a heart attack, producing no ransom, a twenty-year jail term for one of the perpetrators, and an outpouring of public criticism. This was the last major kidnapping operation mounted by IRA supporters which by then had safer ways of raising money. Similarly in Sri Lanka in 1984, a cell of the Eelam People's Revolutionary Liberation Front kidnapped two American aid workers and for their return demanded the release from prison of twenty militants plus $2 million in gold. Denounced even by those whose release they were trying to secure, the group let the captives go without ransom.

Parasites and Petroterrorists

When a guerrilla group switches from episodic activities such as robbery and kidnapping to more stable income sources such as protection payments, it crosses the line from predatory to parasitical modes of fundraising. If predatory fund-raising by guerrillas approximates blue-collar crime, parasitical fund-raising is more akin to white-collar offenses. Probably nowhere is the analogy clearer than in the construction rackets run by Irish paramilitary groups.[55]

During the 1970s and 1980s, the British government spent more than a billion pounds building public housing in burnt-out areas of Belfast. The potential take was sufficient for cells of the Provisional IRA, the Protestant UDA, and even the ultra-radical Irish National Liberation Army to meet periodically to carve up territory and fix fees for services rendered to the construction companies. At the building sites, the paramilitary forces acted as employment agencies, collecting a fee from workers and forcing employers to hire only those designated. Most workers also drew unemployment payments. Not only did the threat of revealing that the workers were scamming the unemployment insurance fund help keep them quiet, but unemployment insurance fraud permitted the paramilitary to offer workers' services to companies for less than market wages, and the companies showed their gratitude by paying the paramilitary a kickback.

The British government had also instituted a tax deferral scheme to help small contractors whose receipts came in irregularly. The result was a market in stolen and forged tax-exemption certificates and tax scams in which the final link in the deferral chain would be a ghost company that vanished when the tax money finally fell due.

As with the Lebanese militias' profiteering from maritime fraud, the Irish paramilitaries' use of construction rackets was the result of a unique conjuncture.[56] However, virtually every guerrilla organization, in its parasitic mode, uses some form of "revolutionary taxation" of the income or wealth of well-to-do individuals or businesses.

Although the Colombian M-19 group was essentially an urban guerrilla organization and therefore, like Italy's Red Brigades, relied on kidnapping and holdups, the other major Colombian groups were (and some still are) powerfully implanted in areas that contained, at peak, a third of the country's arable land. They were able to regularly shake down wealthy landlords, ranchers, and planters, on pain of having crops ruined and livestock stolen. In a similar spirit, the Basque separatist ETA gathered information (largely on the basis of unsubstantiated rumor) about the resources of prominent Basque businessmen to determine what their proper rate of revolutionary taxation should be.[57]

Although these taxes are collected on income rather than on trade, they can depend critically on particular resources. On the Thai–Malay border during the 1960s, the Communist Party of Malaysia financed much of its rebellion by a tax on rubber tappers (people who tap rubber trees).[58] The Philippine island of Basilan became in the 1970s one of the strongholds of Moro (Muslim) separatists, whose links to copra (and rubber) smugglers were so intimate that local skeptics began referring to the guerrillas as copra battalions.[59] In the 1980s in Afghanistan, source of much of the world's lapis lazuli as well as an important producer of emeralds, the Jamiat-e-Islami faction imposed a 10 percent tax on gemstone sales. In the 1990s in Assam, tea planters regularly paid off the ULFA, much to the chagrin of the Indian government, which arrested tea company executives suspected of so doing. Similarly, Colombia's Ejercito de Liberación Nacional (ELN) collects most of its war chest from *petroterrorismo*.

After denouncing the international oil companies for stealing Colombia's oil, the ELN kidnapped oil company executives and destroyed the companies' infrastructure to attack imperialism and deny the government a critical source of foreign exchange.[60] Later the ELN began to "tax" the companies' operations. The companies paid the *elenõs* handsomely both in cash and in construction of roads, schools, and hospitals for the surrounding countryside; in return, the companies were free to produce oil. The largest company of the group, Occidental Petroleum, even put guerrillas on its payroll; their job was to keep other guerrillas at bay.[61] Because a large percentage of the royalties paid by oil companies goes to state governments, the ELN even persuaded some of those governments to pay protection fees and to cede control of land near the oil wells to persons designated by the ELN.[62]

Because of the ELN's insistence on receiving some of its "tax revenue" from oil companies in the form of social infrastructure for the civil population, at a certain point these taxes cease to be primarily a parasitical drain on the formal economy and become more symbiotic. At that juncture they are used to support the expansion of the infrastructure of a parallel economy under construction in the zones of control, and they are administered through a formalized officialdom rather than by armed shakedowns.

The Symbiotic Stage

When the Philippines' New People's Army turned an area into a consolidated zone, it would create a people's government to take charge of civic administration and tax collection, with the guarantee that the local NPA unit would get a special appropriation in the regional budget. The NPA would help the civic administration collect the taxes and sell war bonds, part of whose proceeds would fund the army. And it would get a percentage of capital, property, or goods confiscated from "imperialists, comprador bourgeoisie, landlords, bureaucratic capitalists, and traitors."

Initially all people in the consolidated zones paid a 2 percent tax, often collected at pistol point. This, not surprisingly, proved unpopular. Hence the NPA introduced a radical fiscal reform. Although the population at large was still encouraged to make donations and take out party memberships, the tax burden was deliberately shifted from the poor, who were potential supporters, to class enemies. Landlords were to make large mandatory contributions; logging companies and sawmills were assessed a flat rate per piece of machinery, plus 10–25 percent of their net income. Peasants, on the other hand, were taxed directly only on any increase in income that could be imputed to capital improvements or land redistribution introduced by the NPA government, with a graduated rate of 2–5 percent. The NPA also benefited indirectly from hiring out soldiers as farm workers in return for a fixed percentage of the crop.[63]

Although an insurgent group in a zone of control may still directly tax income and wealth, as did the NPA, more often it shifts to indirect taxation, on retail, wholesale, and international trade, including trade in contraband goods. It may even demand taxes in kind—a percentage of the harvest or the product of mines and forests—which it then markets through obliging brokers and commodity dealers.

Likely the world's most complex system of parallel taxation was that imposed by the Lebanese Forces on the Christian enclave of Lebanon. Although estimates of the annual take from taxation ran as high as $300 million, there is a good chance that the figures were deliberately exaggerated to bolster the legitimacy of the Lebanese Forces as a substitute government and to cover for the amount coming in from more traditional rackets, with drugs possibly high among them.[64] Nonetheless, there were taxes on "government" services. These included a duty on ships unloading cargo in pirate ports controlled by business associates of the militia, a visa fee at checkpoints on people traveling to other parts of Lebanon, and user fees for public beaches. There were real estate taxes on commercial buildings and a hearth tax on private homes. There were sales taxes on private services such as movie tickets and restaurant meals, and on basic goods such as tobacco and cooking oil. Gasoline was taxed three times—at the import, wholesale, and retail levels. Fees for service even included a sum charged to an Italian waste-disposal company to dump 16,000 barrels of toxic waste off the coast and in the mountains—although some was also sold to unsuspecting businesses as virgin chemicals, fertilizers, and pesticides. The plan called for a total of 300,000 tons with payments of $250 per ton, of which 80 percent was to go to the Lebanese Forces National Fund and 10 percent each to two private partners who ran the importing company, but scandal and the end of the civil war cut the operation short.[65]

What was unique about the Lebanese Forces' tax structure, apart from its comprehensive character, was that, reflecting Lebanon's historical role as a free-trading entrepôt and the political power of its merchants, it relied much more on taxing internal commerce than foreign trade. By contrast, most systems of guerrilla taxation depend predominantly on taxing imports to and exports from zones of control.

Frequently the territorial hold of the guerrilla group does not extend beyond a border strip, and even then it may be firm only at night. The frontier between the Irish Republic and Northern Ireland, for example, was (and is) a virtual no-man's-land, with the Provisional IRA (now partially replaced by the even more militant Real IRA) striving to keep it free of Customs and the security services of both jurisdictions. That facilitates smuggling, with the smugglers paying "war taxes" to the IRA or its breakaway factions. Smugglers running contraband between Colombia and Venezuela routinely pay off guerrillas from both the ELN and FARC (Revolutionary Armed Forces of Colombia).[66] Similarly, in the border areas between Albania, Kosovo, and Serbia, the Kosovo Liberation Army (UCK) presides over a smugglers' nest. It collects taxes in cash and in service—the smugglers assist by moving weapons. And individual members run their own rackets, trafficking in refugees, prostitutes bound for European brothels, drugs, and cigarettes.[67]

Granted, in such cases the territorial hold of the guerrilla group may be tenuous. But even partial control of such a frontier, and the revenues it can yield, may be a necessary first step for a guerrilla group to begin converting zones of contention into zones of control.

It was precisely the opportunity to control the Iraq–Turkey border in the wake of the Gulf War that permitted Kurdish rebels to shift from dependence on unreliable outside sponsors (plus the proceeds of kidnapping) to tapping the commercial possibilities of their own territory. The Iraqi refineries that survived Anglo-American bombing produced too much diesel and aviation fuel for Iraq's own use. Yet UN sanctions prevented export of the excess via pipeline to Iraq's pre-war customers. Instead, much of the fuel was hauled by truck to Turkey via Kurdistan. The emerging Kurdish autonomous administration therefore charged transit fees, on both the fuel going out and the cargos of food and general consumer goods coming back. The funds were used for such purposes as paying civil service salaries and buying arms.[68]

Similarly, road traffic, either across the former Soviet–Afghan border or between Kabul and Karachi, long provided landlocked Afghanistan with much of its food and consumer goods. The result in the mid-1980s was the spectacle of two mujahideen groups, the Jamiat-e-Islami and the Hezbe-e-Islami, battling each other for the right to tax truck convoys carrying Soviet and East Bloc supplies to the Communist-led government in Kabul. Even with the fall of the Soviet-backed regime, the contraband continued, providing the Taliban government with a source of revenue that until the late 1990s was rivaled only by taxes on the opium business.[69]

Nowhere was the organization of foreign trade taxes as comprehensive as in Burma (Myanmar), with its plethora of insurgent groups, many of which are now dormant but by no means dead. The reasons lie in a mixture of economics, ethnicity, and geography.[70]

Burma in the early 1960s introduced a socialist economic development model based on tight governmental controls on foreign trade and agriculture. It also tried to Birmanize the country in which nearly half of the population, concentrated in the resource-rich hinterland and border areas, consists of non-Buddhist, non-Birman minorities.

The planning mechanism produced thriving black markets. Apart from subsidized basic commodities such as rice (whose price was three times as high in Thailand), out of the country to Thailand and China would go luxury goods such as teak, perfume essences, rubies, jade, antiquities, opium, and heroin. Back would come ordinary consumer goods, everything from sandals to VCRs, along with arms to keep the insurgents supplied.

Where possible, insurgents would take control of an area that produced one or more of the valuable export goods and then levy taxes on the trade flows both ways. Thus, the Karen National Liberation Army levied a 5 percent tax on all commerce (rice, gems, tin ore, and textiles) crossing its part of the Burma–Thai border. But the most important part of the Karen parallel was, until a mid-1990s Burmese army offensive, the teak trade. Burma contains 70 percent of the world's rapidly depleting teak forests. Not only did the Karens tax (at the usual 5 percent) the clandestine export of Burmese teakwood to Thailand and China, but they oversaw the establishment of many sawmills, whose output financed the purchase of consumer goods for their sub-economy, at the same time the taxes helped pay for the arms to defend it.[71]

An even greater range of activity characterized another Burmese group, the Kachin Independence Army. Apart from sporadic help from China (and, oddly enough, from Taiwan and South Korea), the group derived much of its revenue to support an impressive array of social services by taxing luxury commodities, especially jade. Burma produces the world's finest jade. And although the jade mines were nominally government controlled, corruption was rife, with soldiers often stealing jade from illegal miners and selling it to the same smugglers with whom the illegal miners dealt. Furthermore, the government's writ never really ran beyond the main town. In the hinterlands, the Kachins demonstrated their grasp of the whole range of fund-raising techniques: they stole from government-owned mines (predatory); they protected and taxed the smugglers (parasitical); and they ran their own illegal mines (symbiotic). In other parts of their zones of control, the Kachins similarly organized ruby mining.[72]

Although Burma produces most of the world's finest blood-red rubies, the Kachins' success in tapping the trade inspired a foreign competitor. After being ousted from government in 1979, the Khmer Rouge returned to guerrilla activity, relying mainly on China for arms and on embezzled refugee relief aid for general supplies. But as the 1980s wore on, fears mounted that China would join the United States in imposing on the Kampuchean civil war a settlement that would marginalize their role. The Khmer Rouge therefore began relying more on its own rackets for funding. It was aided immeasurably by the fact that its zones of control included key border crossings, permitting the Khmer Rouge to offer to the smugglers (for a fee) guidance across the heavily mined border as well as the chance to tax the trade each way. This enterprise was aided by the fact that Kampuchea ranked second only to Burma for high-quality rubies and unlogged teakwood forests.

The Khmer Rouge itself did none of the mining—it would have lacked the connections to sell the output. Rather, thousands of Thai miners crossed into the ruby-mining area, with each required to lease mining rights and pay a tax on the output as well as to pay escort and protection fees to whichever subgroup ran a particular area. In addition, large Thai mining companies paid entrance fees, a sum per hectare, and 40 percent of their profits—how that was assessed was never clear. The borders between mining concessions were well defined, with Khmer Rouge officials routinely checking permits and punishing unlicensed miners. As long as the central command was able to impose discipline on local cadres, the rules were fairly enforced; unlike government-run areas, here there were no shakedowns.[73]

The same was true in the lumber business. After Thailand, facing ecological disaster, banned further logging, many companies shifted to Kampuchea. The Kampuchean government imposed quotas and demanded certificates of origin for logs exported, and then officials would add their own informal taxes on top. As a result, Thai companies preferred to pay the Khmer Rouge for rights to valuable hardwoods. The Khmer Rouge charged less and respected its contracts. Indeed, the Thai lumber connection paid yet another, indirect dividend. Once Thai logging companies built roads, the Khmer Rouge found it easier to tax the cross-border trade, which was far more lucrative than the old practice of simply attacking and looting trucks. The connection also attracted small woodworking and furniture factories that could be taxed.[74]

The Khmer Rouge's operations, in fact, contradicted its ideology. Opposed to money and markets, the Khmer Rouge while in government had savagely repressed ordinary commerce, and after its overthrow it had even abolished free markets in the areas into which it had been driven. However, desperate to defend its independence of action, it allowed exemptions for the ruby and teakwood producers in its zones of control. This fiscal expediency is remarkably similar to what prevailed in Peru's cocaine-rich upper Huallaga Valley under the Sendero Luminoso. But it had different results. The Sendero Luminoso retained tight control even in the face of cocaine wealth and was ultimately knocked out by military action, but the Khmer Rouge rotted from within as a result of its very financial success. Increasingly, local commanders resisted demands to ship 80 percent of their earnings to the central command; some agitated for the organization to renounce communism altogether; and others began dickering with the government for an amnesty, provided they could keep their businesses. Eventually corruption and dissent, combined with pending exhaustion of the rubies and the impact of the late 1990s Asian economic crisis on the hardwood market, caused the organization to implode, leaving a remnant to follow a vocation of banditry and extortion at the expense of smugglers and drug dealers crossing their area.[75]

The Myth of Narco-Terrorism

One of the factors that led to the 1990s crackdown on terrorist fundraising is the conviction, born in the early 1980s, that guerrilla groups in the last two decades of the twentieth century fed heavily off narcotics. Beyond doubt, some guerrilla groups do partake of the profits of the world drug trade. It would be a surprise if they did not. However exaggerated the numbers fed to the public, drug trafficking was and remains among the richest components of the world underground economy, and its raw materials originate from areas in which insurgencies abound. Although the usual refrain in the 1980s was that left-wing insurgencies flooded North America and western Europe with drugs to finance purchases of arms from the Soviet Union, in fact, the drug trade, in the best of liberal capitalist tradition, attracted guerrilla groups regardless of their race, color, creed, or political affiliation.

When the remnants of the Kuomintang (KMT) armies, ousted from China in 1949, fell back on the northern Shan states of Burma, they lost little time in getting down to business. General Tuan Shi-wen eloquently explained: "We have to continue to fight the evil of Communism, and to fight it you need an army and an army must have guns, and to buy guns you must have money. In these mountains the only money is opium."[76] The KMT not only collected taxes on all commerce in and out of the area, but it forced local farmers to pay an annual tax in the form of a percentage of their crop. The opium thus collected was run by the KMT to the border and sold to Thai police. They, in turn, arranged for its refinement into heroin and further sale, via Hong Kong–based crime syndicates, first on the local market for smoking-grade heroin and later, with the appropriate quality improvements, on the international market for injectable heroin.

There were two main rivals. One was the Communist Party of Burma, encouraged by China to expand into the Shan states to counter the threat of the KMT. Initially the party relied for the bulk of its funding on the profits from its monopoly of Chinese consumers goods smuggled to Burma. But as China liberalized its trade policy, the Burmese Communist Party lost most of its trade revenue. However, it managed to oust the KMT from some of the best opium-growing areas, which secured an independent source of funds for the party until ethnic rivalry and the corrupting influence of narcotics money caused the party to fracture in 1989.[77]

The role of the Burmese Communist Party pales compared with that of the Shan United Army (SUA). Originally given permission by the Burmese government to run the local opium trade in exchange for fighting communists, the SUA subsequently joined the ranks of ethnic insurgents battling the government. It not only taxed opium (and almost everything else) but diversified downstream into heroin refining. At peak it accounted for an estimated 80 percent of drug production in the Shan states.[78] When its warlord, Khun Sa, surrendered, the government, and the army that runs it, took over the drug tax revenues, while business continued more or less as usual.[79]

Thus, contrary to the narco-communist conspiracy thesis, right-wing guerrillas and nonideological ethnic insurgents have been at least as active as left-wing rebels in profiting from the Southeast Asian opium/heroin trade. Furthermore, during the 1980s and 1990s, Southeast Asia, as supplier of the bulk of the world's heroin, has had a strong competitor, the Afghanistan–Pakistan frontier, where the traffic has always been the exclusive domain of ethnic and religious insurgents on the political right.

In Afghanistan, traditional landlords and religious leaders encouraged their people to grow opium, which the mujahideen military chiefs could tax. The opium was sent across the border into the autonomous Afridi tribal areas of Pakistan, where, in exchange for payoffs to tribal leaders, consortia of Afghan rebel political leaders and Pakistani businessmen were allowed to establish heroin refineries. The heroin was then transported as return cargo in the same military vehicles (which police and Customs were not allowed to open) in which Pakistani military intelligence shipped weapons to the mujahideen. Then the heroin made its way to final market by several routes.

Some was shipped through the port of Karachi. Some was snuck across the Indian border by smugglers sympathetic to or willing to pay off Sikh separatist guerrillas during their 1980s insurgency and then sent to Bombay for further distribution. Some headed west through Baluchistan to Iran, where corrupt members of the Pasdaran passed it off to Kurdish guerrilla sympathizers for further transit across Turkey to Istanbul. From Istanbul, part went to Germany, where dealers often paid protection money to exiled cadres of the bitterly antagonistic Turkish nationalist Grey Wolves and the Kurdish separatist PKK. Alternatively, from Istanbul, some ran up the Balkan route through bits and pieces of what had been Yugoslavia; the bulk of that traffic was soon taken over by supporters of the Kosovo Liberation Army, who were battling the ex-Communist leadership of Serbia.

Nor is evidence of some sort of narco-communist conspiracy any clearer in the center of the world's cocaine trade. It is certainly true that Colombia's FARC, originally the military wing of the Colombian Communist Party, entrenched itself in a region in which some of the biggest drug barons used to operate cocaine refineries. And FARC lost little time taxing the refineries, along with all other businesses in the area. Indeed, drug taxes now rival kidnap ransoms as the most important source of FARC's fiscal resources. But the notion, propagated by the Colombian and U.S. governments, of a strategic alliance in which the guerrillas assisted the narco-barons and were paid for their services in arms is an absurdity.

There is a fundamental long-term incompatibility of objectives between the two groups. The narco-barons were and are capitalist insurgents, seeking to beat or buy their way into a hitherto largely closed social system, whereas the guerrillas are political insurgents seeking to overthrow that system. The two were in frequent conflict over control of territory and over revolutionary taxes, which the drug barons resisted. Such conflicts prompted some traffickers to shift plants closer to Brazil to be free of guerrilla harassment and closer to a supply of precursor chemicals.[80] The myth of the FARC-narc cocaine cartel still provides cover when U.S.-armed and -directed Colombian army units burn down cocaine "labs" (shacks owned by poor peasants), indiscriminately lace large areas with pesticides, and direct death squads against civilians labeled supporters of narco-terrorism.

There is a similar lack of evidence to support the notion of a long-term strategic alliance between cocaine traffickers and Peru's Sendero Luminoso guerrilla movement, which, it used to be claimed, collected anywhere from $30 million to an astronomical $550 million per annum from the coca trade. Granted, in the upper Huallaga Valley where they were deeply entrenched, the *senderistas* encouraged the return to aboriginal agricultural traditions, which included growing coca, and the Peruvian state's U.S.-financed eradication campaigns permitted the guerrillas to make antigovernment, anti-imperialist propaganda. Furthermore, the guerrillas won popular support by organizing peasant co-ops to stop Colombian traffickers from exploiting the growers. The result was higher prices for coca growers, part of which allegedly accrued to Sendero Luminoso in tax revenues. But this was a development cocaine traffickers could hardy be expected to welcome. Nor were they pleased when guerrillas demanded taxes on the import of chemicals and the export of coca paste, along with fees for such services as the use of landing strips. Far from being a sign of a strategic alliance, these activities put the guerrillas on a long-term collision course with the traffickers, who in turn were supported by the army, which lusted after the coca-tax revenues the *senderistas* were collecting.

Furthermore, it is difficult to see how a guerrilla group so vehemently and violently opposed to money and markets could ever effect a close working relationship with ultra-free-enterprising traffickers.[81] Nor could the *senderista* policy of destroying infrastructure of the formal state, including the communications and financial systems, have improved the traffickers' business prospects. And if Sendero Luminoso really earned so much from the cocaine trade, it showed neither any significant symptom of corruption nor any sign of modern, heavy weapons bought on the international black market. The group's arms were almost all taken (or bought) from the army and police; its explosives were stolen from mines by supporters; and its medical and general supplies were contributed by adherents who "requisitioned" them from their places of work.

Finally, the notion that Sendero Luminoso could have been collecting even the lesser amount of $30 million per annum from servicing the coca economy flew in the face of the economics of drug trafficking: returns per unit volume rise dramatically at each stage of the production-distribution chain. Sendero Luminoso, like most guerrilla groups, occupied territory in which only the lowest and most poorly paid stages took place. To collect truly impressive sums, a guerrilla group would have to become directly involved at least with the export traffic in finished product, and it would do best if it could participate in the actual marketing of refined material inside countries of final destination.

Guerrilla groups have made attempts to just that. During the mid- to late 1980s, the Tamil Tigers consolidated control of the Jaffna Peninsula at the northern tip of Sri Lanka, a traditional smuggling base. After they killed off or drove out competitors, the Tigers took over the civil administration and began collecting income taxes from businesses plus sales taxes on petroleum, alcohol, and tobacco. The group also set up a few of its own production facilities and assumed control of the local cement factory, using its output directly for fortifications and indirectly to barter for essentials.[82] But in 1987, the Indian army swept the Tigers out of the city of Jaffna. Deprived of its main source of local revenue, the group had to rely more on overseas sources. That need was enhanced when a Sri Lankan army offensive a few years later also cost the Tigers control of the Jaffna countryside. Some of the gap was filled by contributions from the diaspora, but most exiles were too poor to offer much. Some was filled by well-to-do Tamil businessmen, particularly those in shipping, which permitted them not only to kick in cash but also to run guns and supplies. And part seems to have been filled by heroin trafficking. Benefiting from the absolute dedication of the young militants who courier drugs and run a complimentary traffic in phony documents, the Tamil Tiger heroin rings became a significant force in the wholesale market across western Europe—until they were pushed out by a combination of police crackdowns and competition from the Kosovar networks in the late 1990s.[83]

Another reputed but occasional participant in the downstream drug trade was the IRA. Although the organization was fanatical about keeping Catholic areas of Ulster free of drugs by regularly kneecapping dealers, when it came to international fund-raising, the puritanical zeal of some of its militants seems to have been tempered. In 1986 the U.S. government indicted a Boston-based group that had smuggled more than a ton of marijuana into the United States, reputedly to finance the purchase of U.S. arms for the IRA. And two years later an alleged IRA–Detroit Mafia joint venture to ship Bolivian cocaine to Great Britain was exposed by an informant.[84]

Once again, however, it is necessary to remain skeptical of such associations. Perhaps some individuals took it on themselves to earn money for the IRA cause, with no approval from above; perhaps those individuals cited the IRA simply to raise their own credibility and apparent power; perhaps the entire link was invented by the authorities to taint the organization's reputation among the Catholic population. There were certainly other examples. In 1990 a mugging at knifepoint in London led to the theft of £292 million in bearer bonds. There were tales that it was an IRA job. It turned out that one Canadian, already under indictment for selling fraudulent animal vaccines that had originated in Ireland, bragged to an uncover FBI agent about his IRA connections while trying to unload bonds worth $29 million. Naturally, his primary link with the IRA fled before he could be arrested. In the final analysis, the thieves got nothing, and none of the other principals had any IRA connection. Nonetheless, the affair provided the pretext for a big antiterrorist roundup.[85]

Any role IRA members might have had in international drug trafficking would be trivial compared with that of the Nicaraguan Contras. There were many reasons for drug traffickers to make common cause with the anti–Nicaraguan government guerrillas in the 1980s. Both plied their craft in the same general area. Linking up with the Contra struggle provided traffickers with access to clandestine airstrips and cover for flights carrying drugs into the United States and money back out. Some planes airdropped drugs to small boats, which then ran the stuff into Florida. Some flew directly to U.S. military bases, where no one would inspect a Contra supply flight. On the return flights, some planes carried cash for deposit in Panama, from where it might be wired to Costa Rican banks to pay for Contra supplies.[86] Aiding the Contras also permitted traffickers to play the national security card if things got tough. In one instance the U.S. government returned $36,000 seized from a convicted cocaine trafficker in San Francisco after he produced a letter from Contra leaders stating that the money was for the "reinstatement of democracy in Nicaragua."[87]

Therefore, drug traffickers kicked in cash, planes, or supplies paid for out of drug profits; they paid fees to use Contra airstrips; they hired Contras to guard trafficking installations; and they employed Contras as couriers. There was even a scheme to murder a former U.S. ambassador to Colombia, collect the $1 million reward offered by drug barons, and divert the money to the Contra cause, while blaming the murder on the Nicaraguan government.[88]

Even here, however, although the Contra–cocaine link was true, and useful for those opposed to U.S. foreign policy, it was grossly exaggerated. The flow of cocaine via the Contras was trivial in comparison to total supply, and subsequent claims of a CIA–Contra plot to flood black ghettos in the United States with crack were as foolish as earlier claims that they were behind the $350 billion collapse of the American Savings and Loan Bank system.[89]

Certainly drugs were not the sole source of revenues flowing into Contra coffers. Added to them were the proceeds of embezzlement, tax evasion, political influence peddling, currency black marketeering, and gunrunning. In fact, the money came in so quickly that at one point Contra treasurers, like conscientious corporate executives, invested their surpluses in thirty-day certificates of deposit.[90]

Revolutionary Asset Management

As those Contra fund-raisers discovered, the treasures of the black market present a guerrilla movement with not just with opportunities but also with challenges of financial management. It must make decisions about collecting revenue, hiding money, and investing surpluses so that funds will be available to meet future needs.

The initial decision in revolutionary asset management is selection of the medium of exchange in which to be paid. That decision depends in part on whether expenditures will be local (for example, basic supplies) or international (notably heavy weapons). In turn, the choice of a medium of exchange will affect the selection of targets.

The simplest way to collect revenues is in the form of basic commodities. In the earliest stage, the group might simply requisition supplies for immediate consumption. However, payments in kind need not be reserved for consumption by the group. During its 1970s kidnapping campaign, the Argentinean ERP squeezed from the local Ford subsidiary $2 million worth of medicine, food, and school supplies for distribution to the poor.

Another useful form of payment is arms. That is the form, for example, in which Sikh separatists reputedly collected payment from smugglers for their assistance with moving drugs from the Afghan rebel–run heroin refineries in Pakistan's North-West Frontier Province across the border into India.[91]

Sometimes revolutionary taxes are collected in resalable commodities. El Salvador's FMLN routinely levied a coffee tax on planters in its zones of control that equaled a percentage of their yield. In Burma-Myanmar, much of the taxes imposed on the Shan population by the KMT, Burmese Communist Party, and SUA alike were paid as a share of the opium crop.

When kidnap ransom and taxes are collected in kind, other asset management decisions—hiding the proceeds and investing the surpluses—are taken care of more or less automatically. It is merely a matter of physical storage. Those decisions become more complicated when taxes or ransoms are collected in cash or internationally traded luxury goods.

If the amount collected in local currency is relatively small, it likely poses little difficulty. But a guerrilla group on occasion can be in danger of choking on its own success. When the Argentinean ERP forced Firestone to ransom its local president for $3 million worth of 500-peso notes, the notes filled the armored car the ERP thoughtfully provided. Kidnap ransom also poses another difficulty—the bills are almost invariably marked or their serial numbers recorded. Italian kidnapping gangs used to get around that problem by taking the cash to a casino and having accomplices exchange it and then pass the marked notes to unsuspecting tourists.

Cash, too, might be vulnerable to theft or seizure. Another danger—which has occurred on three separate occasions since the ethnic insurrections began in Burma—is that the government could announce a demonetization of all or part of the outstanding currency, generally the high denomination notes in which black market savings are often held.

The risk of theft, seizure, demonetization, or even severe depreciation (possibly a consequence of the guerrilla group's own success in waging economic warfare) obviously can be minimized if the guerrilla group succeeds in having its assets converted into foreign currency and stored abroad. If the currency in which income is earned is convertible, there should be little difficulty. However, even then the business of currency arbitrage is not without risks. The IRA for a time reputedly used a currency exchange house run by a disbarred lawyer to pick up Irish punts from smugglers who had sold their goods in the Irish Republic; then they converted the punts into English pounds (the currency of Northern Ireland) at a better rate than that offered by the banks. In 1988 the exchange house collapsed, leaving a hole in the books variously estimated at between £500,000 and £1.2 million, of which a large amount supposedly belonged to the IRA.[92]

Unlike the IRA, most guerrilla groups operate in developing countries that have soft currencies and tight exchange controls. Hence getting the money out of the country in which it was earned can be a problem.

One solution is to conduct fund-raising activities in valuable commodities easily sold abroad. Traditionally an excellent choice has been diamonds. It remains UNITA's vehicle of preference as well as the instrument through which the National Patriotic Front of Liberia and its Sierra Leone allies have been funding much of their campaigns.

Other valuable commodities will do as well. When UNITA was on the ropes in the 1980s, it fell back on an area of Angola without factories, mines, or agricultural potential. What it did have was wildlife—it was perhaps Africa's last great reserve. The result was a massive slaughter, particularly of elephants and rhinos, with the ivory and rhino horn joining stolen diamonds and illegally cut hardwoods in barter deals for Israeli and South African arms.[93]

Another currency, reputedly, is drugs. Part of the Lebanese hashish crop used to be negotiated for sale in Cyprus to buyers who simultaneously arranged return cargos of arms. However, these are three-way deals— drugs for cash for arms. Direct swaps of drugs for guns occur only in small amounts at the retail level. While, during the 1982 invasion, Israeli army units were busy conducting house-to-house searches, attempting to strip the occupied areas of their lethal arsenals, members of the anti-Israeli Lebanese National Resistance Front were bartering hashish and opium to Israeli soldiers for their guns and ammunition.

Yet another, even more direct approach is to request that payments of revolutionary taxes be made into foreign bank accounts. Again criminals pioneered the methods. In Italy, kidnapping rings used to target the rich, not only because they clearly could pay higher ransoms but also because they were usually guilty of tax and exchange-control evasion. Therefore the ransom payment could take the form of a wire transfer from the victim's Swiss bank account to the kidnappers' Swiss bank account.[94] Similarly, ETA used to finance operations by extorting money in pesetas from wealthy Basque businessmen on threat of assassination or destruction of their businesses. But when, in the late 1980s, support for ETA flagged and the Spanish police began interfering with its rackets, ETA shifted back to simple predatory activity, successfully kidnapping Spain's richest businessman and having the $5 million ransom deposited in ETA's French bank account.

Perhaps the most sophisticated example of the use of foreign banks was provided by the Philippine New People's Army. "Taxes" from businesses seeking to operate in NPA-controlled territory along with donations from solidarity groups were paid directly into offshore accounts protected by Hong Kong and Singapore bank secrecy laws and were used to support an international training and arms procurement operation based in Japan, Malaysia, and Singapore. The transnational corporations that cooperated in filling the war chest seemed to feel that paying revolutionary taxes to the NPA was not much different from paying an informal tithe to officials of the formal government.[95] Much the same kind of apparatus, again using Singapore as a financial fulcrum, allegedly services the Tamil Tigers.[96]

These offshore accounts are useful not merely as means for financing immediate expenditures but also for creating portfolios of income-earning assets. Although most guerrilla groups, for obvious reasons, cannot engage in deficit financing and must meet their current expenditures solely out of current revenues, some of the wealthier ones, like fiscally conservative states, have, by running budget surpluses, been able to build up asset portfolios. These serve to insulate the group's activities from fluctuations in their current revenues and allow them to fund expenditure obligations beyond those that their current revenues alone would support. It was the PLO's portfolio of financial assets that enabled it to transform itself from merely a successful guerrilla organization to a bona fide government in exile.[97]

In its early days the PLO relied almost exclusively on outside sponsors, mainly the Arab states, which used their financial aid to try to manipulate the Palestinian national movement to their own political ends. By the early 1980s, however, Palestinians, especially those employed in the oil states of the Persian Gulf, were contributing 5–7 percent of their salaries to support the PLO. At the same time, assets held by the PLO—direct investments in factories, real estate holdings, plus stocks and bonds managed through the Swiss subsidiary of the Arab Bank of Amman—were reputedly producing income in excess of $1 billion a year. Although the number could well have been exaggerated by U.S. or Israeli propaganda, it was sufficient to support diaspora schools and hospitals, a diplomatic corps in ninety countries, and a standing army of fourteen thousand, in addition to allowing the PLO to assist the civilian population of Occupied Palestine.

Although assets mean flexibility and independence, they also open a new window of vulnerability. Identifiable assets are susceptible to counterattack by the state. These challenges seem particularly intense now, given rapidly changing financial technology and the increasing commitment of national intelligence agencies to tracing and seizing their antagonists' funds—although how successful the agencies will be remains to be seen. But such countermeasures were also possible in the past. In 1984, for example, the IRA instructed a company to deposit an extortion payment directly into a Swiss bank. The money was wired to the Manhattan branch of the Bank of Ireland. To break the trail, a courier picked up the sum in cash and ferried it to Ireland for deposit in another branch of the same bank. But it was all in vain. The next year the British government traced the money, and the Irish government impounded $2.5 million.[98]

Once a guerrilla movement has succeeded in establishing a zone of control, it has also converted financial into physical capital. This can be a serious threat because the movement's assets are opened up to a different form of attack. Thus, during its 1982 invasion of Lebanon, Israel destroyed $400 million worth of PLO infrastructure and assets in the form of factories, offices, commercial real estate, hospitals, and schools, as well as seizing bank records in an attempt to trace PLO financial assets around the world. To this the PLO responded by liquidating its portfolio of stocks and bonds, and moving the money into short-term, money market assets hidden behind the screen of ghost companies and nominee accounts. The PLO's skill in keeping its assets essentially intact enabled it to survive that disaster. However, the cancellation during the Gulf War of the mandatory deduction that rulers of the Gulf states had imposed, on the PLO's behalf, on the salaries of Palestinian workers, badly hurt the PLO's income just at a time when the costs of supporting the *intifada* were severely draining its resources. This financial loss was one of the main factors that impelled the PLO to sign the Oslo Accords, which probably spelled the end to dreams of Palestinian independence.[99]

Even if a guerrilla group successfully hides its assets from an opposing government, there are other dangers with which it has to contend. In the hot money business, those who seek secrecy have, by definition, something to hide. They are therefore without (legal) recourse in the event of defalcation by their financial agents, in whose name the assets are likely held. Thus, the wealth the Colombian M-19 had accumulated from bank robbery and kidnapping was prudently stashed in a Panama bank. When the group, faced with an army offensive, tried to withdraw some of it, the bank's owner refused. So the M-19 staged a kidnapping of the banker, and the money was released.[100]

Not so fortunate were the Argentinean Montoñeros. Of the $60 million ransom collected in return for the Born brothers, the Montoñeros entrusted $12–20 million to an Argentinean banker running a capital flight business for leading Peronist politicians. The money was stashed in Uruguay, the most common destination for funds fleeing Argentina. Once a month the Montoñeros would call at the banker's office with a suitcase to pick up the regular interest payments. This happy arrangement came to an end during the 1975–76 crackdown by the Argentinean military. The banker fled the country and reportedly died in a plane crash in Mexico, leaving behind a string of broken banks from Argentina to Belgium to the United States. One thing not left behind was the Montoñeros's money.[101]

Insurgency's New Frontiers

In the early decades of the Cold War, the theory that armed insurgency was the result of a Bolshevik conspiracy largely precluded the need to search for the smoking dollar—the Evil Empire hypothesis neatly disposed of both the why and the how. Over time it was partially replaced by the narco-conspiracy: left-wing groups plied the world drug trade, debauching Western youth, to finance the purchase of weapons from a cash-starved USSR—weapons they needed to wreak havoc on struggling Third World democracies. Then, with the fall of the Soviet Union, the rhetoric shifted again. If in the 1960s the bête noir was Che Guevara leading a peasant rebellion, if in the 1970s it was Carlos plotting airline hijackings with a group of urban misfits, if in the 1980s it was Abu Nidhal, the radical Palestinian nationalist (and part-time Mossad agent—although that was never mentioned) sewing mayhem, by the 1990s responsibility for the most egregious acts could be laid at the feet of the dour Saudi fundamentalist Osama bin Laden. Blaming the atrocities of the world on supervillains is not only bad political science and worse foreign policy, but it diverts attention from more fundamental roots of social problems for which the effective solutions are much more complex.

In fact, the old notion that the Soviet Union or the People's Republic of China financially backed a Cold War–era wave of guerrilla activity was simply false. Financial aid given by Communist countries to left-wing guerrilla groups in the 1970s and 1980s varied from minimal (for example, East Germany occasionally offered refuge to fleeing members of the Red Army Faction) to nonexistent. The Soviet Union covertly pumped money into the hands of Communist parties willing to contest elections, not into the hands of insurgent groups. And after the death of Mao, China, hoping to control events close to its own borders, restricted its aid to groups such as the Burmese Communist Party and the Khmer Rouge. Apart from donations from the committed, most financing for left-wing insurgents came first from predatory acts against the uncommitted, then from revolutionary taxation, and finally from the resources of the group's own zones of control.

Indeed, there was little reason for the USSR to aid such insurgents. Apart from the fact that so many left-wing guerrilla groups routinely denounced Communist countries for betraying the revolution, it was never clear just how high Marxism really was on the political agendas of some of these groups. Although a small, urban terrorist group operating in an ethnically homogenous society might have found its ideological raison d'être in an obscure passage in Marx, Lenin, or Mao, some of the serious popular insurgencies seemed to use Marxist ideology as legitimization when in fact their real motives were more mundane.

The politico-ideological veneer was always thin in the case of a group such as the ETA, which invokes the notion of proletarian solidarity to justify creation of an independent Basque homeland in a region of Spain in which the majority of the working class is made up of poor Spaniards from other provinces.[102] The veneer was harder to penetrate in the case of the Burmese Communist Party, which made much effort to politically indoctrinate lower-level cadres. Inevitably, however, the Burmese Communist Party succumbed to Burmese political realities and disintegrated in the face of a military rebellion by the ethnic rank and file against the aging Birman leadership. It turns out that much of the enthusiasm with which the rank and file had devoured the Maoist tracts passed out by their leaders came from the fact that the thin paper was excellent for rolling cigarettes.[103]

The typical self-reliance of left-wing insurgents stands in contrast to the cornucopia of U.S., British, French, and Saudi aid given to right-wing antigovernment rebel forces during the final decades of the Cold War. Yet even here dependence on sponsors was far from absolute. Any sensible insurgent group minimized the political constraints of outside aid by diversifying funding sources. And that, of course, led to the apparent confluence of insurgent and criminal behavior.

It is certainly true that guerilla groups raise money through a variety of illegal methods—from armed robbery to fraudulent diversion of charitable donations to smuggling of everything from rubies to rhino horn, teakwood to tiger skins—and that these methods at least approximate those of ordinary criminals. As with ordinary criminals, too, the sums they supposedly gain are usually exaggerated. Much the way gangsters puff out their chests in pride when the mass media uncritically repeat police hype, guerrillas find bloated figures useful for increasing their significance in the eyes of the general public, whereas the government uses the figures to gain resources, particularly in the form of more U.S. military aid.[104] Gangsters and guerrillas share one other thing—the huge sums they reputedly earn, conveniently for both sides, can never be located.

It is also true that guerrilla activity can degenerate into pure criminality. Once civil conflict has lasted long enough to wreck the civil economy—through physical destruction, collapse of domestic purchasing power, and capital flight—it sets the stage for its own perpetuation. Among other things, long-term civil conflict creates a generation whose only skills, at what should be their peak productive years, are military; they therefore turn easily to criminal activity for survival even after the conflict winds down.[105] That may be the essential kernel of truth in the British government's assessment that Northern Ireland's paramilitary groups have switched their priorities from guns to gold, metaphorically speaking, and that the Troubles racking Ulster since the 1960s have left behind a "mafia" subculture.[106] Similarly, in the border area of Thailand and Malaysia, where the Communist Party of Malaysia attempted to break free of Chinese influence by creating its own network of businesses, peace and amnesty merely meant a switch from a politically driven unofficial economy to a commercially driven one. Even into the 1990s, this parallel economy was still run by old comrades. Although tapping the rubber tappers remained the main source of income, running brothels and smuggling counterfeit consumer goods were major postcapitalist additions.[107] And when Assam's ULFA went into a slump in the early 1990s, former militants used their skills to pull off business frauds, corner construction contracts, and stage armed robberies on their own account.[108]

This criminalization of guerrilla forces is not inevitable, however. When amnesty and reconstruction occur, some groups evolve into bona fide political parties, as happened with the M-19 in Colombia, the FMLN in El Salvador, RENAMO in Mozambique, and the Lebanese Hezbollah. Even the Internal Macedonian Revolutionary Organization, which terrorized the Balkans before World War I by bombing Greek and Turkish targets and shaking down and murdering well-to-do Muslims, rematerialized in the wake of the Balkan wars of the 1990s as a seemingly respectable po-litical party that claimed to be the key to mobilizing for the impoverished homeland a billion dollars of émigré investment.[109]

Indeed, reintegration can take even more spectacular forms. Liberia's General Butt Naked used to lead his Butt Naked Brigade into battle (against rivals like General George Bush and General Saddam Hussein) clad only in leather shoes and a gun—although his men were allowed to wear underpants. Then during one "firefight"—soldiers in the Liberian civil war used to battle with butter knives, golf clubs and even cans of in-secticide if they were short of more conventional matériel—he had visions of God appearing before him. After that he donned a tie and jacket and began preaching peace and reconciliation on behalf of the Soul-Winning Evangelical Ministry.[110]

When a symbiosis between guerrilla financing and criminal activity does occur, it is normally at the end of a failing insurgency. During the course of conflict, there is still an enormous difference between most criminal and in-surgent fund-raising activities—motive. This has profound implications for the prospects of using a follow-the-money strategy to curb and control.

The strategy has two distinct strands. One strand focuses on the appar-ent abuse of front organizations to raise funds in wealthy Western coun-tries. The claim that radical groups from the Middle East, opposed to the Peace Process (an Orwellian term for a deal that leaves Israel in control of most of the arable land and water in Palestine and several million refugees forever excluded from their homeland), were raising millions in mosques across North America led, in 1995, to President Clinton freezing the assets of groups he chose to designate as terrorist. In fact, he set a precedent for much closer monitoring of and interference with any overseas transfer of funds by any domestic educational, religious, or charitable organization with whose objectives the U.S. government of the day might disagree.[111] Not everyone has to worry, however; the deluge of taxpayer-subsidized funds to build Israeli settlements in Occupied Palestine continues largely unabated. Apart from the self-serving selectivity with which the label "terrorist" is used, such crackdowns generally succeed not in reducing fund-raising but in shifting its nature—from open-source donations to under-ground rackets—and making it harder to monitor and control.

The second strand of the strategy, applicable when a guerrilla group has passed beyond the predatory and parasitical stages to consolidate a zone of control, is the use of economic sanctions, which puts the inter-national community in the interesting position of attempting to deny le-gitimacy to political groups through a policy that formally acknowledges their collective existence.

These sanctions were first used in 1993 in an attempt to put the Khmer Rouge out of business. The UN banned the export of oil to and the import of rubies and logs from the group's zones of control at a time when they reputedly accounted for 80 percent of the world's rubies as well as a large share of the global teak and rosewood trade. The sanctions were a flop. Because the Thai army controlled the border and had so many business interests in common with the Khmer Rouge, enforcement was almost nonexistent. The army itself ran the oil smuggling. On the export side, there were many ways to disguise the flows. Thai companies, instead of mining gems on the spot, would haul gem-bearing soil across the border to a central processing point inside Thailand. At the same time, small Thai furniture makers moved into Kampuchea to manufacture on site; the final product was easier to export with false documents, and the migration of the secondary industry enabled the Khmer Rouge to increase their tax returns by capturing part of the downstream value added.[112] Even then logs continued to flow. When the United States threatened to cut off aid to Thailand if it did not stop importing teak and rosewood, obliging officials in Kampuchea issued fake certificates of origin or certified that the logs had been cut before the embargo.[113] Ultimately what shut down the Khmer Rouge financial lifeline was supply and demand— the exhaustion of the ruby mines and the collapse of the hardwood market in the Asia crisis.

Despite the fiasco, the same strategy was repeated with much the same results in a futile attempt to bring the UNITA guerrilla movement to heel. Yet UNITA officials continue to tour the world by using passports issued in assumed names by obliging countries, and the organization's bank accounts are all held by nominees. Nor have efforts to curb the trade in blood diamonds been particularly successful. Other governments have been eager, for a small consideration, to issue phony certificates of origin.[114] Add to that the fact that for hundreds of years, diamond trading has been conducted in total anonymity and the deals sealed by a handshake. Hence once rough diamonds enter the trading circuits, they are quickly washed from hand to hand—until they are cut and sold, at which point the game is truly over. Even if the efforts to isolate blood diamonds eventually bear fruit, the main result will be to allow the De Beers diamond cartel to reassert the power that it temporarily lost to the black market.

There is another way in which the hype over the money trail is a red herring. Even if an insurgent group is effective in financial terms, the path to political legitimacy and power is not paved with gold. Money does not explain why a particular insurgency occurs. Nor is money the only strategic resource an insurgent movement requires. Moreover, its ability to collect reflects many nonmaterial factors—for example, the motivation of its militants and the degree of enthusiasm (or, sometimes, fear) it instills in the surrounding population. True, having enough financial resources is certainly necessary for an effective challenge against the political status quo. But it is far from sufficient. And it does not follow that attacking the financial foundations is the solution to the problem.

Indeed, it is not even clear in many cases just what the problem is. The search for the sources of "terrorist" financing begs the crucial question of whether governments should always and everywhere make the effort. It ultimately depends on the legitimacy of the group's demands and methods compared with the legitimacy of the target government's policies.

The great majority of today's civil conflicts are, and for the foreseeable future will remain, identity conflicts, that is, conflicts involving minority ethnoreligious groups in opposition to policies of some larger political entity. In the Chittagong Hills of Bangladesh, for example, thirteen tribal peoples have been in a state of incipient or open insurrection since the flooding of their lands by a hydro mega-project in 1962 drove 100,000 out of their homes, and then most of the minimal compensation offered was stolen by state officials. In 1975, a military government encouraged the mass migration of these tribes from the lowlands into traditional tribal territory; this precipitated an open rebellion that was financed by war taxes on local businesses and sustained by arms purchased on the Bangkok black market.[115]

This phenomenon—where hill peoples who practice traditional farming see their interests sacrificed to urban interests or subordinated to the drive to impose a cash-crop orientation on agriculture—occurs frequently across Asia. That the hill peoples are often of a distinct religion—in the Chittagong Hills they are Buddhist or Christian, whereas the newcomers are Muslim—can be an exacerbating factor. It is not the cause, however, as the violence in present-day Sumatra (where native peoples under pressure have turned on fellow Muslim newcomers) so well attests. Migrations that precipitate social conflict are usually not the result of ethnoreligious factors. More commonly they are the joint consequence of overpopulation (a word often used as a euphemism for an ecological disaster caused by unsustainable resource exploitation) in one area combined with a drive by the central government to expand cash-crop production, even in wholly unsuitable areas, in order to earn the foreign exchange necessary to cover import bills (including those for arms) or to pay interest and dividends on the foreign debt. Even in the United States, the growth of white militias in the 1980s and early 1990s was ultimately caused more by rural debt, the rising power of the agro-industrial complex, and the growing threat to the viability of the family farm as a socioeconomic unit than by things like anti-Semitism, although, inevitably, it was the latter that attracted the most attention.

It is also true that most "identity" insurrections involve peoples who are poor. Even here, however, it would be foolish to overgeneralize. Poverty is relative and usually subjective. If poverty were the real cause of insurrection, most of the world today would be in flames.

If it is possible to generalize about the real causes of such complex phenomena, they are probably driven by the interaction of two current trends. One is the end of the illusion of the boundlessness of nature, and with it, the myth of the seemingly limitless possibilities for economic growth. As long as everyone's living standard was rising, it mattered little if a favored few, within and between countries, saw theirs rising very much faster. Today, with ever-increasing pressure on biophysical resources that are not merely limited but in many cases being rapidly depleted and degraded, ethic and sectarian feuds are often surrogates for disputes about land and water, fish and forests, minerals and energy.[116] That, too, is destined almost inevitably to become much worse in the near future.

It is true that contests over control of natural wealth have an ancient pedigree. Much of human history could be written around the cycle of a society slashing down forests, draining the groundwater supply, depleting the most accessible minerals, and exhausting the soil to such an extent that it had to colonize or conquer another area.[117] What is different today is that the process is virtually global in scope; the rate is accelerating, and it is occurring in societies in which both numbers and expectations are unsustainably high.[118] And that is exacerbated by another factor.

At one time it was generally accepted that economic growth made social justice financially possible and morally essential. Today, however, short-term economic performance and distributive justice have little in common. The resulting maldistribution of income and wealth has gone beyond the alarming to the obscene. Although the seeds were sown before the end of the Cold War, the apparent triumph of free-market liberalism has made these trends all the stronger. Traditional forms of protectionism, economic and social, have disappeared in the face of the "free" international movement of commodities, services, and money, while fiscal restraints have made it all the more difficult to mitigate the effects. With populations robbed of social and economic security of the type the state was supposed to provide (although too often it did not), sect, clan, and extended family are called on once more to perform the functions formerly assigned to the civic order. Inevitably loyalties are transferred, and those social units can all the more easily become the medium through which to express political frustrations in violent form.

CHAPTER 3

Loose Cannons

Covert Commerce and Underground Finance in the Modern Arms Black Market

Thanks to the drugs that coursed through their territory and the thriving arms bazaar just across the border in Afghanistan, some tribal chiefs in Pakistan's rugged and lawless North-West Frontier Province moved from mud-walled forts guarded by a few kinsmen with bolt-action rifles into marble-floored, Jacuzzi-equipped mansions protected by antiaircraft missiles.[1] Nor are they the only ones for whom smuggling turns mud into marble. Around the world, a similar symbiosis of political insurgency, contraband trade, and arms proliferation has occurred with a frequency that even the National Rifle Association might have trouble applauding.

On the face of it, this bounty from arms sales should not be happening. Peace should be breaking out all over. The Cold War is long finished, and once the impact of a few high-cost, high-tech systems is factored out of the data, the world weapons trade over the post–Cold War era appears to have been in sharp decline. Unfortunately, there are good reasons to read that data in a more pessimistic way.

Gun Smoke and Mirrors

The first reason for pessimism is that the smuggling of technology, reverse engineering of foreign systems, and acute competition among sellers to offer better offset agreements have spread the capacity to make weapons, some quite sophisticated, across the globe. This has greatly reduced the need to buy on the world market.[2]

Second, looking simply at total value misses a dangerous shift in the reasons for the demand. Much of the former Cold War arms boom was not so much preparation for actual conflict as it was history's greatest Potlatch ceremony. Such ceremonies, once common among aboriginal peoples of the Pacific Northwest coast of America, were meant to ensure that political rivalries did not degenerate into intracommunal violence. A man seeking to gain or confirm status would gather and then give away or destroy as much physical wealth as possible, to force rivals to better the performance when their turn came round.[3] Similarly, the Cold War arms boom (to the extent it was not, on the Western side, simply an enormous boondoggle by the weapons industry) involved participants visibly wasting as much national product as possible to stockpile weapons they hoped would never be used, with the objective of spending the other side into surrender.[4] But now, with Cold War restraints stripped away, it is a safe assumption that an increasing percentage of trade is in arms intended for use rather than display or deterrence.[5] The result is more killing power per dollar spent.

Third, part of the measured reduction in total value results from decreases in price, not quantity. A factory-fresh AK-47 used to wholesale for about $125. During the 1990s, a new one could be picked up for $30 or $40 in Russia; a secondhand one cost as little as $8 in Cambodia, the price of a chicken in Uganda, or the equivalent of a sack of maize in Angola or Mozambique.[6] Yet no matter its price, the weapon kills just as effectively. That trend is reinforced by the relative shift from high-cost, high-tech items purchased for reasons of national prestige to lower-tech matériel proven in actual combat and obtainable at much lower unit cost.

Fourth, for strategic and political reasons, governments underreport even their legitimate arms trade, not to mention their trade in components and technology for unconventional weapons. Sellers mingle data on arms with data for civilian products, and buyers misrepresent "double-use" components and technology to make them appear exclusively for benign purpose.

A fifth, yet more disturbing reason why the reduction in measured arms flows may contain more bad news than good is the apparent increase in the amount of arms sales handled off the books through the international black market.

Allergic to Light

The arms business is inherently dirty. Even when weapons are produced within major industrialized countries for sale to their own forces, business as usual means industrial espionage, bid rigging, phony invoicing, faked test-data, and a revolving door relationship involving producer, purchaser, and public overseer that, a century earlier, would have made an American railroad baron blush. All this is encouraged by politicians, who see the arms industry as a job-creation program for their constituents and a source of electoral campaign funds.[7]

Nor are the norms of legal international sales more edifying. In wars for market share, victory often goes to the highest bidder; after all, the higher the bid, the greater the potential kickback to officials of the purchasing country.[8]

Such practices, common early in the twentieth century, became front page news again in the 1970s with revelations that not only did Lockheed Corporation consider qualified as overseas sales agents everyone from convicted embezzlers to accused war criminals but it also reckoned as legitimate sales expenses its contributions to such causes as a phony widows-and-orphans foundation run by the Indonesian air force, electoral slush funds of far-right candidates in Germany and Italy, and the pocket money of a philandering Crown Prince of the Netherlands.[9]

The ensuing scandal left three things in its wake. One was the U.S. Foreign Corrupt Practices Act, which made bribery by U.S. corporations a criminal offense, although its main effect was simply to encourage more sophisticated methods for laundering the required cash.[10]

The second was to educate envious foreigners in the deportment necessary to challenge the United States's dominant position in the free world's arms market. As competition heated up, bribes and kickbacks became near-universal tools of the trade, sufficiently so that Adnan Khashoggi, a veteran Saudi arms-dealer, insisted that all arms manufacturers build into cost estimates an allowance for "noncommercial" expenses.[11]

The third effect was to shift public concern onto a distinctly peripheral issue.

The real question is not why this or that item procured by the military costs so much. Rather it is how so much of society's productive potential became—and remains—captive of an industrial complex dedicated to mayhem and mass murder. This greater corruption—the product of colluding corporations, opportunistic politicians, and a military establishment intent on self-perpetuation—dwarfs in importance the payoffs and padded invoices that are routine in the arms business.[12] Besides, it has never been clear why a clean arms industry is so desirable. In much the way governments whose leaders spend their time stuffing money into Swiss bank accounts can sometimes be an improvement over those capable of carrying out ugly agendas with brutal efficiency, it is arguable that rampant fraud in military procurement could be a blessing in disguise: the resulting cost inflation means fewer weapons can be bought, and those that are will often fail to destroy property or kill people.

However, in the arms business, what truly differentiates a black market transaction from a "legitimate" one is neither fraud on the supply side nor bribery on the demand side (although they may be present as well). Rather, it is the use of covert methods to intermediate between supply and demand, to move weapons one way and money back the other. In a bona fide black-market deal, demand comes from actors who cannot or prefer not to meet their needs on the open market; suppliers impose restrictions on the type or destination of the items being sought; clandestine methods are used to move the weapons from supplier to end-user to mask the identity of some or all of the participants; a substantial part of the cost is due not to physical acquisition of the material but to surreptitious movement of the merchandise; and the payment flows must be laundered to hide their origins or destination. Thus, the essence of a black market transaction is summed up by the fact that black is not a color; it is the absence of light.

Who's Out Shopping?

Until the 1970s, there was a fairly clear distinction between the overt and covert portions of the arms market. In the first, and by far the most important, formal armies obtained weapons from friendly states or state-regulated companies and made payments by a mix of commercial concessions, state-supported credits, and countertrade. In the second, "light" weapons went surreptitiously to "illegitimate" end-users through cash deals. The inference was reassuring: the big, nasty stuff was subject to political control.

In reality, the distinction was never so clean. Occasionally, even formal states bought or sold under the table, and the gunrunner, far from being a freelance operator, was often fronting for a coy government. With apologies to Clausewitz, the arms black market has long been an extension of diplomacy by other, covert means. Nonetheless, the notion that black market dealings were mainly in light weapons was a reasonable approximation to reality, at least until the 1970s. But in a contemporary world in which reputedly it is possible to purchase a tank directly from its crew in the ex–Soviet Central Asian republics or, until recently, have one delivered to the front door of a Beirut hotel, such assumptions are no longer tenable. Given today's supply-side conditions, the main division in the arms market is not the technical one between light and heavy weapons, but the commercial one between transactions that are retail (small scale) and wholesale (in one or both senses of the term). Each is further distinguished by whether end-users employ overt or covert means to satisfy their requirements.

Criminals or "terrorists" (or for that matter, intelligence agents looking for "sterile" equipment) demand light weapons in small quantities, because their acts of violence are generally selective. Such clandestine users can often meet their needs from precisely the same sources as legitimate users do— the U.S. open market, for example—and then arrange to smuggle the hardware to wherever it is going to be used.

Armies, whether regular or irregular, whether done up with all the trimmings or tossed together as ragtag militia groups, also demand light weapons, but in large job lots. Someone interested in the covert acquisition of ten thousand assault rifles will face much the same logistical problems as someone surreptitiously searching for ten antiaircraft guns, and will likely turn to the same set of international traffickers for their resolution. Indeed, the ten thousand assault rifles and ten antiaircraft guns might well make their way to market on the same ship and with payments run through the same obliging banks. Thus, the real issue is not the technical or physical nature of the weapons (the light-versus-heavy distinction much beloved of today's arms control advocates) but the size of the bill their acquisition runs up.[13]

The two sectors of the arms market can be further subdivided by motive of purchase. On the retail market, legitimate citizens seek weapons for defense or display, whereas illegitimate users (criminals, terrorists, and spooks) want them for direct use. In the wholesale sector, there is a parallel difference in motive between those who shop openly and those who have recourse to black market deals.

Regular armies seek weapons on the open market for three reasons: value in use, value in display, and value in foreign bank accounts. The first is straightforward. The second is driven partly by the need to deter external enemies and partly by the need to cow the local population with a display of the regime's military might. Even though the bulk of a modern army's arsenal is useless for suppressing civil disturbances, regimes feel that strutting the armed force in public is (like recalling and reminting the coinage in bygone ages) one of the best ways to make clear who is in charge.

But these two reasons are insufficient to explain why so many states still buy heavily or to account for just what and from whom they are buying. Therefore a third motive seems very much at work, namely, the existence of purchasing officials with large numbers of progeny or secret bank accounts to feed.

In Thailand, for example, the military hierarchy determines which weapons to order, and kickbacks average 15–20 percent of the value of the deal. The money is collected in a lump sum, either directly from the companies or via local arms brokers, and the subsequent scale of payments to officers is nicely staggered by rank. Serving generals can look forward to retirement after three or four years with a nest egg of up to $50 million to see them through their declining years. The cost is, of course, loaded into the final price charged to the Thai taxpayer. Just as such tactics by Lockheed in the 1970s gave Italy formations of high-flying politicians along with fighter aircraft that rarely got off the ground, in Thailand two decades later the result was a logistical jumble of seven types of combat planes and six varieties of tanks, with incompatible parts and different ammunition requirements, some so unreliable they were quickly shifted to training purposes.[14]

At much the same time came a similar imbroglio in Taiwan, after a naval officer, recently appointed director of procurement, was found practicing nautical maneuvers face down in the ocean. It transpired that the efforts of a major Italian shipbuilding firm to get its fair share of a $7.5 billion frigate contract led to the indictment of eight arms brokers, seven senior officers, and a host of bureaucrats.[15]

The principle that the shortest route to arms contracts is via greased palms was also applied in South Korea, whose massively expensive defense procurement program produced, by the end of the Cold War, antiaircraft guns incapable of distinguishing friend from foe, an obsolete radar system, a type of tank that routinely stalled (a blessing in disguise because its firing and navigational systems were not properly integrated), and a naval battery that would not load U.S. ammunition. It also produced the arrest of forty officers and business executives, including two former ministers of defense, in a corruption imbroglio that caused more casualties than the weaponry.[16]

The stereotypical view is that bribery is an unfortunate cost of doing business in "that part of the world." In reality, it is an act consummated by two sets of consenting adults, in private, and to their mutual satisfaction. Thus, in 1988, Great Britain violated its own law forbidding the use of foreign aid to secure military contracts. It offered Malaysia, as a sweetener for a £1 billion fighter-aircraft deal, a £235 million loan to be used for a major hydroelectric project (a project condemned by nongovernmental agencies as a prescription for environmental disaster and by Great

Britain's Overseas Development Association as grossly uneconomic) on the understanding that British construction firms full of Conservative Party stalwarts would get the dam-building contract. Malaysia agreed to pay nearly double the usual cost of the planes to cover kickbacks to Malaysian agents and campaign contributions to the ruling party.[17] Although the deal ended in an embarrassing fiasco, that did not prevent Britain several years later from peddling its wares in neighboring Indonesia—supported by the pledge of foreign aid to build a toll road owned by a company controlled by the daughter of the then-ruling dictator of Indonesia.[18]

By contrast, in the covert part of the wholesale sector, participants have a quite different set of motives for buying weapons and for doing so by underground methods.

Today, black market buyers are no longer merely insurgents and guerrilla armies. They are also aspiring countries blocked from the legal arms market by lack of UN recognition. They are joined in the black market by formally recognized countries that cannot or will not buy openly.

Constituted states might go underground for logistical reasons—to obtain materials others cannot or will not sell them.[19] This is especially the case if it is necessary to break an embargo. Embargo busting was precisely what drove Israel in the 1960s and South Africa in the 1970s to lay the foundation for the modern black market in arms, whose superstructure was then completed by Iran and Iraq in the 1980s.[20]

The motives may also be strategic—to keep a buildup from the scrutiny of neighbors. That was at least one factor that prompted Iraq to obtain, through a global network of front companies and secret bank accounts, the technology needed to create a sophisticated array of conventional and unconventional weaponry.[21]

The motives are sometimes financial. Governments such as those of Iran, Libya, Iraq, or, more recently, Serbia tried to ensure a clandestine war chest, protected by bank secrecy laws in offshore havens, to sidestep punitive asset freezes. Whatever the reasons driving a buyer underground, however, weapons bought covertly are generally intended for direct use in the near future.

A Buyer's Guide to the Arms Bazaar

In the early post–World War II decades, the arms black market was a minor concern. The United States and the USSR dominated the supply of major new weapons systems, for themselves and their European allies. They largely eliminated the potential for a serious black market in second-hand heavy matériel by giving away older models to Third World allies. And the United States kept some control over the market in light weapons by supporting the efforts of an ex–CIA officer, the late Sam Cummings, to stockpile as much of the world's surplus as possible. With ample bank credit, Cummings could move quickly to take weapons off the market. He could then act as a cutout when the United States (or Great Britain) decided to secretly violate an embargo. Not least, his inventory of sterile weapons included East Bloc equipment, which the CIA could call on to equip insurgent forces fighting regimes backed by the USSR. What made the arrangements especially useful was that Cummings never supplied a belligerent without a nod from Washington.[22]

To the extent that weapons did "leak" onto the world market, the transactions were subject at least partially to another, more subtle form of control. Arms brokers and dealers were largely drawn from three interrelated professional classes: ex–arms company executives, veteran senior military officers, and former intelligence agents, most of whom maintained relations with their previous employers. That permitted the major powers, within limits, to turn the heat up or down in a particular region by facilitating or impeding arms deals.[23] Furthermore, free-lancers were mainly brokers, rather than merchants like Sam Cummings, and therefore they were hobbled by the traditional limitations of the black market. It could not assure regularity of supply. It could not guarantee quality. And given the expenses associated with smuggling, laundering money, and paying off officials, black market prices tended to be higher.

During the 1970s, there was some slippage. Financial pressures induced the superpowers to shift to sales of second-tier matériel to wealthier allies in developing countries, who then had an incentive to compare prices and quality. Meantime, competitors emerged in the form of European manufacturers of major weapons. This was the era of the Lockheed and similar scandals, and of the rise of a new class of international wheeler-dealers close to the seat of power in purchasing countries.[24] Nonetheless, the black market per se still seemed a minor concern—until a revolutionary transformation in the 1980s.

Demand literally exploded. Major conflicts raged in the Andes, the Southern Cone, Central America, Southeast Asia, southern Africa, the Horn of Africa, the Levant, the Persian Gulf, and the Arc of Crisis (from Turkey through to Pakistan). Then, in the 1990s, with the dissolution of the Soviet Union and the breakup, actual or pending, of a series of other states that had owed their stability largely to the Cold War system of alliance, came a new set of conflicts.

In addition, the traditional (if sometimes fuzzy) distinction between regular and irregular conflicts, between formal and informal armies, in terms of numbers of participants and amounts of matériel required, largely disappeared.[25] Guerrilla actions evolved into full-blown insurgencies, which in turn became civil wars that might spill over to involve neighboring states, with the demand for weapons rising in step. The result was that if the distinction between light and heavy weapons, or between private and state-related actors, ever had commercial meaning on the black market, in the 1980s that distinction effectively disappeared. Furthermore, over the course of the 1980s and on into the 1990s, a market for upgrade services spread, helping to obliterate many of the military advantages formerly conferred by purchasing new flows rather than secondhand stocks.

There were also accommodating changes on the supply side. One was commercialization of a distribution process previously constrained by politics. That was due in good measure to the number of new entrants into the arms-making business.

For arms manufacturers, foreign sales became essential to maintain production runs long enough to capture economies of scale. Simultaneously, for developing countries, arms production came to be seen as the best way to ensure new technological developments, particularly because some boasted of labor forces that rivaled the skill levels of major industrial countries, yet they could be hired for a fraction of the cost.

Granted any government could directly subsidize civilian development of the same technologies. But, as the example of the major industrial countries showed, subsidizing technological change through the military had a major political advantage—it could be done in the ideologically unassailable name of national security. In addition, by working through the military, countries could not only maintain greater secrecy but also implement a de facto industrial policy, while still nominally adhering to global conventions that called on them to open their economies to the winds of free competition. Furthermore, indigenous production capacity ensured that strategic goals would not be hampered by any of the embargoes that the "international community" imposed reflexively during the 1980s and 1990s.[26]

There were financial incentives as well: the export of weapons became an important earner of foreign exchange. Although in the 1970s, primary product prices had been strong and rising, giving some developing countries the wherewithal to import arms, falling commodity prices in the

1980s encouraged them to economize on foreign exchange through home production, and further encouraged them to earn foreign exchange by exporting the results. This pattern was accentuated greatly in the wake of the debt crisis of the 1980s and the consequent drying up of syndicated loans from Western banks.[27]

Therefore, during the 1980s, the number of states capable of producing high-quality merchandise spread well beyond the traditional alliance systems. To the 1980s' ranks of new arms producers from developing countries were added, in the 1990s, former socialist countries eager to test the principles of the free market in its most dangerous form.

In theory, all the newly produced arms flowing onto the market were subject to control. By the 1980s, all major producing countries (except China) had theoretically accepted the principle that new weapons were only sold with an end-user certificate (or EUC) signed by the aspiring purchaser. The purchaser had to pledge that the weapons were for the bona fide armed forces of that country and that the purchaser would not resell them without permission of the original supplier-state. Only on presentation of a proper EUC was a government supposed to issue an export license to the would-be seller.

The regulations looked wonderful in theory. In practice, however, they ran afoul of a simple principle. Regulatory structures are usually framed if not actually to advance then at least to protect the interests of the regulated, and the regulators are usually drawn from (or aspire to subsequently join) the ranks of the regulated. This is true of many sectors in which private and public interests interact, and it is certainly true in the case of arms. Indeed, it is difficult to avoid the suspicion that the main function of the paperwork that theoretically constrains "legitimate" weapons deals has never been to control the flow of arms onto the world market so much as to allow a supplier to look credibly shocked in public whenever a particularly embarrassing deal comes to light.

Today, obtaining a passable EUC is about as difficult as obtaining a gun dealer's license in the United States, an honor historically denied only to convicted serial killers—who could get around the problem by applying in the names of their pet dogs.[28] Sometimes EUCs are completely faked. That method has the advantage of being cheap, but it also increases the danger of exposure—a fate that befell an Israeli pipeline feeding weapons to Croatia during the Balkan wars. On the basis of a "Bolivian" EUC signed by a nonexistent general, that requested Soviet-model equipment (Bolivia uses U.S. equipment), and that was peppered with Spanish spelling errors, Bulgaria was happy to issue an export license. (At least the letterhead was real—the paper was peddled by an official in the Bolivian government for $300 a sheet.) Only after several shipments did U.S. pressure force an investigation—and a subsequent halt.[29]

More commonly, the EUCs are real. It is a basic proposition in the trade that the signatures of the military attachés of half the embassies in the world are available for a fee that varies from 5 to 12 percent of the value of the shipment. A corollary proposition holds that the farther up the administrative hierarchy the gunrunner goes in search of an EUC, the higher the price but the less probability that the shipment will be questioned.[30]

The EUC was supposed to do double duty: it would restrict to whom new matériel hot off the production line flowed, and it would curb secondary trafficking once officially sanctioned weapons reached their intended destination. Perhaps an EUC made sense when arms suppliers were few, the secondhand market thin, and arms transfers conducted with at least one eye to political advantage. However, the logic was undermined by a combination of commercial greed, political corruption, and, not least, sheer mass of matériel. Even worse, an EUC-based control system rotted by corruption was soon threatened with utter irrelevance by another striking development on the supply side of the market.

There are two distinct ways in which an arms deal can be covert: either its nature can be disguised or its very existence hidden. The first method implies deceiving supply-side regulators (perhaps with their implicit assent) by using faked paperwork. The second implies avoiding the regulatory system altogether. Formerly used only for light-arms deals, the second method has now become the modus operandi in many large-scale transactions as well, mainly because stocks of old weapons may now be more important than flows of new ones in determining availability and setting price.

One simple technical fact makes a big commercial difference. Arms, unless destroyed in combat, can be recycled for decades from war to war. Thus, U.S.-made weapons sent to its allies in Vietnam were captured by North Vietnam in 1975. Subsequently, some were bartered for pineapples to Cuba, which quietly diverted them to a Chilean group of leftist insurgents. The arms were then grabbed in a raid by the Chilean army. In 1991 they were declared surplus and sold off, on the basis of a Sri Lanka EUC, to a Swiss-based firm whose principals included the son of Chilean military strongman Augusto Pinochet. They were then repurchased by members of Chile's wealthy Croatian community to be smuggled to their ethnic kin in Bosnia.[31] Thus, the same stock of arms saw duty as firepower for a formal army, tradable war booty for a victorious belligerent, covert equipment of a guerrilla group dreaming of revolution, part of the stockpile of an army notorious for plotting coups, and a means of strengthening one side in a three-cornered civil war; this last fate was prevented only because the weapons were seized in Hungary en route.

Moreover, the faster new product flows off the manufacturers' assembly lines and the more rapidly the purchasing officials of formal armies can be coaxed, conned, or bribed into accepting model changes, the greater will be the world's supply of usable secondhand matériel. As long as the rate of production of new matériel exceeds the rate at which arms are destroyed in war or rendered technically obsolete, the world's stock of weaponry inevitably will continue to rise.

In addition to being durable, weapons are increasingly substitutable. If the objective of acquisition is to impress the press during National Day ceremonies or to assure a fat corporate sinecure when a general takes early retirement, only the latest models in all their glittering, shrink-wrapped glory will do. But if the point is some quick ethnic cleansing on a border strip, then secondhand will do nicely, especially if it is cheaper and more easily accessible than the new stuff. It is.

The proliferation of conflicts in the last few decades of the twentieth century has led to the emergence of regional distribution centers. Their importance comes not simply from the sheer volume of military supplies poured into them but from the fact that once arms are there, all trace of them is effectively lost. Indeed, intelligence agencies reputedly ship more weapons than required for their immediate purposes to a particular conflict area so that the agencies are free to divert the extras to a politically unauthorized or publicly unacceptable place. Thus, a conflict zone is for arms what an offshore banking center with strict secrecy laws is for money—with the added advantage that anyone attempting to probe the zone's arms business risks considerably more than being declared persona non grata and unceremoniously escorted to the airport.

For retail buyers, there is no need to go far afield to find a regional secondhand market. The United States bears many of the characteristics of a conflict zone, and most flows onto the U.S. market are perfectly legal. Hundreds of manufacturers and legal importers of light weapons sell to tens of thousands of federally licensed gun dealers, who in turn deal so enthusiastically with the general public that, by the early 1990s, there were an estimated two hundred million weapons in the hands of U.S. private citizens.[32] These included followers of David Koresh at Ranch Apocalypse in Waco, Texas, whose stash of rifles, shotguns, and even machine guns was procured legally.[33] Aside from all these arms, there is an additional flow fed by theft from stores, warehouses, cargo carriers, and, not the least, military and National Guard bases.

Whether the weapons are obtained from legal or illegal sources, they are easy to smuggle to end-users abroad. The U.S. market has met the arms requirements of everyone from the paramilitary forces protecting Filipino landlords to the bodyguards of senior Japanese mobsters. It has also serviced political purchasers—for example, Muslim insurgents in Trinidad, Central American rebels, the IRA, and more recently, buyers for Croatia. However, the supply of arms on the U.S. domestic market, even the illegal side, is mostly limited to light weapons in small quantities. Hence insurgent armies and embargoed countries usually shop elsewhere, in those regional supermarkets that handle the full spectrum.

The first arms supermarket to emerge after World War II was in Bangkok, whose dealers were able to offer three decades of surplus ranging from U.S. Vietnam War matériel to Soviet and Chinese supplies for opposing sides in the conflict in Cambodia. The surplus ranged from bargain-basement howitzers to assault rifles selling for less than a pair of designer jeans. The matériel found its way, often via merchants linked to the Thai army, to customers as diverse as Sri Lanka's Tamil Tigers, Filipino Moro rebels, Burmese ethnic insurgents, and the forces of former Shan state drug-lord Khun Sa.[34]

Then came Beirut, which serviced a full range of black market buyers. French gangsters bought light weapons in small numbers through a trafficking ring run out of the French embassy in Beirut, with part of the acquisition cost apparently met by the sale in Lebanon of cars stolen in Europe. Much of the carnage during the early stages of the Liberian civil war was helped by surplus Lebanese light weaponry going to the insurgent National Patriotic Front. And the Croatian army once tried to import helicopters, tanks, and antiaircraft missiles from Beirut, but they were seized by the Serbian navy off Montenegro.[35]

Then came the Horn of Africa. Weapons of all sorts flooded into Ethiopia, Eritrea, and Somalia during the 1970s and early 1980s, so much so that the excess then began flowing out again in the late 1980s and 1990s to nourish conflict elsewhere in eastern Africa. Yet the armies still battling in the Horn showed no evidence of equipment shortage.

More recently, Peshawar, in Pakistan's North-West Frontier Province, emerged as a powerful competitor. There, the combination of billions of dollars worth of weapons shipped by the United States to the Afghan mujahideen, along with a "leakage" rate that may have hit the 65–80 percent range, permitted an overflow to criminal gangs (such as Sindhi dacoits), guerrilla groups (such as Sikh separatists), embargoed countries (such as Iran), and even nonpariah states (such as Qatar, which was searching for antiaircraft missiles the United States refused to supply directly).[36]

Some leakages may have been supplier controlled: there were recurrent rumors of CIA-sponsored diversion to the National Union for the Total Independence of Angola (UNITA) guerrilla movement in Angola and to the Nicaraguan Contras. Some were intermediary controlled: Pakistan's military intelligence supplied several Kashmiri insurgent groups. But many were uncontrolled in the sense that corrupt officials sold to whomever had the money to buy.[37]

Of all the secondhand markets, perhaps the most important was and remains the yard sale of ex–Warsaw Pact equipment. It started with reunification in Germany. With the pullout of the Red Army from East Germany, an enormous amount of matériel was thrown onto the market. Then, when the united German army standardized around NATO models, the equipment of the former East German forces became surplus. One-third of the East German navy was sold outright to Indonesia, top-of-the-line tanks were smuggled to Israel, and 250,000 AK-47s were covertly shipped to Turkey; because Turkey uses NATO equipment, the Soviet weapons were likely used by pro-Turkish paramilitary forces throughout the former Soviet Union.[38]

However large these supplies were, they were minor compared with those freed first by a Soviet–U.S. arms reduction treaty (which, among other things, made no fewer than ten thousand tanks surplus) and then by the collapse of the Soviet Union. Together, these events meant that the greatest stock of military surplus in history was suddenly dumped on the market.

Desperate soldiers, unpaid for months, sold their weapons to obtain essentials. Emerging republics grabbed control of anything in reach— which often turned out to be the very best, because that is what the USSR sent to its troops on the frontiers. Cities in Russia took over local arsenals and announced they were open to offers. The Ukrainian-Siberian Commodity Exchange switched from dealing in grain and oil to selling fighter planes, tanks, and antiaircraft systems. Up to seven trainloads a day arrived in Kaliningrad during 1992 to dump weapons into a compound; no accounting system was in place, and the compound was protected only by barbed wire and underpaid or unpaid soldiers. Not least, downsizing and drastic pay cuts helped attract thousands of Russian military engineers and research scientists to an international market for military expertise in which the respectability of the destination was less important than the size of the paycheck.[39]

Although some of this mass of weaponry stayed in Russia and fell into the hands of criminal gangs, ethnic insurgent forces, and private security firms, inevitably much poured onto the world market. The problem went beyond simply liquidating existing stock. After a failed attempt to promote conversion to civilian production in the final days of the USSR, Russia decided to encourage its arms manufacturers to seek foreign sales. Thus Russia was in the unique position of having the flow of new product from its arms factories competing directly with secondhand stock sold by its military; the result was top-of-the-line matériel at unbeatable prices.[40]

Underbelly of the Beast

If, because of the proliferation of new manufacturers, the corruption of the regulatory apparatus, and the increasing market weight of second-hand sources, the prospects for supply-side control of arms sales seem as remote as the far side of the moon, they threaten to vanish into a cosmic black hole when the capacity of the modern machinery of covert commerce is taken into account. That shift in capacity, too, represents a major change, which an analogy might explain.

Until recently the typical criminal enterprise in, say, the vice rackets, operated in a geographically and socially segregated milieu. When otherwise virtuous citizens wanted to partake of forbidden pleasures, they knew precisely who and where the suppliers were—and so did the police. Consumer, supplier, and regulator all concurred, at least implicitly, on the approximate amounts of the service and on the methods of delivery permitted.

The arms black market used to follow the same pattern. Supplier countries maintained a veneer of respectability by subcontracting an occasional dirty deal to professional gunrunners. Consumers, be they embargoed countries or militants operating independently of state control, metaphorically donned their soiled trench coats to sneak off to sate their appetites in the military equivalent of red-light districts. Meanwhile the intelligence agencies would quietly oversee the process, skimming part of the profits in the form of political capital and disciplining, sometimes terminally, the occasional overzealous customer or greedy supplier.

Today, however, clandestine business activities of all sorts have broken through the traditional constraints, and the methods used have rapidly gained commercial sophistication. From recreational drugs to counterfeit credit cards, from fake designer watches to stolen diamonds, what is at play is no longer this or that individual black market. Rather, there has emerged a set of interrelated black markets with their own sources of supply, their own systems of information, and their own modes of financing.

The result is that a modern covert arms deal might take place within a matrix of black market transactions. Weapons might be sold for cash, exchanged for hostages, bartered for heroin or religious artifacts, or countertraded for grain or oil. The transactions could be handled by middlemen equally at home smuggling rubies from Burma, sneaking counterfeit computer chips into the United States, or dumping toxic waste in Lebanon. The transportation could be entrusted to a company whose headquarters are designated by one of several dozen brass plates on the door of a small Cayman Islands office staffed by a single secretary who watches American soaps the whole working day. Such companies might hire, to haul the arms, ships registered in one of the many flag-of-convenience centers that are the bane of seafarers' unions, marine insurance companies, and UN officials attempting to enforce trade embargoes. The payments could move through a series of coded bank accounts in the name of a network of shell companies protected by the banking and corporate secrecy laws of one or several of those financial havens that are proliferating faster than accountants specializing in tax evasion can keep track of them. And behind it all might well be a complex of (often tacit) alliances between groups as varied as legal arms manufacturers, career smugglers, political party bagmen, "organized crime" families, insurgent armies, and intelligence service agents.

No neater summary of that last principle can be found than in an operation run on behalf of Valsella Meccanotechnica, Italy's leading manufacturer of antipersonnel, antiship, and antitank mines. Until 1984 (when the Italian government banned arms sales to the Persian Gulf), one of Valsella's best-known customers was the Islamic Republic of Iran. After 1984 (until scandal broke), one of Valsella's least-known customers was the Islamic Republic of Iran.

To make loads of weapons disappear from official sight, Valsella called on the services of an Italo-Swiss shipping broker once convicted in a maritime fraud case—he had claimed $500,000 insurance on a cargo lost when a very peculiar storm sank a freighter in an area blessed by balmy weather. (Fortunately, the captain and crew had time to load their belongings into a lifeboat and land safely in Cyprus, while the ship, duly lightened, refloated itself and sought refuge from the storm in a pirate port in Lebanon, where it was repainted and saw service again under a new name.) Sentenced to four years, the broker put his experience in the quick freight business to more personal use: he escaped from a Swiss prison with an ease at first difficult to understand. Shortly after, he resurfaced in Lebanon, offering to arrange arms deals. He assured would-be customers that Swiss banks stood ready to handle the money. Each of the Greek ships he chartered was doubly registered in Honduras and in Lebanon, so they had the ability to change identity on demand.

In 1986, Valsella presented to the Italian government EUCs specifying Nigeria as the proud buyer of 30,000 antipersonnel mines and then called on its broker to do the rest. Although most nautical charts showed Nigeria southwest of Italy, one of the broker's ships headed east. On arrival in Syria, it unloaded the mines for transshipment to Iran. A year later he routed two million mines to Syria via Barcelona, using a Spanish EUC. In the undercover freight business, no less than with legitimate loads, the best way to give good service at reasonable rates is to secure cargoes coming and going. So while Valsella started to prepare its next shipment, the broker went looking for a load of inbound merchandise.

As his ship steamed toward a rendezvous with a waiting shipment of Valsella's mines, the Guardia di Finanzia, the Italian treasury police, suspected smuggling and forced the ship into the port of Bari. A search revealed nothing. Then a tip-off from a guest in a nearby hotel allowed them to locate two types of hidden cargo. One was a load of grenade launchers and rockets of Italian manufacture that had been sold to a Barcelona company using a Spanish EUC, diverted to Syria, passed on to Iran, then run back through Lebanon en route to urban guerrilla groups in Europe. They also found a stash of heroin and hashish for delivery to the local mobsters who ran the port. In the hotel where their informant had been hiding, they spotted a briefcase giving interesting details about the return cargo the ship had expected. In the aftermath, thirty Valsella executives were arrested, although the case against them was later dropped. In all the excitement, one person not picked up was the broker, who for years had been working as a paid informant for the Italian and Swiss secret services in arms- and drug-smuggling cases.[41]

As the Valsella case illustrates, historically there have been two distinct methods by which states exercised supply-side control. One was overt—the legal apparatus enforced by Customs and police. The second was covert—through the secret services, which infiltrated, manipulated, or terminated the activities of those who evaded the first. The problem is that if, today, overt methods of supply-side control have been subverted by corruption or rendered irrelevant by the weight of secondhand sources, covert methods have been undermined not only by the sophistication of modern black markets but by the way the secret services themselves have been compromised by the trade.

From Privateers to Pirates

In the past, the profession of gunrunner tended to draw heavily from the ranks of former intelligence agents, veteran senior military men, ex–arms company executives, and even retired war correspondents. Hence, the un-runners knew the craft at least as much from operational as from com-mercial experience. And most could be depended on to keep a sharp eye out for the direction in which their former ship of state was tacking. Covert arms deals were (and are) an essential part of the art of clandes-tine statecraft at times when the formal government apparatus must have deniability. For example, while the world shook its public head in horror at atrocities in the Balkans and slapped on a general arms embargo, Ger-man intelligence sold arms out of old East German army stockpiles to gunrunners acting for the Croatian secret service while the CIA kept watch.[42]

Furthermore, a stint with the secret services is likely to hone one's skills in such fields as money laundering and document fraud, skills that are also useful in the underground weapons business; Edwin Wilson, one of the United States's most notorious "renegade" agents, was an accomplished counterfeiter of EUCs.[43] But more important, secret services are like the Moonies, the Masons, or the Mafia in the sense that, spiritually speaking, membership is for life. The services maintain old-boys' networks, even to the point of setting up ex-activists in business—with financial institutions, transportation and trading companies, and, of course, arms dealerships—which can complement the work of those remaining officially on the job.[44]

Many arms dealers today still have links to intelligence agencies. That seems true of the hundreds of Israeli gunrunners who conduct their busi-ness through the cover of Swiss, French, German, and British companies, are licensed by the Israeli government, and are supervised by Mossad and Shin Beit. Indeed, it is often impossible—and unnecessary—to know where the spooks begin and the gunrunners end, because part of the job of serv-ing intelligence officers is to spread the word abroad about the goodies Is-raeli arms merchants have available.[45] That Israel is so well represented in the ranks of modern arms merchants reflects the size of its arms industry relative to the economy, its long history of clandestine military relations with some of the world's seediest regimes, its practice of retiring senior officers at the age of forty to peddle arms or mercenary services around the world, and, not least, the enthusiastic support of the only military government in the world that changes leadership periodically by democratic choice.[46]

Today, however, the ranks of the world's gunrunners also include vet-eran cigarette smugglers, toxic waste brokers, metal traders, drug traffickers, and even the occasional defrocked Catholic priest. With the break-down of overt political control, rampant commercialization, and the increased importance of secondhand stocks, the market has ceased to be dominated by weapons experts who understood what their merchandise could do for their customers' political ambitions and been increasingly taken over by traffickers who understand mainly what it can do for their own financial aspirations. That can have embarrassing consequences.

When, for example, China and Israel decided to cooperate in the covert development of some of the missile technology that Israel had borrowed from the United States, the operation was initially complicated by their lack of formal diplomatic relations. The job of providing phony Philippine and Singapore passports to the China-bound Israeli team was given to a small-time Israeli arms peddler operating a Liberian-registered company out of a Hong Kong office. Unfortunately the arms dealer's other business interests—drug smuggling, illicit trade in computer parts, and passing counterfeit U.S. currency—resulted in a police raid that blew the cover of the operation.[47]

In the past, intelligence agencies involved themselves in arms deals mainly to stoke or dampen conflicts. Over time, however, they discovered other advantages, with the result that gunrunning operations linked to the secret services were sometimes undertaken not merely as part of a covert action against some antagonistic government but as an off-the-books fund-raising tool to undermine their own government's oversight apparatus.

In the early decades after World War II, when money was required in a covert operation, it tended to move directly to favored heads of state or to insurgent forces via Swiss and offshore bank accounts. After a series of scandals in the United States and Great Britain over secret support payments to political leaders, deeper cover was required, and the arms market fortuitously evolved in a way that helped meet that need.

In the 1970s, when the major arms manufacturers began their concerted export drive, brokers were expected to kick back part of their commissions. Some of the money went into the personal offshore retirement accounts of officials from the purchasing country. Some went to support covert affairs of state—be they election campaigns, coups, or propaganda campaigns against targeted political figures—thus shrouding outside political intervention in layers of plausible deniability.

Once again, scandal intervened, with a series of exposures of the role of major U.S. corporations in funneling covert action funds overseas. And in the backwash of Vietnam, covert operations fell out of favor. Mass lay-offs and more stringent regulations followed.[48] Then came the 1980s and a rebirth of covert action, which came with a new twist to the game of financing underground politics. The key once again turned out to be changes in the arms market, especially in the mechanics by which prices were set in black market deals.

Paying the Price

In a legal arms deal, the most important element of total cost is the amount necessary to cover the cost of production of actual matériel. If the trans-action is strictly commercial, the purchaser pays a sum sufficient to cover the manufacturers' cost and profit, plus fairly standard charges for ship-ping and insurance, plus a percentage markup for any broker's commis-sion. If there are kickbacks to officials in the purchasing country, they have to be added to either the broker's commission or the manufacturer's cost.[49]

If the kickbacks are to be built into the manufacturer's cost, the first step in a transaction might be for an insider to leak information about ri-val bids to a favored supplier, to permit that supplier to sweeten an offer sufficiently to win the contract. After the contract is signed, all manner of additional "costs" appear. Subsequently, the manufacturer might sub-mit two invoices—the first for public consumption, which specifies the original sum, and the second, which is artificially inflated to cover the re-quired graft. Actual payment of corruption money can then occur in two ways. The most popular used to be by direct cash transfer. In the 1970s, the Paris-based agent of one of the biggest U.S. arms corporations used to wear a double-lined raincoat specially designed to conceal wads of money.[50] However, by the late 1980s, this crude method had fallen into disfavor, at least for major deals. Instead, payments might be transferred through phony subcontracting, "offset" or "consultancy" arrangements, or fraudulent payments for after-sales service.[51]

Working a kickback scheme through a broker rather than a manufac-turer has certain advantages in disguising the trail. A manufacturer's books are subject to audit by the home government, whereas a broker's payments are likely to go through foreign accounts protected by bank secrecy laws. Still, running electoral slush funds via brokers' offshore accounts did not prevent weapons-related corruption scandals from exploding in the face of a host of political leaders ranging from Pakistan's Benazir Bhutto to Bel-gium's Willy Claes to Germany's Helmut Kohl.[52] On the other hand, making covert payments through subcontracts or consultancy arrangements created by the manufacturer confers a certain apparent legitimacy that may throw investigators off the trail. With a bribe properly hidden in an offset deal, it should be almost impossible to unscramble the money flow.[53]

Nonetheless, whether payoffs are added to manufacturers' costs or to brokers' commissions, they represent simply a markup on base price. The deal remains bilateral, and the pricing formula is essentially unaffected. By contrast, in a black market transaction, the pricing process is far more complex. Acquisition of the basic material is only the initial step in a long and complex commercial chain that adds "service" charges at each stage.

First in the chain is the gunrunner, who may be a merchant, not a broker. Therefore, he must either front the money or provide a letter of credit to purchase stock before resale. That will add interest paid or foregone and perhaps charges for issuing letters of credit to the total acquisition cost.

Second, if the matériel is to come from state-controlled supplies, there may be charges to free it. These could include the cost of phony EUCs—the party providing the EUC will have to be squared away with either a fixed fee (typical for fakes) or a percentage of the total (more likely for genuine paper issued by a complicit authority). The costs may also include payments (electoral or personal) to ensure that the selling country's government issues an export license. In addition, obstructionist Customs officials in the exporting country may have to be squared away. It is precisely to eliminate these costs that a black market dealer might turn to the regional supermarkets offering secondhand goods on a come-one, come-all basis. However, given the geography involved and the type of merchandise required, this option is not always possible.

Third, there are costs associated with use of front men and "subcontractors." Multiple intermediaries perform for commercial transactions what multiple transfers through offshore banks accomplish for financial transactions: they hide the trail. Each layer, however, demands a fee. The Israeli gunrunner who tried to use phony Bolivian EUCs to move Bulgarian weapons to Croatia worked through Portuguese and Hungarian arms dealers. Similarly, to hide the trail of massive shipments of explosives to Iran during the Iran-Iraq War, the broker working for the major European explosives manufacturers employed a corporate variant of the old shell game: he sold powder to Yugoslavia and then immediately bought it back.[54]

Fourth are the high costs of transportation. The job of moving the merchandise must be turned over to specialized shipping companies skilled in disguising the nature and destination of their cargoes, and sometimes the very identity of their ships. Typically the ship will fly a flag of convenience and might have to undergo name changes en route. A Bahamian ship might, for example, take on a cargo of Scotch whiskey bound for Italy, run into a "storm," send out an SOS, "sink," and then magically reappear in Dubai, where the whiskey is unloaded to be smuggled into (theoretically alcohol-free) Saudi Arabia. While its owners are still arguing through an insurance claim in London, the ship could undergo a quick name change in Panama and start a new career running Polish guns to the Moro National Liberation Army in the Philippines.

The load must also be carefully packaged. When Chilean army officers cooperated in getting Vietnam-vintage U.S. matériel to Croatia, they revealed more of a sick sense of humor than a sound sense of business in labeling the cargo "humanitarian aid"—and that may have induced Hungarian Customs to open the load.[55]

Declaring a weapons shipment to be auto parts is a common device. One Detroit firm, for example, used to replace drive shafts with recoilless rifles and then ship the real drive shafts as spare parts so that substitution could be made at the other end.[56] Still, this method is not foolproof. During the Iran-Iraq War, one U.S. Customs officer with a military background became intrigued by a shipment of tractor motors equipped with superchargers and consequently broke an operation smuggling tank engines to Iran. However, that did not stop German intelligence a short time later from shipping Soviet-model tanks to Israel in the guise of farm equipment.[57]

Another effective designation is "oil drilling equipment," under which everything from rocket launchers to artillery barrels have been shipped. It was used, for example, for Iran-Contra shipments. Agricultural chemicals, too, are excellent cover; some can even be redeployed as is to make explosives and poison gases.

The cargo should also have a designation consistent with normal trade relations between sending and receiving countries. Just as heroin once moved from Spain to the United States in cans labeled "paella," more recently, light arms went from Lebanon to Liberia stuffed in containers marked "canned vegetables."[58]

Even deeper cover can be provided if weapons are hidden in some cargo, real or nominal, that Customs officers have difficulty searching. Items such as artillery pieces can be loaded into grain carriers, with the grain poured on top. Or, borrowing a trick from drug smugglers, weapons can cross frontiers and oceans in containers of frozen food, with the implicit threat of legal problems if the cargo is opened and spoiled by nosy officials. Weapons can also be stowed in containers labeled toxic or radioactive waste, reducing to near zero the probability of a Customs officer snooping inside.[59]

These choices are not merely a matter of being clever. Some modern arms dealers are also commodity traders who handle grain, oil, and metals, for example. The legitimate business does double duty. It provides physical cover for the cargo and serves as a device for laundering the payments.

Shipping illegal arms may also require hiding the destination by rerouting at sea or transshipping via third countries, either of which deepens the cover while increasing expenses. In Australia's largest-ever haul, weapons were picked up in Yemen, sent to Sri Lanka, loaded on another vessel bound for Singapore, then routed to Fiji via Sydney—where a tip-off led to their impoundment. Even if the arms had made it to Fiji, that might not have been their last stop. One possibility is that they were to be transshipped once more to an anti-Indonesian insurgent force in Irian Jaya.[60]

Although Customs usually does not inspect cargoes in transit, still it is best that a stopover be brief and that nothing be done to attract attention—otherwise additional expenses in the form of hush payments to port officials may be necessary.

Needless to say, circuitous routes also raise the possibility of new charges in the form of transit fees. During the great arms bazaar of the mid-1980s, for example, Portugal was a popular transshipment point. Its officials gained a reputation (whether deserved or not) for accommodating a load for one percent of its value.[61] Not least of the extra shipping costs, the crew must be well paid to assure silence.

Fifth, at the point of delivery, payments may be necessary to assure quiet cooperation at the port of disembarkation. (This may be avoided, however, if the ship is equipped with cranes to discharge the cargo off a mangrove swamp or near a small fishing village, or if the gunrunner can arrange to have the cargo "stolen" on arrival.)[62] To these payments may be added kickbacks to officials responsible for steering the order to the particular dealer—although this is another way in which illegal and legal deals tend to differ.

When the motive for purchase is prestige, as it is so often in the legal market, price is a secondary consideration. In fact, arms bought for display might well be luxury goods—the high price is itself a source of pride. To the extent that corruption is a motive for purchase, a high price may be an incentive. Such corruption could even have a nod from the head of state, who might tolerate senior military personnel receiving kickbacks on the assumption that corrupt officers are less likely to plot coups.[63]

This ceases to be true when states turn to the black market to obtain weapons for direct use. Soft credits and offset deals will be conspicuously absent, and low prices will be an inducement to buy. Kickbacks to purchasing officials may still be necessary, along with payoffs to "skimmers" who muscle in on the deal. But under these circumstances, such expenses are likely less onerous than they might be in regular state-to-state deals. Along with the fact that the gunrunner may have obtained the merchandise on a secondhand market that has no "release" costs, this raises the intriguing possibility that black market deals are sometimes "cleaner" than legitimate ones.

On the other hand, if the customer is a guerrilla group, the closer the group gets to actual power, or the more secure its control of a piece of territory, the more its behavior might approximate a regular government. Therefore, the higher may be the payoffs demanded by its officials.[64]

Sixth, if the deal is being monitored by one or possibly several intelligence services, each may demand a "covert action tax," with the funds used to top up a "black budget." For example, under a joint CIA–U.S. army scheme, codenamed Yellow Fruit, to finance the Nicaraguan Contras during the early 1980s, the army inflated the invoices on arms "sold" to Guatemala and Honduras, among others, and diverted the money to offshore accounts set up for the fledgling guerrilla force. The Central American countries' armed forces were happy to okay the extra charges. After all, the bill was picked up by the U.S. taxpayer through foreign military aid. Any remaining moral qualms were appeased by allowing the local military to skim part of the weapons and by kicking back some of the extra money into the retirement accounts of the commanders. The neat arrangement came to grief after U.S. army personnel decided to levy some service charges of their own, which led to criminal charges and a hasty windup.[65] Into the breech, so to speak, came Iran-Contra, an even deeper-cover operation because it used the inflated invoicing in one black market deal to finance another.[66]

Even after squaring away officials at both ends, meeting the demands of skimmers, and placating the intelligence services, the gunrunner may still not be ready to simply pick up his cash, deduct his expenses, and head for the Alps to bank his profit.

Seventh are additional costs like exchange discounts and commodity brokers' fees. These result from the fact that payments for a black market deal might be made in nonconventional forms—in soft currency, precious commodities such as diamonds and ivory, countertrade deals for items such as oil, perhaps drugs, or even other weapons.

Once all elements in price are reckoned—base acquisition cost; bank charges for purchase credits; fees for documents necessary to release the weapons; transport costs including bribes at both ends, kickbacks due on delivery, covert action taxes, expenses of collection, and so forth—then a profit percentage (including risk premium) must be added. The profit rate will reflect both the pressure of competition and the commercial life expectancy of the gunrunner—who may be hoping for just one quick kill, no pun intended, before the perils of the trade in the form of cheated suppliers, jealous competitors, dissatisfied customers, or angry intelligence services overtake him. The profit rate will also reflect the nature of the client. A state under sanction because the "international community" has chosen to protest its human rights record or its secret nuclear acquisition strategy is an excellent customer. But even better is one placed under embargo in an effort to stop an on-going war. The gunrunner can pick up bargain stock on a glutted black market, then resell it at a fat markup to a hungry belligerent.

The net result is a final sales price that bears little relationship to base cost. It was precisely because of all the additional "service" charges that black market weapons historically tended to be more expensive than their legal equivalents, sometimes considerably more so. That acted as a deterrent to all but the most desperate or best heeled of buyers. For certain types of specialized equipment, the price discrepancy undoubtedly still holds. But for more mundane items, light or heavy, it does not. Today, with the secondhand markets glutted, base acquisition costs for ordinary equipment have fallen so far that there is no longer much, if any, cost deterrent to using the illegal market. Added to this is the fact that relying on supplies from current or former zones of conflict may sidestep any "fees" otherwise required for release of restricted weaponry.

In fact, the price differential contains its own unstable dynamic. An army reckons its cost of acquisition not simply by the price tag of the equipment but also by estimating what that matériel will fetch on the secondhand market when the time comes to upgrade. The lower the secondhand price, the higher the effective cost of new matériel, therefore increasing the temptation to buy old stocks. Indeed, during the recent Balkan wars, the former minister of defense of Croatia (who was in a position to know) complained that he faced prices on the legal market three times as high as those on the illegal one.

This situation, in which the terms of trade turn progressively against the legal market, will persist until covertly available secondhand stocks approach exhaustion—a situation nowhere in sight. When, to the traditional black market advantage of anonymity is added the phenomenon of lower cost and the fact that clandestine traders can now assure rapid delivery, the competitive balance shifts in favor of the black market. Furthermore, unlike in the past, when the black market dealt mainly with light arms, today it can deliver virtually anything. The key question is not whether a load of arms is light or heavy but whether the would-be buyer can afford to pay and whether the seller will accept the particular currency in which the payment is offered.

Settling Accounts

The stereotypical view is that the bill from a legal arms sale is settled by pinstripe-suited bankers after smirking arms company executives have shaken hands with chubby generals whose chests are embellished with self-awarded decorations. By contrast, an illegal one involves men with black eye-patches who exchange a valise stuffed with hundred-dollar bills in a smoky bar—apparently oblivious to the fact that smoky bars are among the best milieus in which to pass counterfeit. In reality, the mechanics of payment are usually a little more complex.

When one state overtly sells weapons to another, payment can be political, commercial, or financial. If political, it takes the form of concessions or favors, for example, permission to use military bases or votes that go the "right" way on UN resolutions. If commercial, the deal might be settled through a countertrade arrangement involving the purchasing country's export goods. Russia, for example, accepted palm oil from Malaysia in payment for arms transferred at a cut rate, which allowed Russia to break into a traditionally Anglo-American market. When China sold aircraft and parts to the Sudan, the bill was covered in part by cotton, gum arabica, sesame seeds, corn, camels, and meat and in part by long-term credits.[67]

If financial, the supplier is usually paid in hard currency via orthodox bank transfers. The buyer simply draws down an official bank balance from its hard-currency reserves held in a U.S. or British institution or from the proceeds of a loan negotiated at market terms.

However, when the supplier state arranges easy credit, financial considerations blend with political-concessionary ones. There is also a tendency with such deals for credits, especially to belligerents, to become progressively softer, until the arms become a de facto gift. This was the unanticipated fate of the war loans made by France in the 1980s to Iraq. It is also the anticipated fate of most U.S. military aid to Israel.

Concessionary terms also figure in trilateral deals, which help provide the real instigator with deniability. When Egypt sold weapons to Rwanda, long a French client state, the bill was picked up by a French state-owned bank. It, in turn, got from Rwanda some cash up front and the pledge of future revenues from tea sales. Unfortunately, guerrillas opposed to the government overran the tea plantations, and the loan quickly turned into a subsidy.[68]

Similarly, deals may involve a mix of commercial and financial aspects—complex offset packages could require the seller to arrange investments in the buyer country in unrelated sectors or to agree to purchase from the buyer country and to resell unrelated goods.[69] Thus, when British Aerospace's product won a surprise victory over a technically superior French competitor in a massive arms deal with Saudi Arabia, Saudi Arabia granted the British-owned petroleum giants BP and Shell the rights to lift and sell more oil. The proceeds were deposited in a trust account run by the British Ministry of Defense. As the project proceeded, the account was drawn down, partly to pay the British manufacturers and partly to pay "commissions" of, reputedly, up to 40 percent into secret Liechtenstein accounts on behalf of members of the Saudi inner circle.

Then, of course, there were additional expenses to reward members of the Savoy Mafia, a group of arms brokers, veteran intelligence officers, and bankers specializing in arms deals, who gathered regularly in a suite in London's Savoy Hotel to talk weapons. Among their recruits (for a mere £12 million) was a thrice-failed accountant named Mark Thatcher who had given up his youthful ambition as a racing driver for a mature vocation as a defense industry procurer—undoubtedly to the delight of his mother, Margaret, who lobbied the Saudis and coaxed her good friend Ronald Reagan into doing likewise.[70]

If the sale is made not directly by a government or its armed forces but by a country's private (although regulated) arms-makers, the terms may still be commercial—with the same possibilities of complex countertrade arrangements. However, most such sales involve strictly financial payments. Banks handle the arrangements as normal trade finance. The would-be buyer opens a letter of credit at the buyer's bank and then presents the letter of credit to the seller. If and when the terms of the contract are fulfilled, the seller cashes the letter of credit at the seller's bank. The seller's bank, in turn, collects from the buyer's bank. The circle is closed when the buyer settles accounts with the buyer's bank.

When a country makes a covert sale to another state, payment may still take commercial form. Secret oil-for-arms deals with South Africa by both belligerents were commonplace during the Iran-Iraq War—two oil-rich arms-poor countries formed natural covert countertrade partners for an arms-rich country under an oil embargo. Whereas legal countertrade deals might require third parties to sell the merchandise, in covert ones, particularly involving strategic commodities such as oil, the swap is more likely bilateral. There may be no need for bank instruments to change hands.

At least part of a payment can also take political form. For example, during the 1980s, Israel supplied U.S. cluster bombs (in violation of end-user pledges) to Ethiopia's former Marxist regime for use against internal dissidents in exchange for the mass migration of Falashas to help replace Palestinians as cheap labor in Israeli construction and service industries.[71]

However, in most covert state-to-state deals, financial arrangements predominate, not least because financial payments are easier to hide than commercial ones. They might involve drawing down a secret foreign bank balance or the covert pledge of (unreported) national gold reserves against supplier-provided loans.

The financial mechanics are more complicated when a primary supplier (a manufacturing corporation) sells to a black market customer, usually an embargoed state. The currency will be conventional—letters of credit issued by obliging banks. However, the money will require laundering. A letter of credit might be issued by a third-country bank that has a (perhaps secret) correspondent relationship with a bank in the buying country. That initial letter of credit might be used as security for new letters of credit issued by yet another bank on behalf of a foreign subsidiary of the selling corporation. Just such an arrangement with back-to-back letters of credit was used to disguise the payment trail when France's Luchaire Corporation sold enormous amounts of artillery ammunition during the Iran-Iraq War.

It should be easy for a serious investigator to unscramble such simple mechanics. But because Luchaire was also making electoral slush-fund payments to bagmen for France's ruling Socialist Party, it likely felt no need for anything fancier.[72] In the covert arms trade, as in any racket, an inverse relationship exists between the degree of political cover and the amount of financial cover required for a deal.

When a private arms merchant sells to an embargoed state, political concessions rarely, if ever, figure among the payment mechanisms. There may be some scope for countertrade in basic commodities—one gunrunner has reported taking live cattle, palm oil, and cotton.[73] But most deals are financial. Payment takes the same form it does when a state or primary supplier is the seller, that is, in dollar-denominated letters of credit washed through accommodating banks.

An international bank can actually play a number of roles—depository, fund transmitter, provider of personal and commercial credit, and asset manager. The bank can even act as fiduciary.

Thus, a deal might have two distinct contracts. For security, the inner contract, which states the terms, including details of payoffs, is stashed in a safety deposit box in a bank, probably in a jurisdiction blessed with tight secrecy laws, or left in the care of the bank's trust department. Indeed, the supervision of bank officials might be essential to guarantee discretion. Both parties, needless to say, feel better if there is only one copy of the contract and it is in neutral hands. (The contract between Egypt and Rwanda explicitly stated, "The buyer and the supplier agree not to show the contents of this contract to third parties.") Meanwhile, an outer contract might, for example, stipulate conditions under which the parties can access the inner contract to study its terms. It might prohibit removal of the contract from the bank without explicit authorization of other parties. Or, more liberally, it might permit photocopying if the interested party cuts off any letterheads and signatures.[74]

Another role is the provision of deposit and transfer facilities, perhaps protected by bank secrecy laws. If the buyer merely draws down a bank balance and remits payments to the seller's account, perhaps passing the payments through several intermediaries for extra cover, the role of the bank is passive. The bank's role might be more active if the arrangements require the buyer to deposit the full sum in advance. In this instance, payments to the seller are made in tranches as the contract proceeds, with agreed-upon neutral parties (perhaps bank officials) determining when sufficient progress has been made.

For a favored customer, the bank may go further. When the Iran-Contra caper looked like it would come to grief over lack of trust between Israel and Iran (Israel insisted on payment in advance, and Iran, burned often by sharp dealers, insisted on a C.O.D transaction), the Monaco branch of the Bank of Credit and Commerce International broke the deadlock. It accepted from Saudi arms dealer Adnan Khashoggi postdated checks issued to him by an Iranian agent and then immediately credited Khashoggi's account. This permitted him, in turn, to pay Israel for the weapons being sold.[75] At this point, the bank moved from passively transmitting payments into actively providing credit, albeit a highly personalized form.

Most private-sector arms deals seem to involve the bank advancing commercial credit. It might be an open line to be drawn upon at will. This arrangement likely is offered only to customers with a long-standing relationship with the bank or to those who have pledged assets to back the full amount. In such a case, the bank can disclaim direct involvement in the actual deal. More commonly, though, arms sales involve dedicated letters of credit issued by the buyer's bank and tied to a specific transaction.

Typically, in an arms deal, neither side trusts the other. This is particularly true if the transaction is underground, because there is no legitimate dispute resolution mechanism: it is difficult for a customer to take a delinquent gunrunner to court or for the gunrunner to sue the leader of a guerrilla group hidden away in the bush. Indeed, a bank letter of credit can be essential on both sides of the market. Arms merchants cannot sell unless they can first buy. And suppliers will rarely provide a private gunrunner with inventory unless he can show an irrevocable letter of credit. The gunrunner, in turn, will probably require a letter of credit from his own would-be client.

Therefore, the seller provides the would-be purchaser with a quote. The buyer must then be satisfied about the reliability of both product and seller. If satisfied, the buyer has his or her bank contact the seller's bank, stating that the buyer's bank is willing to open a letter of credit provided certain conditions are met. With the preliminary agreement made, the buyer's bank sends an irrevocable letter of credit to the seller's bank. The letter of credit might specify delivery time, date of manufacture of matériel supplied, prices, and (perhaps) currency in which payment is being made. It might also stipulate penalties for late or incomplete delivery. In addition, it might require, prior to payment, certification by approved examiners that the goods are as specified.[76] The seller's bank will cash the letter of credit once certain documents are presented attesting to the existence and condition of the cargo and its readiness for shipment.

Before all that happens, banks may be required to perform an additional service. The buyer may insist that the seller post a performance bond for a sum of money to be forfeited if the deal is not completed as stipulated. In this case, the buyer's bank will advise the seller's bank that it stands ready to open a letter of credit once it is in receipt of the performance bond for, say, 5–10 percent of the value of the deal. The two banks then exchange documents. Upon successful completion, the buyer's bank cashes the letter of credit and the seller's bank voids the performance bond. On the other hand, if scandal should break before completion and force an embarrassed supplier to void the transaction, the buyer can cash out part or all of the performance bond at the expense of the supplier. That was the unfortunate fate that befell Austria's Voest-Alpine, which was driven into bankruptcy in part because of a botched artillery deal with Iran.[77]

Sometimes the bank will be perfectly up front about what it is doing. In one case in the early 1980s, an Austrian meat broker in league with a West German arms dealer arranged on behalf of South Africa a shipment of East Bloc arms for the UNITA and RENAMO guerrilla groups in An-

gola and Mozambique, respectively. The order was placed by a South
African front company in Liechtenstein, and the Nigerian High Commission in London provided an EUC, backed by a (forged) affidavit from
the British Foreign Office attesting to its veracity. The International Bank
of Luxembourg telexed Bulgaria confirming it would open an irrevocable
letter of credit and listed the weapons with their prices. The profits, even
after bribes and kickbacks, were up to 60 percent. Alas for the meat broker, his West German partner took off to Miami to a well-protected retirement with all of the commission payments.[78]

Some banks, however, are shy about being seen to finance weapons deals.
When the Atlanta branch of Italy's Banca Nazionale del Lavoro aided Iraq's
armament drive—with $1.1 billion in unsecured credit and $1.9 billion in
dedicated letters of credit—the manager kept a secret set of ledgers on which
the Iraqi business alone was recorded.[79] Alternatively, the parties might mis-
specify the cargo: when the Bank of Credit and Commerce International
agreed to finance a British arms dealer selling antitank missiles to Iran, it
did so with a letter of credit for a load of "fork lift trucks."[80] However, fake
documents can pose a special kind of risk for the buyer.

The covert arms business has witnessed just about every type of scam
that graces the annals of financial crime.[81] For instance, there are advance-
fee frauds. Once a French dealer offered both Iran and Iraq nonexistent
105-millimeter ammunition; Iraq was the first to come up with the requested advance payment, after which the dealer changed his name and
retired to Guadeloupe.[82] In another case, a Portuguese heroin trafficker,
who had attempted unsuccessfully during the Malvinas war to persuade
Argentina that he had antiship missiles for sale, copied official documents
from a sale of fighter aircraft to Jordan and used them to con Iran out of
a big advance.[83]

There are also "phantom cargo" dodges. An Iranian expatriate in London offered Iran eight thousand TOW (tube-launched, optically tracked,
wire-guided) antitank missiles supposedly waiting on a ship across the
Channel. Three Iranian officers sent to inspect the "weapons" (thirty-four
containers of scrap iron) were kidnapped and ordered to send messages
to the London branch of Iran's Bank Melli authorizing payment. When
they refused, the architect of the scheme forged their signatures. When
the head of the London bank balked, he too was kidnapped. The officers
escaped, and Scotland Yard released the banker before any money
changed hands.[84]

Most common, however, are bill-of-lading scams.

In strict theory a letter of credit is not paid unless other documents are
presented along with it. The most important is a bill of lading indicating

that the merchandise specified in the letter of credit has been loaded in good order aboard a commercial carrier. The bill of lading also attests that the goods are bound for the port specified by the buyer. Like the letter of credit, the bill of lading will sometimes misrepresent the cargo—rocket launchers, for example, as oil drilling equipment. If the truth is eventually revealed, the misleading bill of lading gives the bank the same sort of alibi that a phony EUC grants a primary supplier.

However, a fake bill of lading creates an opportunity to defraud the buyer. The cargo may not exist at all, or it may be diverted en route and sold to another customer. The ship may be a figment of the gunrunner's overactive imagination, or it may be sitting in dry dock when it is supposed to be chugging toward the port of delivery. Sometimes the ship arrives with all documents in order, and the cargo, represented on the letter of credit and bill of lading as ice cream or Brylcreem, turns out to be—ice cream or Brylcreem. Ultimately the cost falls on the buyer. For if the correct documents are presented along with the letter of credit, the bank's legal responsibility ends. The seller's bank cashes the letter of credit and demands payment from the buyer's bank, and the buyer's bank then seizes any collateral posted by the purchaser. As a British bank once stated when a cargo of coffee beans bound from Indonesia to Germany turned out to be sacks of gravel, "we are not in the cargo inspection business."[85]

Even a performance bond is not a full guarantee. It may help assure that the proper merchandise is loaded, but it cannot ensure that merchandise or ship will ever arrive. In the final analysis, in the illegal arms business, the ultimate performance bond is the seller's own hide, as some unfortunates have discovered.[86]

Given the many services required, the gunrunner must pick a bank carefully. In racy novels, banks of Switzerland are the sentimental favorites. Historically, there was some basis for that reputation. Even in the late 1980s, when Egyptian intelligence arranged to have an agent ship out of the United States special plasticizers for its missile program in containers labeled, among other things, "fatty acids of animal oil," it set up a Liechtenstein ghost company with a Swiss bank account to finance the purchase.[87]

Switzerland's famed secrecy laws have started to resemble Swiss cheese. Not to fear, there are many other candidates. Belgian companies, in addition to enjoying Belgium's legendary discretion regarding arms transactions, have the reassurance of secrecy laws so tight in neighboring Luxembourg that a bank legally cannot reveal information even if the client requests a waiver. Serbia placed assets needed to break the embargo behind the protective screen offered by Cyprus. Liechtenstein is another prime choice—it is where British Aerospace ran commissions for the Saudi deal. Even Switzerland continues to offer sufficient secrecy to attract not just routine tax and exchange-control evaders but gunrunners as well. In 1994 it was from a Swiss bank that Rwandan exiles financed an arms purchase from South African dealers.[88]

Whether a country's banks are chosen to finance an arms deal does not depend on whether that country hosts offshore banks. "Offshore" does not necessarily mean "bank secrecy." Rather, an offshore bank exists in a regulatory vacuum—it is exempt from its host country's rules regarding interest rates, capital adequacy, and liquidity. Switzerland provided the original model for bank secrecy, yet it is not an offshore center. The world's biggest offshore center is the City of London, where transactions are not protected by bank secrecy law. At best, British banks used to offer confidentiality backed only by the ability of a client to sue in civil court if confidentiality were breached. But even this guarantee has been largely eroded in the on-going hysteria over drug money.[89]

There are places that offer both unregulated offshore banks and bank secrecy laws. But offshore banks operate largely, if not exclusively, in the wholesale sector. They exist mainly to transmit funds from bank to bank or to act as booking agents for loans actually made by their parent banks domiciled in the major economic centers. Therefore, when a gunrunner needs to negotiate credits, he normally does so with a proper bank in a major financial center rather than with some obscurely named insta-bank in an exotic setting. Nonetheless, the offshore banking system can be useful at a later stage. It can whiz money from place to place in a series of deposits and withdrawals to hide the trail behind multiple layers of banking and corporate secrecy.

There is one final service banks can provide. Once a gunrunner has paid off suppliers, settled accounts with the shipping companies, and squared away all the officials, fixers, and skimmers necessary to grease the deal, it is time to enjoy the profits. Then the role of a bank becomes that of fund manager, handling the gunrunner's balances no differently from those of the tax dodgers, stock-fraud artists, heroin traffickers, and cigarette smugglers that make up so much of its private banking department's regular clientele.

Although sellers of arms prefer to work through normal bank channels, that might not always be possible, particularly if their customers are not states, even under embargo, but insurgent groups or warlords in control of bits and pieces of countries.

When a country secretly supplied weapons to an insurgent group, payments used to take political form, mainly if not exclusively. If the group was friendly, payment occurred by destabilization of a targeted regime or by the prospect of concessions when the guerrilla force took power. If unfriendly, arms might be exchanged for hostages or promises that the insurgent group would refrain from actions against the property and citizens of the supplying state. In such cases, deals are rarely direct—the victim country usually has to negotiate through intermediaries whose relations with the kidnappers are better.[90]

Today, undoubtedly, some of those deals are still political in nature. However, with progressive commercialization of the arms market, most states that covertly supply guerrilla groups probably insist on a financial or commercial consideration. But to maintain deniability in such deals, the state usually works through gunrunners. At that point, the payment mechanics become identical to those in straightforward deals between private suppliers and substate buyers.

It is extremely unlikely a gunrunner would accept payment in the form of promises of trade deals or of property and resource rights realizable only when the customers have achieved their political objectives. However, such payment instruments can still figure in three-cornered deals involving insurgent group, arms supplier, and an interested third party. During the Nigerian civil war, there were rumors that Banque Rothschild in Paris had opened a line of credit for Biafra (most of whose budget went to arms) in exchange for future oil rights.[91] During the post-independence conflict in the Belgian Congo, the Belgian conglomerate Union Minière put mercenaries on its payroll to assist secessionists of mineral-rich Katanga Province, and it paid royalties, dividends, and franchise fees ($52 million a year) into the would-be government's bank accounts. The mercenaries were content—their salaries were deposited by Union Minière into (tax free) Swiss accounts, each had a life insurance policy as part of the terms of service, and they were left free to loot in their spare time.[92]

Thirty years later little seems to have changed. When a coup ousted Sierra Leone's head of state and he decided to reverse the verdict, he hired a British "security" firm with a Gibraltar bank account. Into it came payments from a Thai banker, who was reimbursed with the promise of mineral concessions when the old government was restored. Into it, too, came payments from two Canadian diamond-mining companies that had lost their concessions when the government was overthrown. The money was used to buy arms and train paramilitary forces on behalf of the ousted government.

When a gunrunner deals directly with an insurgent group, however, he likely insists on being paid as quickly as possible. In that case the financial mechanics may depend in good measure on just how the buyer manages to find the wherewithal to pay.

In Gold We Trust

Payment can be greatly facilitated if the buyer has outside supporters, political or ethnoreligious. If political, for example, a sympathetic country, the trail can be hidden with a three-way exchange: the intelligence service arranges direct payment to a black market arms dealer, the dealer buys weapons for the customer, and the guerrilla force repays its secret sponsor by political action. This was the method used with most Afghan aid money after donors woke up to the frequency with which direct cash payments to Afghan leaders ended up in foreign bank accounts.

Cover can also be concocted by allowing the quiet diversion of "humanitarian" aid to flow into black market weapons purchases. This technique is especially useful if a country wants to aid a particularly notorious group while ensuring that a potentially outraged public never finds out. A final layer of deniability can be constructed by having the intelligence agency secretly pump money into a private charitable or communitarian foundation, which in turn can arrange to pay the black market dealer, possibly through the front of another nongovernmental organization.

Various ethnic and religious minorities have established such foundations in major Western countries, particularly in North America. (NORAID, a financial vehicle of the Irish republicans in Ulster, is the best known.) Members of émigré communities have sometimes amassed considerable wealth through the activities of "trade diasporas"—international but intra-ethnic, even intrafamilial, networks skilled in moving goods and money past all manner of bureaucratic and political obstacles, including taxes and exchange controls—and can put that machinery to other use, for example, the covert transfer of funds out of host countries to support the politico-military struggles back home.

Nor are these transfers always secret. The former Croatian minister of defense, born in Canada, called on the million-strong members of the North American diaspora to put their money where their hearts were. He stated publicly, "it's all going to war purposes."[93]

Indeed, the governments of major Western countries sometimes assist in funneling such money into black market weapons purchases by allowing donations to be tax deductible. Among those organizations benefiting from such a status in the United States was the late Rabbi Meir Kahane's Institute for the Jewish Idea, whose fliers proclaimed such tax-deductible thoughts as "a Jewish state can never make the Arab equal" and "Israel must create nuclear, biological and chemical weapons for mass deterrent [sic]."[94] Subsequently, the rabbi's son took to training and arming paramilitary groups to make sure his father's notion of religious and charitable activity was not lost to history. Whether that son's own 1999 assassination in Occupied Palestine will interfere with the actualization of Rabbi Kahane's vision remains to be seen.

Payments may take the form of a transfer from the accounts of a registered "charitable," "educational," or "religious" foundation to the accounts of the gunrunner. From the gunrunner's perspective, this is among the most desirable of situations: payment is assured on delivery, and in hard currency transferred through legitimate banks. Alternatively, payment may come from money that exiles have raised from rackets—Tamils, Kurds, and Kosovars running heroin and social security scams in Europe, for example. However, this is decidedly more dangerous. Although payment might be offered in anonymous sacks of dollars, deutsche marks, or Swiss francs, a police investigation into drugs or extortion might also blow the gunrunner's cover.

Moreover, only a few insurgent groups can rely on support from the diaspora. Most must be self-reliant. Furthermore, they tend to operate in countries whose official currencies are soft. In theory, that should pose a barrier to participation in the world arms black market, but the more entrepreneurial groups have had little problem surmounting it.

In the early stages of an insurgency, a guerrilla or paramilitary group can manufacture simple weapons or engage in "tactical procurement" at the expense of the army or police. It might subsequently use the proceeds of ransom kidnapping and bank robbery to buy on local black markets, mainly from disaffected or impoverished soldiers. But at some point most growing insurgent groups find it necessary to tap the international market. It can then resort to "revolutionary taxation" of wealthy individuals and businesses that pay off in hard currency. Or it can become involved in the international trade in contraband goods. Much of the world's traffic in diamonds, rubies, emeralds, lapis lazuli, jade, ivory, and teakwood, along with part of the traffic in looted antiquities, is currently if not actually controlled at source by this or that insurgent group, then at least is taxed by them.

Thus, just as the growth of international smuggling facilitates the physical process of arms supply, it helps insurgent groups find the means to pay for them in a wide variety of forms, provided the gunrunner is willing to cooperate. Although overromanticized, exchanges of guns for gold might well occur—however, the wise gunrunner would carry a bottle of nitric acid to test purity.

Cash is another possibility. Today, as much as 80 percent of U.S. currency lives abroad. Those wandering dollars mean that the old gunrunner's dream about a suitcase of U.S. hundred-dollar bills could well come true—albeit the dream could quickly turn into a nightmare if the stuff in the suitcase is counterfeit. For example, weapons bought by ex-iled Hutu leaders plotting a comeback in Rwanda were partly paid for by fake U.S. currency printed in a Nairobi plant.[95] Nor is that danger restricted to foreign-based deals. While the Reagan-Bush administration ranted in public about a plot by the Sandinista government of Nicaragua to run guns to leftist rebels in El Salvador, buyers for the guerrillas were shopping at U.S. gun shows and, on occasion, paying in counterfeit bills.[96]

Alternatively, because most fund-raising operations by insurgents pay off in the local medium of exchange, the gunrunner might have to accept legally inconvertible currency. This is less a problem than it appears at first glance. Almost any currency, no matter how soft, commands some exchange value in the world's more cosmopolitan financial centers. On the downside, when payments for a large deal are accepted in piles of an obscure currency that has to be renegotiated in Hong Kong or Singapore, there is danger of flooding a thin market and having the deal's profits vanish in a deeply discounted exchange rate.[97]

Accepting payment in a check denominated in soft currency may reduce that risk, although it could add others. Insurgent groups do not open local bank accounts in their own names on which they can draw checks made out to their favorite gunrunner. However, they could have trusted supporters acting as fronts, or they might force corporations and wealthy individuals to meet their revolutionary tax bills in the form of checks payable to the gunrunner. The gunrunner, in turn, could operate behind the cover of a company engaged in international trade in commodities such as oil and grain. Inflating the invoice provides an excellent, almost undetectable instrument for disguising the payment flows. The local bank is likely to clear without question a check drawn on the account of a well-known corporation or prominent citizen and written to pay for legitimate commodities, and the Central Bank or exchange-control authority will be prompt in releasing the equivalent in hard currency, quite possibly at a preferential rate of exchange, to make sure the country's food and fuel requirements are met.

Payment can also be made in valuable commodities. Although it has only recently come into vogue in the West to lament "blood (or conflict) diamonds" and to call for them to be banned, in fact for many years black market diamonds were a major instrument by which West African insurgents bought arms. The diamonds moved along well-established smuggling routes either to Israel or to Antwerp to be laundered through the regular diamond exchanges.[98]

More recently ivory has become a means (although rapidly depleting one) of financing arms imports, not least because efforts to save the remaining elephants have inflated black market prices. The poached tusks are run from African ports to Dubai warehouses to Hong Kong carvers for eventual resale through Japanese retail shops.[99] And until the discomfiture of the Khmer Rouge, scarcely a ruby made it to market from Southeast Asia without the payment of an export tax to either the Kampuchean rebel organization or one of the Burmese ethnic insurgent groups—usually with the cooperation of Thai gem brokers.[100]

Such deals could be bilateral—direct swaps of arms for valuables. However, for many precious commodities, especially rough gemstones, valuations are notoriously variable and the possible source of commercial acrimony between arms dealer and customer. Therefore most such deals (like some legal countertrade) will be trilateral—high-valued commodities for cash for arms. Sometimes they are even more complex. Thus, most of Somalia's annual frankincense crop, grown in an area under control of the Somalia National Movement, is smuggled to the Arab Gulf states and sold at a profit enhanced further by the evasion of (long uncollectable) export duties. Some of the proceeds return in cash dollars to be sold, at another healthy premium, for shillings on the local-currency black market. The shillings are used to buy the popular drug qat, and the qat is used to pay for militiamen and their weapons. Nor does it end there. Much of the food and fuel these armed gangs hijacked or extorted from international aid shipments were sold on black markets in Kenya and Ethiopia, from which both qat and weapons are imported.[101]

Another possibility is countertrade in basic commodities. Although covert oil-for-arms deals are the preserve of formal states buying on the sly, similar arrangements have been made by guerrilla groups (or their sympathizers) using rare woods, tin ore, and coffee. The more widely traded and standardized the commodity, and the more black market activity in that commodity already exists, the easier are the countertrade arrangements. Unlike the exchange of valuables such as gemstones against arms, the exchange of standard commodities means that the black market dealer gives up the potential huge capital gains on resale. On the other hand, standard commodities—not being "hot" like antiquities or subject to huge variations in appraisal like rough diamonds—are, financially speaking, safer to handle.

Another option for the dealer is to take partial payment in the form of other weapons. When a guerrilla force is upgrading, the gunrunner can make additional profit by putting a very low valuation on the trade-ins and then reselling them, sometimes in the legal antique or collectors' market in the United States. In addition, the guerrilla force might supply something that, while irrelevant to the force's own requirements, is of great value to their sponsor. This occurred when agents of South African intelligence offered the Ulster Defense Association small arms and ammunition in return for stealing plans or models of the British Blowpipe missile from the Shortt's weapons complex in Belfast.[102]

There is a popular view that one of the most important means of financing weapons, especially light ones, is to barter for them with recreational drugs. Given the massive production of drug raw material in precisely the areas where civil disturbance and insurgency abound, drugs would seem a natural commodity for a guerrilla group to exploit. And given the wide range between export and landed prices of drugs, the double profit from direct arms-for-drugs exchanges must be a big temptation. For example, some Israeli army veterans who had seen service in Lebanon bought eighteen hundred kilos of Lebanese red, hid it in a consignment of Italian furniture bound for Britain, and planned to use the resulting cash to buy weapons for resale to the IRA—had they not been caught.[103]

Thus, double profits also mean double danger. Furthermore, the notion of a guns-for-drugs swap requires three cautionary clarifications. One is that direct swaps likely occur mainly in servicing small-scale criminal rather than large-scale insurgent demand—as in the barter of locally produced marijuana for imported AK-47s that takes place with increasing frequently in Papua–New Guinea.[104] The second is that even where wholesalers operate in both commodities, the deal is not a swap but rather a matter of selling drugs for cash and then using cash to buy weapons—making the financial mechanics in principle no different from an oil-for-cash-for-arms arrangement. The third is that in most cases, the insurgent group is organizationally (and ideologically) distinct from any geographically contiguous drug traffickers. The main link of insurgent groups to drugs, if any, is taxation of the traffic, along with everything else, in the areas under their control.

Thus, in Lebanon during its long and bitter civil wars, the huge influx of weapons predated the explosive growth of the drug trade. And far from depending on the drugs to finance further additions to its arms cache, Lebanon soon became a net exporter of both. As for the Afghans, given the billions in U.S. and Saudi military aid that poured into their hands, they hardly needed to peddle heroin to finance their struggle. It was more a matter of opium growers and heroin traffickers taking advantage of the collapse of alternative authority in both Afghanistan and Pakistan's North-West Frontier Province to expand their business, and of various mujahideen factions successfully bringing those traffickers under their fiscal net.

From the point of view of the arms dealer, the drug trade may well leave in its wake a lucrative market. However, this is not because of the double profit of directly bartering arms for drugs but because drug trafficking generates so much of its returns, for both the trafficker and any insurgent group taxing the trade, in the form of hard currency deposits in international banks.

From the point of view of an insurgent group, it matters little if funds come from protection fees charged to drug lords, donations of overseas supporters, trafficking in contraband, or revolutionary taxation of corporations and wealthy individuals. If the group can build up assets in the international financial system (and many, from the IRA to the PLO to the New People's Army of the Philippines have done so), then it can finance weapons purchases in exactly the same way that countries do—by using the formal credit mechanisms offered by banks. The sole requirement, which was pioneered by countries buying on the black market, is an easy one—the ability to launder the payment flows.

When the Law of Entropy Meets the Law of the Jungle

The problem of the proliferation of weaponry into the world's trouble spots is clear enough. The solutions are not. Policy can be directed at three distinct levels, not one of which offers a panacea.

First, and most popular, is to attack trafficking, the covert intermediation between the supply and demand sides of the market. As with drug control, governments find that smashing the occasional gunrunning operation permits them to garner lots of media attention while avoiding more serious actions that might involve political risks.

An effective attack on trafficking faces a number of obstacles—apart from the obvious fact that in the absence of measures to reduce demand, restricting the international flow of weapons merely leads countries to develop their own production capacities.

For one thing, unless the will and the means for genuine enforcement exist, the main impact of harsher laws against trafficking will be to permit officials to extract higher bribes rather than to cut the flow. For another, there are glaring asymmetries in national regulations, and these produce a multitude of cracks through which an arms deal can fall. Their presence is scarcely an accident or oversight; they were deliberately created to let certain deals get through.[105] Also, governments, usually through their intelligence services, deliberately divert deals to the black market to give themselves deniability. Therefore their willingness to crack down will be selective, to say the least.

There are also administrative handicaps. Few countries rigorously check exports.[106] The simple rule is that an arms shipment will be intercepted only if there is a tip-off or if the exporter does something particularly foolish. Add to this the fact that some military forces, including those of the United States, are notoriously lax in policing their inventories—perhaps deliberately so to cover up for officially sanctioned diversions.[107] Nor should it be forgotten that the enormous stocks of weaponry accumulated in present and former zones of conflict are beyond the control of any government, even one zealously committed to arms control.

Yet another obstacle is the growing sophistication of the means of evasion—the proliferation of bank and corporate secrecy havens, free-trade zones, and flag-of-convenience shipping centers; the democratization of their client lists; and the rapid diffusion of information about how to use them. If that machinery serves to maintain a steady flow of recreational drugs in the face of ever harsher laws, ever more countries nominally committed to cooperation in enforcement, and ever larger budgets allocated to stopping it, how much easier is it to move weapons, about which laws are vague and inconsistent and genuine international cooperation the exception?

Not least, if the gunrunners are caught, they are, like intermediaries handling drugs, easy to replace. Indeed, it could be argued that any success in the short run makes the problem worse in the long. In almost any black market, the response to regulatory pressure is to increase the number of intermediaries, reduce the size of each load, and find more circuitous means of moving the merchandise, while the overall market continues to serve its clients much as before. Contrary to the common fantasies of police forces, illegal markets are not hierarchically structured under the control of great crime "cartels." Instead, they are anarchic and diffused; underground entrepreneurs come and go; and participants engage in purely ad hoc arms-length transactions with each other.

The difficulties in coping directly with gunrunners have led some arms control enthusiasts to embrace the current fad for attacking the "proceeds of crime," of prying open the secrets of covert finance, and then tracing and seizing the money. This strategy supposedly will deal a deathblow to a trade motivated by the search for illicit profit.

But a bank probably has no useful knowledge unless it offers dedicated letters of credit. Even then, phony documents can hide the nature of the transaction. Furthermore, different banks enter the process in different ways at different times. One may issue credit, with or without knowing what is really being negotiated; another may merely transmit payments from one party to another; others may whiz funds from place to place at the behest of one party; yet another may act as financial manager for assets derived from it knows not where.

In the same vein, law enforcement commonly points an accusing finger at the barrier to investigation supposedly posed by bank secrecy laws. This is at best an exaggeration. There are many degrees of bank secrecy, and most present little obstacle to serious law enforcement. Mutual legal assistance treaties and memoranda of understanding permit the waiving of secrecy and exchange of information. Even where, on paper, secrecy is very tight, it often transpires that the key to penetrating it is no more sophisticated than a hundred-dollar bill. It has long been an adage among users of foreign banks for illicit purposes that real bank secrecy comes not from legislation but from keeping their mouths shut—and using multiple or false passports as identification. Under these circumstances, a bank in New York open to the full force of the law can be just as useful, and just as discrete, as one in Nauru that is legally protected by all manner of ostensible barriers to information flow.

Such secrecy is aided further by the fact that in the gunrunning trade, discretion is a proverb, not only with respect to one's own business but with respect everyone else's as well. By an unwritten code, gunrunners, however anxious to cut each other's commercial throats, rarely rat out each other the way drug dealers routinely do. Even if the gunrunner is a regular informant to the intelligence services, those services are often involved in committing the types of crimes that bona fide law enforcement agencies try to combat, particularly in arms deals.

Finally, even if a country through which a gunrunner's money has passed stands prepared to cooperate in chasing the proceeds, the techniques of effective laundering are now so well known that only the most incompetent or unlucky are caught. The occasional gunrunner might lose his or her bank balance, but as long as there are stocks of weapons for sale and enthusiastic users ready to buy, intermediaries will always be quickly replaced.

None of this is meant to imply that the free market should simply be left to work its magic. Rather, it is a warning that conventional crime control tactics, with their bias toward attacking intermediation, are a sufficient flop in dealing with crimes based purely on individual greed that it would be unwise to expect much result when they are applied to acts in which participants have profoundly political motivations.

In any event, the trafficker cannot operate without someone from whom to buy and someone to whom to sell, which suggests that serious action should be focused on either the supply or demand sides of the market. At all three levels of the supply side—production of new equipment (primary), distribution of old stocks (secondary), and dispersion of arms into the hands of the end-user population (tertiary)—the obstacles to control are formidable.

For decades, governments in the West have used military expenditure as the central instrument in pump priming their economies; therefore, they increased the productive capacity of the arms industry and, with it, the flow of new matériel. Even now, despite the loss of Cold War legitimization, pressure on politicians to maintain elevated levels of military spending have proven hard to resist. Because today's primary flows are tomorrow's stocks, the longer that high levels of military spending continue at home, the larger will be the secondary stock of weapons abroad.

This state of affairs has been complicated by the fact that today, unlike the situation after the two World Wars, conversion of military industries to peaceful purposes is difficult. Although the reasons are partly technical, they include the fact that among arms producers there is an absence of a corporate culture and infrastructure that would allow for success in the civilian sector. Nor have governments been willing to ante up sufficient funds to cover the overhead costs of conversion. Failing a broad commitment to industrial restructuring, governments will find that the only result of reducing domestic expenditures for arms procurement will be that manufacturers will push exports harder.

For producers in developing countries and ex-socialist regimes, the stakes are even higher, and the obstacles to conversion all the greater. Add to this the great irony that a country that built up its arms capacity to counter an international embargo, as South Africa did, celebrated its freedom from pariah status by using that capacity to plunge into export sales.[108]

This problem is exacerbated by the fact that in many countries, the military have their own budgets distinct from those of the state. They get tax exemptions and guaranteed subsidies, or even an assured cut of export revenues. They run their own businesses, military and civilian, legal and illegal—China's People's Liberation Army is particularly infamous in this regard.[109] Therefore, even if arms production is running at a loss, the military can use the profits from their other businesses, or from various kinds of rackets, to subsidize the industry.

Even if industrial and industrializing economies alike could be weaned from their dependence on war industries, that is not enough. Effective supply-side control also requires addressing the accumulated secondary stocks of weaponry. Each time an army upgrades, whether through strategic necessity or greed of purchasing officials, it sells off old matériel. Because the rate of psychological obsolescence in formal armies is higher than the rate of technical obsolescence on the secondhand market, the stockpile keeps growing. The current glut, compounded by the growing ease with which upgrading services can be obtained, means that even if primary flows fall temporarily below the rate of physical depreciation, there will be plenty of secondary stock to fuel conflicts until well into the new millennium. But removing that stockpile from the market seems impossible; if sheer logistics were not enough to defeat any effort, the cost would be.

Furthermore, no program of supply-side control can be truly effective without addressing the tertiary level, the problem of the dispersion of arms to the population at large, particularly in areas subject to insurgency and civil breakdown. Efforts can be made through increased policing, but rarely, if ever, in the face of pressing need have repressive tactics had much success. The main effect seems to be to raise the profits garnered from satisfying the demand. The problem of dispersion of arms also raises the question, rarely addressed by arms control advocates, of whether it is always justifiable to try to disarm populations without guaranteeing the legitimacy of the governments under which they live.

The alternative is buybacks and amnesties to encourage the voluntary surrender of illegal weapons to the authorities. That works sometimes if the state has both power and legitimacy. But outside those narrow borders, the record is spotty. All too often, only junk is handed in. If payment is made, it might be recycled into buying even better arms. Moreover, the most dangerous elements in society, those most prone to using their weapons, are the last to surrender them, if they ever do.

Of course, any global solution requires paying attention to all three levels on the supply side—conversion, destocking, and voluntary disarmament. But none will have discernible long-term effects unless attention is also focused on the demand side.

Demand-side control can take two forms. The most popular is to attack the capacity to buy. Today, economic sanctions are imposed not just on rogue states but on insurgent groups in control of a piece of territory. Time after time, the main result of economic sanctions has been to starve the population at large and ruin the civil economy, while the elite siphon off more national resources to pay inflated arms bills.

The alternative is to attack not the means but the motive. This recognizes that arms are demanded not for their own sake (except by eccentric collectors) but for what they will accomplish. Therefore, control requires addressing the underlying conditions that feed such demand.

The contemporary world has more than its fair share of thugs in power for whom huge arsenals are an instrument for advancing political goals.

And ethnoreligious bigotry is deeply entrenched. But even strutting demagogues require some sort of legitimization, however hypocritical, for their actions, and ethnoreligious bigotry seldom reaches the point of organized violence without some precipitating cause. In all too many cases, the demand for weapons is ultimately a surrogate for the demand for social justice.

Therefore, although not the only factor at play, probably the single most important factor stoking the market from the demand side is the prevailing maldistribution of income, wealth, and ecological capital. What is striking in the world today are the gross and growing disparities in all three. Until these are frankly and fairly addressed, there is little hope of damping the desire of the disadvantaged to seek the tools to rectify those disparities by violent means.

CHAPTER 4

Treasure Island

Offshore Havens, Bank Secrecy, and Money Laundering

To exorcise the demon of money laundering, the United States is leading the civilized world in a crusade that rivals in fervor the anti-Western jihad supposedly proclaimed by Middle Eastern fundamentalists. The State Department hands out brownie points (in its annual narcotics report) to countries according to how well they imitate U.S. legal initiatives. Nor is that mere exhortation. President Bill Clinton celebrated the fiftieth anniversary of the United Nations by denouncing, before the General Assembly, the menace of organized crime and by threatening with economic sanctions countries that "sponsor" money laundering or that fail to bring their regulations into line with "international standards."[1] And the U.S.-run Financial Action Task Force blacklists countries that fail to do so, threatening them with a flight of capital that could spell ruin to their financial systems.[2]

In response, country after country has been coaxed or cudgeled to pass U.S.-style laws that criminalize money laundering, allow governments to find and freeze tainted funds, and enable their forfeiture. Financial institutions scramble to implement special security measures—not to prevent disreputable persons from taking money out of the bank, as in the past, but to stop them from putting it in. Security companies do their bit by peddling fancy (i.e., expensive) software to help those institutions detect nefarious activity. All the while, speakers at conferences held in luxury hotels on island paradises warn executive-class audiences of the threat to the integrity of the global financial system when black and Hispanic crack dealers from big-city centers try to hide their ill-gotten gains in the same haven banks into which these corporate officers stuff their proceeds from the sale of stock options.

Yet for all the fear struck into the hearts of bankers by the image of the furtive figure in a dirty trench coat with a Latin surname and a five o'clock shadow waiting before the teller's window to deposit a Zeller's bag full of crumpled twenty-dollar bills, there is not a shred of evidence that the increasingly intrusive and expensive protective measures intended to combat the supposed menace are effective or even necessary. Stripped to its fundamentals, money laundering consists of a set of acts that are perfectly harmless in themselves; indeed, they add up to little more than usual financial practices, even if sometimes undertaken for unusual reasons. Furthermore, every rational assessment indicates that the sums of criminal money supposedly involved are grossly exaggerated. And far from being a present-day blight, money laundering is actually an ancient practice. Indeed, it might be more deserving than its many competitors of being called the world's second oldest crime—if anyone in the past had thought it was worth criminalizing.

The Second Oldest Crime?

Although the term "money laundering" is relatively new, its practice is not; as long as there has been a need to hide a financial transfer, something like money laundering has occurred. It is a fair bet that the world's first genuine tax code, in Hammurabi's Babylonia, stimulated the imagination of those who sought to grant themselves a rebate. Certainly in late medieval Europe, the outlines of the modern methodology to cloak financial transactions had already taken shape. The main element driving its development was usury law.

Usury, charging interest on loans, occupied in the medieval moral hierarchy a position rather like that of drug trafficking today: more than a crime, it was a sin. As a result, the penalties were severe and of three distinct sorts—civil exclusion, remedial payment, and excommunication—roughly the moral equivalents of today's imprisonment, asset seizure, and subsequent life with a criminal record.[3] Therefore moneylenders used a variety of practices to make interest charges appear something other than what they were.

When merchants negotiated payments over long distances, they would inflate exchange rates to cover interest. They would claim that interest charges were a special premium to compensate for risk. They would make interest costs appear to be a penalty for late payment—while lender and borrower agreed in advance on a delay. They would lend money to the equivalent of a shell company, then take payment, supposedly in profits, even though no profit had been made. All of these tricks, and more, intended to deceive the Church authorities, are the spiritual forebears of today's money-laundering techniques. Back then, however, there was never any doubt as to the target of the law—the offense was how money was earned, not the methods employed to hide it. And the real offender was the person who pocketed the proceeds, not the scribes and clerks who did the paperwork. These were distinctions that modern-day drug war hysteria would largely eradicate. Eventually commercial reality and the impossibility of enforcement prevailed over Church dogma with respect to usury laws; alas, there is little evidence of such developments with respect to anti-money-laundering laws today.

If laundering methods have a long historical pedigree, so, too, does the use of offshore sanctuaries as part of the process. Use of these sanctuaries dates at least from the heyday of North Atlantic piracy in the early seventeenth century.

Prior to the mid-nineteenth century, it was a common practice, in time of war, to issue to merchant ships letters of marque, which in effect were licenses to steal without risking charges of (and drastic punishments for) piracy, provided two conditions were met. First, depredations were to be conducted against ships of specified foreign countries; and, second, prizes were to be brought home to be adjudicated—in Great Britain they were assessed a 10 percent fee plus Customs charges paid to the public purse. There were ways around the second condition: cargoes seized could go unreported; the most valuable portions could be unloaded elsewhere before the prize was taken home; or ships could be ransomed rather than sacked so that technically there was no prize to report. Because all sailors shared in the spoils, there was little incentive to rat out the captain and owners, and in any case, government revenue officers could usually be squared away with a cut.

When in the early seventeenth century, James I ascended the throne of England, the main predator, and made peace with Spain, the main victim, he tried, albeit without long-term success, to ban privateering. In much the way that modern corporations dodge taxes and trade restrictions by setting up brass-plate subsidiaries in offshore havens, for a brief time English ships got foreign letters of marque. But that legal loophole was soon closed: any English subject serving on a foreign privateer became legally a pirate. The result was that fifty thousand sailors, whose main skills were pillage and plunder, were cast adrift, while capitalists who had backed them fretted over lost profits. Many former privateers came together in a pirates' cooperative, joined by adventurous landsmen, political refugees, men fleeing press gangs, and even regular sailors who found life among pirates more comfortable than a career in the English navy. They were supported by some of the same merchants, with the venture capital laundered through obliging fronts as trade credits for legitimate enterprises. Haven countries helped make it work. Some openly welcomed pirates for the money they would spend. And when the time came to retire, Mediterranean city-states, like today's tropical island paradises, competed to have pirates (and their money) take up residence.[4]

Soon, however, the pirates had official competition. Successors to James I restored the legitimacy of privateering, and it remained a common practice by the merchant ships of all major powers in wartime until the middle of the nineteenth century. The big difference was that these officially sponsored pirates had no need to use the available laundering facilities.

Thus, precedents exist, although until well into the twentieth century they were of marginal importance. During the nineteenth century, the doctrine of small government meant low taxes and minimal regulation; at the same time, world trade and financial flows were progressively liberalized—all of which reduced the need for a laundering apparatus. Furthermore, although crimes of a predatory nature were certainly punished, for the most part governments were sensible enough to realize that personal vice was the business of the person with the vice. There were few restrictions on gambling, sex for sale, and alcohol or drug consumption, and those few were rarely enforced. All this would change in the twentieth century.

Three things brought about the transformation. First was total war, which required mass mobilization of resources, both financial and material. Countries compiled data on their national production potential. They also put in place the apparatus, notably higher taxes, for transferring a larger share to the government. And they shifted the fiscal base from taxing commodities to taxing income, which put a premium on evasion.

Second, governments began to criminalize personal vice. The result was that persons earning illegal incomes from serving the forbidden desires of polite society had to disguise the take.

Third, the legacy of World War I—new states with weak currencies and exchange controls, combined with the ever-present threat of renewed hostilities—led to massive flights of capital. Places such as Switzerland, Liechtenstein, and Tangiers found new vocations catering to hot and homeless money. After World War II, numerous imitators spread, first across the Caribbean in the 1960s and 1970s, then throughout the South Pacific in the 1980s, and then into the Indian Ocean in the late 1980s and

1990s. Although most customers were (and still are) transnational corporations and wealthy rentiers engaged in polite (nonindictable) forms of
tax evasion, inevitably the facilities attracted another type of clientele.[5]

All Washed Up

Properly defined, money laundering is a three-stage process. It requires,
first, moving the funds from direct association with the crime; second,
disguising the trail to foil pursuit; and, third, making the funds again available to the instigator, with their occupational origins hidden from view.[6]
In short, disassociation, obfuscation, and legitimation. Thus, money laundering is not burying cash under an oak tree, negotiating a bearer bond
in a Swiss bank, or using a gold bar to buy a BMW. Money is not truly
laundered unless it is made to appear sufficiently legitimate that it can be
used openly, precisely what the final stage of the cycle is designed to
achieve.

Nor is money laundering restricted to big-city heroin traffickers. The
techniques can be employed by small-town used-car dealers who evade
alimony payments or by midwestern evangelical ministers who skim from
the collection plate before jetting off to the fleshpots of Bangkok. If underground entrepreneurs—from stock market manipulators to cigarette
smugglers—must launder money, so too must legitimate corporations, to
disguise a bribe or kickback. Even government agencies have recourse to
the apparatus to break an embargo or fund a coup in some rival state.
Not surprisingly, among the avid users (indeed creators) of the modern
technology for money laundering are the intelligence services of great and
small powers alike.[7]

According to legend, the term "money laundering" was first coined (no
pun intended) in the United States in the 1920s. Gangsters tried to hide
their success from competitors eager to "muscle in," from corrupt police
intent on collecting license fees, and, a little later, from revenue agents,
who discovered that tax evasion charges could be used against those who
beat other raps. The basic strategy involved the takeover of a cash-based
retail service business. The most popular choices were laundries and car
washes—hence the term. The point was to mix illegal and legal cash and
report the total as the earnings of the cover business. All three stages were
combined essentially in one step—money was distanced (physically or
metaphysically) from the crime, hidden in the accounts of a legitimate
business, then resurrected as earnings of a firm with a plausible reason

for generating that much cash. This principle remains the core of most laundering strategies today, no matter how apparently complex.

Despite the stereotypes, most illegal income is not earned in stacks of cash by punks who deal smack on the street corner in the evening and then blow the wad in the wee hours of the morning. The offenses that generate serious money are committed by eminently respectable citizens who run big-name corporations by day and patronize the opera at night. Their take comes in corporate checks, stock options, and kickbacks deposited into offshore slush funds by foreign suppliers. Still, some crooked stuff comes in as cash, and that can pose a special problem.

Aside from the health dangers of the lead fumes given off by large stacks of notes, cash is vulnerable to theft and to seizure by the police. It is also vulnerable to nature. One of the partners in Miami-based Air America, perhaps the most efficient cocaine transportation system in the United States during the 1980s, buried the proceeds in his garden. In short order the humid Florida climate did its work. When they dug out $500,000 to buy a new airplane, the money smelled as if someone had vomited on it. So they had to launder it literally—in the washing machine. When the boss buried his personal money, he took the precaution of first sealing it in plastic pipes.[8]

Large amounts of cash obviously can attract unwanted attention. These dangers are all the greater in the United States, where businesses such as auto retailers, jewelry stores, dealers in collectibles, and various travel and entertainment enterprises are required to send to Treasury a report on sales made for cash and monetary instruments worth over $10,000. Of course, that may be less of a problem than appears at first glance. Certainly it was no deterrent to Thomas Mickens. A New York high school dropout who started retailing crack, he graduated to wholesaling cocaine with sufficient vigor that, by age twenty-four, he owned a yacht, a California condo, and a Long Island home plus other pieces of real estate, along with a sporting goods store, grocery, and laundry. But his real passion was cars, especially his fleet of Rolls Royces. Some were bought with bank instruments, others with cash, and they were registered in the names of relatives and acquaintances, sometimes without their knowledge. It was only a fluke that led to his downfall. A New Jersey state trooper pulled over a Mercedes doing 80 mph in 50-mph zone and located a bag stuffed with $15,000, on which drug-sniffing dogs found traces of cocaine. Yet when queried about their failure to report the sales, dealers insisted that it was their business to sell cars, not to police their customers' behavior.[9]

There are ways around the cash-sale reporting requirements. It is possible to work through cutouts. Someone like U.S. mob boss Sam

"Mooney" Giancana never owned so much as a car in his own name during his entire life—soldiers, family members, and persons who owed him favors acted as fronts, although there was never any doubt who the real owner was.[10] Alternatively, merchants can be coaxed or bribed not to file; forms can be falsified; expenditures can be broken down into a series of smaller sums to evade the reporting threshold; and persons with no record of involvement in illicit activity can be used as fronts. In 1991 the credibility of the reporting regime received a major blow when routine police work led to a big New York jeweler laundering for a cocaine ring. In thirty-nine months he had filed 1,685 reports covering tens of millions of dollars, of which more than 30 percent were faked. He simply filled in the names of well-known customers as the sources of the cash, and no one at his bank or the Treasury thought any more about it.

Use of cutouts, however, can preclude full enjoyment of the fruits of underworld labor. And the other tactics carry risks: a merchant can turn informant, falsification of forms or breaking down the sums to evade reporting thresholds can lead to severe penalties, and front men can abscond with the goods or the money. Hence, an underground entrepreneur might prefer a formal laundering technique.

If the sums are relatively small or episodic, the race track is useful. Winning tickets can be purchased for cash at a small premium. Winners might be especially eager to sell if winnings are reported to the tax collector. To be sure, this simply transfers the tax liability to the underground entrepreneur. But the bite can be reduced by collecting discarded losing tickets as proof of business costs.[11]

Much the same occurs with state lotteries. Persons with illicit money hang around the offices where payouts are made and purchase tickets (paying a small premium) from winners who arrive to collect. This technique is particularly desirable when winnings are tax-exempt—it is hard to present masses of losing lottery tickets as proof of "costs" to cut the tax bill. By presenting a ticket for payment, a money launderer can have illegal money neatly converted into a respectable check drawn on the state lottery corporation.[12] One man bought winning tickets at a U.S. state lottery, then reported that he had to share the prize with three others—who paid him with drug money and retired with a twenty-year state annuity.[13] There have even been brokerage rings that buy winning tickets en masse for subsequent resale to persons with money to launder.[14]

Granted, use of a lottery makes laundering dependent on the luck of the draw—and the willingness of a winner to sell a ticket. But similar results can be accomplished at will through a stock or commodity broker. In exchange for cash, put through brokerage company accounts in the name of the house, the broker simultaneously buys long and sells short (or the reverse) the same security or commodity. Whichever way the market moves, there is a capital gain and an offsetting loss. The broker destroys the record of the losing trade and returns the funds in the guise of a capital gain to the client, less a double commission and some hush money.

Similarly, someone can purchase a piece of property. The publicly recorded price, set well below market value, is paid with legitimately earned money in usual bank instruments. The rest is paid in cash under the table. The property is resold for full market value and the money recouped, with the illegal component appearing as a capital gain.

Going one step farther, a run-down building can be acquired using partly legal and partly illegal money, and the workers to renovate it hired for cash (further dissipating the illicit funds). Because their earnings are tax free, the workers will not be inclined to talk. The building can be sold for a double capital gain, due in part to the original undervaluation and in part to the renovations. Alternatively, the building could be a rental property. Not only can illicit money partially fund its purchase, but more can be laundered by reporting it as rent payments. Inflated rental returns further puff the capital gain realizable on final sale. Or they can be the basis for a higher assessment to justify a bank lending more money, which the entrepreneur can use to buy yet more buildings.[15]

Such techniques can be employed only episodically and, usually, for laundering relatively small sums. No one can appear lucky at the track too often, and substantial capitagains can lead to questions about the start-up funds. To cover continuing flows, the best candidates are still the retail service industries. They generate (or rather, can credibly seem to generate) large amounts of cash on an on-going basis. Services have a major advantage over physical goods. In manufacturing; the flow of input bears some technical relationship to the flow of output, which facilitates the task of determining what revenues should be. But in services there is only a fuzzy relationship between cost of physical input and value of output. Just as services are the best sector through which to evade taxes (by underreporting income), so they are also the best sector through which to launder money (by overreporting income). The process has been rendered easier by structural changes in modern economies.

In this supposedly post-industrial age, the proportion of GNP accounted for by the retail service sector has been rising sharply. With it has come a shift in employment away from secondary manufacturing by large firms and toward services in which the scale of plant tends to be much smaller. The result is a proliferation of exactly the type of small, service-oriented firms that provides an ideal environment for money laundering—with the critical proviso that the sums each washes must remain relatively small for the operation to avoid attracting attention.

Car washes are still used—albeit they should avoid the mistake of one firm in the United States whose books showed that it had serviced two hundred vehicles on a day when a blizzard had stopped all traffic. Restaurants are good choices—who knows what great economies on raw material a talented chef can achieve? At worst the restaurant risks a municipal fine for watering the soup rather than a criminal rap for washing cocaine money. Used-car dealerships have been known to offer discounts to customers who pay in cash, while reporting the car as sold at full cost to create space for some bent money. Even better is a video rental shop—the physical input, the stock of videos, is fixed and subject to slow depreciation, whereas the number of times each video is rented out for cash can be inflated virtually without check unless the police try to count the customers leaving the store. And unlike with a car wash, the worse the weather, the more credible a large flow of business is likely to be.

Better still are bars, where total receipts are about as easy to fake as the results of a Florida election—particularly because the authorities are more likely to worry about how much tax the owners are evading rather than how much they inflate their taxable earnings to cover for a money-laundering operation.

This example, of course, raises an obvious problem. When illegal cash is mixed with legal receipts and the combined sum reported as legitimate earnings, taxes must be paid on the total. But the bite can be reduced by padding the payroll with ghost employees (simultaneously providing cover for people employed in the racket that generates the illegal earnings), by inflating the cost of inputs, and by puffing figures on breakage and spoilage. A restaurateur, or a dealer in perishables, can easily exaggerate losses if the objective is to skim cash and evade taxes rather than to launder. In fact the two can be mutually reinforcing. A vending machine company, for example, can divert stock to black market sales, the owners over-report sales to wash money, and those who purchased the stock sell it for cash and dodge taxes.

A domestic cash-based retail service business can serve to effectively combine in one milieu all three stages of a laundering cycle. By physically running cash through the business, the launderer separates criminal money from the act that generated it. By reporting the money as earnings of that business, the launderer hides the trail. Then, once the firm's tax returns have been approved, the money can be used openly by the persons who initiated the operation. Nor, contrary to a belief widely held by politicians, police, and public alike, is there any need for such operations to work strictly in cash.

In 1979 Elias K. set up a contracting business and took out a loan from a local credit union, nominally to buy supplies for his firm. The borrowed funds were diverted to buy drugs from wholesalers, and the drugs were retailed to customers, who were instructed to pay not in cash but in checks made out to the contracting company. Elias endorsed the checks over to the credit union, using part of the proceeds to service his loan while declaring the rest as profit. Regular loan payments plus healthy profits made Elias an excellent credit risk. The credit union was happy to lend him more money, which he used to buy more drugs. In short, a respectable financial firm created a revolving credit line to keep a trafficker supplied with inventory and simultaneously washed his profits. What was most remarkable was not that the scheme functioned through the same financial instruments as a strictly legal business—any criminal operation with a suitable business front could do likewise. Rather it was that Elias ran such a sophisticated operation largely onshore at a time of explosive growth of offshore financial havens, albeit he was careful to send part of his profits abroad before decamping himself.[16]

Don't Leave Home without It

When the sums become larger and law enforcement nosier, the laundering process will likely involve an international dimension. At that point the three stages—disassociation, obfuscation, and legitimation—become logically and chronologically distinct.

The international cycle begins with the funds being moved out of the country of origin. In the United States there are two special barriers, which other countries, under pressure, have begun to imitate. One demands that each time $10,000 or more in cash or bearer instruments is deposited in (or withdrawn from) a financial institution, a currency transaction report (CTR) be filled out, identifying the depositor and explaining the origins of the cash, with a copy sent to the U.S. Internal Revenue Service for scrutiny. Once the money is in the bank, the depositor is free to convert it into cashier's checks, money orders, or wire transfers and move it abroad. But because there was a deposit report, supposedly there is a paper trail. Alternatively, should the person decide to bypass the formal financial system, each export (or import) worth more than $5,000 in cash or monetary instruments must be accompanied by a currency and monetary instruments report (CMIR), which is filed with U.S. Customs and provides information similar to that on a CTR.

Faced with such barriers, would-be travelers, or their money, have a number of options—flying over, digging under, sneaking past, or just sweet-talking their way around. The most notorious method is one that police officers, speaking in hushed tones that convey a mixture of fear, respect, and misunderstanding, refer to as the underground banking system.

THOSE INSCRUTABLE ORIENTALS

In fact, the underground banking system uses standard banking techniques—the lateral transfer and the compensating balance—common in legal transactions, particularly in countries in which there are exchange controls or legally inconvertible currencies. The basic idea is simple. Assume that business 1 in country A owes $X to business 2 in country B, while business 2 in country B owes $X to business 3 in country A. To settle the debts without compensating balances, business 1 would send $X to business 2 and business 2 would then send $X to business 3. This requires two international transfers and four distinct withdrawal and deposit transactions. To settle the debts with compensating balances, business 1 in country A merely settles the debt owed by business 2 to business 3 in country A. Now there are only two banking transactions, from the account of business 1 to the account of business 3, and no international transfers. Generally the mechanics are more complex, the sums do not exactly balance, and the exchanges are multilateral. Still, the basic principle remains, the practice is commonplace, and legitimate brokers specialize in the arrangements. Such transfers are common, for example, in the foreign exchange business. A currency house might accept a deposit of dollars, say, in New York, then instruct a German affiliate to make the equivalent in deutsche marks available in Frankfort; sometime later, a reverse flow will balance out the original transaction.

In a so-called underground banking system, much the same process occurs. Someone in country A who is seeking to move funds abroad contacts the underground banker and deposits a certain sum. The underground banker sends a coded message to his or her correspondent abroad, telling the correspondent to credit the equivalent of the deposited sum (less the fee) to a foreign bank account set up for the person seeking to move the money out of country A. The offsetting transaction occurs when someone else abroad attempts to move money into country A.

The spread of such a method is often linked to the growing tendency for ethnic and religious minorities of non-European extraction to take root in the West and for transactions to take place across borders but within an extended family or ethnic group. Although touted as a new phenomenon and a symptom of the emerging borderless world, so-called trade diasporas have existed since ancient times precisely because of barriers.[17] Typically, entrepreneurial members of a trade diaspora make no distinction between social and economic life. Their business firms are extensions of kinship structure, with leadership that reflects the extended family hierarchy, which can extend across continents. Not only might they feel ill at ease with banking institutions in the host country, but sending money to and from their places of origin could be complicated by poor financial infrastructure or exchange controls back home.[18]

True, the underground banking system can be used for criminal purposes from time to time—so can life insurance companies and nursing homes—but it has benign origins. The most currently infamous version, the Chinese underground banking system (*fei ch'ien* or "flying money"), was invented not as a means to permit money to evade the sight and the grasp of the authorities but as a tool to facilitate taxation. The emperor needed a secure means to move tax money from the provinces to the capital, while tea merchants coming to the capital faced the insecurity of a long trip back once they had sold their produce. Therefore, the merchant deposited money from tea sales with the office each provincial governor kept in the capital, for which he was given a certificate. On his return home, the tea merchant presented the certificate and was paid out of locally collected tax receipts, thus eliminating the danger and inconvenience to both parties of having to transport money over long distances.[19] It then remained for the overseas Chinese diaspora to wed informal banking institutions with the technique of flying money in a context of mistrust of formal banks, political turmoil, and persecution of Chinese minorities— and so the Chinese underground banking system was born.[20]

Wherever significant trade diasporas exist, so does some sort of underground banking system. That the Chinese and, to a slightly lesser degree, the Indo-Pakistani (*havalah*) systems are more widespread reflects the extent of emigration. That they work efficiently reflects the degree to which ethnoreligious solidarity can be backed by clan loyalties and interwoven obligations: the ultimate sanction is the threat of exclusion. However, there are instances in which fear plays a more important role in assuring that contracts are respected.

Although it has a long history, Colombia's black market peso-exchange system is today breathlessly described as "the single most efficient and extensive money-laundering 'system' in the Western Hemisphere."[21] It originated with a simple problem. Colombia had, until the 1990s, tight exchange controls that restricted money on the way out, and high Customs duties on many commodities on the way in. It also had an enormous demand for U.S. goods—raw materials, machinery and equipment for factories, and bootleg booze, cigarettes, and blue jeans for bargain-hunting consumers. Furthermore, travelers to the United States were severely restricted in the amount of dollars they could take out, while wealthy Colombians searched for a way to get their savings out of the reach of the local tax collectors. The result was a huge appetite for black market dollars.[22]

Meantime, excess dollars in search of a way back home piled up in the United States. Some were the savings of the large Colombian émigré population, who wished to remit back to their families but out of sight of the fiscal (and U.S. immigration) authorities. Some were the proceeds of illegal exports to the United States of legitimate commodities such as coffee and emeralds, which were subject to Colombian government restrictions and controls. Some came from cocaine and marijuana sales. Naturally it was the third group that attracted all the attention.

In between stepped the *cambista*. A cambista would bid for cash in the United States, offering to pay for it by depositing the equivalent in pesos, at an agreed black market rate, in a bank account in Colombia. Then the *cambista* instructed his representative, an underground money broker in the United States, to take possession of the cash. As soon as the broker received the amount, he informed the *cambista* in Colombia, whereupon the lateral transfer-compensating balance mechanism swung into operation. The cambista released the peso equivalent, less the agreed charge, to the person who wanted to get the money out of the United States. The cambista then attempted to introduce the U.S. cash into the U.S. financial system. He or his broker either sneaked it into bank accounts through the front of a cover business or they smuggled the cash out of the United States and then brought it back for deposit through use of wire transfers or cashier's checks. Once the money was in a U.S. dollar account, the funds would be sold again—this time to a Colombian businessman seeking to import goods from the United States. Everyone exited smiling. Smugglers and émigré workers got their money home; tax and exchange-control evaders got their money out; Colombian businesses in need of raw materials, parts, and equipment got access to foreign exchange at a discount; and Colombian dealers in contraband goods obtained supplies at a double advantage (no taxes and cheap dollars) over legitimate importers.

CASH AND CARRY?

Although lateral transfers play a role, there seems little doubt that most funds that bypass the formal banking system en route to foreign havens go out in cash. Sometimes items such as gold or other collectibles can substitute. Diamonds are a possibility, although not for amateurs—who end up buying at retail and reselling well below wholesale. Similarly, rare stamps. A block of 1918 U.S. air mail stamps (rendered especially rare because the image was mistakenly printed upside down) sold in 1991 for $1.8 million.[23] Even the most committed follow-the-money zealots would have difficulty making it a crime to fly out of the United States carrying air mail stamps. Whatever object is chosen, it should be of high value in relation to bulk—therefore physically simple to smuggle—and easy to sell at destination.

Cash, however, is far more common. There are clear advantages to working with high denominations—the 1,000 deutsche mark and 1,000 Swiss franc notes are favorites in some areas, whereas in Southeast Asia the 10,000 Singapore dollar bill commands a certain allegiance. On the other hand, more obscure currencies are distinctly dangerous. When the Royal Canadian Mounted Police, fired up with big-note envy, successfully lobbied the Canadian government to withdraw the C$1000 note, they probably did criminals a favor; anyone trying to pass such a note abroad would attract more attention than if the currency came equipped with flashing red lights and warning bells. The only evidence of "widespread" criminal use of the C$1000 bill the Mounties could offer was the result of one of their own sting operations, when they had pressed the notes on their cocaine-dealing clients.

Despite the inconvenience of a relatively low denomination, the worldwide favorites are the U.S. $50 and $100 bills. Perhaps 75 percent or more by value of U.S. currency, that is, more than $300 billion worth, is in circulation outside the United States.[24] In growing numbers of countries it is the official currency. In others, it circulates along with and sometimes in preference to the national currency. And in many countries, even if retail transactions on domestic black markets are conducted in local currency, U.S. notes, especially in $50 and $100 denominations, are in great demand to conduct covert wholesale transactions, hide international transfers, and hold underground savings.

This poses a dilemma. The $50 and $100 denominations cost the U.S. government an average of 2.5 cents per note to print. Hence, as other countries suffer increases in black marketeering and tax evasion, as they watch their own currencies displaced and, along with them, the ability of their national governments to finance public works through the printing

press, the benefit pours into the hands of the U.S. Treasury at a rate of $15–25 billion per annum—the amount in interest the United States would have to pay on the equivalent borrowed money. Yet simultaneously, the export of U.S. currency makes its own anti-money-laundering initiative more difficult.[25]

In theory, Customs reporting requirements are a barrier to the export of cash. In reality, they are largely useless. Indeed, it is hard to avoid the suspicion that their main function is to provide the illusion of action, to preclude the United States from being denounced as hypocritical when it berates other countries on their weak anti-money-laundering effort, while it happily banks the benefits of its own exports of hard cash.

When flying, a traveler can simply stow cash in check-in baggage, although that is recommended only for travelers who are using airlines that have a reasonable reputation for getting bags to the proper destination. More commonly, money travels in hand luggage, which makes airport security equipment a potential problem. Still, money can be disseminated artfully so that the contents appear innocent to those operating scanning equipment. Or it can be wrapped around a torso—a practice that will continue until some enforcement agency persuades Congress to authorize mandatory x-rays for all departing passengers.[26] Perhaps the main danger is that some U.S. airports are patrolled by drug-sniffing dogs, and most U.S. currency is tainted with traces of cocaine.[27]

Nor does the movement have to involve scheduled passenger service. Palettes of cash have been delivered by cargo plane. And professional smugglers carry money south in small aircraft en route to pick up shipments of cocaine and marijuana to haul back.[28]

Movement by land is easier. Although the United States–Mexico border is, in theory, tightly patrolled, so many commercial and private vehicles (not to mention light planes) cross it each day that it is trivially simple to move a load of cash. Indeed, in the early 1990s, U.S. agents discovered an air-conditioned, lighted tunnel under the border.

The Canadian frontier is even more porous. There are numerous crossing posts where rarely, if ever, is there a guard. Furthermore, if money is entrusted to a courier company as a commercial package, the company assumes the contents are what the customer claims—to open the packages would violate a contractual obligation. And Customs waves the vehicle through.[29]

Best is by boat. Outbound luggage is not checked unless there has been a tip-off.[30] It suffices to mark an item as cabin luggage, turn it over to porters, and then wait for delivery—after which the individual might spend a leisurely crossing, alternating between shuffleboard on a sunlit

deck by day and counting cash in a stateroom with the curtains drawn by night.

The money can also go in cargo containers, which are not normally subjected to outbound inspection. Even if they are opened, it is rare anything would be found. Although currency has been discovered in everything from barrels of textile dye to cryogenic containers of bull sperm, again the only real danger is a tip-off.[31]

Such subterfuge may not even be necessary. There are Canadian border crossings where U.S. guards exist but the proper forms do not or where individuals who offered to report were waved through by officers bored or engrossed in a big league baseball game. Some people file for much less than they carry out on the assumption that Customs officers will not bother to count, and if they do, the difference can be imputed to an honest mistake. Others, by contrast, enter the United States with a certain amount but report a much larger sum. They can leave again carrying the sum they reported on the way in, using their copy of the original CMIR as proof of the benign origins of the money.[32] But sometimes these tricks are superfluous. The self-promoting Cuban launderer Ramon Milian-Rodriguez, who bragged of handling $50–100 million per month and managing billions in "cartel" assets, told a rapt U.S. congressional hearing that "By filing the forms we were always able to justify large amounts of cash on our persons." The Customs agent would look at it, say thank you, and toss it on the pile.[33]

Even if the probability of being caught is not very high, it does exist. Therefore, to further reduce the risk, it maybe useful to turn the job over to professional couriers—albeit the fee can be stiff. Airline staff, for example, not only get priority passage through Customs, but they are usually on sufficiently good terms with airport security that they are almost never checked. Hence they are a popular choice to carry everything from contraband booze to tax-free diamonds to valises stuffed with high-denomination currency notes.[34]

Usually couriers are chosen for their ability to maintain a low profile—that is, by their behavior or appearance or destination they do not stand out from the crowd. On the other hand, when Chicago mob kingpin Sam Giancana sent one of his lieutenants to keep on eye on the mob's interests in Hollywood, the lieutenant was instructed also to be on the lookout for movie stars to run errands. "They make great bagmen," Giancana said. "Everybody's too busy being dazzled by a star and askin' for their autograph to ask what's in a briefcase."[35]

Similarly, few Customs and immigration officers want to be seen harassing priests. The practice of using them as couriers dates back at least

as far as World War II, when priests were about the only people who could cross lines with ease, and the Vatican ran a lucrative capital-flight business couriering cash, gold, jewelry, and securities on behalf of the faithful.[36] Sam Giancana also used to employ a priest with the appropriate name of Father Cash to tuck money under his robes and run it to Panama, Italy, and Switzerland.[37] The practice is not dead; in 1994 a ring arranged for drug money to be funneled from Houston, Los Angeles, Chicago, Miami, and Puerto Rico to New York before being couriered to Zurich by two Hasidic rabbis.[38]

CORPS DIPLOMATIQUE—CONTRABANDISTE DISTINGUÉE

In the hierarchy of desirable couriers, diplomats rank highest. Diplomatic status confers three distinct advantages.[39] First, the embassy and sometimes the consular grounds (which could be the backroom of a corner convenience store) are off-limits to law enforcement, making them useful places for storing money prior to moving it out.

Second, the diplomat is immune from arrest. The Vienna Convention of 1961 tried to reduce abuse of diplomatic status by differentiating official from private acts and awarding different levels of immunity to various classes of diplomats. Thus, consuls are immune from criminal prosecutions only when acting in their official capacity, whereas ambassadors have total immunity for everything from unpaid parking tickets to first-degree murder. However, in practice, even consuls effectively have blanket immunity, provided they are accredited by the country in which the event occurs. Except in the very unusual event that the country that conferred diplomatic status strips it away, the worst that can happen to a diplomat is for he or she to be declared persona non grata and expelled.

The third advantage is the diplomatic pouch. Normally used to carry classified documents, passports, encoding equipment, and the like, the pouch is sealed, usually with wax or lead, and, if clearly marked as diplomatic, it cannot be subjected to an ordinary Customs search. If Customs suspects contraband, the pouch can be inspected only with consent of the diplomat. Because a diplomat cannot be prosecuted, and harassing one might cause an international incident, diplomatic bags are typically waved through, along with the diplomat's personal luggage. Furthermore, in those few cases in which a country blocks a diplomatic package, it generally refuses entry, not exit, which is what concerns the cash courier.

As a result, the diplomatic pouch is ideal for moving not just cash but drugs, weapons, diamonds, Swiss watches, stolen artworks, looted antiquities, and even black market nuclear materials. In theory diplomats are only allowed to import legitimate goods, and even then only enough for personal consumption. Of course, different people consume different goods in different proportions. That, at least, was the claim of a North Korean diplomat caught in Sweden with two and a half million duty-free cigarettes.

Instead of hiring a diplomat, it may be possible for the entrepreneur to personally achieve that status, saving costs while adding an extra layer of personal protection. This can be done by securing a fake diplomatic passport—forged, stolen, or issued by a country that has since changed its name. (Ceylon no longer works but British Honduras will do the job; clerks simply see the word "Honduras.") However, there is no need for fraud when genuine ones are readily available, often at affordable rates.

Two things make the acquisition of diplomatic status easy today. One is the sheer number of new countries without the means to support a world-wide diplomatic core and therefore eager to grant diplomatic status to persons preferably, but not necessarily, of the same ethnic background, provided they will serve their ancestral or adopted homeland for free. Second, some countries sell such status to large investors. The process of acquisition can be bilateral—someone requests a posting from a country—but that is slow and unreliable. It is better to work through a brokerage company; the higher cost is more than compensated by speed and selection. One firm in Lugano, for example, arranges full-fledged ambassadorial posts, along with foreign passports and Swiss bank accounts. Another in London, whose main business is setting up offshore companies, can arrange consular appointments in several European and South American countries for about $50,000. Yet another in Costa Rica specializes in North American postings for persons willing to represent various Latin American countries. Because spouses and children of diplomats have the same status, adults have arranged to be adopted in order to secure immunity, sometimes from current prosecutions. Incidentally, the Lugano firm also arranges adoptions to nobility for the appropriate fee.

Despite its attractions, diplomatic status is not foolproof, as many an amateur has found to their regret. Diplomatic passports facilitate movement of "diplomat" and luggage but confer immunity only if that diplomat is formally accredited to a particular country.[40]

It is precisely to offset the ease of export of bulk cash that the United States pressures certain countries whose banks have acquired a reputation for accepting "suitcase currency." (The island of St. Maarten used to have four armored cars a day meet planes from the United States; in the same spirit, the Cook Islands once ordered four thousand bill-counting machines, almost all sized for U.S. notes.) Undercover agents film clients and sometimes infiltrate the bank, and the governments of the host countries are subjected to threats of economic retaliation. That has had some impact. But so many places readily accept U.S. dollars in their parallel foreign exchange markets that such efforts just change temporarily the geographical distribution, not the fact that money movers easily sidestep U.S. currency export controls by using cash.

E-FINANCE: CYBER-THREAT OR TECHNOHYPE?

The ongoing transition between a cash/bank paper economy to one based on electronic money has led to the emergence of new techniques for the clandestine movement of funds.[41] Alarm bells are ringing around the world over the threat of "cyber-laundering"—even though no one has yet found a single instance. In theory, there seem to be valid reasons for concern. Not only can enormous sums be squeezed onto a microchip, not only does the technology of peer-to-peer transfers permit complete bypassing of the formal banking system, but there seems to be nothing to prevent someone with millions on their smart card from sauntering right past a Customs agent staring forlornly at a stack of irrelevant CMIRs—nothing except the fact that a chance brush past a magnet might wipe the card irretrievably clean.

It is important to take today's technohype with not just a grain of salt but with most of the shaker. Each generation, it seems, has optimists who tell the world that its technological achievements are unique to the point of constituting a veritable revolution. Each also has pessimists who warn the world that those technologies will create massive new problems for the institutions of governance. Obviously modern technology can have a major impact on economic exchanges—illegal as well as legal. But the effects of today's electronic communication and mass-based cheap and rapid international transport of goods and people are easily exaggerated compared with those of the technological achievements of past centuries.

The telegraph in the mid-nineteenth century, for example, not only permitted the creation of a genuine world market in which all traders had access to the same price information at almost the same time, therefore transcending the constraints of location, but it gave crooks a fancy new tool. Brokers used fast access to data to trade on privileged information, and scam artists used it to rig markets. From the start, too, telegraph companies worried about hackers and the security of telegraphic fund transfers—in a manner little different from current concerns voiced about Internet commerce and finance.[42] Yet none of this was incompatible with the ability of the state either to enforce criminal law or to collect taxes sufficient for its needs.

Much of the fuss made today about electronic funds transfers, for example, can be put into perspective with a simple comparison. On the one side, calculate the time required to send a bill of exchange or purse of silver coin by sailing ship across the Atlantic in the period up to the early nineteenth century and compare it with the time required to make a telegraphic transfer once the first transoceanic line was laid in the mid-nineteenth century. Then calculate the relative time saving represented by the switch from telegraphic (electrical) funds transfer to electronic funds transfer in the latter half of the twentieth century. In the first instance, the difference was truly revolutionary; in the second it was, for practical purposes, trivial. For all the technohype, the person has yet to be invented who can respond to information in nanoseconds.

Granted, there is more to e-finance than speed. But whether it poses a serious threat to law enforcement's attempts to follow the money depends on what form it takes.[43]

One form of e-finance already in wide-spread operation consists of no more than the use of ATM machines for transfers and bill payments, along with standard debit cards that permit clients to credit directly a merchant's account from their own. These are simply more convenient (and, for banks, more profitable) ways to conduct regular bank transactions. It is true that a standard debit card can be carried across borders with no legal requirement for reporting. But because the funds have to be in a bank before they can be transferred via a debit card, they pose no more impediment than an ordinary credit card to auditing anyone's transactions.

A second, not yet widely used but spreading in popularity, is the smart card (or stored-value card). Not much different in principle than a standard phone card, these are loaded at a regular financial institution and spent in a normal retail outlet or unloaded at another financial institution. They, too, pose little or no challenge to law enforcement.

A third is genuine digital cash, in the shape of bytes stored in a hard drive. However, even if, in a sense, paper money does grow on trees, e-money cannot emerge suddenly from cyberspace. The funds loaded into the hard drive originate from a bona fide financial institution—and they eventually end up in yet another financial institution. It is, of course, possible that nonbank institutions can, much the way some barter houses or local trading networks do now, initiate their own special purpose moneys and therefore bypass the existing financial system. But networks so created have to work on trust, they will almost inevitably be small scale, and by definition they will be localized, which means they are incapable of permitting money to flee to sunnier climes without first being converted into normal bank instruments.

However, there is one potentially serious problem. The technology of electronic purses, even though still minimally used, permits transfers from one smart card to another. Those transfers can also go via telephone or modem. The technology, too, permits payments to be disembodied: a transfer leads to a deduction from the card and a confirmed payment into a merchant's account, with nothing to link the two. This has obvious implications for tax collection. It might also ease the building up of untraceable offshore nest eggs. An audit trail can lead from the entrepreneur's bank account to his or her smart card but not to the final destination, which could be an offshore bank or trust company.

Granted, even with peer-to-peer transfers, anonymity is assured only if adequate levels of encryption can be employed. It is one thing to hide the name of the payer from the recipient merchant but quite another to hide it from a government agency intent on cracking codes. In the near future, however, encryption technology may advance beyond the effective capacity of government agencies to defeat it. For a long time the military and intelligence forces had a virtual lock on the sophisticated stuff. But the end of the Cold War also ended most restrictions on international flows of technology and released large amounts of talent skilled in encryption and related matters into the private sector. Furthermore, there are the growing ranks of computer whiz kids dedicated to developing encryption-for-the-masses technology, partly out of ideological commitment to defeating Big Brother but more often just for the thrill of it.[44] The object of their concern may not even be just drug cops or tax authorities; it could also be commercial creditors, potential kidnappers, divorcing spouses, or libel lawyers hired by someone angry about an item posted on a web site. Nonetheless, the result is the same.

True, virtually any encryption can be broken—but at the expenditure of often considerable, even enormous, amounts of time and money. As a result, the authorities prefer to chase nonencrypted transfers.[45] The resource issue becomes even more of a problem given that the target is not a single enemy agent boring into the bowels of the Pentagon but many thousands of underground entrepreneurs intent on keeping their financial profiles as low as possible.

You Can Still Bank on It

Whichever route is followed to smuggle out the money, once it is abroad, it can be plunked into an accommodating bank and the matter, barring bad luck, should be at an end. However, most transfers occur not through underground banking systems, cash, e-money, or even gold or bearer bonds but through orthodox bank instruments. In theory, the requirement of a CTR for each deposit (or withdrawal) of $10,000 or more in cash or monetary instruments should be more effective as a barrier to illegal money movements than is the CMIR. Yet there are many ways of evading it.

SLEIGHT OF HAND

The first, and probably most effective, is to convert cash into checks before making a deposit. Checks do not require special reporting—the check itself provides a paper trail. Therefore underground entrepreneurs hang around bars and cash workers' paychecks, sparing them a trip to the bank, which would cut into their drinking time. Formal check-cashing services do the job even better. Common in poor neighborhoods, they cash unemployment or welfare checks for clients who either do not have access to standard banking facilities or have outstanding debts and therefore risk having the proceeds of the check grabbed if they negotiate it through their bank. Instead of drawing cash out of a bank, an event that triggers a CTR, the check casher uses illegal money as working capital to cash clients' unemployment and welfare checks. The checks are then deposited in the company accounts. The balance, less a service fee, might be withdrawn again in the form of a cashier's check, for example, and given to the underground entrepreneur—who is then free to carry or mail it out of the country or even deposit it in his or her own domestic bank account. Even simpler, the check casher might simply sell clients' checks to the entrepreneur, who deposits them directly into his or her own account.[46]

However, the check casher may prove dishonest, expensive, or on the police payroll. Better for the entrepreneur to introduce the cash directly into the bank.

The classic method is to "structure" the transaction, that is, the money is broken up into a series of deposits each under the reporting threshold. Then the money is either wired abroad or drawn out again in cashier's checks, which are easy to hide and negotiate outside the country. Even in a country in which a CTR-type report is not required, structuring makes sense because any large cash transaction is likely to attract unwanted attention.[47]

Successful structuring requires attention to logistics. It would be foolish to make every deposit for exactly $9,999, yet the smaller the sums, the more time-consuming the process. Structuring is easiest where banks are packed closely together. Couriers have to be changed frequently, have no criminal records, and attract little attention. That need was apparently the inspiration for the Grandma Mafia, a group of six middle-aged women, all grandmothers, who moved from bank to bank buying cashier's checks with drug cash.[48]

When it became clear to U.S. authorities that structuring was often used to evade the CTR regime, the reaction was threefold. First, the act of breaking up deposits to evade the reporting requirements was itself criminalized—even if the money and the individual were otherwise innocent. Second, restrictions were imposed on who could buy cashier's checks, as were new requirements to record identities of purchasers of bearer instruments. Third, the U.S. Treasury developed a computer program to scan bank records for unusual patterns of cash deposits under $10,000.

The first, of course, was only a problem if the individual were caught, a fate more likely to befall the novice, or the innocent, than the experienced. The second could be circumvented by use of a fake ID, which can be easily purchased on the black market if one does not own the necessary, simple technology—albeit some can be subject to computer verification if the bank bothers to try.[49] As to the third, in an age agog at electronic wizardry, a program to detect unusual deposit patterns seemed an especially good idea—until a wiretap accidentally picked up representatives of a Hong Kong–based ring bragging to potential clients about a counterprogram to structure deposits that fooled the Treasury computer.[50]

Another option is to get on the list of those exempted from filing CTRs.[51] Some types of business are automatically exempt because they normally generate large amounts of cash—in effect, exempting the category most useful for laundering. Some can be exempted by the banks on their own volition, although they have to establish an exemption limit appropriate to the business. Some exemptions require Treasury permission. Whichever, once a firm is on the list, the business can be sold and the exemption automatically transferred to the new owners.

Assuming an exemption is not forthcoming, it was, and likely still is, possible to bully or bribe bank officers into ignoring reporting requirements.[52] In a cute subvariant, bank employees fill out the paper, put a copy in the bank's files, and throw away the one destined for the IRS. If agents come calling, the banker can claim that failure to mail in the form was an oversight or that it got lost en route, while using the bank's own copy to demonstrate honest intent.[53] This problem, obviously, is one that can be reduced by a complete switchover to electronic filings.

These tricks are especially likely to prove successful when dealing with small and weak banks that are desperate for business and therefore happy to accommodate cash-heavy customers. It is also reasonable to suppose that the propensity of banks to ignore reporting requirements varies directly with the state of the economy, falling in good times and rising when the financial sector is squeezed between high deposit rates and bad loans. Furthermore, with the decentralized banking system typical of the United States—a plethora of independent banks, often with only one or a few branches—it is possible for an entrepreneur to secure control of a bank, thus assuring that no potentially troublesome paperwork reaches the wrong hands.

All these—and many more—evasion techniques suppose that most underground entrepreneurs fear filling out the CTRs. Even if true, if the money is to be deposited only once or a few times in quick succession and then wired to distant havens, the entrepreneur might use a fake ID to fill out the required forms, hoping that by the time the forms are checked, he or she (and the money) will be long gone, perhaps to repeat the operation at another bank. Once money has been deposited, the clever entrepreneur might leave a small sum in the account to keep it nominally active and make it look legitimate.

Indeed, it may well be that the entrepreneur really does not have to take the risk and bear the expense of false ID. It may well be that the system is so clogged with indigestible information that the easiest solution is just to make the deposit, fill out the form, and forget the whole thing.[54]

For a long time U.S. banks regarded the reporting requirements (which date to 1970) as a nuisance to be ignored. Then in 1985, a scandal (conveniently timed with the introduction of a new anti-money-laundering law) erupted involving the Bank of Boston, one of the most prestigious older banking institutions in the country. It was suddenly discovered that among the happy beneficiaries of the bank's laissez-faire attitude were the don of a New England crime group and the local chapter of the Irish Republican Army. In the wake of the scandal and the heavy fines imposed on the bank, filings began to climb rapidly. Bank after bank 'fessed up and accepted their responsibility, in the process paying fines that could be either charged against taxes or simply passed on to consumers of bank services in the form of higher fees. Then the opposite problem emerged. Within a few years, there were so many millions of CTRs backlogged in warehouses that the rats likely would get to them before the Treasury analysts.[55]

Even if all forms could be scrutinized in a timely fashion, however, and by analysts who actually understand the nature and operation of illegal financial markets, it is unclear a priori what they would reveal—in part because no one knows how many of the reports are simply faked. But the main problem is that launderers obviously structure their activities to approximate as closely as possible legitimate transactions; it is the unlucky and the incompetent who are caught. Anyone making enough criminal money to fill out the forms on a regular basis is surely smart enough to have legitimate-looking cover in the form of a business that would be expected to generate large amounts of cash. Therefore, unless the law is already on someone's tail for completely independent reasons, financial reports make little difference, and therefore filling them out is rarely a serious security threat.

However, running a business that seemingly explains a large amount of cash deposits is not enough. If the objective is to move the money through the formal banking system and then out of the country, there must also be a good reason for the international transfer. An entrepreneur could use a company that engages regularly in international trade in goods or services. A clever laundering operation would assure that any "payments" to supposed suppliers abroad are in odd rather than round sums and that those sums are not repeated. It might also divide the payments between "suppliers" in several countries, alternate between wire and written forms of remittance, and ensure that the nominal recipients appear to have sound business reputations. This is best done with services—for trade in goods implies that something concrete is acquired in exchange for the money being spent. However, money can also be moved through institutions in which there is no commercial activity whatsoever, and therefore no need to show any proof, physical or documentary, of a quid pro quo to justify the transfer abroad.

THE HOLY NETWORK

In 1988, while trying to trace the U.S. activities of a money launderer from Cali, the FBI stumbled onto a seemingly perfect cover for both accepting cash and sending money out of the country. The arrest of two Israeli bagmen led to a Seattle Hasidic rabbi who confessed to accepting large sums, breaking the cash down into amounts below the reporting threshold, depositing it in bank accounts held in the name of his religious institutions, and wiring it abroad, some to financial havens, some to Israel. In addition he had helped set up a courier system to run cash to Panama and Israel. Still, his lawyer pleaded, the rabbi was motivated by the best of intentions: he thought the money belonged to Iranian, Argentinean, and South African Jews trying to get it to Israel. The court apparently agreed that although it is an extremely serious offense to violate U.S. money-laundering laws, breaking tax and exchange-control laws in other countries, particularly when Israel is the beneficiary, is less important than repeated parking violations. The court sentenced the rabbi to thirty days of community service.[56]

The case was not an aberration. For years the FBI had been trying to crack a network—embracing New York, Miami, Montreal, and Tel Aviv, and with subsidiary links to other cities—run by Hasidic Jews who used yeshivas as fronts for laundering allegedly up to $200 million a year. The Hasidim would place the money in New York branches of Israeli banks, claiming it was from cash donations to religious institutions, and collect a commission for themselves and for the participating yeshiva.[57] Subsequently the money whizzed to Panama, Colombia, the Cayman Islands, and Israel. One of the launderers, then hiding in Israel, noted to a reporter: "Only the laws of the Torah dictate our conduct, and there is nothing in them which prohibits laundering money." The reporter pressed on, "But the money comes from drugs." To which the response was, "Yes, but we are allowed to turn a blind eye and to say that because the money passes through many hands before reaching us, it does not really come from drugs. Most of us do not launder money for the drug dealers. But I would say that I do not have a moral problem. I usually get the money from a person like yourself, and that makes my conscience clear."[58]

The investigation was a long and painful process. The FBI was only too aware of how it would be denounced if word got out its agents were running undercover operations against ultra-Orthodox Jews. There was also the efficiency of the system. The kingpin was apparently a former Mossad officer who, from his Tel Aviv office, ran it as slickly as any intelligence operation, with safe houses for the couriers and a system of informants providing counterintelligence. Not least was the difficulty in finding informants. As one participant noted, "If a Jew would dare to speak to Gentiles about Jewish money laundering, he knows that he would be ostracized for his entire life." Indeed, the FBI's first investigative attempt collapsed in 1991 when the person hired as a Hebrew translator tipped off the targets. The translator, it seems, had been sufficiently uncomfortable tracking Jewish criminals that he consulted a rabbi, who concurred that taking down the drug-money-laundering ring would constitute an attack on Israel and advised him to warn those whose activities were being monitored.[59] A later attempt was more successful.[60]

In 1994 yet another laundering scandal involved Hasidic rabbis. The head of an ultra-Orthodox sect in Los Angeles who found himself in deep financial trouble after a real estate collapse tried to cover the hole first by trafficking in stolen cashier's checks. When the FBI floated in an undercover agent posing as a drug trafficker, they discovered the rabbi had a second scheme to restore his fortunes. He bragged to the agent that his couriers could fly up to $5 million a week to New York, where it would be turned over to Hasidic diamond dealers who operate strictly in cash and seal all deals with a handshake. After putting the money in their accounts, the diamond merchants would wire it to Switzerland. Then it could return to the United States in the form of payments into the accounts of the rabbi's religious institutions. To put the operation at the drug dealer's disposal, the rabbi wanted only 30 percent of the laundered amount. Alternatively, he offered to buy the drug money outright by using checks forged on the bank accounts of a local insurance company. And in case the FBI agent was feeling insecure, the rabbi's principal accomplice in the scheme offered to sell the agent a batch of assault rifles.[61]

Even that was not the end of the story. In 1997 another FBI operation nailed two Brooklyn rabbis and a group of Colombian drug dealers. The rabbis took cash from the dealers, broke it down into sums below the reporting threshold, put it into yeshiva accounts, and then offered the dealers checks written on those accounts. The proceeds were used to purchase aircraft appropriate for drug running, or it was sent off to safety in Switzerland.[62]

Seeing the World

Once the money is sent abroad, it is time for stage two of the laundering cycle—moving it through the international payments system to obscure the trail.

Contrary to stereotypes, only a rank amateur would arrive at the front door of a Swiss bank with a suitcase of high-denomination U.S. notes and demand to open a "numbered" account.[63] That would both begin and end the would-be launderer's life of crime.

Certainly Switzerland has plenty of appeal as a financial haven. It is stable politically; the Swiss franc is strong; the country plays a major role in the world gold market; and it has a variety of banking institutions. Some are powerful global players that combine commercial and investment banking with fund management and brokerage services. Some are small, discreet private banks that are specialized in handling the affairs of the "high-net-worth individual."

In the early years, the cornerstone of Switzerland's appeal was its bank secrecy laws, which made it a criminal offense for a bank officer to reveal information about an account holder. The Swiss would waive secrecy on the request of another government if there was serious evidence a depositor might have committed an offense that was also a crime under Swiss law, but because Switzerland had no exchange controls and treated tax evasion as purely a civil matter, the great majority of probes were blocked from the outset. Even when the Swiss agreed to allow foreign police access to bank data, they insisted that the police ignore any evidence of tax evasion.[64]

During the late 1980s and the 1990s, however, the Swiss authorities signed various treaties in which they agreed to cooperate with other countries in matters of criminal investigation. They then moved to freeze the accounts of persons suspected of crimes ranging from embezzlement by heads of state to insider trading to bribery. They abolished the practice of allowing a lawyer to substitute his or her name for that of a client as the beneficial owner of an account. Indeed, the Swiss highest court ruled that when lawyers act as fund managers, their transactions cease to be protected by attorney-client privilege. Switzerland also made money laundering a crime per se. It later tightened the law to require that all financial institutions, not just banks, report suspicious transactions on pain of imprisonment of their officers.

Of course, given the size and historical reputation of the Swiss financial system, much criminal money undoubtedly still seeks refuge there. But the smart money is undoubtedly subjected to a prewashing elsewhere—in any of the more than forty jurisdictions in the world currently offering the protection of various types of bank secrecy. These various types of secrecy include:

- Accounts in which the client must reveal his or her identity but officials of the bank are bound by law never to reveal it without court authorization.
- Accounts coded in such a way that only the top management can know who the beneficial owner is, and secrecy laws prevent management from revealing that information.
- Accounts protected by bank secrecy law and by nominee ownership in which the nominee and the beneficial owner are connected by civil contract or simply by a bond of trust (or fear).
- Accounts in which a lawyer interposes between bank and client, thereby protecting the client's identity, first, by bank secrecy law and, second, by a layer of lawyer-client privilege.
- Accounts in which the client can request (perhaps under pressure from law enforcement) that the bank lift the protection of bank secrecy law.
- Accounts in which bank secrecy law forbids that the bank reveal information, even if the client so requests.

- Accounts that are completely anonymous in that no employee of the bank can possibly know, unless the clients themselves reveal it, who the beneficial owners are.

Secrecy can be further facilitated by avoiding use of signatures. In Hong Kong, for example, it was possible to open a "chop account." Although the senior officers of the bank knew the identity of the account holder, all deposits and withdrawals were conducted using a special seal or stamp. In Southeast Asia, the historical standard has been a piece of elegantly carved ivory. Some Caribbean haven banks offer a similar service to Americans, but with a suitable cultural adaptation—depositors transact their business using rubber stamps with images of Goofy and Mickey Mouse.

Except in the case of totally anonymous accounts, however—a species currently threatened with extinction—bank secrecy can be waived by any financial haven in the event of a criminal investigation. It can also be broken by bribery or espionage. As a result, the most fundamental rules in money laundering are to avoid contact between the bank account and the databases police are known to search, to use private mail drops, and to keep one's mouth shut. These rules also demand that illicit money be held not by an individual (even in a "numbered" account) but by a corporation. Therefore, before sending money to the haven of choice, the launderer will probably call on one of the many jurisdictions that sell offshore corporations, that is, corporations licensed to conduct business only outside the country of incorporation, free of tax or regulation, and protected by corporate secrecy laws. There are many options, although the traditional favorites have been Liberia, the Cayman Islands, the British Virgin Islands, and especially Panama.

Panama was born to serve. It was created in 1903 when the United States, seeking a location for a canal to span the isthmus, sponsored a revolution in the most northerly province of Colombia. The next year legislation to entrench the U.S. dollar as the new country's currency was drafted, appropriately enough, by the U.S. secretary of war.[65] Panama subsequently put in place the infrastructure for free-trade facilities and a flag-of-convenience ship registry. It passed its first bank secrecy law in 1917, tightened it in 1941, reinforced it with Swiss-style coded accounts in 1959, and strengthened it further with offshore banking legislation in 1970. Soon it was not just the largest offshore center in the Americas but almost a Central Bank to other countries' offshore banks—they would accept deposits, then move the money to Panama. The official status of the U.S. dollar played a doubly facilitative role. It assured financial stability. And because 20 percent of the business of the multi-billion-dollar free trade zone is usually conducted in cash, once suitcases full of dirty dollars arrive in Panama, they become indistinguishable from the proceeds of normal activities such as cigarette smuggling or embargo busting. Not least, Panama was perhaps the hemispheric pioneer in corporate secrecy laws and in setting up an instant corporation manufacturing business. Local lawyers create companies in job lots, peddling them to customers as varied as Fortune 500 corporations "avoiding" taxes to Colombian drug smugglers evading detection.[66]

An insta-corporation can be made to measure or purchased off the shelf. The second is preferable. Not only is it usually cheaper to acquire a secondhand company, but the fact that it has a history of activity increases the appearance of legitimacy—provided it was not formerly used for trafficking heroin. Once the corporation is set up in the offshore jurisdiction, a bank deposit is made in the haven of choice in the name of that offshore company. In this way, several protective layers are built between the entrepreneur and the law enforcement authorities: one level of bank secrecy, one level of corporate secrecy, and possibly the additional protection of attorney-client privilege if a lawyer in one of the haven countries, preferably a different haven country than the one that hosts the company, has been designated to set up and run the company.

In addition, some laundering schemes use yet another layer of cover, that of the offshore trust. There are some legal reasons for the establishment of offshore trusts (mainly estate planning), some dubious ones (such as dodging decisions of a bankruptcy or divorce court), and a few that are clearly criminal. When the owner of assets conveys their ownership to a trust, those assets cannot be seized by creditors. Offshore trusts are usually protected by secrecy laws and often contain a "flee clause," which permits, indeed compels, the trustee to shift the domicile of the trust whenever the trust is threatened—by war, civil unrest, or law enforcement probes. The obvious disadvantage is the nominal loss of control by the owner—in theory, a deed of trust is irrevocable, and the former owner can influence but not control the actions of the trustee.[67]

Although usually trusts are restricted to countries with an English Common Law tradition, the major exception is Liechtenstein. More a family corporation than a country, Liechtenstein had been ruined economically by the dismantling of the Austro-Hungarian Empire after World War I. In 1930, partly with a view to recovery and partly with a view to finding an effective way to manage the family fortune, the ruling family steered the country into the tax haven business. Then, after World War II, they accelerated the process. Today Liechtenstein's three leading industries are, appropriately enough, false teeth, sausage skins, and shell corporations.

The country has other attractions. It boasts no political entanglements and the Swiss franc as its currency. And it has a unique legal infrastructure. Its *anstalt*, unlike most trusts, is a commercial entity capable of doing business; it permits the transferor of the assets to be the ultimate beneficiary, thereby undermining the notion that a conveyance is irrevocable. Liechtenstein also offers a *stiftung*, a trust in which the founder can at any time change his or her mind about the nature of the provisions, although this trust cannot conduct any commercial activity.[68]

Today those advantages are much diminished. The very term *anstalt*, which by law must appear in the company name, now serves as a red flag for foreign revenue authorities and law enforcement officers. That means greater competition from the "asset-protection trusts" offered by many former and current British dependencies. If suitably set up, such trusts can convey the advantages of the Liechtenstein model without attracting the attention. Assets could be conveyed to an offshore company; control of the company could be transferred to the offshore asset-protection trust; the person transferring the assets could arrange to be appointed manager of the company; and the trust deed might stipulate that the transferor had the right to buy the assets back again for a nominal sum, thereby respecting the letter of the law of trusts while trampling all over its spirit.

Whatever the exact form it takes, the offshore asset-protection trust creates yet another layer of secrecy and security in a money-laundering scheme. And it can be complemented by yet more tricks and devices.

For example, companies can be capitalized with bearer shares so there is no owner of record anywhere—the person who physically possesses the share certificates owns the company. The share certificates might then be parked in a safety deposit box in a Channel Islands trust company that has no other connection to the individual who set up the laundering operation. However, bearer shares must be paid up in full, and they can also be lost; for that reason, some experts counsel that it is preferable to simply use regular shares registered in the names of trusted proxies.

There can be multiple systems of interlocking companies all incorporated in different places, forcing law enforcement officers to proceed from jurisdiction to jurisdiction to peel them away like layers of an onion. In one case the City of London Serious Fraud Squad spent years unscrambling a network of companies. When they reached the end of the trail, all they found was a Liberian shell that the owner, figuring they deserved a pat on the back for getting that far, had thoughtfully named "Congratulations Inc."

Alternatively, each asset—including a yacht and a Miami condo—could be held by a different offshore company with no obvious connection.

Thus, in the event of an investigation, the authorities might be satisfied if they got their hands on only one.

There can be multiple bank transfers from country to country, with each transfer protected by secrecy laws that must be breached one at a time. Better still, transfers can be disaggregated into smaller amounts and routed through different channels before being reunited. And the trail can be broken on occasion, with the launderer picking up the money in cash from a bank in one place, redepositing it in a bank somewhere else, perhaps in a different currency, and then wiring it to yet a third location. This is even better if the entrepreneur cloaks each transfer behind a different identity, perhaps using multiple passports.

For yet another layer of cover, entrepreneurs concerned about possible leaks in bank secrecy can make it truly ironclad—by owning the offshore bank through which they run their money.

Shark Bait

There are skeptics who insist that owning an insta-bank is like buying a title of nobility—pure foppery of no use in achieving greater financial privacy. On the other hand, there are those who claim it has many advantages.[69] The bank is unlikely to balk, or holler for the cops, if the owner turns up with a suitcase of cash or tries to deposit checks issued by clients under false names. Because the launderer is the direct beneficiary, there are unlikely to be serious objections to hefty fees for high-quality service, particularly if they can be deducted against taxable income back in the launderer's country of domicile. The bank could take title to the owner's property, which would help render it immune to court action by estranged spouses, defrauded business partners, tax authorities, or police. That is just for starters.

There is also prestige, which can be turned to business advantage, from flashing a bank director's or president's card. And the bank itself will always stand ready to provide the owner with a glowing reference. Granted, a very small institution might not inspire much international respect. But the apparent size can be increased by the simple device of lending assets to spouses or friends, who immediately redeposit them. Done many times, this can have miraculous effects on asset volume and "earnings" shown on the bank's books, particularly because obliging rent-an-auditors abound in haven jurisdictions. Even better, one insta-bank can beget another. It is easier and much less costly to set up a bank in some of the more heavily regulated jurisdictions if the applicant is another bank rather than an individual or commercial corporation.

Some advantages are more tangible. Banks often grant each other discounts on commission charges for stock or bond purchases or other financial services. Interest rates on loans, too, tend to be lower if the borrower is another bank. Even better, any deposits the bank happens to attract from outside can be lent to the bank's owners at prime minus prime. Ownership of a bank even permits interest-free loans from creditors. If the owner settles debts with checks drawn on the offshore bank, it will take six to eight weeks for them to clear, and in the meantime the money can be put to other uses.

Nor is this the end of the list. Items such as unfinished (or purely imaginary) condo projects in tropical retreats, "insurance" policies, or fake stocks and options are much easier to sell if the pitch includes a bank guarantee. The bank can issue letters of credit to persons whom more straight-laced institutions would refuse, and then collect fat fees. It can attract deposits by promises of high rates and secrecy, and then divert the money; the type of clientele attracted is unlikely to be in a position to complain. Because an offshore bank is, by definition, immune from national credit controls, it can run an international loan-sharking business, charging extortionate rates to desperate borrowers. And a truly enterprising owner can get the bank to issue a certificate of deposit (CD), pledge that CD to another bank as collateral for a loan, and then disappear with the money.

Such uses of insta-banks date back at least to the 1960s, when four Americans, one with a history of charges (although no convictions) for check fraud, opened the Bank of Sark on a three-mile-long chunk of rock in the English Channel. It sold policies from its one hundred captive "insurance" companies, peddled offshore mutual funds, and dealt in bank instruments such as international cashier's drafts, then commonly used for bank-to-bank settlements. If buyers of the drafts were unsuccessful in cashing them directly in unsuspecting banks elsewhere, they could be pledged as "collateral" for loans. Some were even used to buy automobiles and pay phone bills.[70]

The Bank of Sark lasted for about $40 million. During its era, and for some years later, it had few emulators. It was not until the 1980s when the pleasures a pvileges of bank ownership came seriously into vogue.

Some people seeking that status are content with an offshore company with the word "bank" in its name but without a banking license. One such company was European Overseas Bank Ltd. of Grenada, owned by a woman who ran a Houston loan-brokerage firm—when she was not trying to dodge efforts by the Bahamian police to arrest her for real estate fraud. She would spin tales of her family wealth to reassure clients that the advanced fees they paid for loans were secure. She collected nearly $2 million from sixty would-be borrowers, none of whom saw a penny of the supposed loans, before ending her banking career with a seven-year prison sentence.[71]

Although the uproar caused by sham banks has, in theory, caused regulators to monitor them more closely and to issue warnings when unauthorized persons use the term "bank" in their business's name, some escape through the cracks. One promoter recommends that if the potential clientele is German-speaking, for example, the would-be banker set up a Cayman Islands company (or, for that matter, an even cheaper one in Delaware), with "Kreditanstalt" in its name. To British or U.S. officials, there would be no offense because the company does not call itself a "bank," whereas the German-speaking clientele would see what the promoter wanted them to see. If the potential pool of customers were English-speaking, the company could be called General Bank Supplies Inc. or even the Douglas Fairbanks & and Savings Corp.

Still, to get the full advantage, it is necessary to acquire a properly licensed bank. There are two routes. One is to apply directly to a haven jurisdiction. That reduces costs but is slow and uncertain. The alternative is to obtain one directly off the shelf, primed, and ready to go. For nearly two decades the most renowned primer was Jerome Schneider.[72]

Schneider began his business career by hacking into computers of Pacific Telephone, ordering equipment, and diverting it to accommodation addresses, where henchmen were waiting to unload it on the black market. He was caught and briefly jailed, but on his release he set up WFI Corporation in Los Angeles, a vehicle initially used for selling Cayman Islands shell companies before it branched into the insta-bank business.[73] His first stops were Anguilla and St. Vincent, then Montserrat, a little later the U.S. Pacific trust territories, then the Caribbean again; these peregrinations depended on the reaction of local authorities to British or U.S. pressure and to the outrage of those swindled by Schneider's clients.[74]

Schneider would acquire bank licenses wholesale, then retail them. His seminars preaching the virtues of an offshore existence were well received—so much so that one U.S. federal agent attending such a seminar spotted undercover investigators from three other agencies in the audience.[75] From 1976 to 1991, Schneider sold between six hundred to seven hundred banks along with offshore insurance companies and mutual funds. Although his average bank price was about $35,000, in 1991 he advertised a special clearance sale of Bahamas banks for only $9,900 each.[76] By working through Schneider, in a few days an aspiring banker could have a prelicensed institution in a tax-free jurisdiction with strict bank secrecy laws, usually with no minimum capitalization, blessed with a low annual renewal fee, with preprinted letters of credit and CDs, and even the possibility of shares held by nominees or issued in bearer form. Lack of experience was no obstacle: WFI could arrange for an international management company to run the show.

Although several jurisdictions licensed insta-banks, none achieved the notoriety of Montserrat. It owed its start to the happy confluence of two forces. One was British stinginess. Eager to reduce the aid sent annually to its Caribbean colonies, Britain encouraged local leaders to emulate the success of the Cayman Islands in developing financial services.[77] Not only did Montserrat offer bank secrecy, but it soon offered the banks themselves. That caught the attention of the second force—the whirlwind marketing efforts of Jerome Schneider. Together they assured that by the end of the 1980s, Montserrat, an island of about 14,000 people (before it was devastated by a volcano), was the proud host of nearly 350 "banks," with approximately 200 of them sold through Schneider's efforts. If the bank was purchased directly from the government, the initial license fee was only $3,000, and the annual renewal cost another $8,000; however, the first year's cost rose to $30,000 or more if the bank was obtained through Jerome Schneider.[78]

Apart from ease of acquisition, there were many other attractions to locating in Montserrat (or any other British colony). Such a location conveyed to potential clients the impression that the banks were underwritten in some way by the Bank of England, if not by the Queen herself. And the island gave its banks bipartisan support: the chief minister, who was also the finance minister, signed their licenses, and one of the leading opposition figures ran a law office that administered fifty-three of them.[79]

Some of Schneider's clients were other banks. When Panama came under U.S. pressure to clean up its drug-money-laundering act, some of its banks created an additional level of cover through Montserrat affiliates. But most customers were entrepreneurs. They included "Brother Eduardo" of the Circles of Light Church, who solicited donations from Americans to help "starving children all over the world." He promised to invest their donations in a scheme that would generate a forty fold return. Some thirty thousand people sent in more than $3 million to the brother's First American Bank before the FBI broke up the operation.

There were those who criticized Schneider's work. But he was ready to defend it right to the top. Before a committee of the U.S. Senate, he insisted on the upstanding character of his customers. Some, he claimed, did not even use their banks as banks; they just "keep them as status symbols, like having an extra Rolls Royce in the garage."[80] Of those who did use the banks for business, Schneider cited, as an example, J. David Dominelli.

Dominelli, who ran a foreign exchange operation in the United States, took Montserrat by storm, promising to invest $40 million in local development. He certainly had the money, even though it was not his own. His pledge of a 40 percent rate of return attracted $120 million from twelve hundred investors from across the United States. The funds were deposited in Dominelli's Montserrat insta-bank, then diverted to high-return investments such as luxury cars, wild parties, and real estate loans to friends. When the operation crashed, $80 million went missing. Dominelli was later given twenty years of leisure to pursue his studies of high finance.[81]

Jerome Schneider took the demise of Dominelli and his bank in stride. Among his later efforts were Chase Overseas, Deutsche (Suisse) Ltd., Manufacturers Overseas Bank Ltd., and World Bank Ltd. There was even one that made a virtue of calling itself exactly what it was—Blue Sky International Bank. Some of Schneider's Montserrat creations achieved a notoriety beyond their names. The Commonwealth Overseas Bank bilked a British missionary in East Africa out his savings by selling him worthless CDs. The owners of the Union Bank of Commerce, with a paid-up capital of $2.00, attempted to borrow $4 million from a British bank; they offered as collateral a $5 million CD issued by their bank six weeks after it had been officially closed by the Montserrat authorities. Owners of the Zurich Overseas Bank ran advanced fee scams across the United States. Would-be borrowers were apparently undeterred by the fact that the bank's physical facilities consisted of a fax machine underneath the bar in a Montserrat tavern owned by one of the bank's proprietors.[82]

Alas, success bred jealousy. Under British and U.S. pressure, Montserrat revoked licenses of the three most notorious and sent warning letters to sixty-two others. However, the chief minister commented: "I still think the banks are a good idea." Refusing to be appeased, the British staged a constitutional coup d'état. Control of international financial matters was taken away from elected officials and vested in the Crown-appointed governor. Interestingly, a year after losing office, the chief minister himself was charged with conspiracy to defraud the government. Montserrat ultimately closed down 220 banks.[83]

Of course Montserrat was not alone in the Caribbean insta-bank business, or in the scandals. Bargain hunters may have preferred Anguilla, where set-up costs were lower but the quality of the company perhaps higher. It was in Anguilla, for example, that former U.S. Secretary of the Treasury Robert B. Anderson parked fees he earned as financial counsel to the Reverend Sun Myung Moon when Moon was facing tax fraud charges. Anderson also advised his other legal clients that the U.S. banking system was unstable and that they too were better off depositing their savings in his Commercial Exchange Bank and Trust. There, Anderson assured them, they could find the benefits of "absolute client anonymity" in a "tax-free environment" prior to the funds being recycled back into (also tax-free) investments in an energy project run by another business associate. Unfortunately the Anguilla bank's co-owner was convicted of money laundering; the manager of the energy venture pleaded guilty to a fraud that swallowed up $4.4 million of the depositors' money; and in 1987, Anderson himself was convicted of tax evasion along with violations of banking law.[84]

Another person to appreciate the benefits of Anguilla banking was Rabbi Joseph Prushinowski. This leader of a small Hasidic sect first earned his financial credentials in Britain in the early 1970s, where, using fictitious invoices from his import-export company, he stiffed the value-added tax authorities for $600,000. In 1975 he turned up in New York City, where he used phony financial statements from two trading companies to secure from Manufacturers' Hanover Bank a $300,000 loan, which he never repaid. Even better, he deposited in his account bogus checks drawn on foreign and out-of-state banks supposedly worth $4.3 million and persuaded the bank, while it was waiting for the checks to clear, to grant him a $1.25 million overdraft. He was arrested in 1977 but fled to Canada. Arrested again in 1981, he was sent back to the United States, where he copped a three-year sentence. Out of jail, he tried valiantly to fight extradition proceedings started by the British government, pleading variously that the offense charged was not extraditable and that in a British jail he would face the cruel and unusual punishment of starvation because all they would offer him was "unclean" food. Unimpressed, the judge ordered the extradition. In the interim, however, the rabbi had fled to Israel to renew his rudely interrupted financial career, this time in the offshore sector. On his new theory, instead of using fictitious financial statements and drawing bogus checks on real banks, he would use legitimate financial statements to open accounts in real banks, then deposit into them checks drawn on completely bogus banks.[85]

Soon "checks" on his Union Bank of Anguilla were turning up in the hands of banks and commodity brokers on three continents. Repeating his Manny Hanny success, for example, the rabbi deposited $3,725,000 in phony checks with the Bank of New York and was granted a credit line of

$1 million. The next year he closed the Anguilla bank and vanished. But in 1987, using another alias, he opened two more banks in Anguilla and used them, with the assistance of another rabbi later convicted of money laundering, to run a check-kiting fraud against Bank of America in Los Angeles. A short time later Prushinowski moved his financial headquarters to Grenada, where his Republic Bank became the centerpiece of a $250 million property scam in London. Meanwhile, as the arrest warrants piled up, Prushinowski remained safely ensconced in Israel, where his money and political influence kept him from harm. To each query from police forces around the world the Israeli government insisted it could not find the "robbing rabbi."[86] He was finally arrested in 1998 but never extradited.

Not all the insta-bank activity occurs in the Caribbean. Even before Jerome Schneider started touting the virtues of the U.S. Trust Territories in the South Pacific, Tonga had gotten a jump on bank wholesalers by selling charters to favored individuals. The first was an American named John Meier, who fled the United States ahead of a civil suit that charged he had embezzled several million from Howard Hughes and a criminal prosecution that charged him with tax evasion. Arriving in Tonga, Meier wooed the king with promises of economic development—airports, luxury hotels, shipbuilding, and the like—and talked his way into a diplomatic passport, a ninety-nine-year monopoly on merchant-banking activities, and a charter for the Bank of the South Pacific. But when Meier failed to deliver and the United States put pressure on the kingdom, the bank license and diplomatic passport were lifted. Meier was later arrested in Vancouver and extradited back to the United States.[87]

That was not the end of Tonga's adventures in the insta-bank trade. A short time later an institution with a similar name, the International Bank of the South Pacific, was chartered by a Mormon bishop with a passion for sports memorabilia. He attracted deposits from fellow Mormons by promising high rates of tax-free interest; he recycled the money back to the United States into a local sports museum and other ventures, and then emptied the contents of the museum along with the bank account before absconding.[88]

In the meantime, Jerome Schneider had come calling, albeit his main interest was the North Marianas. In short order he purchased fifty bank licenses and resold thirty-eight of them, stressing the fact that his banks combined two virtues: they were impervious to the U.S. tax collector, yet their deposits were protected by the U.S. Federal Deposit Insurance Corporation.[89] One of his contented customers was a California father-son team, David and Mark Pedley; together they opened the Merchant Bank and Trust Company of Saipan in 1982, at a time when Mexico had imposed exchange controls and the peso had started to nosedive. Their prime targets were Americans who had sneaked money off to Mexico to evade U.S. taxes, only to find that their dollar deposits were forcibly converted to pesos and that the funds were reconvertable only at a very unfavorable rate—an action that might also expose them to the IRS. The father-son team came to the rescue: they offered the American tax dodgers, as well as some Mexicans seeking to get money out of the country, a deal in which, in return for their pesos, they would be immediately lent back 50 percent in U.S. dollars, while the rest was supposedly invested in U.S.–dollar CDs. The CDs were well secured—by $10 million worth of State of Texas Veterans' Land Bonds, purchased for six cents on the dollar with forty years to maturity. That sufficed to coax out of their investors $14 million, of which $6 million was skimmed by the promoters in profit.[90]

With all the bad publicity, the United States took the opportunity to press the local government to raise sharply the minimum capital requirements of new banks and to review the licenses already granted. None of Schneider's thirty-eight were renewed. A few years later came the collapse of Montserrat's offshore banking sector. Hence, in 1991, Schneider announced he was getting out of the bank brokerage business. He cited tightening regulations as the reason.[91] But he may also have felt the heat from new competitors for a shrinking market. Some came from a Dutch broker operating through a post office box in Gibraltar, who sold banks in the Caribbean and South Pacific for between $12,000 and $15,000. Even worse, the Nauru International Services Corporation (of Arizona) in 1990 started offering banks on that Pacific island for a mere $7,500.[92]

Nauru is scarcely a tropical paradise. A former British colony, it faced depletion of the guano mines, which had long provided the main source of hard currency. Meanwhile, ecological destruction from the mines precluded much tourism. Hence the government, in desperation, decided to promote the financial services sector. Aided by the fact that its currency was the Australian dollar, it soon became a major center for offshore trust companies, and a little later it acquired a reputation for hosting the cheapest insta-banks in the world. Although holders of a license had to show within two years a paid-up capital of A$100,000, that requirement could be met simply by having another institution attest to the money's existence. Although Nauru offshore banks were in theory forbidden to accept retail deposits, no one checked. And although Nauru is hardly prime territory from which to launch a career in international banking, the bank-licensing procedures provided easy access to more desirable ones. For A$3,000 a promoter acquired a Nauru bank license, then applied for a Vanuatu license in the name of the Nauru bank. Although a private individual had to demonstrate paid-up capital of US$150,000 to get a Vanuatu license, a banking institution had to show only $10,000. Once the Vanuatu license was approved, the promoter could sell the Nauru charter and recover the initial fee, or possibly even make a profit.[93] Indeed, the attractions of Nauru were such that ten years after he was supposed to be out of the business, Jerome Schneider has his records seized by the IRS during their investigation of a fraud allegedly involving a Nauru bank Schneider had sold for $70,000.[94]

Thus, one way or another, the underground entrepreneur has the opportunity to improve the banking service he or she receives, and perhaps pick up a little business income on the side, through the device of the insta-bank, although an entrepreneur intent on laundering money might well find that pulling off an international letters of credit fraud from some exotic location does little to reduce one's financial profile. This process of improving bank service can be taken one step further: in addition to an insta-bank, the entrepreneur might acquire an insta-country to host it. Even before the great bank rush of the 1980s, there was already a movement afoot, among those dissatisfied with the services of existing haven countries, to have new ones made to order.

Just Add Water and Stir

From the vantage point of the new millennium, the notion of creating a country no longer appears far-fetched. During the last decade of the twentieth century, countries seemed to come into existence at a rate suggesting a conspiracy between cartographers and atlas publishers. Yet in the 1970s and 1980s, when the world was living in a Cold War–induced geopolitical freeze, the antics of insta-country manufacturers were seen as idiosyncratic, if not insane.[95] Furthermore, back then they peddled not the "ideal" of ethnic nationalism but something more practical—the desire to mold banking and tax law in congenial ways. Most of the efforts of would-be founding fathers focused on microstates, particularly tropical islands lacking natural resources, in the hopes that no one with clout in the world arena would care much if a small piece of territory took on new management. For those attempting to create such new countries, there were several blueprints they could—and still can—follow.

STATE OF MIND

The most elementary model is the spiritual state, although this type is more typical of tax evaders than sophisticated money launderers. In the United

States, survivalist groups of all political hues dot California and parts of the Midwest. Some have opted out of society completely. By definition, they enjoy the ultimate in bank secrecy because they rarely, if ever, have occasion to enter a bank's premises. Some—those with a libertarian ideology that looks forward not to the political liberation of all races or creeds but to the fiscal liberation of a handful of middle-class whites—variously denounce the tax and regulatory system as unconstitutional, form barter networks, insist that gold is the only legal money, and revel in public confrontation with the fiscal and monetary authorities.

So it is with Americans who follow "Christian common law." Because their objective is to end all legal obligations to the existing government and create their own communities, they feel that it would be an act of desecration to pay taxes. Besides, they argue, because they are ambassadors of Christ on earth, they have diplomatic immunity. Still, their faith does not entirely preclude worldly pursuits. One devout community created the Common Title Bond and Trust, which issued "sight drafts" to members seeking an ordained legal tender. Unfortunately Uncle Sam did not share their views on diplomatic immunity, and one of their ministers ended up in jail for using a sight draft to buy farm machinery.[96]

Sovereignty, followers of Christian common law might argue, is a state of mind. But as their minister's fate illustrated, it also helps to have a piece of territory with its own legal and monetary system, or at least its own militia force to keep "revenooers" at bay. That was the objective of the most notorious of the far-right tax protest groups that flourished in the United States in the 1980s, although they went into decline (or perhaps just deeper underground) after the mid-1990s.

Unlike the Farmers' Liberation Army of Kansas, the National Freedom Movement in Montana, the United Tax Action Patriots in Texas, or the Silent Brotherhood of Washington, Posse Comitatus spread across several states. Midwestern farmers were a natural target of the Posse's recruiters. During the 1980s, when heavy debts and low prices led to widespread farm bankruptcies and foreclosures, Posse members would show up to block farm tax-auctions and disrupt foreclosure sales.[97]

Posse Comitatus was less an organization than a collection of small groups of like mind, whose members individually might also support the ideology of other associations, such as those fighting abortion or gun control. Adherents were survivalists. Well armed and trained to use firepower, they stored not just weapons but freeze-dried and nonperishable goods as part of their preparations for Armageddon. Their work was not purely defensive, however. As followers of the Identity faith, which sees Americans as the chosen people and the United States as the promised land, their objective was to save America from the coalition of Jewish Communists and "money czars" that holds it captive.[98] If there were a year in which such captivity began, they would say it was 1913, which saw both the creation of the Federal Reserve system to monopolize the issuance of paper money and the introduction of the income tax. Posse members are impelled by their principles to target both. One Posse stalwart, Gordon Kahl, before he was martyred in a gunfight with IRS agents, claimed that income taxes form one of the ten principles of the Communist Manifesto.[99]

Individual members' actions against the tax system vary. The archbishop of the Posse-affiliated Life Science Bible Church, for example, spent two years selling ministerial credentials, and the tax exemption that supposedly went with them, before being jailed on twenty-one counts of tax fraud.[100] Others attended special evasion seminars, where they were advised to, first, close all bank accounts, dissolve any corporations, and wait a couple years for records to become dormant; next to tell employers to stop deducting taxes at source; and then to identify themselves publicly as "sovereign" Americans. Finally, they were to stop filing tax returns or to file with only their name and address, perhaps with the Posse statement of principles attached. Some went further. They used cash and barter to avoid detection of part of their transactions, created bogus family trusts or inflated other deductions, or created their own special deductions such as a substantial downward "conscience adjustment" on the sum due. Once again their tactics were not purely defensive. A favorite ploy was to file forms telling the IRS they had paid certain sums to certain people—usually judges, law enforcement agents, or even other IRS agents—to trigger tax investigations of the targeted individuals.

The monetary system, with its banks and paper money, was almost as repulsive to them as was the income tax, particularly because the monetary system assists the government in enforcing the income tax. Because, as they saw things, the only legal money was gold and silver, any income received in paper money or by check was by definition not taxable. Therefore Posse members employed barter, using in particular a system of barter houses that stretched across several states. These houses, which kept their membership lists confidential, permitted members to convert cash into silver bullion and gold coin, without receipts or records. If the member chose to keep bullion on deposit, any affiliate could pay bills on his or her behalf; if the member needed cash, the barter house stood ready to buy back a portion of the silver and gold. Although the barter houses maintained regular bank accounts, transactions were conducted in the name of the house, not individual members, thus preserving their anonymity.[101] As with the tax system, the monetary order was also a target of more aggressive action, although with less than happy results. In 1988, Posse's director of counterinsurgency was arrested in a scheme to print up to $100,000 per week in fake U.S. notes, smuggle them abroad, exchange them for bona fide foreign currencies, sneak the foreign money back home, and exchange it into U.S. currency—with the proceeds used to finance paramilitary activities.[102]

SHIP OF STATE?

The success of spiritually defined nations in laundering money is decidedly limited. Therefore some take the process of asserting sovereignty a step further, using the "ship of state" model. This model involves sailing a vessel into international waters and proclaiming independence. Then the vessel can be used for gambling, unregulated securities trading, the dispensing of banned therapies, and so forth. If the authorities of a nearby jurisdiction decide to interfere, the captain of the ship of state can simply weigh anchor. One user of this method was Scientology-at-Sea.

The Church of Scientology was founded in 1957 when L. Ron Hubbard, a successful science fiction author, declared to his followers that he had visited heaven—twice. He used the resulting revelations to build a religion whose operational headquarters were in Liberia. The church bragged of a maze of subsidiaries and ten million followers worldwide, although skeptics put the actual number at a tiny fraction of that figure. For a potential convert, the theological process started with a free personality test, which inevitably revealed that the person had serious problems. Next came an "auditing" session to probe the nature of those problems, costing upward of $500 an hour and paid in the form of a donation rather than a fee for service, which would have imperiled the church's tax-exempt status. Then came the sale of self-improvement courses. Meanwhile the church's parishioners formed a captive clientele for Hubbard's many books and pamphlets. Much of the proceeds flowed out of the United States, the church's main market, to Switzerland, Luxembourg, and Liechtenstein, with "priests" as couriers.

The idea of casting off earth-bound constraints seems to have originated when Hubbard realized that in an earlier life, he had been Cecil Rhodes. During the late 1970s, he had tried to set up in white-ruled Rhodesia, then under siege for its unilateral declaration of independence from Britain. Hubbard had planned to dig up all the gold and diamonds he was convinced Cecil Rhodes had hidden and, more immediately, to buy a luxury hotel, then going for cheap, in Salisbury, from where he would operate a Scientology-for-the-well-heeled affiliate. When that plan failed, Hubbard himself declared a form of unilateral independence. For the next several years he sailed around the world in search of buried treasure, ministering to the faithful, and fleeing to another safe harbor if local authorities got nosy.[103]

There are obvious drawbacks to this route to national independence. Floating clinics, casinos, and even churches may have worked in the past, but no one has yet succeeded in getting a ship of state plugged into the international financial system as a sovereign actor. Even if cyber-technology solves that problem, another serious one remains. The last two decades have seen a dramatic resurgence of piracy, a profession whose practitioners might well find a floating country, with its foreign exchange reserves locked in the ship's strongbox, a target too tempting to pass up.

HOSTILE TAKEOVER BIDS

Given these problems with countries that are either states of mind or all at sea, founding fathers have tried to persuade existing states to sell off a piece of territory. If that scheme has failed, they then might have tried a hostile takeover bid; that is, they might have made a grab for a chunk to create their own country, or they might have tried to "persuade" an existing microstate to change its laws. The underlying logic is that there would be little chance of an outside police agency penetrating the country's secrecy laws if the founding fathers were standing, assault rifles in hand, just behind the president's desk when he takes that phone call from Washington.

These pioneers fall into several discrete professional categories—career mobsters, mercenaries, securities swindlers on the run, ultra-right-wing ideologues, and ex–intelligence agents—in various combinations. Their objectives are more standardized. From the new or reformed microstate, they seek passports, concessions for casinos, and charters for banks, perhaps with some free-port privileges or a locale for a gunrunning business. There have even been cases in which the main objective was to turn the captured islands into bases for busting sanctions on apartheid-era South Africa. The ideal haven country would be one blessed with the following characteristics:

- bank secrecy that cannot be waived even at the client's request;
- low or nonexistent income and capital gains taxes;
- no deals for sharing tax information with other countries;

- offshore trusts;
- instant corporations;
- tight corporate secrecy laws;
- excellent electronic communications;
- a large tourist trade to help explain major inflows of cash;
- a free-trade zone that uses a great deal of hard currency;
- circulation of a major world currency, preferably the U.S. dollar, as the local money;
- well-paid financial sector employees who are difficult to bribe;
- a geographic location that facilitates business travel to and from rich neighbors;
- a time zone that facilitates communication with world money centers;
- a government willing and able to resist outside pressure;
- perhaps a flag-of-convenience shipping registry;
- and also helpful, a history of use of the haven by the CIA to fund covert action.

The role, therefore, of founding fathers is to try to make the new home and native land approximate as closely as possible that ideal.

One of the earlier attempts to buy a new country was the handiwork of William Mellon Hitchcock, Wall Street broker, partial heir to the Mellon family fortune, and chief financial planner for the Brotherhood of Eternal Love, a California tax-exempt religious foundation that police later accused of peddling fully half the LSD flooding the U.S. market during the 1960s.[104] Hitchcock had first moved the drug profits to the Castle Bank and Trust in the Bahamas. It seemed a safe choice. Not only were there tight secrecy laws to protect the assets, but the bank had been set up by a former CIA officer, who balanced his concern with secret finance with a continued interest in covert politics. His former colleagues used the bank to finance part of the CIA secret war against Fidel Castro. But its three hundred American clients also included Hollywood stars, porn magazine publishers, and a prominent rock group.[105]

When the IRS moved in to close what it called the biggest tax evasion caper in U.S. history, the CIA intervened to block the investigation. Still, Castle Bank, its cover blown, moved to Panama. Billy Hitchcock, sensing the unhealthy interest the U.S. authorities were taking, also abandoned the Bahamas. First, he shifted both his own and the Brotherhood's money to a small bank in Switzerland, with which Hitchcock, in his stockbroker guise, had already built up a solid relationship. Later, he decided to make it really safe by helping the Brotherhood create its own country.

The target was Clipperton, a waterless flyspeck seven hundred miles off the Pacific coast of Mexico. A French possession since the mid-nineteenth-century guano boom, the island had had human inhabitants only during World War I; while France was otherwise preoccupied, Mexico had sent a group of "settlers." When Mexico itself got embroiled in civil war, it forgot to send supplies. The colonists spent some time murdering each other before the French sent a ship to remove the survivors. In the acid-enhanced imaginations of Billy and the Brotherhood, Clipperton was to be an independent republic with an economy on the LSD standard. Their main production facilities would relocate there, and it would become a tax haven, banking center, and money laundry. So Hitchcock decided to send an emissary to France to see if they could buy it. He gave the emissary $2,000 in walking-around money. The emissary landed in France and just kept walking.

Soon thereafter, one of Hitchcock's couriers was caught with $100,000 in cash. The courier decided to sing. But the song was not about LSD. Rather it concerned illegal stock trades through the Swiss bank. The ensuing scandal brought a hasty windup of the bank and reputedly wiped out much of the profit the Brotherhood had hidden there. Furthermore, Hitchcock was in midst of a nasty divorce, and his soon-to-be ex-spouse started talking publicly about his interest in psychedelics and Swiss bank accounts. After writing a check to the IRS to cover back taxes and a fine, Hitchcock did a deal. He pleaded guilty to two counts of tax and securities violations and received a five-year suspended sentence in return for becoming the star witness in the trials of the leading Brotherhood members.

In the 1970s and on into the 1980s, the most energetic promoter of insta-countries was Robert Vesco, the often-crowned king of American white-collar crime. Even before he went on the lam with about $225 million allegedly looted from a system of offshore mutual funds, Vesco dreamed of fathering a country. In his vision, citizenship would be held not by people but by international corporations, while Vesco's own holding company would exercise virtual sovereignty. He tried a number of locations. During the left-wing revolution in Portugal in the early 1970s, Vesco plotted with right-wing planters and American mobsters, with the apparent support of U.S. intelligence, to make the Azores, the strategically placed Portuguese islands in the Atlantic, independent and a headquarters for gambling, offshore banking, and anti-Portuguese covert action. Thwarted, he hatched similar plans for bits of the Bahamas and Costa Rica, for tiny islands off the coasts of Haiti and the Dominican

Republic, and even one in the South Pacific. At one point he even conceived the notion of buying the *Queen Elizabeth II* and anchoring it off Panama as a floating casino and money laundry.[106]

Vesco's wackiest scheme was for a slice of the island of Barbuda, itself a sliver of sand politically linked to Antigua, to become the seat of the Sovereign Order of New Aragon. Members of this "chivalric" order would be wealthy tax-dodgers who would receive both a knighthood and the right to settle on Barbuda. After that scheme too failed, Vesco took refuge in Cuba for "medical treatment." There were rumors that besides helping the Cubans evade the U.S. embargo, his projects included a plan for an offshore center on Cayo Largo where persecuted people, or at least their money, would be given sanctuary.[107]

But of all the insta-country architects to grace their era, none marched across the world stage with as light a heart or as heavy a foot as Michael Oliver. A Nevada real estate promoter and a fervid anti-Communist who made a fortune speculating against the U.S. dollar during the Vietnam War–era currency crises, Oliver held political convictions that told him paradise on earth would consist of a state without government, an economy founded on totally free enterprise, and a monetary system based on gold. After an abortive effort to get the British to cede control of the Turks and Caicos Islands for a free port and gambling scheme, a bid for the Coco islands off Puerto Rico, and even a claim for some World War II antiaircraft platforms in the English Channel, in 1972 he and his colleagues turned their attention to the South Pacific. The target was Minerva Reef, part of the Tonga group. It was to be the ultimate in tax and bank secrecy havens— not least because the entire reef disappeared under a meter of water at every high tide. Oliver recruited settlers (an Ohio oilman and a California lumberman) who landed (at low tide) to run up the flag of the Republic of Minerva. Oliver thoughtfully arranged for a dredge ship to try to heap up enough sand to keep the settlers dry. Meanwhile, declarations of sovereignty had been mailed around the world. One recipient was the king of Tonga, who, in a fury, handpicked the toughest criminals from of the local jail, loaded them onto his personal yacht along with a couple of artillery pieces, and booted the settlers off the reef.[108]

Down but not out, Oliver's next target was Abaco, two neglected islands in the Bahamas group. From his South Pacific experience, Oliver had learned an important lesson: there is no point declaring independence without the muscle to back it up. Hence he called on Mitchell Werbell III, an ex–CIA agent, gunrunner, and trainer of mercenaries, for assistance. Werbell was to arm a local force to spearhead the drive to independence.

In preparation, conferences were held on the islands to preach libertarian philosophy. But Werbell himself was arrested on charges he had attempted to sell machine guns to Robert Vesco to further that founding father's own schemes. Torn by internal dissension, the Abaco Independence Movement died of its own accord a few years later.

By then, however, another opportunity had opened back in the South Pacific. The New Hebrides, a French-British colonial condominium, was slated for independence, although under unhappy circumstances. The main Melanesian party had demanded the expropriation of uncultivated land held by French settlers; French settlers were also worried about being overwhelmed by English speakers; and the French government was concerned lest agitation for independence spread to New Caledonia, where France had major mining interests. But salvation was on the way in the form of Jimmy Stevens, a former bulldozer operator and self-appointed priest of a cargo cult, who liked to appear in public in flowing robes and a billowing white beard, and surrounded by his harem. Stevens appointed himself head of a secessionist party on the island of Espiritu Santo. He had plenty of support—by members of the cargo cult, who expected Stevens to expedite the return of an airborne messiah bearing enough refrigerators, radios, canned fruit, and whiskey for everyone; by French planters, who saw him as a counterpoise to Melanesian radicalism; and by Michael Oliver.

Oliver, by then relocated to Amsterdam, in conjunction with some right-wing monetary cranks, had created the Phoenix Foundation to advise Stevens and to funnel money to him. Oliver also drafted a Declaration of Independence and wrote up a constitution based on free enterprise, individual liberty, a gold-based monetary system, and the right to bear arms. Meanwhile, the Phoenix Foundation minted gold and silver coins with Stevens's head stamped on them, and from Amsterdam, the emerging world center for securities fraud, it sold shares in a development corporation to run the economy after independence.

When the great moment came, the New Hebrides government called on Australia for military aid; the independence movement was crushed and Jimmy Stevens tossed in jail. Yet, ironically, soon after independence, as the Republic of Vanuatu, the government of the ex–New Hebrides passed laws to create an offshore banking system, a quick ship's registry, and an instant corporation business, thus laying the foundation for its emergence as the South Pacific's most important financial haven. As for Michael Oliver, he was last reported on the Isle of Man in the English Channel, chatting to residents about the advantages of independence from Britain.[109]

None of these attempts to create a new microstate from scratch have come to much. Founding fathers had more luck when they tried to take over and convert an existing island paradise into a tax haven, money laundry, and smuggling center. But even in those instances the record is far from universally positive.

In 1979, for example, Patrick John, the leader of the Labour Party on the recently independent ex-British colony of Dominica, got caught in a scandal over a secret deal for the Caribbean island to host a refinery to smuggle oil to apartheid-era South Africa, then under embargo. As a result, he lost an election. The next year he received an offer of military aid to restore him to power, from Nordic Enterprises Inc., a company founded by North American white supremacists. In return they wanted the usual— tax concessions, passports, casinos, and, of course, the right to set up banks. But they also wanted to settle Dominica with members of the pure Aryan race. To give the project a little local color, so to speak, they hired to assist the military operation the Dreads—marijuana-trafficking members of a Rastafarian sect who, unlike most of their mellow co-religionists, periodically ventured down from the hills to rob banks and shoot up government installations. However, ten heavily armed Ku Klux Klansmen were arrested in New Orleans before they could set sail, Patrick John and local ringleaders were jailed, and the Dominican government passed a new antiterrorism law targeted at the Dreads.[110]

One place where this sort of scheme almost worked was the Seychelles. Wrested from France by Britain during the Napoleonic Wars, the Seychelles for decades was a forgotten colonial anachronism in the Indian Ocean. Then came the June 1967 Middle East War, which closed the Suez Canal. Subsequently, much of Europe's oil supply flowed in supertankers down the East African coast past the Seychelles. That provided a fillip for the ambitions of Chief Minister James Marcham. He envisaged a brilliant economic future for the islands as a tourist mecca and a trade entrepôt, as well as a tax haven and an offshore banking center modeled on the Channel Islands, to complement its growing role as a U.S. intelligence listening post.

Britain, however, was committed to withdrawal east of Suez. Hence, despite Marcham's opposition, the islands were granted full independence in 1974. Because that precluded the Channel Island model, Marcham tried another. "My dream," he claimed, "was to turn the Seychelles into a small Switzerland, taking advantage of our geographical position and staying out of the tug-of-war of power politics." For a time it seemed to be working. European and Middle Eastern money flowed in, and Citibank announced plans to open an offshore branch—until Marcham was ousted in a coup launched by his prime minister, René Albert, whom the CIA had already typed as a Communist agent, and the dream seemed destined to oblivion. Fortunately others were prepared to keep it alive.[111]

The coup led to a panic flight of capital. Arriving in the turmoil was Giovanni Mario Ricci, a millionaire Italian businessman, who wooed the government with tales of big investments in tea and coffee plantations and in luxury hotels.[112] There was a catch: the government had to make the islands into a tax haven and allow him to launch the first offshore banking facility. In response, the Seychelles abolished taxes on offshore companies, passed bank and corporate secrecy laws, and even legalized casino gambling. Then came a new vocation.[113]

One day in 1981, an all-male group of tourists landed, sporting on their T-shirts the symbol (an overflowing tankard of ale) of the Ancient Order of Froth Blowers, a British fraternal order devoted to the assistance of deprived children. When an overcurious Customs officer opened a piece of luggage and discovered a machine gun, the group transmuted into mercenaries (ex–Green Berets, former British SAS troops, and Rhodesian army veterans) led by "Mad Mike" Hoare, survivor of many of Africa's wars and coups. After a shoot-up in the airport in which their own plane was wrecked, most of Mad Mike's merry band hijacked an Air India jet to South Africa. They left behind a shaken head of state, suddenly aware of South Africa's growing interest in his island home.[114] Apart from hiring another mercenary to take charge of his personal security, René Albert became party to an appeasement plan that involved a truly Byzantine set of actors.

One of the fellow Italians whom Giovanni Ricci entertained in his island retreat was Francesco Pazienza, who had worked for SISMI (Italian military intelligence) as a money launderer and liaison officer with the Italian underworld. Pazienza was also party to a plan to subvert the Italian government, a plan that not only precipitated the greatest political scandal in Italy's postwar history but also contributed heavily to a series of its most important financial crises. Under indictment for subversion, embezzlement, fraudulent bankruptcy, forgery, and terrorism, Pazienza decided to take a well-earned vacation in a tropical paradise in 1984. From him came the idea of setting up in the Seychelles a bunkering station to fuel ships and planes bound to and from South Africa and to act as a transit station for moving cargoes of crude oil in violation of the embargo. To Giovanni Ricci, this was an especially interesting prospect because South Africa paid premium prices for embargoed oil and the Seychelles, equipped with bank secrecy laws and a tax haven status, lay directly on the main oil route from the Persian Gulf. It was also interesting to South Africa, which realized that the islands could make an excellent general transit facility for goods bound to and from South Africa, with their origins and destinations blurred by phony labels, circuitous itineraries, and banking and corporate secrecy laws.

Indeed, the Seychellois spirit lived on after the fall of the apartheid regime. When, in addition to losing the business from sanctions busting, the country also faced the closure of the U.S. space tracking station, its number three earner of foreign exchange, in 1996 it passed the Economic Development Act. This law granted immunity from prosecution and from asset forfeiture to all persons (except those who committed murder or trafficked in drugs—in the Seychelles) who invested a minimum of $10 million on the islands. They were even offered Seychelles diplomatic passports. A global howl of outrage forced the embarrassed government to back down.[115]

CYBER-STATES IN MOTION

All the fuss about creating new countries on bits and pieces of territory, it could be argued, is old-fashioned. In this postmodern age, one step beyond the insta-country with a fixed address is the cyber-state of no fixed address. And none have better captured the supposedly borderless nature of today's global economy than the Ecclesiastical Sovereign Dominion of Melchizedek, named after the biblical priest who blessed Abraham. The insta-country has claimed everything from a tiny, uninhabited island three hundred miles off the Pacific coast of Colombia to an atoll that is part of the Marshall Islands to a piece of reef sixteen hundred miles south of Tahiti with more than nine times the disadvantages of Minerva—it is nine meters underwater at high tide and never sees the surface even at low. Melchizedek has even asserted rights to a large slice of Antarctica, while insisting that its spiritual headquarters is in Jerusalem. Prudently, it keeps its computer server in San Francisco.

Although Melchizedek insists that its mission is God-given, the origins of the Ecclesiastical Sovereign Dominion seem a little more profane. It all began with Currentsea, a company set up in 1970 by an environmental activist who claimed he was going to levy a tax on the output of all offshore oil-drilling operations and spend the money to protect the world's oceans. For a long time no one took it too seriously, except for David and Mark Pedley, the father-son team who had used one of Jerome Schneider's Pacific insta-banks to run the Mexican capital-flight scam. David wrote the Melchizedek bible, before allegedly dying in a Mexican jail, while Mark, who got out of a U.S. prison in 1990, took control of Currentsea, secured a listing on the over-the-counter market in New York, and in short order was back in business—taking the occasion to change his own name to Branch Vinedresser.[116]

One of the country's first acts was to float bonds. It chartered an accounting firm whose board of directors included Mr. Harvey Penguini of Rockefeller Plaza, South Antarctica, to provide full financial statements for the two Panama companies handling the issue. In turn each of those companies provided more than $1 million "worth" of bonds to a Guernsey broker to try to sell to or swap. When that failed, the rest of the $2 billion issue was apparently abandoned.

Apparently nonplussed by the refusal of the international financial community to take its bonds seriously, Melchizedek had recourse to a more traditional way of financing government responsibilities. It decided to issue $10 billion in "equicurrency." To those who questioned the country's financial solvency, one of its spokesmen had a platinum-clad response; he would display a one-pound bar worth $6,500 and assure his audience that there were thirty-three tons more, valued at $440 million, to back the currency. To further bolster its finances, the country began selling bank charters along with a raft of insurance companies. Not least, it created a network of ambassadors. Indeed, they were more than just ambassadors. Anyone donating $2,000 to the new country received both ambassadorial rank and a bank charter. Soon shell banks were attempting to use Melchizedek paper to collateralize loans, and its ambassadors were peddling drafts on Melchizedek-chartered banks from Hong Kong to London to the United States.[117]

Heading Home

Once funds have been moved through the international financial system—via offshore bank accounts held in the name of shell corporations owned by offshore trusts housed in existing or made-to-measure financial havens—and moved sufficiently so that their origins are extremely difficult to trace, it is time for money laundering to enter its third stage, that of getting the money home again, to be enjoyed as consumption or employed as capital.

It is possible for money to return disguised as foreign investment. An indeterminable proportion of the supposedly foreign money pouring into stocks, bonds, or bank CDs in major Western countries is actually "round-tripping." Residents sneak it abroad and then run it back through off-shore companies to give it the appearance of foreign investment, and therefore avoid or greatly reduce taxes. Nor is this a game played purely in rich countries. During the 1980s, when Latin America was rocked by a crisis of capital flight and many countries were unable to repay their foreign debts, smugglers or tax dodgers with offshore nest eggs could buy their country's foreign debt on the international secondary market at, say, 10 percent of face value. Then, when the country, under pressure from the International Monetary Fund, decided to privatize state assets, it would offer to swap shares in state corporations for government bonds held by foreigners. So drug money, or something similar, would end up neatly invested in a public utility, factory, or mine. The entrepreneur gained the original (dollar-denominated) profits from the contraband, the capital gain from any devaluation of his or her national currency (which capital flight itself exacerbated), the additional premium from buying foreign debt instruments on the cheap, and then any further gains from obtaining choice state assets at bargain prices—all in the name of economic efficiency and "liberalization" of financial markets.

Although foreign investment has its attractions, it also has a disadvantage: the interest, dividends, and capital gains earned must be sent back out again to maintain the illusion that the investment funds are of foreign origin. But the underground entrepreneur usually wants to use the earnings publicly back home.

There are several techniques to make that happen, with the choice dependent in part on the sums involved and the regularity with which money is to be repatriated. The actual form in which it returns—business or personal checks, money orders, wire transfers, or whatever—is not the central issue. What counts is adequate cover to explain its origins.

In some cases it may not be necessary to have any cover. If the objective is merely to finance regular living expenses, nothing more is required than a credit card issued by a foreign bank. Either the issuing bank automatically pays the balance due out of the money kept abroad or money is wired periodically from one foreign bank to another to settle the account. Such a card can also give access to ATMs, and the transaction with the machine can remain confidential, because the ATM needs no other information than a card number to process the transaction.

It is possible to take confidentiality a step further. Some banks issue a debit card that is effectively anonymous even to the issuing bank. When the applicant opens an account, there is no need for references or a local address as long as the applicant is a nonresident, and the applicant can fill in a signature card with any name he or she chooses.[118]

From the point of view of automaticity and confidentiality, debit cards issued by foreign banks protected by bank secrecy laws are superior to credit cards, particularly if the credit card's issuing institution keeps its records in the United States, where they can be suborned or subpoenaed. However, even a normal-looking credit card can be converted into a de facto debit card if it is secured. A secured card requires that the holder deposit with the issuing bank collateral equal to the credit line. Although usually such a card is issued to those who are bad credit risks yet need the card for such purposes as reserving hotel rooms or renting cars, it can be useful to anyone, however flush, who seeks to lower his or her financial profile. Because the credit line is secured by the collateral, the applicant needs give virtually no financial details. It is even better if an offshore trust owns the account on which the card is issued.[119]

Even better is a totally anonymous cash card, usable in virtually every ATM in the world, that draws on a dollar account kept legally separate from any offshore account, with the ATM account periodically credited out of the offshore one.[120]

Perhaps best of all is an offshore-sourced smart card, maybe several. With the appropriate sums programmed onto the cards, they can be used free of any ongoing electronic link whatsoever between issuing bank and user. When they need to be topped up, they can simply be mailed back to the bank.

Alternatively, bills incurred in one's place of residence can be settled by an offshore bank or, even more discretely, by an offshore company. In fact, persons seeking to use at home illegal money held abroad need not even bother to set up their own offshore accounts and shell companies. There are firms that advertise their willingness to handle all of a client's major payments—utility bills, car loan installments, mortgage payments, and so forth. The client makes a deposit into the firm's offshore account and sends bills or payment instructions to the firm. Indeed, the firm will go further and handle automatically all banking requirements. Requests for payment can be sent directly by the billing company to the firm, provided the client has deposited enough money to cover them. The firm will also clear, through its own accounts, checks made out to the client or the client's business, and it will credit the balance to the client's account for a small per annum plus a fee per check.[121]

Visibility can also be reduced by use of a payable-through account. Instead of securing a license to operate in a particular country, a foreign bank might open a correspondent master account with a bank in the host country. This is often done in the United States, where foreign banks have had increasing difficulty getting approval to operate. (Of course this is the same United States of America that has been busy bullying other countries to admit its banks to their financial marketplaces.) After opening such an account, a foreign bank would allow its clients to draw checks on it. The account remains legally in the name of the foreign bank, so although there is a paper trail, an immediate glance would show only the name of the correspondent bank as the beneficiary and user of the payable-through account.[122]

Alternatively the entrepreneur might decide to open his or her own account and bring home some or all of the funds for direct deposit. Of course the account is then susceptible to law enforcement probes. But as long as the money comes back in nonbearer instruments, there is no need to report the flow. And if the money is placed in a non-interest-bearing account, there is no report to the revenue authorities.

If further insulation is required, it is possible to fake the identity of the recipient. If, during the money's world tour, the entrepreneur picked up an extra passport or two, these can be used to open up a tax-free non-resident's bank account and the money used to pay living expenses or even to invest in securities—with the requirement that the interest and dividends be "repatriated." The documents are easy to acquire; Bangladesh, Belize, Cape Verde, Peru, Sierra Leone, St. Kitts, and Uruguay, to name but a few, have a long-standing practice of selling their passports. More countries are steadily adding their names to the list; for a while the Ukraine, for example, offered a bargain passport for a mere $1,000. Israel offers instant citizenship, and quick passports, to Jews from anywhere (while denying full civil rights to Christians and Muslims who have lived in Palestine for millennia). As with the diplomatic variety, these passports are most easily acquired via brokerage firms that advertise regularly in publications such as the *International Herald Tribune* and *The Economist*.[123] Although some of these documents are not so useful for traveling, they can work to open bank accounts and gain the equivalent of offshore status right at home. Needless to say, once the tax-exempt account is opened, money should be deposited by wire or by regular bank instrument. Because the objective is to minimize attention, turning up with a suitcase of hundred-dollar bills is definitely a no-no.

Similarly, the money could be sent to a relative, nominee, or cutout in whose name all expenditures would occur and purchased assets held. A variant on this scheme involves immigrants' "investment funds." Just as money can leave the country in the form of unrequited transfers, for example, to religious and charitable institutions abroad, or as remittances to family members living abroad, so too it can return with a landed immigrant. This has become more common as countries compete for the pool of wealthy individuals willing to move to wherever the grass seems greener and the tax rates lower. Thus, the entrepreneur might smuggle money abroad, then have a relative or friend bring it back as part of a claim to landed immigrant status, a claim backed, of course, by the entrepreneur, who will attest to the would-be immigrant and even guarantee support money if required.

All these tricks, however, have a downside. Once the entrepreneur starts to make expenditures (the reason why the money was brought home), he or she still has to account for the sudden improvement in living standards. And using cutouts poses risks, as well as being a lot less fun.

It is also relatively simple to bring the money back in the form of valuable commodities. However, there is an asymmetry here. Precisely the factor that makes diamonds, for example, useful for moving money covertly out of a country makes them less than ideal for moving it overtly back in again, namely, that the diamond trade operates in cash. More dependable in this regard are art and antiquities, which can be bought on the black market abroad, then legally imported and sold. This permits the individual to deposit in a bank account a check issued by an art and antiquities dealer. Even better, the individual can donate the work to a local fine arts museum in return for a receipt for a tax-deductible contribution perhaps grossly inflated by complicit evaluators. That way the money comes in the cleanest possible form—a tax refund check issued by the government.

To be sure, such antics are not foolproof. They might account for the immediate sum in the bank, but a careful investigation might lead to questions about the origins of the money used to purchase the diamond or the artifact. However, there are alternatives that avoid such difficulties.

One is to bring the money back disguised as casino winnings. Money could be wired from the underground entrepreneur's offshore bank account to a casino in the Bahamas or the Dominican Republic, for example. The casino pays the money in chips; the chips are cashed in; and the money is repatriated via bank check, money order, or wire transfer to the entrepreneur's domestic bank account, where it can be presented as the result of good luck. The method is neat, but it has two disadvantages. One is that because the casino has recorded the money coming and going, it cannot provide evidence of losses to offset the gains, and therefore, in some jurisdictions, the money brought home might attract income tax. The second is that the trick is usable only sporadically: "winning" too often could attract attention.

Another option is to receive the money as a bequest from an offshore trust, perhaps set up some years before by a recently deceased maiden aunt. Indeed the trust could be genuine—the underground entrepreneur having set it up with himself as beneficiary using fake ID or a complicit lawyer. Of course, that procedure is better employed in a jurisdiction without gift or estate duties, and it can only be used once.

Another option is an international real estate flip. Here the entrepreneur "sells" property to a foreign investor—who is, in reality, the same person working through one or several offshore companies. The sale price is suitably inflated above acquisition cost, and the money is repatriated as a capital gain on a smart real estate deal. If the property is a personal dwelling, there is, in some jurisdictions, an added bonus—the capital gains are tax free. Like the casino caper and for the same reasons, international real estate sham sales can be used only on an occasional basis.[124] The same limitation holds when the entrepreneur "sells" a domestic corporation to an offshore company that he or she secretly owns.

Preferable to bogus real estate sales are bogus capital gains on options trading. Unlike real estate, securities are more likely to be traded regularly. In fact frequent securities transactions, each with modest capital gains, are less likely to attract unwanted attention than the occasional big score. The trick is to "buy" and "sell" a currency, commodity, or stock option back and forth between foreign and domestic companies. The onshore company records a capital gain and the foreign one a capital loss. This works even better if the foreign company is incorporated in a country with secrecy laws. Such a wash trade is perfectly safe because the domestic authorities cannot audit the books of the offshore entity. And because the entrepreneur is his or her own client, the danger of complaints to the relevant securities commission would seem to be eliminated.[125]

Needless to say, there are all kinds of interesting subvariants. They include, for example, scams in which holdings are scattered among several shell companies, then traded back and forth. This both clouds the trail and builds up potential interest by genuine outside investors. It might then be possible to unload bogus shares on some unsuspecting third party, collecting a capital gain in the form of a fraud premium. This is best practiced at the expense of other offshore asset holders who, given the probable origins of their money, are unlikely to complain to any authority, even if one could be found with jurisdiction to investigate. It is never clear, with offshore boiler-room schemes, where the con job ends and the wash job starts.

For truly regular flows, the entrepreneur might arrange to collect the money in the form of income rather than gambling receipts or capital gains. Personal income is easy to arrange. The entrepreneur simply has him or herself hired by one or more of his or her offshore companies as an employee or, better, as a consultant. In effect the entrepreneur can pay him or herself a handsome salary or generous consulting fee out of the offshore nest egg and perhaps throw in as extra a company car or a condo in some prime living spot. Granted this attracts the highest personal tax rate, but that can be partially offset by having as much of the "consulting fees" as seems credible paid to cover "expenses" that are then deducted from the taxable component of the income.

Alternatively the entrepreneur could choose to repatriate the money as business income. It is merely a matter of setting up a domestic corporation and having it bill an offshore company for goods sold or services provided. If commodities are the chosen vehicle, it is safer that they actually exist and are overvalued (if on the way out) or undervalued (if on the way in), rather than completely fake. It is easier to argue with Customs inspectors about the declared value of a good than to explain a shipment of empty crates or how a load of computer parts turned into a box of scrap metal. If the goods are "sold" abroad, they can be dumped—on the black market or, if they are largely junk, into the sea.

Needless to add, sham commodity deals to launder money can be linked to insurance scams, especially if the insurance company is incorporated offshore and secretly owned by the underground entrepreneur. Money then returns home as compensation for a lost or hijacked cargo.

Billing an offshore company for services rendered eliminates the problem of Customs inspection, but it possibly complicates explanations for a tax audit. Here the difficulty is precisely the reverse of that posed by a purely domestic money-laundering operation conducted through a retail services business. In the domestic case, the objective is to inflate sales revenues by mixing illegal with legal income, and the inability of the auditors to establish a clear relationship between costs of inputs and the value of output is a distinct advantage. But with repatriation from abroad, the income flow arriving through orthodox banking channels is undisputed. Rather, it is incumbent on the entrepreneur to prove the validity of deductions. With physical goods, there is always proof of actual purchase of material directly related to the return flow of money from sales; with services, the links are much more tenuous.

Probably neatest of all, the money can be brought home in the form of a business "loan." The entrepreneur arranges for money in an offshore account to be "lent" to his or her onshore entity. Even better, once the loan has been incurred, the borrower has the right to repay it, with interest, effectively to him or herself. Therefore, the entrepreneur can legally ship even more money out of the country to a foreign safe haven, while deducting the "interest" component as a business expense against domestic taxable income.

Indeed, there is no need to actually create an offshore company. In a variant on the back-to-back loan used in legitimate business, money deposited in a foreign bank in the form, for example, of a CD can be pledged as collateral for a genuine loan that the bank then makes to an onshore individual or business entity. The disadvantage is that interest earned on the CD is likely lower than that charged on the loan—unless the entrepreneur owns the bank. However, even if the loan is negotiated at arms length through an independent institution, the interest problem can be partially offset by the fact that it is tax deductible at home; the result is simply to reduce the net profit on the transaction. With this arrangement, should the entrepreneur decide to default on the loan, there is no fear of the bank undertaking legal action for recovery; it merely seizes the pledged CD.

The cover can be deepened by a back-to-back CD technique. The entrepreneur gives the money to the company arranging the loan. The company deposits it in a bank in the firm's own name, receiving from the bank a certificate of deposit. The company then issues its own certificate of deposit on behalf of the entrepreneur, which provides an extra layer of confidentiality because the client's name does not appear on the bank's books. The new CD will be either in the name of the entrepreneur's offshore company or, if no such entity exists, in bearer form. Furthermore, even when issued as a bearer instrument, the client has the assurance that if anyone but the entrepreneur attempts to cash that particular CD, the company will refuse to honor it until contacting the entrepreneur for confirmation.

The process can also work using domestic real estate as collateral. There is a firm in Costa Rica that specializes in setting up discrete back-to-back personal loans to assure the tax deductibility of the interest. The firm will even allow clients to use the firm's own offshore companies. The client arranges to borrow from a friendly offshore company, with interest payments and term of the loan set at anything the client wants, because the company is "lending" to the client funds the client had already contrived to smuggle offshore. If the loan is personal, the loan company will take as collateral a mortgage on the client's house. Uncle Sam only allows income tax deductions for interest payments on personal loans if they are incurred to buy or improve a personal home. Once interest and principal payments are received by the loan company, it either arranges to send them right back again or diverts them into the client's offshore account, less a small fee for service.

When a loan is structured in this way, not only can the client take a tax deduction in the form of the interest the client is effectively repaying to him or herself out of taxable income, but the client now has a mortgage on his or her home that is held by a lending institution, meaning the lender has a first lien on the asset, ahead of the tax collector, commercial creditors, or a divorce-inclined spouse. And because it is the client's own money that made the mortgage loan, it is the client who holds that preferred mortgage. It is rather like the government paying the client to protect the client's own property from seizure.[126]

Clever though they seem at first blush, back-to-back loans present one big danger. Every revenue officer in the world—with police investigators not far behind—knows full well that no bank lends without collateral. Therefore they take loans made to domestic entrepreneurs from offshore or international banks as evidence of undeclared assets.[127] The risk can be reduced by working through an international bank that has a domestic affiliate. The collateral is stuffed in the bank abroad, and the bank there instructs its local affiliate to initiate the loan, which attracts much less attention. In a sort of back-to-back loan and lateral-transfer jumbo package, the more money the entrepreneur can sneak offshore, the more money the onshore bank can lend.

Using any of these "loan-back" techniques, and the neat device of repaying the offshore loan at the expense of the tax collector, the entrepreneur can not only close the money-laundering circle but actually increase its diameter.

Of course, none of these techniques is foolproof. In one notorious case, drug-derived cash was smuggled across the United States–Mexico border to a foreign exchange house in Monterrey. The foreign exchange house sent it back again for deposit under its own name in a bank on the Texas side. Then two officers of the private banking department of a prominent institution created Cayman Island companies with bank accounts in Switzerland and New York. They used the drug money on deposit abroad as collateral for loans to the traffickers to finance investments in meatpacking, computer distribution, car dealerships, a video chain franchise, country clubs, and real estate in both Mexico and Texas. As additional cover, the drug dealers made sure that their $29 million investment portfolio was held in the name of a front man. Alas, it was not the best choice—a Mexican gas station attendant. The case ended with American Express Bank assessed a record fine of $32 million and two of its officers in jail.[128]

Who Regulates the Regulators?

Contrary to protestations about the equity and efficiency of the free-market system (routinely heard from academic economists with their generous salaries guaranteed, often by the state, for life), tight financial regulations are essential to protect societal interests. Historically they have had three functions. One was to assure the liquidity and solvency of the system—liquidity was the responsibility of the Central Bank, solvency that of the superintendent of financial institutions or equivalent office. A second was to protect institutions against theft and fraud by employees, clients, or outsiders; this function was largely the domain of the criminal justice system. A third was to defend clients against malfeasance by managers; this task was handled by regulatory bodies such as securities exchanges, with the criminal justice system as the final guarantor. But over the last two decades there has emerged a fourth function: protecting society against crimes by clients, through or with the complicity of financial managers and their institutions. This function not only revolutionized the role of financial regulation but transformed relations between client, banker, and police. In the past, client and banker formed an implicit alliance against police probes, whereas in the present, police and bankers (even if unwillingly) form a silent cabal against possible client misdeeds. The new function differs from the earlier three in another important way. In the past there were simply defined objectives (preventing liquidity crises, robberies, or abuses of trust, for example) and clear criteria for success. But the new regulatory function requires routine monitoring of transactions that pose no threat to the institution or the client; indeed, such monitoring may be against both their interests. And it requires an endless proliferation of regulations, although its target is at best vaguely defined and ever moving.

The process began with an attempt to examine deposits of cash in banks and to scrutinize the export of cash instruments abroad. When it was realized that people could also convert their cash into gold, diamonds, furs, boats, and fancy cars, there came regulations that required reporting of cash sales of luxury and durable items. Then came tightened rules to prevent structuring and to restrict the purchase of cashier's checks. Next came more recording requirements for wire transfers. Mandatory suspicion transaction reports followed shortly. As concern spread about the possible illicit use of nonbank financial institutions, enhanced scrutiny was extended to everything from brokerage firms to check-cashing services, from exchange houses to wire transmitters. More recently the fear frontier shifted to private banking and use of correspondent accounts. Today law enforcement frowns in contemplation of the seemingly endless laundering capacities of e-money and the Internet.

Each shift in emphasis has usually been preceded by a (conveniently timed) scandal or a televised congressional hearing featuring the usual hooded witnesses telling tales of counting stacks of greenbacks in back rooms. Each has been accompanied by claims that as a result of increased vigilance on one front, the frontier of money laundering has shifted to another, requiring yet more vigilance on other fronts. Indeed, new regulations are now demanded to anticipate the next frontier of money laundering—just in case. By the same argument, the fact that any bank is a potential target of armed robbery justifies the requirement that every would-be depositor submit to a retinal scan and a rectal search before being allowed through the front door.

In reality, there is no shifting frontier of money laundering. From the very beginning, money laundering occurred using exactly the same methods, and passing through exactly the same institutions, as legitimate finance. As a result, it is not only extremely difficult to detect and deter, but attempting to do so imposes a regulatory burden whose social costs probably now far exceed any benefits in terms of crime control. Not only is that regulatory burden increasingly heavy but it is also misplaced, and nowhere more so than in efforts to deal with the purported menace of financial havens.

The very term "haven" should probably be purged from the vocabulary. Much like the term "organized crime," it suggests aliens plotting evil against polite society, when, in reality, haven jurisdictions emerged largely to serve the requirements of the very countries that have now so vociferously turned against them.

During the 1960s and later, the big industrial countries believed that having branches of their financial institutions and transnational corporations operate in haven countries actually improved domestic regulation, because it meant that they could impose tax and other regulatory standards appropriate to their domestic situation without harming the competitive position of their business institutions abroad. Therefore "onshore" countries were willing to tolerate, even encourage, this development, as long as the offshore centers remained within their sphere of influence (most are British territories, former British colonies, or U.S. trust territories), there was no perception of egregious criminal conduct, and domestic businesses were not seriously threatened by competition from low-tax jurisdictions.[129] The result was a powerful lobby of financial institutions and corporations from major countries to whom offshore booking facilities and the potential to incorporate subsidiaries in tax havens were essential to maintaining a competitive edge. To them were added fund management facilities, again mainly subsidiaries of the big international banks, as international private banking grew in importance and as banks of other countries, notably those of the United States and Canada, challenged the traditional Swiss and British lead.

Today, however, across the world, taxes are slashed, regulations liberalized, exchange controls abolished, and reserve requirements lifted. As a result, big banks and large corporations no longer have the same need for offshore facilities. The havens have lost their most powerful allies and are now exposed to the full force of the lethal combination of law enforcement zeal and political correctness. First came a war on drugs, then a war on corruption, and now a war on harmful tax competition.

The term "haven" also suggests that illegal incomes have decided to stash themselves permanently abroad while their owners periodically jet down to enjoy the palm trees and watch the flying fish. A better term would be "financial R&R center" to capture the fact that they are simply transit points. Funds flow in from the major industrialized countries, and then flow back out again, usually to the places from whence they came. Money laundering, it must be recalled, is a three-stage process that starts and ends at home. This suggests that the focus should be on the rich countries that generate, transmit, and receive the funds. For law enforcement or tax purposes, virtually all the necessary information is already held inside the banks of the country concerned. But rather than demand that politically powerful domestic banks routinely yield full information to the authorities on demand, politicians take the easy route of beating up on a handful of island jurisdictions that have almost no effective way of fighting back.

Finally, it is simply not true that the so-called havens resist law enforcement cooperation out of greed, complicity, or bloody-mindedness. Some, like the Cayman Islands, well entrenched as an offshore booking center for international wholesale transactions, can afford to be more cooperative in chasing down the more blatant forms of criminality without seriously endangering the financial services sector. Switzerland is certainly cooperative today compared with its historical reputation; it has criminalized such activities as insider trading and money laundering, imposed asset freezes at the request of foreign countries on the allegedly ill-gotten gains of certain heads of state, restricted bank secrecy in general, and signed a series of mutual legal assistance treaties. However, smaller and less established places are often holdouts against pressure to breach the secrecy rules behind which their financial services industries have grown up, precisely because they have little alternative. Such pressures threaten the loss of income and jobs, and the possibility that business will flee to other havens less amenable to pressure—in exchange for nothing. It remains a remarkable fact that almost every country whose farmers grow cannabis, coca bush, or opium poppy is offered international aid to break the addiction. But to date no one has offered the haven countries any kind of financial crop-substitution program.

CHAPTER 5

The Underworld of Gold

"Gold" is more than a word—it is an incantation. It conjures up many images: Spanish conquistadors slaughtering aboriginal peoples while plundering the New World; masked highwaymen waving down coaches at pistol point to relieve passengers of purses bursting with coin; big-city sharpies in top hats hawking claims to acres of empty sand while gold fever rages in the boondocks; and shifty Levantine merchants sitting cross-legged before heaps of glittering jewelry while water pipes bubble in the background.[1]

But that was supposed to be history. Well before John Maynard Keynes, in the 1930s, declared gold a barbarous relic, its role as a regal symbol of wealth seemed destined to recede. Modern banks seemed to provide all the financial services of gold with none of its disadvantages—limited supply, vulnerability to theft, and physical bulk. After World War I, country after country, and then the international financial system itself, cut back on use of gold. In the early 1970s, the price of gold, long guaranteed by official monetary demand, was freed to follow the market, just like any other commodity. Gold, it seemed, was destined to be relegated to a few industrial uses, whatever monetary cranks might think. Any residual governmental interest could be imputed to institutional underdevelopment, while private urges were written off to superstition or vanity.

Yet today, despite new gold fields as well as technological advances that permit profitable extraction of much more from old ones, every ounce finds a ready market. And the historical images have merely been airbrushed with modern tones—Brazil's *garampeiros* massacring Yanomani Indians; robbers trussing up guards at the Brink's-Mat warehouse at London's Heathrow Airport; gold scam artists trolling North American middle-class suburbs for suckers; and Dubai smugglers loading *dhows* with tiny bars for a quick run across the Indian Ocean.

Part of that persistence is simply the result of strength of tradition. But the ease with which ever-rising production gets absorbed is also a result of the growth and spread of a global underground economy. Whatever the vagaries of gold's role in legitimate transactions, its function as an anonymous and highly liquid instrument for covert transactions and hidden savings remains, like the metal itself, untarnished by time or institutional change.

As a result, those who enter the underworld of gold come face to face with smuggling, capital flight, tax evasion, money laundering, counterfeiting, and investment fraud, not to mention ecological devastation and the occasional act of pure genocide.

The Midas Syndrome

Traditionally the most important destination for gold has been the world's Central Banks. Although for years major Central Banks have been net sellers, those of other countries still want to add to their stash. Even to satisfy this most apparently legitimate source of demand, gold can be bought for both overt and covert reasons. Some countries use it to adorn the statistics of foreign exchange reserves, whose figures they publish to impress (or mislead) international creditors. For others, the virtue of gold is precisely the opposite: it is an ideal asset of last resort because, quietly held in a Central Bank's vaults or secretly stored abroad, it is untouchable in the event of an embargo or an international credit freeze. Just as, during the seventeenth and eighteenth centuries, stocks of precious metal were referred to as "the sinews of war" by European state-power theorists, so too today these metals are a means to acquire weapons and strategic commodities when subterfuge is essential.[2]

BURIED TREASURE

Gold's usefulness in the acquisition of strategic supplies is a lesson of World War II, when Hitler's forces looted gold across Europe. Seizing the gold was only the first step. Before it could be used to purchase essential supplies, its origins had to be disguised. Coins were simple—they bore no serial numbers. But bars required care. Reichsbank specialists resmelted them, stamped them with a pre-war date, and shipped the bars to Switzerland or, less often, to Sweden, Portugal, and other neutral countries, with fake documents and letters of assurance that the gold had been legitimately acquired—although most of the recipients were in a position to guess, if not know, that the assurances were bogus. The gold was then swapped for strategic supplies or pledged as collateral for trade credits.[3]

Although at the end of the war most of the gold and other valuables taken by the Nazis were recovered by the Allies, before the plunder could be returned to its owners another looting operation occurred. Thefts and misappropriations by Soviet and U.S. military personnel of precious metals, jewels, and foreign currencies totaled approximately $30 million (at then-prevailing prices), and theft of gold bonds totaled approximately $400 million worth. Although few if any of the bonds were ever successfully negotiated, virtually none of the gold, jewels, or cash was found.[4]

The same thing apparently was happening to another treasure trove on the other side of the world. During World War II, the Japanese plundered religious shrines, government reserves, and museums, as well as private citizens, bankers, and even rich gangsters across occupied Asia. The speculation at the time was that the hoard (named Yamashita's Gold after the Japanese admiral nominally in charge) was worth $3 billion (or more than $50 billion at current prices), with the gold portion alone totaling four thousand to six thousand tons, although, as in all cases of fabled hoards, the sums have behaved magically—much like compound interest—growing with each iteration. However much there really was, it was collected in the Philippines, and those responsible for hiding it were murdered once the job was done. It has never been found, officially, although there are stories (some put out by the ex-president himself) that it formed the basis of the reputed wealth of the late Ferdinand Marcos.[5]

Similar considerations are at work today when countries face economic embargoes or the ire of their creditors. Peru, in the mid-1980s, fearful that its refusal to keep up interest payments on its foreign debt would lead to seizure of its financial assets abroad, quietly liquidated them, converted them to gold, and brought the gold home. China rode out a post–Tiananmen Square credit cutoff by recourse to its gold reserves. Iraq and Libya secretly employed theirs to undercut sanctions. Vietnam used gold for international transfers during the period when the United States refused to permit it to clear dollar balances through New York.[6]

In a similar spirit, political leaders might create a hidden treasury in anticipation of the need to finance a comfortable retirement or stage a comeback. Yamashita's loot was not the only gold to bring luster to the Marcos saga. After the president fled the Philippines on a U.S. Air Force jet for a Hawaiian exile, his successors claimed that much of the Central Bank gold was "missing." About the same time, twenty tons of gold unexpectedly turned up on the Japanese black market. There unofficial gold dealers usually offer sellers a rate equal to about 90 percent of the world price; then they resell to registered dealers, who in turn melt and recast the gold and unload it on the open market in their own names.[7]

If it is true that Marcos made off with Central Bank gold, he was merely following precedent. In the 1960s, Indonesian president Achmed Sukarno reputedly created a "revolutionary fund" of $750 million in gold bars (now worth about $15 billion), which he stashed in London, Geneva, and Tokyo.[8] Similarly the late emperor of Ethiopia, Haile Selassie, bought gold produced in his southern provinces at half the world market price. It was shipped to Switzerland, where it was refined; part was to be held in bars in the emperor's accounts and part sold, with the proceeds invested in everything from a Swiss watch factory to an Alberta cattle ranch.[9] The revolutionaries who seized control claimed to have found among the emperor's hastily abandoned effects a letter from his bankers asking him to defer sending more gold because they had run out of storage space. Like most stories about ousted leaders, particularly when told by successor regimes facing the lethal combination of an empty treasury and inflated public expectations, this one has to be viewed with the same critical detachment as that employed for evaluating a used car offered at a bargain price.

Apart from gold purchased for political reasons, overt or covert, a large chunk of its annual world production is bought up by industries such as electronics, dentistry, and jewelry. Here, although the end use is legal, the supply method sometimes is not. In the old Soviet Union, dentists working for cash on the side were one of the largest sets of customers for gold stolen from the alluvial diggings of Siberia. In countries as varied as Italy, Turkey, and India, much if not most of the gold used by the jewelry industry has been smuggled in to evade taxes, tariffs, or outright prohibitions.

In total, all the world's official monetary and industrial demands would still annually take off the market only about half the new supply. The rest is absorbed privately. Like paper currency, gold can be used to buy goods and services, speculate for a profit, or save for emergencies. But financially speaking, it is sterile, that is, a non-interest-bearing asset. So why the lure?

Legitimate holders may distrust paper, fear for the stability of depository institutions, see gold as a hedge against inflation or devaluation, or simply have a precious metal fetish. Some may also see it as the ultimate survival tool: televised newscasts of the aftermath of the 1995 Kobe earthquake showed an elderly woman triumphantly pulling from the rubble of her house an unscathed gold bar.[10] All of these motives can also apply to illegitimate holders, who may have additional reasons as well. For them, gold can be a medium for covert transactions (to finance black market dealings, escape exchange controls, or launder money), an investment device that escapes wealth and capital gains taxes, or a secret fund for such emergencies as the need to change domiciles quickly ahead of an arrest warrant.

BLACK GOLD

As a medium of anonymous exchange, gold has many fans in many places. Among the users in North America can be found survivalist sects and far-right tax protest groups convinced that existing governments are illegitimate and that the established economic order is slated soon to collapse—although not before governments have run amok confiscating private wealth. One of the most militant in the United States, Posse Comitatus, created a system of barter houses whose membership lists were confidential and where members could convert cash into silver bullion and gold coins without any records being kept of the transaction. If a member chose to keep bullion on deposit, any of the affiliates could pay bills on that person's behalf, and if a member needed cash, the barter house stood ready to buy back a portion of that person's silver and gold. Transactions with banks were conducted in the name of the barter house, not in the names of individual members, thus protecting the members' identity from the tax authorities.[11]

The fan club also includes drug traffickers halfway around the world. Gold from Hong Kong, for example, is smuggled into Nepal and swapped for heroin. Those on both sides of the transaction are happy. Inside Nepal the local price of gold is kept high by taxes and tariffs, whereas the local price of heroin is low because the country is a crossroads for the supply routes out of both the Golden Triangle and the Golden Crescent. The gold smugglers reap one type of profit; the heroin smugglers reap another—and anyone plying both trades at once feels blessed with a virtual Midas touch.[12]

Gold is equally useful as a vehicle for flight capital. After the fall of South Vietnam, the victorious Communists expelled en masse ethnic Chinese, who tended to support the old regime and whose members had dominated local black markets. Of course the truly rich had already stashed their wealth in Hong Kong and Singapore and fled with or in advance of the U.S. forces, whereas the less well to do formed subsequent waves of boat people. Loaded onto ancient freighters, fishing boats, and even rafts, for which they had paid an average toll of nine gold rings, they put to sea to face storms and Thai pirates.[13]

Once in the United States, some found that old habits died hard. Gold, in small wafers made in Vietnam and bearing the stamp of well-known goldsmiths, was smuggled in to circulate as underground currency.[14] But what comes in can also go out. As part of its on-going program of economic warfare, the United States imposed tight controls on the amount ethnic Vietnamese living in the United States could send to families back home. As a result, some hired professional couriers to smuggle out their remittances, sometimes in cash and sometimes in gold.[15]

The United States was not alone in finding that gold could undercut restrictions on the international flow of funds. Turkey, until a decade ago, had tight exchange controls as well as limits on the amount of domestic lending denominated in foreign currency that a bank could conduct. In 1984, senior officials of three of the largest banks were charged with buying sixty to ninety tons of gold on the black market, using Turkish lira, and then smuggling the gold out of the country and selling it for dollars and deutsche marks. The proceeds were wired home, increasing their banks' foreign asset holdings and permitting the banks to make more foreign currency–denominated loans.[16] That case was of direct concern only to the Turkish authorities. But a few years later the unique role of the Turkish gold market in the region's underground financial movements was again in the news, this time all over the world.

The unraveling began in Los Angeles in 1986 when a man checked in for a Pan Am flight to Europe, only to be assessed excess baggage charges. He protested though eventually relented. The altercation, however, assured that the ticket clerk would remember him. So when she saw him, a few minutes later, buying a ticket on a KLM flight, she notified the authorities. When they retrieved the bag he had checked onto the Pan Am flight, they found not a bomb but $2 million in small bills. He confessed it was cocaine money en route to a Zurich firm of money changers run by the Magharian brothers, two Lebanese-Armenians who had taken refuge in Switzerland. That same year, independently, Swiss police arrested a Turkish smuggler and his Italian accomplice with one hundred kilos of heroin and morphine, and found on them the phone number of the very same money changers. From there the trail led, via Turkey and Bulgaria, into the boardrooms of the three biggest Swiss banks and on up to top levels of the Swiss government.

The fulcrum was the gold-jewelry section of the Istanbul Grand Bazaar, a place where gold is so entrenched in social and economic life that rents are reckoned in it. There, gold-jewelry shops have long run a parallel banking system catering, on the demand side, mainly to businesses seeking illegal foreign exchange and, on the supply side, to people wanting to quietly convert foreign exchange they were bringing into Turkey. These included tourists seeking a better exchange rate, families of Turkish émigré workers in Germany trying to avoid taxes on money sent home, and drug smugglers.

Since the 1980s, one of the main transit routes for Afghan heroin has led overland across the Golden Crescent to Istanbul, where the Turkish *babas* arrange to smuggle it, via the Turkish or Kurdish émigré community, to western Europe. Cash from drug sales was shipped back to Istanbul. Then the Magharians in Zurich entered the picture.

Turkish jewelers gathered masses of banknotes, mainly dollars and deutsch marks, and then sold them to the Magharian brothers. The notes were packed into false floors on buses or into trucks loaded with people or produce, then driven into Bulgaria. Apart from the cover provided by more than four hundred thousand vehicles crossing the Turkish-Bulgarian border every year, security was enhanced by handfuls of cash to police and Customs. In Sofia, notes were counted at a safe house provided by the Bulgarian state intelligence service—which reputedly took a modest $1.00 to $3.00 per $1,000. Then the notes were turned over to couriers from Switzerland, who took them, accompanied by Bulgarian police, to the airport for a quick flight to Zurich. In Zurich the money was deposited in accounts opened in the big banks in the name of the Magharian brothers. Then the return leg of the circuit began.

Part of the hard currency was wired back to Turkey into the hard currency accounts of Turkish import-export firms, which repaid the Magharians at the black market rate in lira, which the Magharians then used to buy more dollars and deutsch marks in Istanbul. But approximately a third was converted directly into gold. The gold was turned over to couriers who carried it to Sofia, paid a $60 per kilo commission to Bulgarian intelligence, then hid it in trucks and buses for the trip to Istanbul, where it was delivered to jewelry shops. On arrival, part went to jewelers as a fee for service, part went to drug traffickers as profits, and part was sent farther east to pay for Afghani and Pakistani opiates.

Of course the Swiss banks had made careful inquiries about the source of the money before allowing the Magharian brothers use of their facilities. They were informed that the money came only from innocent activities such as tax evasion and capital flight. Having received the assurance that their customers' foreign business was sufficiently shady to yield a high return, yet insufficiently so to invite any local legal headaches, the banks warmly welcomed the Magharians. Crédit Suisse issued a letter of reference to help them secure residence permits, lobbied Swiss embassies abroad to secure visas for their couriers, advised the brothers on setting up a shell company, and allowed one of the bank officers to hold a power of attorney over a Magharian account. The Magharians, in turn, handed out to Crédit Suisse officers gifts as varied as oriental carpets, high-priced car radios, and all-expenses-paid vacations in Greece. With such business rapport, the two brothers had little trouble running more than 1.4 billion in Swiss francs through Crédit Suisse and 600 million more through its two main competitors before disaster struck.

It came in the form of unfortunate incidents in Los Angeles and on the Swiss–Italian border, which brought U.S. narcotics agents snooping. When the U.S. authorities probed their Swiss counterparts about the operation, the Swiss minister of justice placed a hasty phone call to her husband, advising him to resign as vice president of the firm supplying the Magharians with gold. When news of that phone call leaked out (by one account, through a National Security Agency wiretap), the ensuing scandal forced the minister to step down and led to unanimous passage by the Swiss parliament of a law making money laundering a criminal offense.[17]

ALL THAT GLITTERS . . .

Apart from its use as a covert medium of exchange, gold has been eagerly sought for short-term speculative gains. It used to be that whenever the world political climate turned sour or the stock market tanked, there would be a flight to gold, egged on by "investment counselors" with an ideological and financial interest in touting the virtues of gold as the refuge of last resort.

However, the last time world events precipitated a dramatic run-up was after the 1979 Soviet invasion of Afghanistan. Gold reached an all-time high of more than $800 per ounce, only to collapse by 1981 to $350, from which level, come hot war or cold peace, it has experienced only modest and short-lived recoveries. Indeed, the 1990–91 Kuwait crisis and Gulf War shocked gold bugs by leading to a fall in the price.

Still, even declining prices opened up opportunities for a reverse alchemy scam. The architects of such deals took investors' money, promising them that their gold was safely stored and redeemable either whenever they wanted or, more commonly, after some fixed future date. As long as prices kept falling, the operations ran smoothly. Few people wanted out, preferring to keep their bullion "safe" until the market turned around, and those who did demand redemption could be accommodated by buying new bullion at a lower price than the one at which the bullion had been invested. In the interim, the rest of the money could be diverted by the organizers wherever and however they wanted.[18]

One such operation in Fort Lauderdale was set up by two brothers who started their professional careers as hair dressers, graduated to selling jewelry, then went into the precious metals business, lured by dreams that gold would make them owners of the world's largest corporation; instead, it sent them to prison. Before that happened they managed to attract twenty-three thousand investors with offers of below-market bullion if clients would wait for delivery. In the meantime, the brothers spun off the money into enterprises such as interior decorating and yacht chartering. When the company was closed in 1984, its warehouse in which clients' gold was supposedly stored contained thirty painted wooden blocks shaped like gold bars. Some $75 million was never found.[19]

That collapse spooked the market and helped bring down one of the Fort Lauderdale operation's main competitors, an operation set up by a former telemarketing manager with no experience in precious metals. Still, it attracted a large clientele, helped by slick promotional brochures attesting that the firm dealt only with top-name metal, that it insured with Lloyd's, and that it stored the metal in one of the best-known facilities in the United States. And it kept customers happy with professional-looking monthly account statements. After the Fort Lauderdale crash, however, clients began demanding their gold or attempting to liquidate holdings. Eventually the firm's president killed himself, and the firm collapsed with $60 million worth of clients' gold "missing" from its Utah vault.[20]

Despite the failure of the gold market, since 1980, to perform as gold bugs insist it should, people with more money than sense continue to fall victim. Events such as stock market crashes still set off a rush for new types of fools' gold.

One popular scam is the dirt pile swindle. Promoters use doctored assay reports to induce investors to buy unprocessed earth, nominally bearing, for example, twenty ounces of gold, for a total price of $5,000—meaning they would get their gold, once it was extracted, for the equivalent of $250 per ounce, approximately one-third less than the market price. These scams are often further embellished with fake gold-purchase agreements with refiners and pictures or maps of the mine site. One case in the early 1980s involved a triple whammy, using three companies owned by the same set of scam artists. One operated a mine and offered to sell piles of aggregate to investors; a second undertook to transport the material to refiners and arrange the extraction of the gold and silver; a third took on the job of calling investors to alert them to the market opportunity, to present them with glowing geological and assay reports, and to assure them that any investment would yield a tenfold return with no risk. The geological and assay reports were faked; the mining project had never existed; the picture on the prospectus was of a coal strip-mine; and although the promoters were in Florida, they used an Arizona number to convince investors they were on site.

In all such scams, the investors are told they have simply to wait a year or two for the processing to be completed.[21] Years later they are still waiting. And they are joined by another group attracted by the development of new technologies to extract residual gold cheaply from already worked-out ore. Thus a Florida firm, formerly in the oil sands business, changed its name and began selling black volcanic sand from Costa Rica from which it would extract gold using a unique chemical "digestion machine" developed by a man who became the firm's president. It was a hard sell, even if the person chosen to peddle the stuff had a sufficiently good sales record to have been convicted of tax fraud and banned from securities trading.[22] A few years later, a Toronto businessman was sentenced to jail for selling "gold delivery contracts" to investors who were told that gold could be obtained from low-cost producers at half the market price, and a pair of Florida sharpies pleaded guilty to conning money from investors in a bogus scheme to recover microscopic ore from an old Nevada mine.[23]

It is even possible, from time to time, that the deception is unintentional. Although no one is likely today to buy a shipment of iron pyrites (the classic fool's gold), in 1994 villagers from a mining area of India tried to peddle semiprocessed uranium yellowcake, convinced by its color that it was gold. Fortunately the police intervened before any would-be investors got burned.[24]

IN GOLD WE TRUST

More important than the lure of short-term speculative gain is the attraction of gold for long-term savings, a demand satisfied in various proportions in different countries by coins or small bars or even crude jewelry. Although much of the value of finely wrought jewelry is due to craftsmanship, the market value of most crude ornaments is almost entirely due to gold content.

Some of the factors that predispose people to hoard gold are deeply rooted in local culture. In places as varied as Korea, Morocco, and the Indian subcontinent, the practice of giving gold at events such as birthdays and marriages persists, reinforced in some Muslim countries by the fact that women expect gold as insurance against divorce-induced poverty. Furthermore, in India, where tradition prevents inheritance of property by female children, their future is provided for by gifts of gold.[25] There too, as in other countries whose banking institutions are underdeveloped, mistrusted, or indifferent to the poor, the village goldsmith fashions and sells simple jewelry and small bars, and functions as a moneylender, accepting the same gold back as collateral for loans during metaphorical rainy days—albeit demand for his services is likely higher during periods of drought than during a climatological harbinger of a good crop.

Some factors are more modern. Currency instability or lack of deposit insurance may lead to a preference for gold. In some Islamic countries, religious opposition to interest payments may incline people to put money into gold rather than financial institutions in the hope of capital gains.[26] In countries in which the "black economy" is very large but there are effective barriers to laundering illegally earned money through financial institutions, gold is an obvious place to stash savings. Added to these motives is the fact that even legitimately earned savings held in gold promise freedom from wealth and inheritance taxes. It is mainly the threat of such taxes at a time of rapidly rising wealth that explains why, since import restrictions were lifted in 1973, the Japanese have been able to sleep more comfortably on mattresses stuffed with more than fifteen hundred tons of gold. And it was likely more than merely respect for gold's history as a religious icon that led members of the notorious Aum cult to store twenty-two pounds of it, along with nerve gas ingredients, in their Tokyo headquarters. Meanwhile, on the other side of the world, Italians, with their deep aversion to taxes and grand reputation for romance, combine the two rather neatly by manufacturing two to three times as many tax-free wedding rings annually as there are marriages.

Certainly not least as a source of continued appeal is the fact that gold is (usually) easy to liquidate during emergencies. For example, in Iraq after the Gulf War, when direct destruction compounded by sanctions brought much of the population to, and even beyond, the point of starvation, the poor and the middle class sold their gold to buy food. The rich, however, shipped their gold abroad in defiance of Iraqi exchange controls. They either stashed it or used it to purchase essentials, which they re-imported and sold on the black market at huge markups.[27]

So, too, in Armenia. In the wake of the collapse of the USSR and war with Azerbaijan, destitute people queued up to sell their gold jewelry so they could survive in an emerging market economy in which the fastest growing sector was composed of pawnshops. In the face of nominally stringent laws restricting the export of valuables, "suitcase merchants" would borrow cash from their families or on the informal loan market, buy gold at 30 percent below world price, melt it down, have couriers carry it to trading centers such as Dubai, and then repatriate part of the profits in consumer goods for resale at crisis-inflated prices.[28]

These examples illustrate a fundamental truth about the secondary market for gold: it is a class-based redistributive mechanism that works inversely to general economic conditions. In good times, the poor stockpile gold (or, if they cannot afford gold, silver); in bad, they shed it. The rich do the opposite. For the poor, gold represents emergency savings; for the rich, it is a tool for currency hedging or capital flight.

Yet gold has disadvantages. In large amounts it can be cumbersome. The 1975 spectacle of South Vietnamese struggling to clamber aboard U.S. evacuation helicopters with suitcases of gold was apparently not un-

derstood by rich Kuwaitis who had to abandon their gold to Iraqi in-
vaders in 1990. Yet after the Iraqis were expelled, so much jewelry flooded
into Kuwait that those responsible for hallmarking (stamping to attest
purity) could not keep up with the demand.[29]

The Gold Diggers

From the supply side, the role of gold in the global black market economy
begins, appropriately enough, underground. The job of bringing the gold
up out of the ground falls to both capital-intensive, multinational mining
companies and, increasingly since the early 1980s, small-scale, labor-
intensive "informal" ones, which now account for at least 25 percent (possibly much more) of world production.

Although all gold mined each year enters the formal refining and distribution network (before half again disappears underground, figuratively
speaking), the impact on host countries of the two types of mining is quite
different. Large companies, typical of major producers in South Africa,
the United States, Canada, and Australia, where either deep or open-pit
mining is the norm, are easier to monitor. Even here, though, there are
opportunities for theft, sufficiently so that in the year 2000, spokespersons
for the South African gold-mining industry claimed that profits were cut
by fully a third as a result of theft. Gold can find its way out of the official
channels at all levels of the mining hierarchy. At the bottom, literally and
figuratively, are the black miners, who know which pieces of rock to hack.
Next come (usually white) operators of equipment that is designed to collect small bits of gold residue. When old processing plants are disman-
tled, sometimes the recovered gold covers the full replacement cost, unless one of the skilled workers gets to it first. Logically, the most tempting
target would be the official refineries, but they are the best protected.
Hence most of the stolen material takes the form of rough or semiprocessed gold, which is then processed further in underground refineries in the black townships. Although it is possible to "fingerprint" gold,
detecting tiny differences in consistency, to determine its origin within
South Africa, once it takes flight to Europe, the game is over.[30]

If this kind of problem besets large-scale mines in which already tight security is backed up further by the specialist gold-and-diamonds branch of
the South Africa police, it is far more difficult, in fact usually impossible, to
control small mines operating in widely scattered alluvial fields. From such
deposits, typical of Brazil, China, Russia, and many other countries, much,

if not most of the gold is usually smuggled onto the world market. The miners evade state purchasing monopolies and contribute little or nothing to a country's tax receipts or foreign exchange reserves.

FIELDS OF DREAMS

Despite the propensity of small companies to smuggle, some countries, China and the Philippines among them, deliberately encourage independent prospecting, partly to keep people from swarming to the cities and partly in hopes of increasing national gold reserves. The first works well; the second poorly, if at all.

Brazil, at the start of its great depression and financial crisis of the 1980s, accelerated the opening of the interior, keen to shift the unemployed out of the urban slums and into the gold fields, where they would make trouble only for the Indians and each other. The authorities also hoped that despite their problems controlling the activities of the alluvial miners, the miners might provide desperately needed foreign exchange. Hence, into the Brazilian Amazon, later spilling over into Venezuela, Guyana, and Bolivia, flowed waves of *garampeiros,* who, by the mid-1990s, totaled over one million—at huge social and ecological cost. Although Brazil's gold output skyrocketed, pushing the country into the major league of producers, the rush also led to the emergence in the Amazon of a free-wheeling transnational economy in which gold became so central that workers' wages, policemen's bribes, and suppliers' bills were paid in nuggets or dust; in which claim jumping, armed robbery, and extortion became routine; and in which a parallel black market supplied teenage sex slaves for the brothels.[31]

Among the richest finds were those on the Brazil–Venezuela border, lands of the Yanomani Indians, the last major unassimilated tribe in Latin America. When the miners were queried about the frequency with which Indians were murdered, they either insisted the stories were a plot by transnational mining companies in league with the Vatican to deny them their livelihood, or they boasted that they had learned how to treat Indians by watching American cowboy movies.[32]

Equally deadly has been the ecological impact. Swathes of forest have been cut or burned, and watercourses have been fouled with waste oil from machinery along with perhaps two hundred tons per year of mercury.[33] Large mining companies that have abandoned the practice of mercury amalgamation, supposedly on ecological and health grounds, have made a public display of virtue by criticizing "free miners" who work in areas the big companies want for themselves. In reality, however, it is a matter of pick your poison, because the big companies have greatly in-creased production through heap leaching, which dumps cyanide into the ecosystem—a fact brought home in a dramatic way by the massive spill of cyanide solution into the Lapus-Somes-Tisza river system of Romania and Hungary by an Australian company in 2000.[34]

Many alluvial miners fit the stereotype of the informal entrepreneur, that is, they pay no taxes, hold no legal title, and use no real capital equip-ment beyond shovels and pans. But there are many who use bulldozers, are supervised by people with cellular phones, and conduct operations that might even be monitored by computer. Far from independent, most of these miners end up working for "owners" of deposits, usually rich former *garampeiros* or urban businessmen looking for a profitable place to invest some illegal money. The lucky ones become *porcentistas,* but most are *diaristas,* that is, working for a daily wage.[35]

As a result, few who mine get rich. The average wage in Brazil's gold rush country was once estimated at one-seventh the amount paid to black workers in South African mines.[36] The wages or shares miners do get are spent quickly—on booze, cocaine, prostitutes, and for a few, luxury cars. As in all gold rushes, past, present, and undoubtedly future, the real money goes either to a handful of rich investors who buy control of op-erating claims or to suppliers of food and capital equipment, vice traffick-ers, and those who purchase and resell the gold.

Although the gold rush has been successful in keeping perhaps a mil-lion more people from crowding into urban shantytowns, it has been less so in bolstering Brazil's foreign exchange reserves. The garampeiros ac-count for far more of Brazil's annual gold production than do legal companies.[37] However, not only does most of the potential gold output get lost through use of low-tech processes, but at least half of the amount actually recovered ends up not with the Brazilian government (for a long time, the government paid less than world market price and in local cur-rency) but with illegal gold-buying networks run by those who can pay in dollars, liquor, or drugs. Or it ends up with *canteiros* who have pro-vided supplies to the miners on credit against a pledge of their future out-put. They might crudely refine it before reselling—some to Brazilian jew-elers, but most to smugglers who spirit it out of the country.[38]

Sometimes the gold goes out via human carriers on scheduled airlines. But most is shipped abroad in the same light planes that ply the cocaine and general contraband trade. In gold rush country, thousands of take-offs and landings occur per month, with no radar or emergency equip-ment, no inspections for mechanical safety, and, of course, no filed flight plans. Finally, in 1996, the Brazilian government capitulated, cutting taxes and licensing private gold buyers. But because garampeiros pledge their production in advance to suppliers linked with smuggling networks, a big chunk still takes underground routes out of the country.

One destination is Paraguay, the paramount smuggling center of Latin America, from which, in return, come duty-free consumer goods. Even more important is Uruguay, the principal hot money haven on the continent, which manages to export annually approximately twenty to thirty tons of gold without risking the social or ecological consequences of a single gold mine on its territory.

Brazil is not alone in sustaining massive losses through smuggling. Guyana, too, created a state monopoly for the purchase of locally produced gold (and diamonds), and it insisted on paying in local currency at much less than the world market rate.[39] Larger and more visible mining operations declare only a small percentage of their total output, while bribed officials look the other way. Small ones declare nothing at all. Agents of Guyanese buyers (the biggest of whom, allegedly, have political protection) take suitcases of dollars into the interior, then charter light planes to haul the gold to the capital, thus eliminating the risk of being ambushed in the jungle on the way back. Then the gold is sent abroad, mainly to the United States. Some of the gold also flows to Brazil, whose merchants service the Guyana gold fields, in payment for supplies, including cocaine and marijuana. From there, some goes directly to Uruguay. Some also goes to Barbados, where, despite Guyanese government complaints, a discrete free market welcomes the gold. But most seems to join the émigré worker circuit en route to the United States.

Elsewhere in Latin America the same story unfolds. In 1983 Venezuela, facing losses estimated at 70 percent of total output, banned private sales and centralized marketing—with such effect that the next year its estimated loss had risen to 90 percent.[40] By the early 1990s the situation had reached the point at which the air force was ordered to bomb the airstrips and jungle camps of the overflow of Brazilian garampeiros; the action was rationalized as a war on drugs and guerrillas. Costa Rica, too, reckoned losses at about 70 percent from gold sold on the local black market or smuggled via Panama.[41] And in Bolivia, although the official production level in 1989 was 3.4 tons worth $43 million, unofficially production equaled another 30 tons worth $400 million, much of it smuggled out with the connivance of government officials and army officers.[42] Not without reason is the South American product referred to in the trade as smuggler's gold.

Despite that accolade, the same story is repeated elsewhere. So it was in former Zaire under Mobutu Sese Seko, the president-for-life who is now dead. Apart from directly owning a large gold concession (one of the first targets of the rebels who overthrew him in 1997), reputedly he once arranged for the Central Bank to print new banknotes, which he then used to purchase black market gold. If true, the president was merely joining the fun. Almost all of the country's output is sneaked by traders across the country's many borders. One destination is Zambia, where officials at the Saudi embassy used to take time off from strenuous diplomatic duties to exchange raw gold for dollars. Those dollars would be traded by the gold smugglers on the black market for Zambian currency, and the Zambian currency would then be resold again at an additional profit for Zairian banknotes. Another destination is Brazzaville in the Congo Republic; gold joins the former Zaire's diamonds in a constant stream across the Congo River. Then ex-Zaire's gold, in the form of fine gold dust or crude bars, winds up in the hands of European brokers, who in turn send it to Swiss banks for refining. Yet another destination is Kenya, where the government even attempted to maximize returns by granting an official monopoly to a group of gold smugglers.[43]

Father afield, the Philippines has been swept by gold fever since the early 1980s. Most of the product is spirited out by Chinese smugglers, perhaps with high-level assistance. Certainly back in the Marcos era there were rumors that the president employed covert buyers to sop up the black market gold to bolster his overseas retirement savings plan—tales that he had found Yamashita's Gold might well have been a cover. But probably the country in Asia most afflicted by free mining is Indonesia. On the island of Sulawesi, the miners can show, to anyone who asks, mining permits stamped and signed by local officials—even though the area was leased long before to an Australian company. Similarly, on the island of Kalimantan, the same company found its diggings surrounded by Indonesians on motorcycles; after each dynamite blast, they would roar down and grab pieces of ore. Forced to abandon several of its mines, the company then saw them overrun by free miners, behind whom stand dealers who pay about 30 percent of the world price and supply the miners (earning on average the equivalent of one dollar a day) with mercury to poison themselves and the environment.[44]

SALTED SAMPLES AND WATERED STOCK

Granted those who dig are poorly remunerated. But that does not preclude a gold rush from making fortunes for some who avoid dirtying their hands physically as distinct from metaphysically. In words that still resonate, Mark Twain once described a gold mine as a hole in the ground with a liar on top. Every so often stock markets, particularly in Canada, where listings are notoriously easy to obtain, are driven into a frenzy by rumors that some promoter has stumbled across King Solomon's mines, perhaps the most geographically peripatetic mother lode in history. The price of shares of junior gold companies is particularly volatile: the shares are issued for pennies, so small changes in the world price of gold can cause enormous price movements, and the resulting rash of speculation feeds on itself. How much more so if the invisible hand of the free market spends some of its time dialing numbers on sucker lists or writing hyped prospectuses, fraudulent geological reports, or phony assay results.

Thus, two swindlers working out of Toronto bought a defunct Costa Rica mine with only traces of gold, set up a Panama "mining company," then peddled shares using the phone lines of a U.S. telemarketing firm and lists of potential marks bought from other conmen. Those who seemed interested got market bulletins from the supposed mine and were bombarded with calls purportedly from Costa Rica. If a client refused, he or she received a call a week later with a report the stock had risen. Once the client bit and sent money to Panama or Costa Rica (which promptly was wired back to Toronto), the client was rewarded with fake share certificates and interim reports. If clients tried to cash out, they found that the share price had mysteriously dropped from $3.00 to 25–50 cents.[45]

Using technological breakthroughs, real or imaginary, to hype shares is also a frequent occurrence. For example, in the early 1970s two McGill University professors conducting research on gonorrhea and spinal meningitis discovered how the human body stores iron to protect itself from disease. They attempted to isolate the biochemical mechanism and then tried to use it to extract metals such as gold from seawater or from the cyanide sludge left behind after gold-bearing rock is crushed. Desperate for funds for their research, the two were introduced to a Montreal promoter, Irving Kott, who used claims about the technology to run boiler room scams out of Amsterdam, until the Dutch authorities raided his operation and shut it down.[46]

Although boiler room sales, with or without technohype, can work well, today most scams are accompanied by would-be geological reports and assay results. An imaginary geological report was the key to the enterprises of Pier Luigi Torri, an Italian playboy who left home just ahead of an arrest warrant. He wanted to make the trip in his own yacht, but it had been impounded by the Financial Guard as part of a large fine for exchange-control evasion. However, he persuaded a friend to pay the fine to free the yacht and then left in a hurry, pursued by the friend seeking compensation. Somewhere in the Atlantic, the yacht had an accident. Torri managed to get to England safely, but he was disappointed when a marine insurance company refused to pay up. For a while he pursued a respectable career as an offshore banker, riding out a miniscandal when one of his banks was discovered to have been used by an Italian fascist group to wash ransom money. Then he linked up with two Italo-Canadians in a gold-mining project in British Colombia. A glossy brochure insisted that the company, discretely incorporated in Panama with a Cayman Islands address, held claims to part of a gold-bearing area from which ore worth no less than $288 billion had already been extracted. The company's own concession reputedly contained nearly 900 million ounces of gold, silver, and platinum—no small feat for a property that consisted of a waterlogged shack on a small piece of logged-out scrubland. Proof of the veracity of the claims could be found in the rapid rise of the shares—from $1.00 to $32.00 in a matter of weeks. It just happened that all the shares were traded through two Anguilla banks owned by Pier Luigi Torri. In case potential investors were still skittish about risking their funds, they could monitor the progress of the shares regularly on the Offshore Stock Exchange, run by a friend of Torri's through his own Caribbean insta-bank. While waiting for investors to grab the $326 million of stock on offer, one of Torri's banks issued $1.5 million in bank drafts, which a member of the gold scheme used to buy two airplanes from Cessna. After the drafts bounced, the police came calling. The gold scam collapsed. Jailed, Torri managed to grant himself temporary leave of absence through the roof ventilator of his cell, although he was later picked up in New York and shipped back to Britain for trial, eventually copping seven years.[47]

Assay reports also can be completely fictional. In 1997, on the basis of drilling three exploratory holes, one Vancouver firm claimed to have found five million ounces in Nevada, driving the shares from $8.00 to $34.75. When a Nevada mining official challenged the results, the company presented independent confirmation by another company whose unique assay technique no one else possessed. The testing firm was run by someone who did not have an assayer's license but did have a previous conviction for securities fraud. Later it turned out the geological formation could not possibly have held gold and that the assay results were based on salting the samples in solution.[48]

Salting can be accomplished in several ways. When a core sample is ground for analysis, gold flakes can be sprinkled on it, but this is problematic because gold flakes are not part of rock. It is usually better to dissolve the gold in a cyanide complex and then spray the solution on the raw core before or after it is ground, or add it to the test solution.[49]

So it was with a North Carolina promoter who had a long history of regulatory scrapes. In 1987, he coaxed Adnan Khashoggi, the Saudi arms broker, to put his signature to a press release extolling a piece of desert in

Mali as the location of the world's last great gold reserves, perhaps the legendary King Solomon's mines themselves. Although this effort never got much beyond a breathless prospectus, ten years later the promoter was back in business, this time with a company called Timbuktu Gold Corp. The second time around he needed more credibility, which he gained when someone inadvertently dropped bits of crushed Krugerrands into boxes of worthless rock samples prior to testing. Before that accident was discovered, all manner of investment counselors "herd" the message and bought in, usually with other people's money, convinced this would be the next Bre-X.[50] In a sense they were right.

Within three years Bre-X's billing changed from the greatest gold discovery in history to the greatest mining fraud of the century. Alas, it cannot claim either distinction. At heart it was just another salting operation that happened to get out of hand.

The saga began when a couple of geologists posited new theories about the geological forces that explain the location of the world's gold deposits. Those theories led them in succession into the jungle of Kalimantan, the swamp of Indonesian politics, and the sewer of Canadian stock exchanges.

Kalimantan does have gold, lots of it. For centuries the indigenous peoples have panned riverbed deposits. But the gold was nowhere near the site pinpointed by the theories of Bre-X geologists. Drilling began, with zero results. Soon there was danger that the operation would be shut down. At that point Michael de Guzman, who ran the field operation, decided to buy more time—and, in Kalimantan, time, like everything else, is best purchased with gold. So he sought out a merchant who sold supplies to the alluvial miners and in exchange bought their gold. Over the next three years, de Guzman spent about $21,000 to purchase sixty ounces of river gold. At night he would carefully measure gold to match it to ground-up rock from the drill cores, taking care to change the concentrations. Then the salted samples were sent in for analysis—with increasingly spectacular results. Initially it seems that the point of the salting was to keep development money flowing until gold was actually found. It wasn't until disappointment followed disappointment that the scheme degenerated into a deliberate stock-market swindle. Even then most, perhaps all, of the Bre-X executives, apart from de Guzman, apparently had no idea what was happening. Certainly there was no inkling among other mining companies or the crony-capitalists who surrounded the Indonesian president; the result was a series of hostile and high-profile takeover attempts that only served to further consolidate the Bre-X claims in the public mind. As usual, expert stock shills trumpeted the company's fantasies—its claim to 200 million ounces would have given it 8 percent of the world's gold supply in one deposit. And the labs testing the ore managed to completely overlook not just the occasional red flag but a field full of frantically flapping banners.

The finer an ore sample is ground, the higher should be the concentration of gold revealed in subsequent tests, but in this case the proportions remained constant. Although alluvial gold appears in grains large enough to be visible to the naked eye, underground deposits should be in flecks so small they cannot be seen—but those in the Bre-X samples could be. Furthermore, gold and silver occur together in nature. With surface gold, the silver leaches out; with underground gold it remains. In the Bre-X samples, there was no associated silver. But the shares rose to dizzying heights before de Guzman's mysterious death brought the entire edifice crashing down, wiping out about C$5 billion in stock "value."[51]

GOLDENBERG AND THE GOLDEN TOUCH

Of course there are those who avoid any contact with something as crude as rock, preferring, like medieval alchemists, to transmute base paper into pure gold. When some imaginative entrepreneurs did that in Kenya, they managed to take the Central Bank for a $210 million ride.[52]

It began when the government of Kenya decided to create special incentives for export industries. Companies expecting to receive foreign currency in payment for exports could borrow in Kenyan shillings from a commercial bank, the equivalent of 15 percent of anticipated foreign currency earnings before the goods even left the country; then they could borrow another 20 percent while awaiting payment after the goods were actually shipped. The commercial banks in turn could apply to the Central Bank for compensation. Of course, the transactions were not completed on faith—firms that received preshipment finance had to provide documents attesting to the existence of the foreign orders; those that received export finance had to show invoices detailing expected payments as well as airway bills, and, in the case of mineral exports, certificates of inspection from the commissioner of mines.

There was not exactly a mad rush to take advantage. One applicant was a fishing company already technically insolvent.[53] The only other was Goldenberg Corporation, privy to an open secret.

Although Kenya produced little gold and no diamonds, it was a major transit point for gold and precious stones smuggled out of neighboring countries. However, what was smuggled in could also be smuggled back out. Along with the contraband just passing through went most of Kenya's own gold production. Therefore the government listened carefully when Goldenberg made an offer that was hard to refuse. It promised to export (and repatriate the foreign exchange from) no less than four hundred kilos of gold per month, whereas Kenya's official production was about one hundred kilos per year. All it wanted was a five-year monopoly on the export of gold, diamonds, and jewelry—plus other goodies that would be specified in the future. For Goldenberg, the monopoly would make it more difficult for anyone to contest its figures because there would be no immediate basis of comparison.[54]

To secure the preshipment financing, Goldenberg presented documents attesting to orders from two firms in Switzerland and one in Dubai. The Swiss firms did not exist, and the Dubai one had never heard of Goldenberg. To secure export financing, Goldberg had to show the Central Bank a number of forms and documents. In one instance it presented both a Customs form attesting that jewelry had left the country on a certain date and a certificate from the commissioner of mines verifying that the same goods had been inspected nearly two weeks later. A check of one of its invoices showed that Goldenberg was selling gold abroad for eleven times the world market price.

In strict theory, foreign exchange in payment for the "exports" should have been coming back into the country and then turned over to the Central Bank. Goldenberg solved part of that problem by using the money from preshipment credits to buy foreign exchange on the local black market, then claiming it came from exports. Part was solved by misdeclaring money from the partners' own local businesses. Although the regulations stipulated that export earnings had to be invoiced in foreign currency, the Central Bank never blinked when some of the export invoices declared earnings in Kenyan shillings. At one point a Goldenberg-controlled bank sent to the Central Bank sixteen bundles of cash in five different currencies on four different business days, all allegedly payments received for a single export consignment.[55]

Indeed, things got easier a year later when regulations were changed. Instead of turning foreign exchange over to the Central Bank, exporters could keep it in special accounts in a commercial bank, then draw on it freely when they had bills to pay abroad. If those exporters also owned the bank, so much the better. All that was necessary was for the bank to tell the Central Bank that the foreign exchange existed, even if it did not. As further cover, banks controlled by Goldenberg's principals lent money back and forth to create the appearance they were all receiving remittances from foreign customers. Even better, when questions began to be asked, officials in the Central Bank faked the books to hide a hole that eventually totaled $210 million. When the International Monetary Fund looked closely and discovered what was afoot, Kenya faced a credit cut-off and one of the biggest political scandals in its history.[56]

FROM RED TO GOLD

Smuggling from smaller countries of Africa, Latin America, and Asia can have an enormous impact on their foreign exchange reserves, but it has little effect on world supply.[57] However, that is not true with suppliers the size of China or Russia, where unpoliceable alluvial fields and sophisticated smuggling networks coexist.

In China, the combination of economic liberalization, high returns from mining compared with those from farming, and the general weakening of state authority has meant that the alluvial fields, producing nearly one hundred tons per annum, have became the fiefdom of rival gold lords. Drawn from the ranks of the Muslim minority and commanding or buying the loyalty of thousands of peasants, these local chiefs, often with separatist leanings, are linked to smuggling syndicates through family ties. They sometimes brag of firepower greater than that of local representatives of the central government, and they enhance that firepower by providing weapons and training for miners in their territory. As in Brazil, the hundreds of thousands of peasant miners leave in their wake deforestation, erosion, mercury contamination, and the destruction of rare wildlife.[58]

Although some black market output stays at home to supply underground jewelry manufacturers, a great deal makes its way to Hong Kong, where, ironically, it helps pay for a return flow of finished jewelry smuggled back into China by the same syndicates. Efforts to enforce the state monopoly—raising the price, cracking down on smuggling rings, even threatening to invoke the death penalty—have simply made the smugglers more ingenious and added to the ranks of covert gold buyers, corrupt party cadres, government officials, and even undertakers. Cadavers, real or false, stuffed with gold, are carried in coffins out of the producing areas, accompanied by the required entourage of weeping relatives.[59]

Large though it is, the drain of black market gold out of China pales in comparison to that from the ex–Soviet Union, which has long been second only to South Africa among world producers. In Uzbekistan, Kazakhstan, and Siberia, the gold fields are now run by "mafias" of ex–party apparatchiks and regional warlords, which represents a dramatic change, given the role gold mining has played in Soviet history.

Although Russia produced gold before the October Revolution, the real drive came under Stalin. Fascinated by the role of gold in opening the American West, Stalin saw gold as a tool that, at one and the same time, would consolidate Soviet control over Siberia, kick-start strategic industrialization in an area far from vulnerable frontiers, and eliminate any threat to the USSR's financial position that could be precipitated by a Western credit freeze. Although forcible collectivization was imposed on the peasantry in the western areas of the Soviet Union, free enterprise (assisted by slave labor from nearby prison camps) was the watchword in gold. All this would change, however, when Nikita Khrushchev came to power. Not only did he amnesty many prisoners, but, with Soviet agriculture weakening, Soviet gold had to be sold to purchase wheat. Thus began a long process in which the huge gold stocks built up by Stalin were drained off.[60] To try to offset the loss of free labor, the state required some prisoners to remain for a while as cheap wageworkers, and it offered the private sector additional incentives to expand. To attempt to ensure that all gold output was sold exclusively to the state monopoly, the state kept stores in the gold-mining areas well stocked, even in the face of shortages elsewhere, and it made gold legal tender for purchasing supplies. There was some diversion of gold onto the domestic black market, but it was of little concern. The amounts were small, and the main buyers were dentists who did a little drilling on the side plus jewelers who ran a small underground industry.[61]

Then, in the 1980s, the black market widened. By the end of the decade fully two-thirds of officials of the mining cooperatives had been disciplined, and some were imprisoned—to no real effect. Huge amounts of gold were embezzled and state-owned equipment routinely hijacked for private use. At the receiving end, the customers were members of the general urban population who were seeking a safe refuge for their savings or a place to stash black market earnings.[62] Furthermore, control of the gold resources (and of diamonds) became central to the struggle over the future of the Soviet Union. When Boris Yeltsin took power in Russia, he asserted Russian ownership over natural resources. The ensuing concession of de facto control to the republics was perhaps the first major step toward Soviet dissolution.

With the end of the Soviet Union, the situation degenerated into a free-for-all. Freelance miners flooded into the alluvial fields, raising their share of total production from 35 to 60 percent, and the smuggling rate jumped to at least 25–30 percent of total output. This time, however, the black market gold was destined for the world rather than the internal market.[63] Perhaps it would have made little difference to Russia's foreign exchange position if the state monopoly had captured all the production. For although smuggling was draining raw gold from the alluvial fields, much of the gold successfully collected by official channels and then refined was stolen by senior bureaucrats and their business allies and sold abroad.[64]

A Touch of Refinement

Ultimately both officially produced and smuggled raw gold end up refined by the same respectable institutions, which also package it for resale—some for the legal and some for the illegal market. The first step in the refining–manufacturing chain is the production of what are called good delivery bars, which average four hundred troy ounces and are at least 99.95 percent pure. Although almost any smelting firm can make gold bars, only members of the London Bullion Association—a group that originally consisted almost entirely of British firms but that now includes ones from the Americas and Asia as well—have the right to produce the type of bar acceptable on the London market. Each comes with a serial number and the stamp of the refiner.[65]

The delivery process is actually more symbolic than real. For many years the City of London (because of its connections with South Africa, the United States, Canada, and Australia) dominated the wholesale market, with five firms meeting twice a day in London to fix the world price. But since the late 1960s, Zurich has been a powerful competitor for the physical trade. South Africa, the world's largest producer, shifted its marketing from London to Switzerland to protest a British arms embargo, and the Soviet Union followed. The advantages of a Swiss trading forum included lack of exchange controls (which the British maintained for more than twenty years after World War II), neutrality in world affairs, (formerly) tight bank secrecy laws, and Switzerland's long role as the world's most prestigious financial haven. However, whether from London or Zurich, good delivery bars are sold to Central Banks, government mints, and private firms in the secondary manufacturing business.

COIN OF WHOSE REALM?

Part of world production is converted from good delivery bars into coins—South African Krugerrands, British Sovereigns, Canadian Maple

Leafs, U.S. Eagles, Chinese Pandas, and so forth. The clientele includes survivalists holed up in log cabins in the American West, with bags of dried beans, boxes of ammunition, and sacks of gold coins in their larders. It includes people in certain high-risk professions—one veteran gunrunner advises those entering his trade to carry a survival belt of gold coins, although his personal preference is for a wad of U.S. cash.[66] It includes ordinary citizens. In 1994, when the police, looking for evidence of payoffs, raided one of several homes of the former head of the Italian Ministry of Health's pharmaceuticals division, they found, in addition to one hundred small bars of gold, six thousand gold guineas, thousands of Krugerrands, and old Russian and Roman coins—an interesting haul from a governmental official of a country in which private investment in gold had been illegal since 1936. The clientele for gold coins even includes jewelers. Especially in the Middle East and southwestern Asia, coins are sometimes strung into inexpensive jewelry, thereby doing double duty: they can be worn by the final purchaser as an ornament, and a coin or two can be plucked from the chain to be spent when need arises.

Some people are so eager to acquire coins that they do not bother to pay for them. Once in London a group contacted two dealers to purchase £700,000 worth of Krugerrands. Payment was to take place by bank draft. On the day the purchase was to close, couriers arrived at the coin firms with the drafts and waited patiently while clerks phoned the issuing bank to confirm the details. This task satisfactorily completed, the coins were handed over. It turned out that the drafts were excellent forgeries, and the phone lines had been intercepted, with the result that the confirmation call was rerouted to a house holding accomplices, who were pleased to attest to the authenticity of the drafts.[67]

The advantages of gold coins—ease of handling, supposedly assured value, and the prospect of capital gains—attract many people willing to pay for those advantages, particularly the elderly and those who routinely find their way onto hit lists peddled back and forth by telemarketing companies. The scams are fairly predictable: sales of fake or grossly overvalued coins, often with phony buy-back guarantees; demands for down payments of up to 50 percent, with the company then packing up and disappearing; and so forth. Perhaps the cleverest instance of actual counterfeiting occurred (if it really did) sometime after 1986, when the Japanese government commissioned ten million coins to commemorate the sixtieth year of Emperor Hirohito's reign. Given the occasion, the government decided to make this particular coin, the first minted in Japan since the 1930s, risk free. Hence it guaranteed that although each coin contained only ¥40,000 worth of gold, investors could sell them back to the government at the issue price of ¥100,000 should the value start to fall on the open market; on the other hand, should the price rise, investors could sell the coins on the open market. Not only did the scheme promise big profits ($3.5 billion) to the Japanese Ministry of Finance, but by cleverly routing the purchase of three hundred metric tons of gold through New York, the ministry created an illusory improvement in the United States–Japan yawning trade deficit, which they hoped would help appease U.S. politicians clamoring for trade restrictions.

The scheme was also an opportunity too rich to be missed by private-sector entrepreneurs, who reputedly stamped two tons of gold into counterfeits, each, like the originals, containing ¥40,000 worth of gold. The counterfeits were so good that they fooled even the Bank of Japan, which had minted the real ones. The coins were sold to banks for the full government-guaranteed price. At the end of the process, the Ministry of Finance admitted to accumulating more than $70 million worth of the fakes, setting off a police hunt that seemed to go nowhere.[68] Indeed, it proved impossible to convince some coin dealers there had actually been any counterfeiting. There were wild stories, however, that the gold to make the fake coins had been supplied by Saddam Hussein to his allies in Lebanon, and they in turn had run the stuff via Cyprus to Switzerland and then to Japan. Whatever the truth, the rumors led to a collapse in confidence in the coins and a massive cashing in at the guaranteed price. The government's next coin issue in 1991 was much smaller and contained 50 percent more gold.[69]

Coins aside, much of the world's gold production is broken down into smaller bars: the kilo bar, about the size of a package of cigarettes and much in demand in richer industrialized or oil-producing countries; the ten-tola bar, the size of a matchbox or a large chocolate candy and tailored especially for the Indian subcontinent; the tael bar (actually several sizes), a wafer of gold, eagerly sought in the Far East; and a range of other, more exotic and less widely used shapes and sizes.

Initially the manufacture of secondary bars was dominated by Johnson-Matthey Bank, the only member of the original five London price-fixers to possess its own refinery. So trusted was the Johnson-Matthey stamp that gold merchants in the Middle East sometimes refused to accept any other product. Among other advantages, Johnson-Matthey small bars were made with rounded edges so they would not tear the canvas body-bags used for smuggling or, for that matter, cause internal damage if couriers chose to hide the gold in more private parts. The firm's competence in mass-producing small bars also made it the target of the greatest gold heist in British history.

THE GANG THAT COULDN'T LAUNDER STRAIGHT

It began in 1983 at London's Heathrow Airport with a raid on the Brink's-Mat warehouse. The security firm had just taken delivery of three and a half tons of gold in kilo and ten-tola bars, worth £26 million, along with platinum, one thousand carats of diamonds, and $250,000 in traveler's checks. Although an informant ensured the quick arrest of those who did the job, the actual robbery had gone like clockwork. Amateur hour struck only during the subsequent stages, when associates of the arrested robbers attempted to sell the gold and launder the money.[70]

The easiest solution would have been to smuggle the loot abroad and sell it, at a hefty discount, in a no-questions-asked bullion market whose experts would facilitate its reentry into the normal flow of gold trade. Perhaps intimidated by the volume or put off by the size of the necessary discount or just lacking the required information, those trying to unload the stuff decided to handle the matter at home. Apparently valuing expertise above prudence, they turned the loot over to a man already under investigation for gold smuggling.

The first problem was that the gold had Johnson-Matthey markings attesting to its purity, and the kilo bars (although not the ten-tola ones) had serial numbers. Therefore, the man in charge of passing the gold went to the Channel Islands to buy a batch of kilo bars, stashing them there and returning only with certificates of purchase so that if he were ever caught in Britain ferrying bars of the stolen gold to a smelter, he had good cover. However, he had made such a commotion in the process of assuring that the certificates for the Channel Islands gold did not have the serial numbers noted that the bank reported his visit to the police. The report provided one of the first leads. And if the cops needed any more help, the gang was happy to oblige.

The expert gold-washer approached a friend who ran a small refinery, apparently unconcerned that his friend's firm had already achieved notoriety for evasion of value-added taxes. The friend melted down the gold at home to remove the serial numbers and then took it to his business to resmelt it, where he adulterated it with silver and copper so it could pass as scrap. As cover, the smelting firm placed advertisements in trade publications offering to buy scrap gold at prices that were much above the industry standard—making the firm the talk of the trade.

Soon it was not just other gold dealers who were commenting on the sudden improvement in the smelting firm's fortunes. The firm paid for the Brink's gold in cash, and that required so many banknotes (in the final analysis, more than £10 million) that the firm's bank had to hire extra staff and arrange emergency shipments of notes from the Bank of England.

To hide the origins of the gold, the firm arranged phony paperwork to show the gold had come from two companies that collected jewelry trade scrap. One company was already defunct, however, and the other belonged to someone convicted of smuggling imitation gold coins into Britain. The smelting firm would telex a large sum to the firm run by the coin smuggler, ostensibly in payment for the gold; the coin smuggler would withdraw the money from his bank in cash and then hand it back to the smelting firm after deducting a fee.

After the gold was resmelted and adulterated, it was sent to a government-run assay office. Duly certified as to its purity, it could be sold to unsuspecting precious metal brokers, who in turn resold it to reputable firms, some to the jewelry trade, and some even back to Johnson-Matthey. As buyers of the resmelted gold poured money into the smelting firm's bank account, it would withdraw the money and purchase yet more Brink's-Mat gold bars from the thieves, who then had to worry about what to do with all the cash they were accumulating.

The solution was to move the cash covertly offshore, prior to bringing some of it back to Britain through regular banking channels to invest in the London property market. But that, too, required professional assistance.

To handle the laundering cycle they contacted another expert who had already attracted a great deal of unwanted attention. The West German police had made inquiries after the would-be launderer had conned local businessmen in a commodity futures scam; the U.S. Drug Enforcement Administration (DEA) was investigating his role in moving money on behalf of a Florida marijuana ring; the British police had noted his involvement in a swindle in which a British charitable foundation had been used to whiten millions from around the world; and he had come under suspicion as a possible money launderer for the IRA.

Not least of the examples of the gang's sense of discretion, when the police were investigating one of the suspects, they came across two rottweilers owned by the suspect's wife and proudly bearing the names Brinks and Mat.

In the final analysis, virtually all the participants were caught. But only eleven gold bars were recovered. Of the money earned from the sale of the others, by the end of 1995 some £20 million was either seized or frozen pending further court action—although the estimate was that by then the loot, properly invested, would have accumulated to nearly £70 million.[71]

By the time the Brink's-Mat robbery occurred, London, and Johnson-Matthey, were already losing their dominance of the small-products business. Indeed, they came close to losing the gold trade in its entirety. In 1984 the banking arm of Johnson-Matthey collapsed after a series of commodity swindles in Nigeria; the collapse threatened confidence in the gold pool and forced the Bank of England to rescue the firm.[72] It was bad timing. By then all three big Swiss banks had their own refineries turning out a full range of smaller bars, and Switzerland hosted a group of Middle Eastern gold firms, one of which brought the Swiss gold trade some new publicity.

Mahmoud Sharkachi had been among Beirut's best-known gold and foreign exchange dealers, pioneering a line of small ingots designed to cater to Middle Eastern demand. Given his long relationship with the Swiss banks that had provided his gold, Sharkachi relocated to Zurich when he was forced to decamp during the Lebanese Civil War. Although initially he was refused residency, that decision was reversed as a result of a recommendation from the intelligence bureau of the Zurich police. During the next few years, Sharkachi repaid that confidence by taking the chief on hunting trips to Bulgaria and by collaborating with Swiss intelligence in tracking "Arab terrorism."

Under the auspices of the patriarch's sons, the firm expanded, with its own network of couriers and direct access to the tarmac of Zurich airport. Its gold exports to the Middle East some years hit thirty tons.[73] And its money-changing business had a list of satisfied clients that reputedly included the CIA: during the Afghan war, the CIA allegedly got from the firm 25 million Swiss francs worth of Afghani and Pakistani currency at black market rates to make its covert action budget stretch a little further.[74]

The Sharkachi firm's business was not without setbacks. In 1983, one of its Turkish clients was fingered in a major heroin case. Arrested in Austria, he jumped bail and disappeared. But the revelations prompted the Swiss government to freeze the firm's bank accounts. That presented a challenge to the firm's vice president, a well-connected Zurich lawyer who just happened to be married to the future Swiss minister of justice. The Zurich lawyer lobbied successfully for the freeze to be reversed.[75] Hence it soon was business as usual, until two of Sharkachi's associates managed to precipitate a far more serious scandal.

When the Magharian brothers arrived in Zurich, they were taken under the Sharkachi wing. The doyen of the firm lent them use of his courier network and Bulgarian contacts during the first few difficult years, when they were conducting business out of a hotel room that had been booked using false Greek passports. Then he helped them on their way with a $1 million loan. He also supplied them with much of the gold that they smuggled into Turkey on the return leg of the operation that came to such a spectacular end a few years later.

Now You See It, Now You Don't

From Switzerland (and from lesser wholesale centers), there are several distinct ways in which gold, in shapes and sizes suitable for the retail trade, meets the final customer.

One is for the money to come to the gold—greatly facilitated by Switzerland's long-standing (if no longer accurate) reputation as the world's top financial haven. For further encouragement, the Swiss banks created an account in which the holder makes deposits and receives a passbook denominated not in currency but in ounces of gold. Legend has it that the gold account was pioneered by Geneva's Banque de Crédit International (or ICB), an institution set up in the 1960s by a former Israeli gunrunner who numbered among his satisfied customers the Israeli Mossad, U.S. mob boss Meyer Lansky, Bernie Cornfeld's scandal-wracked Investors' Overseas Services, and a number of African potentates anxious to set something aside for retirement.[76] ICB crashed after an Italian real estate debacle in 1974, but the idea of the gold account proved more durable, so much so that other countries have followed suit. Austria offers both gold bullion and gold coin accounts. Even better known in this area is Singapore, which offers such accounts to, among others, members of Indonesia's hugely wealthy and chronically insecure Chinese business class.

HOME DELIVERY

Most of the time the flow is in reverse, that is, the gold goes out to meet the money. One of the liveliest flows is that between Switzerland and Italy: 30–50 percent of the gold absorbed by Italy's huge jewelry business (Italy is the world's largest jewelry exporter) is smuggled from Switzerland. From there it can end up in the oddest places. In 1994, for example, Italian police cracked an operation in which drug money from the United States was sent to Italy to buy about one ton per month of gold and gold jewelry. The jewelry was shipped to the Colon Free Trade Zone in Panama, and from there it was smuggled to Colombia to be resold for pesos.[77]

Actually moving the merchandise requires professional couriers to deliver gold to customers in countries whose governments impose high taxes or other restrictions. As in any form of covert financial movement, the most desirable courier is one who possesses a diplomatic passport. In the days when priests wore robes, priests were also good choices: their robes would literally cloak contraband, and few officials wanted to be seen publicly harassing a priest—except in some countries.[78]

After seizing the West Bank portion of Palestine, Israel closed or sharply restricted commercial banks that had long serviced the area. The objective was to divert the business to Israeli banks, but the unintended result was to divert more business into an underground financial system built around moneylenders who smuggled Swiss gold across the Jordan River. In 1987, during a crackdown, Israeli border officials stopped a car carrying the Greek Orthodox patriarch of Jerusalem, a man who combined religious with diplomatic status, and seized $1 million worth of gold along with some heroin.[79] But, perhaps to prove there was no religious discrimination involved, a few years later a pair of Yeshiva students, equipped with vests stuffed with gold, who had been regular runners for gold and foreign exchange dealers in Jerusalem, were arrested at Ben Gurion Airport.[80]

Couriers for smuggling syndicates are usually well trained, but the business also attracts independent amateurs. So it was with a London gem dealer. Eton- and Oxford-educated, he had moved in the best circles before the prospect of fun and profit brought him into partnership with a Bombay merchant in a gold-smuggling plot that soon degenerated into insurance fraud. The idea was to finance a shipment of gold from Geneva to Bombay, sell it at a 25–30 percent profit, and then invest the proceeds in gemstones to be smuggled back out for resale at another handsome markup. Unfortunately the gold shipment was intercepted by Indian Customs. So the principals came up with a plan to recoup their losses. They flew to New York with bogus invoices for nonexistent emeralds, rubies, and sapphires and arranged for someone to "rob" them. Then they presented a claim to Lloyd's of London and received £1.8 million in compensation—before insurance investigators broke the case.[81]

Much more important than direct delivery is the indirect trade in which the Swiss (and British) banks ship gold openly and legally to regional distributing centers, from which the actual smuggling takes place. Whether or not a country has the honor of being among those centers depends on a mixture of financial opportunity and physical geography.

The archetypal center for gold smuggling, as for so many other things, was probably Tangier during the days when it was an international city. Surrounded by mountains and with no resources except its geographic location at the northwestern tip of Africa and its entrepreneurial energy,

Tangier had a legal infrastructure of secret bank accounts and instant corporations, and a tax system in which basic goods for local consumption
were taxed more heavily than were luxuries bound for re-export. Tangier
also hosted a thriving foreign exchange market. After servicing black marketers and spies throughout World War II, Tangier found other things to
occupy its time when the shooting stopped. European countries tried to
finance their reconstruction by use of high sin taxes, particularly on cigarettes, and attempted to stop the drain of foreign exchange by restricting gold purchases. Hence the two favorite commodities for the Tangier
trading community became cigarettes and gold.[82]

With the London gold market closed until 1954, the Swiss banks
moved into the vacuum. They shipped increasing amounts of gold to
Tangier, which resold some it to other regional distributing centers such
as Curaçao, Montevideo, and Beirut. Tangier also served its own retail
clientele, of which the most important group resided in France. The
French were (and still are) renowned for their appetite for gold. During
World War II, the Germans had created a special police force, one of
whose principal tasks was to ferret out hidden hoards in occupied
France, but at the end of the war France was reckoned to contain three
hundred tons more than at the start.[83] After liberation, the purchase of
gold remained illegal for French citizens, and the frontiers were well po-
liced. However, it was easy to move large-denomination franc notes to
Geneva, convert them to dollars, buy gold in Zurich, export it openly
to Tangier, and then arrange for it to be smuggled into France by small
planes, which would parachute the gold down to isolated areas that the
French resistance used for refuge during the war. In fact, the Swiss banks
began stashing large amounts in the Tangier port zone (at peak, more
than fifty tons) in anticipation of orders. They would also sell either registered or bearer certificates redeemable in gold in Tangier. For the more
sophisticated investor, they even sold futures contracts on the
stockpile.[84]

The decline of the gold traffic was an omen of the pending demise of
Tangier itself. France reopened its gold market in 1948, and although it
was still illegal to import and export the stuff, controls were relaxed
enough that the gold could be smuggled directly from Switzerland. Then,
in 1949, South Africa began selling gold on the free market, driving down
prices enough that the returns from smuggling sometimes ceased to cover
costs. The deathblow came with the reopening of the London market in
1954, which ended Tangier's role as a re-export center. Shortly thereafter,
Tangier was politically reintegrated into Morocco. Its spirit, however,
lived on elsewhere.

During the 1960s and early 1970s, the Royalist government of Laos, unable to raise sufficient money from business, personal, or resource taxes and finding the population suspicious of its paper money, turned to gold. It encouraged import of gold both for local sale and for smuggling throughout a region in which the Vietnam War had caused black market demand to explode. Taxes on the traffic provided at peak 40 percent of the public revenues.[85] But the end of the Vietnam War, the victory of the Communist Pathet Lao, and the rise of Hong Kong and Singapore combined to put Laos out of the gold-smuggling trade.

An even larger distribution center that fell on bad times was Beirut. For many years, before the outbreak of the Lebanese civil war, Beirut imported kilo bars either to manufacture jewelry and fake gold coins or to sell directly throughout the Middle East. From Beirut, gold would be smuggled into Turkey and Egypt, whose restrictions on gold imports drove up the black market price, or it would be sold legally in the Arab Gulf states.

Among the pioneers of the Beirut trade during its go-go years just after World War II were members of the Safra family. They imported gold from London and Zurich, sold it to Kuwaitis and Saudis, and then, according to an idolatrous biographer, "laughed at the suckers who paid their big markups," calling them jackasses and other flattering things. The Safras were apparently surprised when, in the wake of the first Arab–Israeli conflict, their presence in Beirut was less than welcome. Later, in New York, they founded Republic National Bank, which for a time dominated the gold coin and industrial bullion business in the United States. And in Switzerland they set up the Trade Development Bank, one of whose sidelines was attracting Jewish flight capital from and exporting gold back to the Middle East. Until the introduction of airport security machines, their couriers could be found winging their way across the Middle East, with gold strapped in body bags.[86]

Ensuing years of civil war ensured that others followed their lead in abandoning Beirut. Many gold-dealing firms moved to Switzerland. The Armenian jewelers moved en masse to Los Angeles. Dubai came to dominate the Gulf states' trade. Turkey developed its own smuggling route from Switzerland via Bulgaria. Even the Egyptian trade was lost, partly to direct imports from Europe and partly to a newly emerging gold market. From Jordan, gold dealers already servicing the black markets of Israel and Occupied Palestine ran Swiss gold overland across Palestine into Gaza, and from there smuggled it into Egypt to be sold for Egyptian pounds. The cash was ferried out, again via Gaza, and used to pay Egyptian workers in Jordan and the Gulf states. Those workers, in turn, arranged for the cash to be secretly remitted back to their families in Egypt, free of tax or government scrutiny.[87]

Jordan's main role has been that of redistributor of Swiss gold throughout the Middle East. Since the 1980s that function has been performed in western Europe by Luxembourg, a fairly recent entrant into the business. Luxembourg's break into the wholesale gold business was neatly timed to coincide with the victory of the Socialist Party in France and its ban on anonymous gold trading.[88] Although the French ban was later repealed, Luxembourg has not lacked customers, mainly because of the high (and differential) value-added taxes on gold in most European Union countries, including Britain. Thus, while British banks try to regain ground lost to the Swiss in smuggling gold into the Orient, Luxembourg banks do a fine trade selling to smugglers taking the stuff into Britain.[89]

One notorious ring, whose leader earned the nickname Goldfinger, worked with a fleet of identical Honda Integras, specially chosen because the car had a design feature that facilitated the hiding of gold. Gang members would head for Luxembourg up to three times a week, swapping vehicles or simply changing license plates, before driving on board the Dover–Calais ferry. Once in Luxembourg, they would hide fifty kilos in the fenders, drive the car back as far as Calais, and leave it for a courier to bring home, while the original drivers went across as foot passengers before picking up an identical car in Dover. The ploy of changing drivers and either vehicles or license plates sufficed to fool Customs long enough for the ring to manage the tax-free import of more than £35 million worth of gold before it was busted in 1992.[90]

Once the gold was in Britain, the job of quietly disposing of it was entrusted to gang members well known among London's discrete community of Indian jewelers. In Britain, these jewelers play the role of parallel bankers common in India. Even second and third generation immigrants from the Indian subcontinent go to jewelers to buy gold by weight, tax free, and to leave money on deposit. This sort of transaction requires that the jewelers have a steady supply of cheap gold. The busting of the Goldfinger ring in 1992 was undoubtedly a setback—but only a temporary one.

Four years later another, nearly as large operation was uncovered. This time the jewelers had made an especially clever choice of courier—a U.K. policewoman. The courier traveled every other weekend to Brussels in different used cars, bought kilo bars (claiming they were bound for Dubai and therefore tax exempt), hid them in her car, and delivered them to the jewelers. Some 107 trips and three tons of gold later, the scheme had netted profits of more than £3 million by evading British value-added tax.

However, centers such as Luxembourg or Jordan have had and will likely continue to have only a small role in relation to the total world gold trade. They tap rich but strictly limited markets. There are two others, though, that have long had the good fortune to be in the right place at the right time.

PEARL OF THE PACIFIC, GOLD OF THE ORIENT

One center is Hong Kong, whose tax-free, no-questions-asked gold market (in competition with Singapore's) feeds black market demand across Southeast Asia. Actually Hong Kong's direct role in gold smuggling is fairly recent. Until the mid-1970s it was illegal to import gold into Hong Kong. But even during those years of gold drought, Hong Kong, because of its role as the most important Southeast Asian laundromat for dirty money, played a central role in financing gold smuggling to and from other localities, not the least India.

It was a fortuitous but fortunate confluence of circumstances. In 1963, as a result of war with Pakistan, India moved to preserve foreign exchange by banning the import of gold—except under closely controlled circumstances. About the same time the U.S. buildup began in Vietnam. Between these two otherwise unconnected events, Hong Kong provided a golden link.

Inside Vietnam there were, at peak, up to half a million U.S. military personnel, creating one of the world's most lucrative black markets for drugs, sex, arms, diamonds—and gold. Prices were better if payment was made in U.S. dollars rather than Vietnamese piastres, which encouraged U.S. soldiers to import and spend hard currency or bank instruments. On the other hand, with war raging, capital was skittish. To attempt to prevent massive flight, the government of South Vietnam imposed exchange controls. With black dollars pouring in to finance illegal domestic consumption and black dollars ready to flee to finance illegal offshore savings, a great entrepreneurial opportunity was at hand.

Many different people, ranging from "massage parlor" operators to U.S. army officers to agents of the Deak-Pererra foreign exchange firm played the currency black market. The most sophisticated was a group of Indian Muslims from the Madras area who were linked by extended family ties, intracommunal trust, and international financial connections via Hong Kong. The racket worked in three different ways.

Sometimes the Indian money changers just bought U.S. currency at the black market rate and then smuggled it directly to Hong Kong. Sometimes, in exchange for coded chits, U.S. soldiers wrote them checks with the name of the payee left blank. These checks were sent to New York. Once the checks cleared and the funds were deposited in the money changers' New York account, the chit was settled inside Vietnam in piastres at the black market rate. The U.S. funds were then wired from New York to the money changers' accounts in Hong Kong. Sometimes the money changers worked through the system of military pay certificates (MPCs), which is how the soldiers drew their pay. The MPCs could be converted by the soldiers into money orders to remit home.[91] So the Indian money changers would pick up MPCs on the black market, arrange for insiders at the U.S. military post office to convert them to postal money orders, cash them in the United States, and again have the money wired to Hong Kong. One way or the other, the funds that reached Hong Kong bank accounts could be used to buy gold in Switzerland or Dubai. Then either the gold would be smuggled back into Vietnam to be sold on the black market for more piastres and thus continue the cycle, or, even more profitably, it would be smuggled into India, where the government restrictions had driven the price well above the world market level.[92]

When Hong Kong itself moved directly into the gold business, India was initially one of its largest customers. But geography soon triumphed over sentiment, and Hong Kong lost the India trade to Dubai. Still, it has not lacked for customers. One is South Korea, whose government has long tried to break with the old tradition of giving gold as gifts and with the modern tradition of avoiding taxes. The country mysteriously manages to satisfy the demand for about 200 metric tons of gold a year, although its total domestic production per year is 1.2 metric tons and its measured net imports equal another 10 tons. Although in some countries gold is quietly offloaded by night, in South Korea most gold is handled by legitimate gold dealers who, using the cover of legal imports, bring in far more under the table. In 1995 the police cracked the biggest gold-smuggling ring in the country's history, seizing in one lot gold worth $145 million and arresting several officers of the country's biggest gold dealership.[93]

Yet another of Hong Kong's loyal customers is Bangladesh, which imposes tight exchange controls and severely restricts its citizens' right to hold gold, to the delight of gold merchants, smugglers, travel agencies selling airline tickets, and Bangladeshi Customs officials, who shake down couriers for bribes or steal their gold.

One of the most ingenious smugglers was Mr. X, a successful owner of several profitable businesses inside Bangladesh; these included dry cleaning and laundry shops, video rental stores, and a popular restaurant, all of which provided cover for his couriers, who were nominally employed in them, and served to launder the proceeds of his gold trade. The gold circuit started in Saudi Arabia, where Bangladeshi expatriate workers sought to get money home to their families at better than the official exchange rate. Also in Saudi Arabia was a business associate of Mr. X, who would collect workers' savings in hard currency and remit the money to a bank account in Hong Kong, where Mr. X's local associates would convert it into gold. Mr. X would dispatch couriers to pick up the gold and then fly home, each carrying about two kilos. The return trip was carefully coordinated with Customs officers who had been bribed to let Mr. X know when they would be on duty. At the gold's arrival, Mr. X would arrange for it to be sold to local jewelers. And the receipts, in local currency, were simply declared as part of the operating profit of Mr. X's legitimate businesses.[94]

SMUGGLERS' CREEK

Whatever riches the Bangladesh trade offered Hong Kong paled beside those that the rest of the Indian subcontinent made available to Dubai. The tiny sheikhdom of Dubai forms part of the United Arab Emirates but has little oil. Formerly the country was the center of the world pearl industry, but the market was ruined, first by the Great Depression, then by the Japanese invention of the cultured pearl, and then by massive oil pollution of the Gulf waters. Now its wealth comes principally from trade and from the blessings of geography. With the best harbor within striking distance by small boats of Iran, Pakistan, and India, Dubai became a regional smugglers' supermarket, its warehouses stuffed with watches, synthetic fabrics (long restricted in India to help the local cotton and jute industry), electronics, auto parts, whiskey, perfume, cigarettes, and pornographic movies; at the same time, its appetite for gold (virtually all in ten-tola bars) has at times equaled or exceeded that of Hong Kong.[95]

The Dubai government only issues trading licenses to the minority of residents actually born in the country. But recipients can sell those licenses to Indian and Pakistani merchants. These merchants can then purchase gold (and silver) from local branches of the big Swiss and British banks.

Smuggling precious metals requires serious capital, but it is easy to attract investors (of both legitimate and black money). The risk is small. Traditionally an outside investor's money is not exposed on a single voyage but spread across several. With widespread bribery of police and Customs on the other side, as well as rivalry between Customs and coast guard officials, the seizure rate by Indian officials has historically been very low; in fact, when the gold goes by sea, pirate ships may pose a greater danger than do Indian or Pakistani law enforcement officials.[96] To further reduce risk, one firm in Dubai would sell loss insurance at 15 percent of the value of the load.[97]

Next in the hierarchy come the smuggling syndicates charged with the actual logistics of moving the gold. They sometimes cooperate with each other in transportation, while remaining fiercely competitive in marketing.[98]

If the cargo is only gold, it can go by plane, be carried by personal couriers, or be hidden in baggage or cargo. Customs and police on the subcontinent have turned up gold stuffed inside fruit, hidden in the lining or false bottoms of suitcases, flattened into foil and placed instead of film in cameras, powdered and either dissolved into chemicals or poured into soft drink cans, hidden in the frame or tires of bicycles, melted into machine parts, tucked into corset belts, concealed in cookies, molded into flasks, water pipes, and dishes, as well as being shoved into the private parts of couriers.[99]

The choice of couriers is equally varied. Well-spoken, educated young men seem preferred, although more and more women have been found plying the trade. Usually they are native to the place of arrival, although everyone from Somali transients to the son of a president of Sierra Leone have been caught.[100] The general rule is that a courier is to be inconspicuous. But one of the most important Indian smugglers who trafficked in heroin and weapons as well as gold invested his proceeds in the Bombay film business. He used to bring well-known actors on all-expenses-paid junkets to his corporate headquarters in Dubai. Presumably, on the return journey, Customs officers would be more interested in shaking a famous hand than poking up a famous butt.

Although airline passengers suffice for carrying relatively small lots, historically most gold crossed by dhows. With interiors easily converted to haul almost any kind of cargo, and drawing little water, these ships can go almost anywhere along the Arabian, African, and Asian coasts as the occasion warrants. They can alternate between motor and sail, depending on the need for speed versus distance. The mechanics of a dhow are very simple, making for low maintenance costs and ease of recruitment of crew—who work for very little. As a result, they have become something of a seaborne informal sector, plying the region with cargoes of everything from whiskey (for dry areas such as Saudi Arabia), to ivory (smuggled out of East Africa for eventual sale to Hong Kong carving shops), to qat (the recreational drug of choice in the Horn of Africa), to gold to feed the voracious Indo-Pakistani demand.[101]

Traditionally the dhow sailed near the Indo-Pakistani coast (Pakistan's Makran coast was the favorite) and waited in international waters for fishing boats, which in turn would haul the cargo ashore. Eager to help were local villagers, who earned more by aiding smugglers than by fishing. From the village, the gold was stuffed into false floors in cars or trucks (registered under phony names) for conveyance to Karachi or to Bombay, historical center of India's black economy, or some other urban center in the area, to be redistributed to local black market gold dealers.[102] In the final stage, the gold went to jewelers or village goldsmiths, who retailed it to a public assured of double protection. The jeweler-goldsmith mixed the smuggled gold with legal, making it difficult to differentiate. This was made all the more so because ten-tola bars bear no serial numbers, and Customs receipts for legally imported gold could be bought on the black market.[103] And the final customer usually received not bars so much as crudely wrought jewelry, possession of which was easier to explain.

All of these layers of intermediation—gold merchants, smugglers, black market distributors, and goldsmith-jewelers—were essential for moving gold into the hands of the public. There was as well a complementary financial circuit. In India and Pakistan, gold is retailed for rupees. In Switzerland and Dubai, gold is wholesaled for dollars. Because Indian and Pakistani rupees were, until the mid-1990s, legally inconvertible, there was an obvious hole to be filled.

BALANCING THE SCALES

Over time, India and Pakistan have paid for their gold in several different ways.[104] In early post–World War II years, when the Indian rupee was legally convertible, it was easy to cover the cost through direct export of currency. Even after they ceased to be convertible, Indian and Pakistani currencies could still be traded at a discount in Arab Gulf states. The notes could be resold to émigré Indian and Pakistani workers, who might carry them home to their families at the end of their contracts, although inconvertibility made this expensive and awkward.[105] Since the restoration of convertibility, it seems that Indian currency is once again being exported in bulk to buy gold.[106]

The next simplest method was through the normal foreign-exchange black market. Someone in the market would exchange foreign banknotes and traveler's checks from tourists or business visitors, and even personal checks drawn on accounts held abroad by local businessmen, into rupees at the black market rate. The hard currency instruments could be resold to smugglers and exported to pay for gold.

More important was phony invoicing of trade accounts. Merchants would report to the exchange-control authorities that imports cost more, or exports yielded less, than they did. The excess could be stashed abroad and used, among other purposes, to finance gold imports.

Another technique was to acquire hard currency through the smuggling of valuables such as antiquities, rare animal skins, and gemstones out from India, and to a lesser degree, out of Pakistan. As India began making its mark as a diamond cutting and polishing center, a triangular relationship developed. Belgian banks would finance the import of raw diamonds to India; the diamonds were finished and smuggled back to Belgium. The foreign exchange earned from resale of diamonds would be sent to Dubai and used to buy gold, which was smuggled into India. The resulting rupees could then be used to buy more raw diamonds.[107]

For a time, silver was important. So much silver drained out of India into Dubai that, during the late 1960s and early 1970s, Dubai was officially the largest supplier of silver to the world market. Indeed, the relative values of gold and silver in India reflected the pattern of what is euphemistically called economic development. As the rich got richer, raising the demand for gold, the poor got poorer, forcing them to disgorge hordes of silver in order to survive, so the profits on smuggling silver out sometimes exceeded those from smuggling gold in.[108] However, even at peak, silver could not have covered anywhere near the cost of gold imports. Furthermore, after 1980, world silver prices began to fall sharply, and the flow went into reverse: Dubai imported silver openly from the rest of the world and smuggled it, along with gold, into India.

Fortunately for the gold business, about the same time silver began falling in price, the boom in Afghan heroin began.[109] Moving down from refineries in Pakistan's North-West Frontier Province, most was exported overland through Iran or by sea from Karachi or smuggled along Baluchistan's Makran coast. But some joined the flow of contraband (everything from whiskey to betel nuts to AK-47s to huge amounts of gold) crossing the border with India, to be taken to Bombay and then exported to European destinations.[110] Once the drugs were sold, the money could be wired to Dubai to cover the cost of gold smuggled into India or Pakistan.

Of all the techniques available, none has been as important as the Indo-Pakistani underground banking system. The emergence of the modern *havala* banking system reflects a series of events—economic, political, and legislative.[111]

India, like China, both before and during the era of European domination, was dotted with informal banking and financial institutions, ranging from village moneylenders to rotating credit associations. However, their role as deposit and loan institutions was overwhelmingly local.[112]

In India (and Pakistan) the havala system evolved partly to bring long-distance financial services to rural areas not served by banks, which in any case were largely mistrusted as British colonial institutions even in the cities.[113] With the spread of a Indian trade diaspora, first to East Africa during the British colonial era, the system moved with it, handling remittances from émigré traders to family members back home.[114] Then came World War II.

Not only did price controls and rationing lead to the emergence of major black markets, but the British encouraged the growth of institutions that specialized in smuggling currency. The *havaladars* helped the British not only by identifying Axis agents and anti-British Indian independence militants, but, with the support of a banking infrastructure set up for them in Madagascar, they ran money covertly into Axis-occupied or Axis-controlled areas to finance Allied intelligence operations. After India achieved independence, the British authorities took the records of the operation with them, bequeathing to the Indian authorities a fully operational currency-smuggling apparatus just when India was promoting a policy of economic autarky.[115]

The chaos of partition further entrenched the parallel banking system. Out of British India came two intensely hostile states, faced with the problem of resettling millions of uprooted people forced to abandon property on opposing sides of the cease-fire lines. Because there were no formal financial relations between the two countries, people turned to the underground banking system to liquidate property and move assets from Pakistan to India and vice versa. It was likely that through their role in handling the financial mechanics of postpartition resettlement, the havaladars created the public trust that stood them in good stead in the decades to follow.

The next stage came with the 1963 war with Pakistan. Attempting simultaneously to conserve foreign exchange, discourage hoarding, reduce tax evasion, and eliminate a major symptom of social inequality, India passed the Gold Control Act, which effectively banned gold imports and severely restricted individual holdings—oblivious to the fact that during wartime, even more than during periods of severe inflation, the demand for gold historically has gone up dramatically. This was all the more true in countries in which traditional uses of gold were as deeply entrenched as they were in India and where, for most of the population, banks were alien institutions until the 1940s or beyond.[116] The result of the Gold Control Act was to call into existence a gold-smuggling infrastructure that soon linked up with, and gave a new urgency to, the underground banking system.

That link was further consolidated by the growth of demand for gold. Many factors contributed. They included the impact of the Green Revolution and cheap-labor industrialization, which increased the wealth of the middle classes at the expense of the poor, and therefore shifted the distribution of income in favor of the class most prone to buying gold. That was combined with the general growth of the black economy across India and Pakistan in the 1970s and 1980s.[117] Another factor was the boom in drugs and diamonds in certain areas. Put all of these together and they provide much of the explanation for the fact that even toward the end of the 1980s, when the financial infrastructure of India was rapidly modernizing, the middle classes invested in gold at about double the rate they invested in the stock market, and the accumulation of middle-class jewelry and small gold bars (anywhere from 7,500 to 10,000 metric tons) represented the largest single block of savings inside India.[118]

However, although those factors explain the demand side, something else equally important was at work on the supply side, namely, the oil boom in the Arab Gulf states. There, a huge work force of émigré Indians and Pakistanis was paid in hard currency. If they remitted earnings to families through the orthodox banking system, the money would be converted into rupees at the official rate, and the authorities could trace the flow for tax purposes, present and future. At the same time, Indian and Pakistani gold smugglers had a problem. They bought gold in exchange for hard currency, mainly U.S. dollars, but were paid in rupees. In the absence of an alternate mechanism, the rupees would have had to have been converted to hard currency inside India at the black market rate and the hard currency physically smuggled back out again. Into the breach stepped the havaladars.

Earnings by émigré workers in hard currency were collected in the Arab Gulf states and turned over to the gold exporters. Indeed, Pakistani émigré workers in the Gulf states did not have to go far to find a willing banker; their representatives would set up outside the post office, the Pakistani embassy, or Pakistani banks and advertise their rates quite openly, although the usual pattern was to rely on a money changer linked into a personal network of friends and relatives. The gold would move across to India or Pakistan. There, the gold importer would pay (directly or through an underground banker) the equivalent sum to the family of the émigré worker in rupees at the black market rate. No monetary instrument had to pass across borders or oceans. It was neat, efficient, and above all, almost untraceable.

As with the Chinese system, the guarantee of performance is primarily family or group loyalty and only secondarily the threat of violence. The core operators come from the same set of small villages in the Punjab, Tamil Nadu, Sind, and Gujarat states—the last had seen the greatest historical development of parallel banking institutions as well as one of the heaviest rates of out-migration. Any recruit into a network has to be from the same village as the banker and be sponsored by someone already involved. Recruits undergo rigorous training, including the ability to withstand physical interrogation, and are then put to work, initially as couriers. Money is picked up and delivered, door to door, at a rate that varies from 15 to 30 percent. But the actual international movement of cash is rare; the key is compensating balances between two havala bankers in different places. Despite the Hindi origins of the term "chit," neither coded receipts nor other sorts of tokens are essential—many havala bankers operate purely by verbal understandings.

The obvious answer to the gold-smuggling problem in India was to abolish the Gold Control Act and permit free imports, on the widely held theory that where there is no law, there is no crime. In fact, the government of India in the 1990s did heed demands for liberalization.

Liberalization for India meant allowing nonresident Indians to each import up to five kilos of gold, provided they paid a seemingly modest import duty in foreign exchange. The result was less a curb on smuggling—initially smuggling actually may have increased—than a change in its form. Each returning nonresident Indian was now a potential courier for the gold-smuggling rings, and they shunted back and forth between India and Dubai, changing passports each trip. Not only were the duties charged sufficient still to justify smuggling, but the smuggling syndicates offset the fall in profit rates on gold by diversifying their loads. More watches, electronics, and other high-valued items were brought in, while more heroin went out, because profits on a return trip carrying heroin were more than enough to compensate for any reduction in profits from the gold. Not least, the influx of legal gold in one way actually made the problem worse, because it became harder to identify gold that had been smuggled.[119]

Along with liberalization of the inflow came recourse to an old gambit that had been tried unsuccessfully three times in the past—the sale to the public of gold bonds. Under the terms of the 1993 gold bond issue, holders could deposit their gold in exchange for a five-year bond and be repaid the principal in gold along with a small cash interest when the bond fell due. All interest and capital gains would be tax free. And the bonds would be transferable as well as usable for collateral for bank loans. Certainly not least appealing was the government's pledge that there would be no questions asked about the origins of the gold or the origins of the money used to buy the gold. Specifically, there would be no enquiries under the laws pertaining to Customs, foreign exchange, or income and wealth taxes. Faced with all these incentives, Indians responded by depositing with the government a grand total of 35 tons (out of a possible total hoard of 7,500 to 10,000).[120]

Meantime the Pakistani government also tried to address the issue. It granted one company a monopoly on the right to import gold legally for the jewelry industry, and the company allegedly showed its appreciation by kicking back $10 million into one of the many slush funds controlled by the husband of then-president Benazir Bhutto.[121]

The Indian government moved in a somewhat more effective way to at least partially address the issue at source. It created a system whereby workers in the Middle East could buy gold certificates directly from Indian government agencies, take the gold certificate home, and then obtain their gold from one of the state bank offices at the airport.

But in all its policy responses, the Indian government ignored the virtually iron rule that governments that have made the initial mistake of imposing such severe restrictions as to call into existence an infrastructure of smuggling then make an even greater mistake when they simply capitulate to it without addressing explicitly both the culture of evasion and the apparatus smugglers had created in response to previous regulations. Thus, gold smuggling may have been considerably reduced—by 1999 the government claimed it accounted for only the magic 10 percent of remaining gold imports. But smugglers simply loaded more whiskey, porn movies, and consumer durables onto their dhows. Furthermore, there was ample business for the parallel bankers. As long as wealth taxes existed, money brokers would wander the camps in the Gulf in which Indo-Pakistani expat workers lived to offer parallel transfer services.[122] With mass migration beyond East Africa and the Gulf, both to Britain and to less traditional destinations such as North America, the havala bankers simply put their connections to work on virtually a global scale. Even within India and Pakistan, they could replace the business lost through gold liberalization by handling capital flight on the way out, and drug money, bribes, support payments for the guerrilla movements in the Punjab, Assam, and Kashmir, along with ordinary émigré workers' remittances, on the way back. Much like the Chinese underground banking system, the Indo-Pakistani model is so embedded in culture and socioeconomic reality that muddled efforts by law enforcement to deal with it inevitably come to naught. In any event, India reacted to a post-liberalization upsurge of gold imports—in 1998 Indians spent more on gold than on cars, bicycles, motorcycles, fridges, and color television sets—by hiking the import duties once more and thereby giving the smugglers another lease on life.[123]

The Golden Fleece

In the final stage of gold's travels from the ground to the consumer, the metal (whether smuggled or legally obtained) has to be put into the hands of citizens enraptured by its beauty, worried about social upheaval, frightened by the specter of financial collapse, or merely irked when their government dares to tax their hard-earned money to subsidize shiftless welfare bums.

At the retail level, the gold market involves a double relationship with the consumer: it sells the refined product and usually stands ready to buy it back again. Unlike commissions on diamonds, those on the repurchase of gold are not especially high. The liquidity of the market is partly the result of a worldwide connection between the local refineries and the major world suppliers of pure gold. A jeweler, for example, can take two kilos of scrap gold of 16.8 carats purity to a local refiner affiliated with Johnson-Matthey; the gold is then assessed, and the customer can pick up the equivalent, about 1.2 kilos in 24-carat gold, on the next business day at almost any refinery in the world with a Johnson-Matthey link. Even gold manufactured into jewelry commands a ready resale market. So Michel XX discovered when he got into credit card fraud in Bangkok.

A Québecois by birth, Michel XX moved to Thailand in the early 1980s, married a local women, and soon learned the language, which gave him a signal advantage when he went into business with a local fence. The scheme operated as follows: Scouts working at the post office would search the mail for credit cards. Michel and other shoppers then headed to gold-jewelry shops to buy; his knowledge of the language meant that if a merchant got suspicious and called the police instead of the credit card company for verification, Michel could take a powder. Even then the threat was not very severe, because the team was making payoffs to a senior officer of the Bangkok police. The gold and jewelry acquired with the stolen credit cards were then resold to other jewelry stores for about 90 percent of the value of the gold, no questions asked. Michel's proceeds were safely invested in things such as a pig farm whose title was in the name of his wife's family. When Michel and his scouts tried to freelance, the boss ratted on them. But Michel soon bought his way out of prison, scrambled across the border into Malaysia, and made his way back to Montreal.[124]

Given the anonymity, portability, and high liquidity of gold, together with its stable value, it is not surprising that at the retail level, the gold business, already heavily compromised by smuggling and tax evasion, is a prime target for further criminal infiltration.

BLACK MONEY, WHITE GOLD

One of the most spectacular examples of theft came when two women joined the flow of Russian Jewish émigrés to the United States in the early 1980s. Taking jobs with a jewelry manufacturer in Manhattan, the two were soon regarded as model employees, even arriving for work early each day—before the company's metal detectors had been turned on. Once inside, they loaded up with jewelry, trundled it past the dormant detectors, and stashed it in their lockers before returning faithfully to work for their statutory minimum wage. Meanwhile confederates were kept busy selling the jewelry, carting the cash to Switzerland, and then wiring some back—to be invested in property and small businesses, including, appropriately enough, a car wash. In the final analysis, the ring stole $35 million worth of gold and gold jewelry, enough to drive the firm that had employed the women into bankruptcy.[125]

Because gold and jewelry retail operations generate such large amounts of cash, they are natural vehicles for laundering. Gold firms can act as fronts for depositing money in financial institutions, they can play a role in recycling proceeds back from offshore havens, or they can run full-service pickup-wash-and-delivery operations.

One of the more interesting schemes was run by a coin dealer in New York. During the 1979–80 price run-up, his reputation expanded across the state and beyond, not least because he was fencing much of the gold stolen in his area. High school kids would break into houses, steal gold and silver, and then line up in front of his store to unload it. He managed to end that phase of his career, however, with nothing worse than a short jail stint for income tax evasion. It was time to upscale.

In 1989, the coin dealer set up dummy shops in the Manhattan jewelry district to which couriers from across the United States would arrive each day with drug cash in shipping crates and duffel bags. The money would be picked up by courier and taken to his main branch in a small town in Rhode Island or to a subsidiary location in Los Angeles. Those firms would deposit the cash in various banks, convert it into cashier's checks made out to dummy firms nominally in payment for gold or diamonds, and wire it to foreign bank accounts controlled by Colombian traffickers, less the coin dealer's handling fee—which could range up to 10 percent. Eventually his large cash deposits attracted attention, and the suspicious banks tipped off the feds. The coin dealer was arrested in Geneva carrying $500,000 in cash.[126]

Somewhat more elaborate was the operation run in the Boston area by Bay State Gold and Silver Exchange. One of the many retail buying businesses to spring up during the price hikes of 1979–80, Bay State owed its existence to the generosity of a man who later gained fame as the head of a New England drug-trafficking network. He smuggled cash to the Bahamas and deposited it in a bank account belonging to Premium Investments, a firm that boasted among its shareholders the wife of one cabinet minister and the islands' chief political fixer. Premium Investments then lent through open legal channels some $800,000 to Bay State's promoter to get him started in the precious metals exchange trade.

Bay State did not deal with the public directly but chose to work through middlemen, who were delighted with the arrangement. Not only did Bay State offer excellent prices, but it paid cash on delivery and gave the middlemen perks such as consulting fees and interest-free loans. Once Bay State got the precious metals, it resold them to refiners and deposited the proceeds in its bank account. Then it withdrew money in cash from its bank account and used it to purchase yet more gold and silver from the middlemen. It was all quite orderly and clean—on the surface.

But, of course, the trafficker using Bay State had reasons for his investment beyond a desire to aid the progress of American entrepreneurship. Cash from drug sales was infiltrated into Bay State's coffers, which enabled it to buy yet more gold on each subsequent cycle. The drug money could then reappear as proceeds of the resale of gold to the smelters, part of which the trafficker withdrew in cash and part of which he arranged to have wired through ghost companies to offshore hiding places.[127]

Although the coin dealer had been content merely to use his firm as a front for dealing with the banks, Bay State went one better, actually using the drug money as part of its bullion trading capital. But neither could hold a candle to La Mina, which combined retail and wholesale jewelry operations, gold bullion importing and refining, and even futures trading in perhaps the largest and most elaborate money-laundering operation ever seen in the United States.[128]

THE ALCHEMISTS

The operation began in 1986 when a Uruguayan precious metals broker was approached to help solve the problem posed by the cash Colombian cocaine dealers were piling up in Los Angeles. He dreamed up a scheme of laundering the money through sales of Uruguayan gold. Uruguay's gold mines are a fiction, but its gold exports to the United States, which are based on smuggling raw gold into Uruguay from Brazil, are real enough. Or at least they were until this broker got busy.

To start, he took control of a Montevideo bullion and currency house; then he went to Los Angeles to set up shop in the jewelry district. In stage one, the dealers delivered cocaine cash to his Los Angeles company. The broker used the money to buy scrap gold at premium prices from local jewelers. The cash was then deposited into banks by the jewelers and accounted for, properly, as the proceeds of the sale of scrap gold.

The gold was top quality, whereas gold from South America is generally of a lower purity. Therefore, in the next stage, the broker arranged to adulterate the gold with a small amount of silver to make it appear South American. Simultaneously, he ordered "gold" from his Montevideo affiliate, and his Uruguayan associates would ship up gold-plated lead bars. Hence, the broker could sell his real but locally adulterated gold to New York banks and dealers, waving the Customs declarations as proof of its South American origin. Then the broker would instruct the New York purchasers to wire payment for the "gold" to Montevideo, from whence, behind the screen of Uruguayan bank secrecy laws, it made its way to Colombia.

However, soon the cash flowing in exceeded the ability of the original jewelers to provide scrap gold. Furthermore, the broker was pressured to handle money from Houston and New York as well. So he recruited two Armenian wholesale jewelers in the Los Angeles jewelry district. They sold him scrap gold, and they took direct delivery of the coca dollars. The biggest flow came from New York. There, in its jewelry district, false-front "jewelry" stores were set up as collection points. The money was stashed in boxes labeled scrap gold. The boxes were insured for the full value of the cash they contained, and all taxes due on the "gold" were paid before it was turned over to Brink's or Loomis for transportation to Los Angeles. On arrival, the boxes were delivered to one of the Armenian jewelry firms. The money was put through counting machines and then sent, partly by courier but mainly by the Los Angeles jewelry district's regular armored car service, for deposit, along with regular business receipts, in accounts at various banks. From these accounts, money sufficient to cover the declared value of the boxes, less a commission, was wired to New York, either directly or sometimes via Costa Rica, to avoid the appearance of too many large wire transfers to the same destination. From New York, the money was wired again, nominally to cover the cost of gold imports. Originally it went to Panama, then later to Uruguay and

London. From all three points, the final destination of most of the money was Colombia.

As the amount of cash handled by the Armenian jewelers grew, so did the amount of gold they had to sell to the broker to generate the cover required. That meant they had to keep buying new gold to replace that being sold to the broker, and the broker in turn had to find a market for the gold he was buying from them. An obvious opportunity beckoned.

The key link was the Florida refinery. At first, it would buy gold from the broker, resmelt it, and then sell it to legitimate buyers. Then came a slightly more sophisticated arrangement. The Florida refinery would sell the gold to a gold brokerage house, which then directly sold it back to the Armenian jewelers. In the meantime, the Florida refinery, on orders from the Montevideo exchange house, would wire money to Panama. Next, to cut the costs of transporting gold across the United States, the broker began stashing the gold in custodial accounts so that only the title to the gold would have to move back and forth. In the final refinement, all traces of physical gold were eliminated, with all trading in contracts for nonexistent gold.

It was almost perfect. Every required form, from Customs declarations to express company waybills to bank cash transaction reports, was scrupulously filled out without any reaction from the Treasury officers supposedly monitoring them. Then bad luck struck on several fronts. The Armenian jewelers had been making large cash deposits in ten Los Angeles banks. Nine were content with the fact that as long as the required cash reports were filed, the banks had fulfilled their legal obligations. But the compliance officer at the tenth was more curious. She noted that most of the firm's business was wholesale, not retail, and that in the wholesale jewelry business almost all transactions are conducted by bank check, whereas the firm sometimes had couriers with up to a million dollars or more arriving at the bank weekly. The compliance officer passed her suspicions on to the IRS.

Simultaneously, problems were brewing in New York. A Loomis employee noticed through a hole in one of the boxes that it contained not scrap gold but cash. When he inquired, he was told by the recipient firm that customers were shipping cash because interest rates were higher in Los Angeles. Loomis reported the incident to the FBI.

Last, but hardly least, a money broker for Colombian traffickers was busy in Atlanta negotiating with undercover DEA agents running a sting operation. He complained about their high rates and slow service, and he told them they needed to study the modus operandi of his own favorite laundry, La Mina, more closely. They heeded his advice.

Black, White, and Gold

Governments have long attempted to interfere with the gold market. Whereas historically the motivation may have been the association of gold with the deities or its role as a symbol of sovereignty, in more modern times the reasons have been much more mundane.

Developing countries see the propensity of the public to hold gold as both a threat to the growth of a modern banking system as well as an impediment to the government's capacity to collect taxes. Gold holding, too, tends to be visibly associated with social and economic inequality. And from the point of view of the government's financial position, gold is a double threat: it drains away foreign exchange when it is covertly imported, and it acts as an excellent vehicle for undermining exchange-control laws when it is secretly exported.

In industrialized countries, where most restrictions on private gold holding were long ago eliminated, governments regard private acquisition of gold as primarily a fiscal challenge and private use of gold as primarily a monetary challenge. The problems are twofold. Governments in the West have been finding income taxes increasingly difficult to collect.[129] As a result they have shifted the tax burden more toward consumption taxes. But consumption taxes are regressive. Hence, to maintain a veneer of fairness, some governments impose heavy excise taxes on luxury goods, gold jewelry among them. The result is to stimulate underground traffic. At the same time, illegal gold trading creates a parallel monetary system, effectively outside government control, that can facilitate the laundering of criminal money.

Nor are the producing countries immune from problems. From Brazil to Indonesia, governments inherit the ecological and social costs of alluvial mining, while the gold takes flight. And from Guyana to Russia to China, gold rushes undermine the authority of the state and corrupt some officials.

The difficulties posed by gold are evidently large, whereas the success of policies designed to address them are considerably smaller. One obvious problem is that restrictive policies can run afoul of deep-rooted habits in consuming countries in which gold has long had traditional uses.

Another is that efforts by governments to restrict or heavily tax the international flow of gold run counter to current ideological fads, which tend toward greater freedom of trade and smaller degrees of government regulation.

Yet another problem is that in most countries, gold offenses are usually not taken too seriously. When ex-president Fernando Collor of Brazil was facing possible impeachment on corruption charges, he argued in his own defense that the $6 million in unaccounted-for wealth that was at the heart of the scandal came not from bribes but merely from smuggling gold. When, in 1991, a U.S. narcotics agent faced trial for drug trafficking and money laundering, he similarly attempted to explain away the $2.6 million in his Swiss account as fees earned from an Italian jewelry firm in return for his aid in smuggling 11,800 pounds of gold chain into the United States duty free.[130]

Likely the most important factor is that intermediation between the supply and demand sides of the black market equation is managed by a formidable alliance. Many of the same respectable firms and institutions that operate on the legal side of the business also absorb smuggled gold and oversee the process of getting the refined product into forbidden hands. Meanwhile, the actual trafficking is managed by individuals and groups who honed their skills smuggling everything from cigarettes to heroin to AK-47s.

"Gold," insisted no less an expert than Christopher Columbus, "is a wondrous thing. He who possesses it is lord of all he wants."[131] Not only does it command the means for the good life, but it blesses those who have it with a touch of divinity. When Columbus added, "By means of gold one can even get souls into Paradise," he knew whereof he spoke, having so dispatched countless Indian souls in his personal quest for glowing fame and golden fortune. The allure of gold remains as strong today as it was in Columbus's time. It is beautiful to behold, although reflected off its glittering surface are images of smugglers, investment scam artists, drug dealers, gunrunners, pirates, and thieves, who represent the ugliest face of modern commerce.

CHAPTER 6

Washout

Follow-the-Money Methods in Crime Control Policy

Once upon a time, not so long ago, the Harlem pimp with a diamond stickpin, seated behind the wheel of a fur-upholstered Cadillac convertible, seemed the quintessence of criminality. If the pimp wound up in the slammer, justice was declared done, and no one paid much heed to the fate of the stickpin or the Cadillac. Today the public's imagination is more likely titillated by the image of the Colombian narco-baron reclining in a gold-plated bathtub while lighting Havana cigars with hundred dollar bills—until the Feds kick down the door, hustle the manacled trafficker off to a waiting paddy wagon, and then proceed to ransack the place. As panels are ripped off the walls, contents of drawers upended onto the floor, and feathers from the king-sized mattress sent flying, it becomes clear that their real target is not the trafficker—after all, drug dealers breed like mosquitoes in a tropical swamp. Nor is it the stash of dope chilling in the fridge beside the Dom Perignon. It is not even the loaded Uzis stacked menacingly in the front hall. What the narcs are really after is that Adidas bag stuffed with greenbacks, which they eventually find tossed casually into the corner of a clothes closet.

Over the last fifteen years there has been a quiet revolution in law enforcement. These days, instead of just closing down rackets, law enforcement goes after the earnings from crime on the theory that confiscating the yield removes both motive (profit) and means (operating capital) to commit further crimes. Therefore a new offense—money laundering—has been added to the statutes of many countries. Tougher reporting requirements have been imposed on financial institutions. And law enforcement agencies now host special units responsible for arresting not malefactors but bank accounts, investment portfolios, houses, cars, even Rolex watches. These initiatives are closely related. Detailed records create a paper trail that aids in tracing criminal money, while anti-money-laundering laws create new offenses to justify its seizure.[1]

To various degrees in various places, the new laws have undermined traditional presumptions of financial privacy, muddled civil and criminal procedures, and opened previously confidential tax records to police probes. Particularly in the United States, these laws have reversed the burden of proof, smeared citizens with the taint of criminality without benefit of trial, and converted police forces into self-financing bounty-hunting organizations.

Some might argue that all this is a necessary response to an overarching social evil. Others might agree in principle that such a strategy can help deal with a very serious problem, but they criticize its worst abuses. Yet others might suggest that the entire exercise is simply insane. For despite lurid tales of great criminal hoards in the hands of great criminal hordes, no one really knows how much criminal income and wealth exist, how illegal gains are distributed, or how deleterious their impact on legitimate society really is. Nor can anyone say with any confidence what impact a follow-the-money strategy might really have on its target, although they can point with more confidence to its pernicious side effects.

Licensed to Loot?

There is nothing new about the notion that criminals should not profit from their crimes. However, in the past, if the state wanted to seize a citizen's wealth, it had to prove, beyond reasonable doubt, first, that a person had committed a crime and, second, that the target assets came from that crime. That dual standard was something of an obstacle.

The solution to that obstacle turned out to be civil forfeiture, something perfected first in the United States and now being imitated in other countries. Instead of charging a person with a crime, which would require that the state prove its case beyond a reasonable doubt while the accused had protections such as right to counsel and defense against double jeopardy and self-incrimination, the government could move directly against a person's property. Not only did property have no civil rights, but the government could go after it using a civil (balance of probabilities) standard. Better still, police could seize property on probable cause, the weakest of all legal criteria, on the basis of nothing more than hearsay from paid and anonymous informants. Once accused, property was presumed guilty unless its owners could find the financial wherewithal and produce the evidence to prove its innocence. Furthermore, even if the government chose to first bring a criminal case against the owner and lost, it could re-litigate the same facts in a civil trial against the property, reassured not only that it had depleted the owner's resources but that it faced a much lower burden of proof. Best of all, after 1984, U.S. police forces were given the right to keep what they grabbed.

Five factors accounted for U.S. law enforcement's fixation with chasing the money. One was the apparent failure of "targeting up." This theory holds that it does little good to nail and jail easily replaced subordinates in hierarchically structured criminal organizations when the top management is still on the loose. Hence the strategy became one of going after the capos. The only problem was that that strategy seemed not to make any real difference either. Just as much cash seemed to get blown in illegal gambling dens, just as much weed got toked up in college dorms, and just as many otherwise prim and proper citizens abandoned wives and children in the dead of night to cruise the streets in search of forbidden carnal delights.

The resilience of the criminal marketplace might have convinced some that the notion of crime controlled by a grand conspiracy of swarthy men whose names were suspiciously difficult to pronounce was Hollywood fiction. It might have suggested that the crime world was really populated by an anarchic collection of small-time operators more intent on ratting out each other than laying tribute at the feet of a local godfather. It might have conveyed the notion that rather than huge amounts of capital under the control of great criminal cartels that stashed it in obliging financial institutions, most illegal profits were distributed in small amounts of cash among a host of petty wheeler-dealers who kept the dough stuffed in socks under their beds, when they did not immediately fritter it away on booze, drugs, and flashy living. And just maybe the appropriate deduction might have been that as long as a demand for illegal goods and services existed, someone was going to find it profitable (thanks to the way criminalization drove up the price) to supply that demand.

Instead, the accepted explanation became that not only were mob bosses more replaceable than previously thought, but even if not replaced, they had little difficulty continuing to run their businesses from prison.[2] That seemed to argue in favor of arresting and de facto jailing the one thing presumably indispensable—the money that provided the motive and the means. The head of the U.S. Drug Enforcement Administration (DEA) put it squarely before Congress in 1978, the year his agency was given the right to proceed by civil forfeiture against both "proceeds of crime" and funds supposedly destined for use in narcotics offenses: "We recognize that the conviction and incarceration of top-level traffickers does not necessarily disrupt trafficking organizations; the acquisition of vast capital permits regrouping and the incarcerated trafficker can continue to direct operations. Therefore it is essential to attack the finances that are the backbone of organized drug trafficking."[3] This theme was parotted by other law enforcement officials with a frequency and vehemence that contrasted remarkably with the lack of evidence offered to support it.[4]

The second reason for shifting attention to the money trail was the conviction that the Western world was being flooded with narcotics and that, as a result, the worldwide drug trade raked in gross earnings of at least $500 billion per annum, of which the United States alone accounted for $100–120 billion. Added to this presumably enormous take from drugs were the proceeds of a host of other rackets. Indeed, this great wealth in the hands of alien "cartels" posed a threat much beyond the merely economic. For example, Colombia's so-called Medellín cartel was described by influential *Washington Post* columnist Jack Anderson as "a subterranean superpower that threatens U.S. security." And he insisted that the U.S. government should "call upon" all other countries to adopt emergency laws and treaties to confiscate drug money.[5]

Of course, there was (and is) lots of funny money washing around the world economy. Most, though, comes not from peddling kiddy porn or designer drugs but from tax and exchange-control evasion on money of legal origin. All that those frightening statistics really prove is that it is not necessary to take the square root of a negative sum to arrive at a purely imaginary number. But the objective was not to illuminate the shadowy world of crime so much as to enlighten politicians about the need for larger law enforcement budgets and more arbitrary police powers. Therefore those magic numbers assumed the status of religious cant and were rarely revised, except heavenward.

A third reason for the new law enforcement approach was the triumph of the ideology of fiscal restraint—Wall Street's term for a combination of tax cuts for the rich and government expenditure cuts for the poor. During the 1980s, out-of-control military spending had driven the U.S. budget deficit to record highs. Simultaneously, drug consumption, and therefore the presumed untaxed wealth of drug barons, supposedly hit its peak. It was also a time when the principle of universality of access to public services—the idea that all citizens had a right to have their basic needs met regardless of economic status—was under attack and when user fees for things the government formerly had provided for free were becoming more common. Along with that trend came demands for privatization of public functions. If users were to be expected to pay full cost for hospitals, schools, and other services formerly considered public rights, it took only a small shift of logic to apply that principle to crime control, particularly given that criminals were notorious free-riders. This was articulated in 1982 before the U.S. Senate Judiciary Committee by a senior official of the U.S. attorney general's office:

> OFFICIAL: The potential in this area is really unlimited. My guess is that, with adequate forfeiture laws, we could . . .
> SENATOR: We could balance the budget.
> OFFICIAL: There clearly would be millions and hundreds of millions available.[6]

Closely related was a fourth factor, a change in the attitude toward the causes of crime. For some time, academics and activists alike had urged that the focus should be on eradicating the environmental factors that drove people to crime. But in the new era of free-marketeering, the cant changed to favor punishment of individual evildoers. If, according to the old view, economically motivated crime was largely the consequence of unequal social and economic opportunity, then the government would be expected to correct the imbalance. But if, according to the new view, it was the work merely of bad people, there was no need to address the existing distribution of wealth and power. Thus, the criminal came to be viewed not as a complex product of psycho-socio-economic conditions but as a simple cost-benefit calculator. It followed that crime could be addressed by merely tilting the likely outcome of such a calculation to reduce the potential profitability of the criminal's actions and to incapacitate (by stripping away economic assets as well as by imprisonment) those who failed to heed the initial warning.[7]

Fifth was a fundamental shift in the nature of the crimes being targeted, which had subtle but enormously important implications, many of which are still not fully appreciated.

In the early part of the twentieth century, a wave of Puritanism swept North America. It was composed of many elements—a revolt by small town and rural America against the decadence of the big cities; WASP racism against immigrants who were associated with offensive behavior (Chinese with opiate use, Irish with whiskey, "Hindoos" or Mexicans with marijuana); the flexing of muscle by an emerging middle-class feminist movement, which saw predominantly male vices as a threat to family values; and an emerging political reform movement denouncing saloons (which functioned as working men's political clubs) as centers of vote buying and election rigging. The consequence was a concerted effort to criminalize personal vice.[8] Gambling, buying sex, using recreational drugs, and even the consumption of alcohol were criminalized, or if the activity already was a criminal offense, the laws pertaining to it were more systematically enforced. No longer would cities be permitted to host red light districts in which otherwise legitimate citizens could temporarily sate their appetites before returning to a world of respectability. All this was cheered on by prominent industrialists and their yes-men from the economics profession, who saw in the curbing of personal vice a means of reducing workplace absenteeism and therefore raising productivity and profit.[9]

In response there was a dramatic change in the direction of law enforcement. For the first time, the main thrust of police action shifted from combating predatory offenses (robbery, extortion, embezzlement, and the like, practiced at the expense of an unwilling public) to attacking market-based crimes (in which underground entrepreneurs attempted to service the forbidden consumption needs of a complicit public). Although both types of crime are lumped together in the criminal code, the economic nature of each is profoundly different and therefore so is the appropriate attitude of the authorities toward the profits derived from each.

Predatory offenses involve the redistribution of existing wealth. The transfers are bilateral, involving victim and perpetrator, although others may be involved in subsequent handling of misappropriated property. These transfers are also involuntary, commonly using force or the threat of force, although deceit may suffice. The victims (individuals, institutions, or corporations) are readily identifiable. The losses are also simple to determine—a robbed (or defrauded) person, institution, or corporation can point to specific money and property lost. Because the transfers are involuntary, the morality is unambiguous—someone has been wronged by someone else. Therefore, over and above direct punishment of the guilty party, the justice system's response is restitution to the victim of his or her property.

By contrast, market-based crimes involve the production and distribution of new goods and services that happen to be illegal by their very nature. The exchanges are multilateral, much like legitimate market transactions, involving (among others) producers, distributors, retailers, and money managers on the supply side and final consumers on the demand side. Because the transfers are voluntary, it is often difficult to define a victim, unless it is some abstract construct like "society." Therefore there are no definable losses to any individual from the act itself (although there may be from indirect consequences of the act; drunk driving is an obvious example).

Predatory crimes are crimes purely of redistribution of existing wealth; they do not generate new goods and services, and therefore they do not increase total income flows. Barring indirect consequences such as the costs of increased security (which could be argued either way), their net effect on Gross National Product (GNP) is zero. By contrast, market-based crimes involve the production and distribution of new goods and services. Judged in strictly economic terms, these crimes should have a positive impact on GNP. Indeed, it is now standard procedure in many countries to try to estimate the value of underground transactions in both legal and illegal goods and services, provided they are based on consensual exchanges, and to add that value to their existing national income data to get a better picture of just how "well" their economies are doing—yet another factor that makes the moral issues involved considerably fuzzier.

Because there is no definable victim to whom restitution is due, law enforcement has had trouble articulating what should be done with the proceeds of market-based offenses. With an awesome leap of logic, the position was taken that because both types of crime involved illegal activity, there was a close analogy between stolen property and illegally earned income, with the proviso that the victim in the second case was society. This rather forced analogy rationalized statues that would make guilty parties forfeit their gains to society (or its guardians).

These five factors combined account for most of the enthusiasm with which the United States embraced the follow-the-money doctrine. But to them must be added an explanation as to why it was so imperative for the rest of the world to follow suit.

On the Track of the Black Greenback

Across the world, U.S. banknotes, especially the fifty- and hundred-dollar denominations, are greatly in demand for conducting covert transactions, for hiding international financial transfers, and for parking underground savings in a safety deposit box, sticking them in a wall safe, or burying them in a garden plot. Not only does the resulting seigniorage—$15–25 billion per annum—effectively return to U.S. government coffers a good chunk of the money it pays out in foreign aid to poor countries whose tax cheats and smugglers are particularly hungry for U.S. dollars, but the United States gains indirectly. Persons habituated to thinking of the physical greenback as their primary haven against political and financial uncertainty will, by inference, come to see U.S. dollar deposits and investments in U.S. securities as the most logical place for their longer-term savings as well. Furthermore, raising the prestige of the U.S. currency encourages more legitimate trade to be financed through dollar-denominated instruments. That reinforces the competitive position of U.S. banks and pays additional returns to the United States in the form of increased invisible earnings on its international trade balance. All this strengthens the U.S. dollar on international exchange markets and assures that the world's richest country continues to be a net beneficiary of the savings of poorer countries.

In addition, for decades U.S. exports of goods sagged relative to imports. The gap in the commodity trade account had to be covered by importing capital (much of it based on capital flight from, and tax evasion in, other countries) or by running a large and growing surplus in services—the payments earned by U.S. consulting firms, insurance companies, banks, and similar enterprises all over the world. At the same time, the biggest growth sector in financial services has been private banking, that is, managing the portfolios of those euphemistically termed high-net-worth individuals. Traditionally dominated by Swiss and British banks, this field by the 1980s was one that the major U.S. banks were eager to exploit. Standing in the way were those pesky anti-money-laundering rules, which made the United States the least attractive of the major jurisdictions to foreign clients seeking confidentiality.

Therefore the United States faced a double dilemma. The physical acceptability of its banknotes undermined its own anti-laundering effort. At the same time its efforts to impose tighter regulations on its own banks threatened to scare off the world's super-rich, who wanted to hold the bulk of their assets denominated in U.S. To the rescue rode Senator John Kerry with an amendment to a 1988 money-laundering law; the amendment required the U.S. Treasury to negotiate with other countries the imposition of reporting regulations similar to those in force in the United States. Senator Kerry was quite clear about the danger: "If our banks are required to adhere to a standard, including offshore, and other banks do not and rush for deposits in those [U.S.] banks, we will have once again taken a step that will have disadvantaged our economic structure and institutions relative to those against whom we must compete in the marketplace."[10]

Thus, instead of restricting the export of U.S. banknotes, so beneficial to the Treasury, or watering down the U.S. reporting regulations to attract more foreign fund management business to U.S. banks, the strategy was to force other countries to impose, on their own banks, the administrative costs and competitive disadvantages of U.S.–style reporting regulations. Initially those reporting regulations were demanded for all cash transactions conducted by foreign banks in U.S. dollars over the $10,000 threshold. During the 1990s, other countries have been pressed to adopt such rules for cash deposits and withdrawals even in their own currency.

Nor was this demand merely moral exhortation. Behind the Kerry Amendment and subsequent measures stood the threat that foreign banks would be barred from use of the U.S.-controlled international wire transfer (CHIPS) system, something that would have crippled their international competitive position. The screws were tightened in 2001 when the U.S.-dominated International Monetary Fund and World Bank took their first steps to making loans to countries facing fiscal and financial crises provisional on those countries adopted IMF- or World Bank–approved anti-money-laundering controls.[11] Even in the late nineteenth century, the great age of financial imperialism, powerful creditor countries only imposed their own legal standards on debtor countries in order to assure repayment of debts, not to force them to bring their criminal codes into line with those of the creditor countries.[12] In response, with the enthusiastic support of their own police forces, country after country bowed to U.S. pressure.

Right on the Money?

The proceeds-of-crime approach to crime control rests on three premises: first, eliminating criminal gains acts as a powerful deterrent; second, taking away ill-gotten funds prevents criminals from being able to infiltrate and corrupt the legitimate economy; and third, removing the money also takes away the capital to commit future crimes. In addition, there is the underlying moral principle that no one should be permitted to profit from crime. All together they appear to provide a compelling rationalization. But appearances can be deceiving.

The deterrent theory is at best an oversimplification. Professional criminals, presumably the ones of most concern, are motivated by factors other than money—the sheer thrill of the act or the desire to show off their cleverness or daring. Moreover, most people who earn a substantial percentage or all of their income from illicit activity seem profligate spenders. This trait may reflect in part inherent hedonism, in part the urge to impress peers and partners, and in part the ever-present threat that their careers might be shortened by competitors or regulators. The stronger the asset-seizure provisions of law, the stronger this already inherent propensity to earn-and-spend is likely to be, leaving little for law enforcement to seize. Furthermore, because it is no mystery that the bulk of the career-criminal class is made up of down-and-outs rather than billionaire narco-barons, losing assets simply forces them to repeat the acts that generated the money, because professional criminals tend not to have a particularly wide range of vocational alternatives. Granted, some certainly save. But criminals, no less than other entrepreneurs, have a learning curve: if they are burned, they are more likely to learn better techniques for hiding and laundering than to switch careers.

There are even circumstances in which asset seizure, far from cleaning up crime, might encourage more of it. People tend to manage their income differently, depending on its source. Many who are dourly scrupulous with their wages will happily fritter away lottery winnings. With illicit income, too, the prevailing principle seems to be "easy come, easy go." A study of Oslo prostitutes, for example, showed that they carefully budgeted money from legitimate jobs or welfare but blew their illegal earnings on drugs, booze, and fancy clothes, even if their legitimate income was insufficient to cover their family's basic needs.[13] Under these circumstances, asset seizure would take not the illegal but the legitimate part of their earnings—hardly an incentive to give up a life of crime. Furthermore, asset-seizure laws discriminate in favor of a criminal who spends all his or her money on high living, versus the one who, while committing the same offenses, might use the proceeds to buy a house for aging parents or to invest in U.S. Treasury bills to help finance the War on Drugs.

Perhaps the ultimate repudiation of the deterrent notion is the simple fact that the United States, the country in which the proceeds approach is used most intensely, boasts a higher percentage of its population behind bars than does any other country except Russia. Yet it also remains the world's richest market for the forbidden products criminals peddle.

The second rationalization is that seizing proceeds stops criminals from infiltrating and corrupting legitimate business. But this too is, at best, an exaggeration. Apart from the fact that a fairly obvious question—Just how much criminal money is out there?—has to be answered before any rational judgment can be made about the threat it poses, it is also necessary to ask why criminals would wish to invest in the legal economy. There are actually several reasons, with radically different consequences.[14]

One reason is that some criminals, especially aging ones, want to provide for their future. Not only is their reason for investing in the legitimate sector benign, but so too their methods. They will work through bona fide investment houses to make passive investments in high-quality securities that convey no control over the issuing enterprise. There may be a moral objection to the principle of the criminal so securing his or her profits, but there is no reason to suspect that in so doing, the criminal will control or corrupt legal markets.

A criminal may also decide, in anticipation of death, arrest, or retirement, that he or she wants to transfer wealth to members of his or her biological rather than criminological family. Ensuring an inheritance requires, first, moving assets into the legal economy. Although the actual investments may be slightly different than those chosen for the entrepreneur's own retirement, the reasons, the methods, and the consequences are equally harmless to the legal economy. Indeed, a case could be made that this is actually positive. If the United States had taken seriously the notion that the sins of the fathers are visited upon the sons, it would have deprived itself not only of its most media-genic president but also of the first attorney general to raise the battle against the bogeyman of organized crime to the status of a national crusade.

Alternatively, the criminal entrepreneur might seek to reduce risk to his or her income by diversification into an active legitimate business. Legally derived income is much less vulnerable to disruption by criminal competition or regulatory pressure. Presumably the more insecure the source of illegal income, the greater the strictly financial need for an independent source of legal income, and therefore the greater the incentive to create a legitimate alternative. But for this strategy to be effective, the business must be run in an impeccably clean manner: criminal methods should be avoided, and the business should not be used as a front for illegal operations or for laundering criminal money.

In all three cases, the integration of criminally earned assets into the legal economy does not threaten the integrity of legal markets. In all three cases, the acquired assets, financial or commercial, must be kept clear of association with their underworld origins. That poses a dilemma for crime control policy. If the objective is to punish past acts committed by the criminal entrepreneur, then the logical policy is take away from the criminal those legitimate assets acquired using illegitimately earned income; precisely how they should be taken away is a separate issue. If the objective is to prevent recidivism, there is actually a case to be made for leaving the criminal in possession of those assets, to encourage a shift from illegal to legal activity. And if the objective is not to address this or that malefactor but to attack the criminal marketplace as a whole, the correct policy might be to encourage actively the movement of criminal assets into the legal economy. These kinds of transfers simultaneously reduce the assets of the underworld economy while raising those available to the legal one.

On the other hand, some of the reasons criminals chose to shift money to the legal parts of the economy are not so benign. A legitimate business might be used, for example, to support underworld operations. That, in turn, can take three different forms.

One is to provide laundry facilities. By running illegally earned income through a front company, the criminal entrepreneur gives that income an alibi. However, money laundering is not a means of earning criminal profit (except by a professional launderer) but of redirecting profit after it has been earned. Once laundered, the money might be used to bribe a judge or hire a professional assassin. Or it might be used to make payments into the criminal's retirement savings account. Yet in crime control measures, no distinction is made.

Another similar possibility is that a business front can provide the underworld entrepreneur with tax cover. Legitimate citizens take their total income, calculate taxes due, and then decide in what proportion to consume or save the remainder. Underworld entrepreneurs work in reverse—they estimate how much after-tax income they wish to have visibly available to consume, save, or invest, and then they calculate the level of pre-tax earnings of the front enterprise to sustain the after-tax total. All criminals who expect to remain in business for any length of time should undertake such an exercise, however informal, unless they have exceptionally strong police or political connections or their incomes are so low that they have virtually no fiscal vulnerability. By itself this introduces no serious distortion into the operation of legal markets. Indeed, on one level it is beneficial, because otherwise untaxed income is exposed to the fiscal authorities.

Yet another possibility is that a front operation directly supports underworld rackets. It might function as a place through which to peddle stolen or smuggled merchandise or from which to traffic drugs, sell snuff movies, or run an illegal gambling enterprise. However, what is involved is a veneer of legality to disguise continued illegality. Whether used for laundering, tax cover, or logistical support, the front company, which appears to be part of the legal economy, operates in reality as the apparatus of enterprise crime. Therefore it can hardly be said to be corrupting the legitimate sector.

Where the threshold is unambiguously crossed and criminal entry into the legitimate economy becomes unambiguously harmful is when the criminal uses investments in the legal economy not as cover for on-going crimes but as a direct source of criminal profit. In this instance the criminal takes underworld techniques—a reputation for violence, a willingness to bribe regulators, the capacity to extort kickbacks from suppliers, and the means to reduce through intimidation both labor costs and competition—into the legal economy in order to squeeze higher profits out of the legal business than would be possible using strictly legitimate methods. Here (and only here) is it possible to say with conviction that criminal assets corrupt a legal business. However, it still cannot be said a priori that career criminals do more to undermine the integrity of legitimate businesses than do legitimate businesspeople who employ illegal means to achieve the same ends. Yet no one suggests preemptively seizing their assets to head off that result.

The third reason for attacking proceeds is based on the premise that deprived of financial resources to maintain a flow of product to their customers, crime "cartels" would be quickly put out of business. There is an obvious problem with this theory. Asset seizure targets the firm, not the industry. For every firm knocked out, others are eager to enter or expand. To the extent that any one criminal firm is affected, it is unclear whether it will reduce the scope of a criminal market or just as change the identity of those who earn the profits. Furthermore, to the extent that crime markets offer credit to underworld entrepreneurs, repeat offenders fresh from prison will probably have the least problem securing loans to get back into business. They have the proven experience, the best contacts, and the reputation for not singing to the regulators—otherwise they would not have clocked prison time. In the criminal sector of the economy, capital consists of personal contacts at least as much as it does of money. And the kind of trust such contacts represent cannot be bought—it can only be earned.

Nonetheless, money is a necessary, even if not a sufficient, condition for enterprise crime. Unlike the deterrent and corruption-of-legal-business arguments, the notion that depriving a criminal of operating capital will seriously impair illegal markets merits further consideration. How important it is as a criminal justice objective depends in good measure on how much criminal money is really floating around.

The Numbers Racket

Absolute sums in isolation are meaningless as guides to policy. To truly determine if an attack on proceeds has any discernible impact on the criminal marketplace requires some basic calculations and a preliminary clarification.

It is necessary to differentiate criminal income (i.e., proceeds) from criminal wealth (i.e., assets). Granted the first is necessary to produce the second, but it is not sufficient. Income is what is earned from rackets, and much of it is dissipated in meeting costs. If the objective is to stop criminal income, then the only way to do so is to close rackets—which makes the new law enforcement method really no different from the old. But if the objective is to deter through eliminating motive and means, the focus must be on net income or profit, and in practice the target must be the wealth that has accumulated as a direct result of net income or profit from previous offenses. Rationally, the procedure should be called profits-of-crime, not proceeds-of-crime.

Therefore, to determine how effective is a profits-of-crime policy, it is necessary, first, to find the ratio of seized criminal wealth to total criminal wealth, both at the beginning and again at the end of the test period, in order to assess how big a dent is being made in underworld resources. Properly speaking, that ratio should be calculated for every year in the period under review—to reduce the possibility that the first or the final year is for some reason anomalous. If the ratio is rising, then net assets available to criminals are falling. But the ratio by itself does not suffice to prove the success of the policy.

Second, it is also necessary to compare the rate of growth of criminal income with that of legal income to ascertain if the chunk taken out of criminal wealth is actually affecting adversely the ability of illegal markets to service their clientele. If the growth of criminal income begins to slow relative to that of legal, or if it falls absolutely, then clearly something besides general economic conditions has affected the criminal sector. If nothing else has radically changed on the law enforcement front, it might be reasonable to impute that change at least partially to the net loss of criminal assets.

Without both types of data—changes in the amount of available criminal wealth and the relative growth of criminal and legal income—no defensible conclusion about the impact is possible. The question is, can those two calculations actually be made?

The first piece of data required is the value of seized assets. In theory that should be simple to find. In fact it is not. The figures announced by the police are generally their guess about the value of properties frozen. These reported sums must immediately be deflated by eliminating double or multiple counting. This is especially a problem with bank data. A sum of money might have been wired from one bank to another, but instead of merely reporting the net deposit, police may add together every intermediate deposit and then announce the total. Asset values must also be deflated to take account of outstanding debts; this is particularly a problem when dealing with mortgaged property. In general the (rarely reported) value of the final forfeiture is usually substantially less than the (enthusiastically reported) value of the initial freeze for several reasons: the initial amount may have been exaggerated for public relations purposes; some assets presumed to exist could not be found; some assets depreciated badly in police custody; or ultimately a judge or jury could not be persuaded that there was any link between the assets and the offense. Furthermore, all innocent property inadvertently (or sometimes deliberately) caught in the net should be deducted. If a teenager is caught smoking a joint in the backyard, and the parents' house is forfeited as an "instrumentality" of crime, it makes little sense to include the value of the house in a calculation purporting to show how much criminal wealth is being taken out of circulation—although that is precisely what U.S. reports on the value of seizures attempt to do. Indeed, surveying the multiplicity of horror stories to emerge from U.S. asset-seizure programs, it is hard to avoid the impression that a very large share of the property grabbed by police has nothing whatsoever to do with crime, either as proceeds or as instrumentalities.[15]

Assuming that the value of seized criminal wealth could be satisfactorily calculated, the figure has to be compared with the total amount of criminal wealth in existence. Even the roughest guesstimate of that amount requires several steps. First, it is necessary to arrive at some approximation of total criminal income flows. Second, a certain profit rate must be imputed to those flows. (This is especially problematic because in practice profit rates vary widely not only among different rackets but among different practitioners of the same rackets.) Third, and particularly tricky given the propensity of criminals to blow all their earnings, a certain percentage of the profit must be assumed to be saved and therefore available to accumulate as assets each year. (Why not the magic 10 percent?) Fourth, those assets must be cumulated over time, while imputing a certain rate of return (if held in financial form) or depreciation (if held as durable goods) or potential speculative gains / losses (if held as precious stones, high-priced artwork, mink stoles, or the like). Difficult though steps two through four might be, they are useless unless the first step is taken. The problem here is that attempting to estimate criminal income flows is a task that would have caused Hercules to apply for early retirement.

To be sure, there are many people on the job, churning out an impressively wide range of impressively large numbers as evidence, it is claimed, of a huge and growing problem. This is not because of a conspiracy to exaggerate. Rather, there is an implicit consensus among members of a large-number coalition. This community is comprised of law enforcement agencies whose powers and budgets increasingly depend on the perceived threat of large-scale (read large-dollar-value) crime; informants who have a vested interest in puffing their own importance by inflating the significance of the information they are imparting; criminals eager for peer and public esteem; the mass media, which long ago discovered that sensationalism linked to crime sells exceptionally well; politicians who raise their profile by posing as anticrime crusaders either to appeal to their constituents or to attack the other side; and the research community, whose grants usually depend on them finding a suitably "large" problem to study.

Finally, with respect to macrodata problems, aggregate figures, even if reasonable, are simply that—aggregate. By themselves they give no clue as to the number of beneficiaries or the distribution of the sums among them. Therefore they can provide little or no information about how criminal enterprises are structured or how criminal markets actually work.

Police, press, and public alike prefer to believe that crime is typified by large organizations making huge profits and plotting to infiltrate legal markets to distort them to criminal ends. Facts on the ground have repeatedly shown the opposite. Constrained by lack of access to the formal capital market, inability to employ mass marketing techniques (which attract attention), rapacious attention of competitors, susceptibility to false and misleading information flows, and constant threats from the police, the criminal firm typically is small and unstable and, for the most part, generates low and sporadic profit.

The difference is important. Clearly even large amounts of criminal income distributed among a host of petty wheeler-dealers pose much less of a threat to the integrity of legal markets than does massive infiltration of money in the hands of a few criminal titans. The more widely distributed the proceeds, the greater the likelihood of it staying on the street, being blown on the purchase of luxury goods, frittered away in prestige-enhancing entertainment of peers or playmates, or lost by gambling. If nothing is known for certain about the nature, size, and strategic objectives of the criminal operations earning the money, then even if the ratio of seized assets to total criminal assets is rising, it is impossible to say whether the criminal market has been adversely affected by a policy of targeting illegal wealth. For example, if seizure values are skewed upward by a few large catches in a marketplace dominated by many small "firms," there is likely little impact on the ability of the criminal marketplace to satisfy its customers—others will simply expand to fill the void. In all likelihood, the criminal marketplace has both large and small "firms" represented, although in what proportions no one has the faintest idea.

Finally, nothing can be safely concluded without taking into account the intent of the criminal entrepreneur with respect to asset management. If the objective of a criminal accumulating criminally derived assets is to further a life of crime, taking away those assets might have a positive effect—even if it goes no farther than merely changing the identity of the players in the criminal marketplace. But if, instead, the objective is one of the more benign possibilities, such as investing in the creation of an alternate and legal source of income as a prelude to retirement from the underworld, seizing those assets can hardly be construed as an unambiguous contribution to crime control.

Up Close and Personal

Even if little can be accomplished with the macro approach to estimating, surely effective data on a local or regional level can be obtained from particular incidents. By inference, these data—which can come from informants, actual cases, or sting operations—should also give some clues about the distribution of criminal income among various enterprises and individuals.

Informant-derived information is especially problematic. The criminal milieu has more than its share of pathological liars and acute paranoiacs, not to mention people who have lived so long in the shadow world of deceit and deception that they cease to recognize any border between fact and fantasy. The credibility of the information is especially dubious when informants have a vested interest (in terms of direct payment, license to continue their own rackets, or reduced sentences) in exaggerating the importance of the information they are peddling.

Case-driven information should, in principle, be more reliable, but here there is a major distinction between information about predatory versus market-based crimes. With predatory offenses, establishing the value of misappropriated property is fairly straightforward. The victim has an incentive to report—with some danger of exaggeration if an insurance company is expected to cover the bill. What the victim loses, the perpetrator gains—albeit if it is physical property, the returns to the perpetrator from resale to a fence are likely much lower than the replacement cost to the victim (or insurance company). With a market-based offense, however, there is no victim to complain. If caught, a perpetrator has a vested interest in minimizing the amounts earned. The accused will face charges for the particular incident for which he or she was caught, not for the sum total of all the income that might have been earned over a career in crime. Whereas a particular heist in a predatory crime might generate a very large sum, and be rarely repeated, in an enterprise offense the predominant pattern is for most incidents to involve small retail sales—the real payoff comes from multiple iterations.

Thus, when someone is arrested for a market-based offense, they have a strong vested interest in hiding the extent of the operations—unless they turn informant, in which case they will tend to exaggerate the size and importance of other people's activities. The impact of asset-seizure laws accentuate both effects: the arrested person tries to hide his or her assets, whereas the informant is sometimes rewarded on the basis of how much of other people's assets are seized.

Nor is the situation better with information that originates from police stings. Police are subject to legal and financial constraints that predetermine the form of their sting operations. Because stings are exceptional and apply to only a narrow part of highly segmented markets, the best they can yield is a view of what might be going on in that particular segment, which might have little relevance to any other segment. Furthermore, by participating in the market in a particular way, police action can function to steer the marketplace into directions it might not have taken left to its own devices. Once the police sting operation ceases to affect the structure and operation of a particular marketplace, it might revert to its original forms, leaving the police with a view that reflects little more than their own preconceptions.

Probably the biggest single problem in working with incident-derived data is that even if the data were not distorted by informant fabrications, by the deceit of malefactors, or by the peculiar circumstances of police stings, the results may still be meaningless from the point of view of the market as a whole. Simply put, there is no market for illegal goods and services. There is merely a series of more or less interconnected regional submarkets. For a genuine market to exist, there must be a free flow of information, commodities, and money within it. Within legal markets, the role of the regulators is to guarantee that free flow. Within illegal markets, the role of the regulator is to do the opposite. Hence, data derived from one case likely reflect conditions in one regional submarket (which might be no bigger than a city street) and little more. Consequently, it is impossible to extrapolate from individual cases to the "market" as a whole, and, at best, it is very difficult to use prices and quantities from any one case to compute overall numbers representative of the size of trafficking in a particular good or service.

Even if all data problems are satisfactorily solved, there is still a fundamental failing in the entire exercise: it is not at all clear what the numbers prove. With predatory offenses, a successful law enforcement strategy, by definition, means that relative to some appropriate base of comparison, the number of offenses should diminish. Predicting what will happen to the value of goods taken in each incident is more problematic. From the point of view of the victim there is no a priori reason that the sums involved per offense should change. But from the point of view of the perpetrators, they will. To the extent that law enforcement also targets fencers of stolen goods, fencers will discount the risk by lowering prices to the thieves. Nonetheless, whether returns to thieves per incident stay the same or fall (they certainly will not rise in response to a law enforcement blitz), the net effect of successful law enforcement is that the number of offenses, and possibly the number of perpetrators, will decrease, and so too will the total value of illegal property transfers.

However, with market-based offenses, the opposite is true. As enforcement becomes more effective, the number of participants might well rise. Here there is an important distinction between a legal and an illegal enterprise. In a legal enterprise, the more the firm can dispense with intermediaries, the more it can internalize their share of the profit. But in an illegal enterprise there is the opposite tendency. Criminal entrepreneurs respond to the threat from law enforcement by increasing the number of defensive layers of intermediation between themselves and their customers. To reduce risks, they are forced to diffuse earnings among a large number of others, simultaneously reducing the danger of being caught with large accumulations of criminal capital. At the same time, the physical quantities involved in each transaction should fall—more participants each handling smaller quantities. Yet prices should also rise in response to greater risk. Because presumably the demand for criminal goods and services is somewhat inelastic, the value of goods and services traded actually increases in the face of successful law enforcement. Because the profits are distributed across more participants, there is no way of determining a priori if the net income of each participant should rise or fall.

Hence, unlike predatory crime, in which large and growing numbers of incidents or values of involved property are a sign of a law enforcement crisis, with market-based offenses such things are more likely a sign of law enforcement's success. Therefore it is absurd for law enforcement to use large numbers representing the apparent value of illegal economic transactions as an indicator of the need for more resources or greater arbitrary power to deal with the problem. The opposite conclusion could as easily be drawn: The larger the number, the more effective is existing police action and that less the need for any drastic change.

Maytag or Washboard?

The difficulties of interpretation of evidence apply not just to primary markets for illegal goods and services but also to the secondary market in laundering services. There have been attempts to estimate the total amount of money being laundered not just within particular countries but worldwide. Efforts to make such calculations by using world balance-of-payments data have been useless—a fact that does not prevent the results from gaining considerable currency, provided they are big enough to attract attention. The numbers for the current account (goods and services traded) even for legal transactions are full of statistical anomalies: reported prices are warped by efforts to evade taxes and exchange controls, and quantity data are distorted by smuggling, quotas, and embargoes. Data on international trade in services are even worse.

Nor have direct calculations been much more successful. Take for example the usual approach to calculating the drug trade, widely (perhaps erroneously) believed to be the largest single chunk of the illegal economy: first, estimate the size of the world drug production; second, figure out how much of the product actually gets to market; third, estimate total revenues; fourth, calculate drug profits; and fifth, pick a number to represent what percentage of those profits requires laundering. Out of these calculations comes the total amount of drug money supposedly needing to be laundered, which is then compared with total financial flows. On the basis of such methods, it has been claimed that 2–5 percent of world Gross Domestic Product represents laundered money.[16] The figure might just as easily be 20–50 percent or 0.02–0.05 percent. Given the credibility of the methodology, the only thing that can be stated with certainty is that the actual figure is not likely to be less than 0 percent or more than 100 percent.

Working with specific incident-derived data is also problematic. Almost all information comes either from those who got caught, who, by definition, tend to be the more incompetent, or from police stings. This produces the usual problems of unrepresentative or distorted data. Indeed, it is possible that money-laundering stings are welcomed by serious criminals. A few subordinates are sacrificed and some of the money lost when the operation is taken down, but in the meantime the perpetrators have been guaranteed a laundry service that is remarkably efficient (because it is, by definition, immune to regulatory troubles).

This problem aside, optimally, money-laundering cases should yield three different kinds of information—the amounts being laundered, the fees charged, and the methods employed. There are difficulties with all three.

In terms of sums, there is often double or multiple counting of bank balances, at least at the initial freeze stage. There is also the problem of commingling. For cover, illegal money is put in bank accounts in which much, probably most, of the funds are of legal origin, but when the funds are seized by law enforcement, the total is reported as the "proceeds of crime."[17] There is also the problem of money being deemed guilty by association. In an incident that has been replicated several times subsequently, a U.S. citizen, himself above suspicion, had a Miami bank account frozen on the grounds that he had bought dollars from a Colombian money changer who traded with other money changers, some of whom allegedly serviced drug dealers. The government's position, which the courts have upheld, is that once drugs are sold for cash, that cash—no matter in what manner or how often it changes hands—is still owned by the government. "That's the underlying theory," proudly proclaimed the chief of financial investigations of the DEA.[18] Just how this sort of seizure advanced the cause of removing the profit and the operating capital from crime was never explained.

But even without data problems, it is unclear what the numbers show. Even if seizures of assets in laundering cases are rising, the result is meaningful only in relation to the trend in the total value of criminal assets being laundered. Lacking such figures, there is no evidence to support a judgment on the results one way or the other. Even worse, assuming the ultimate objective is not to fill the coffers with forfeited booty but to prevent and deter crime, then, judged in such terms, the most successful and the least successful antiproceeds programs would have exactly the same results—small value of seizures and small numbers of arrests.

There is, however, another indicator that the police cite as proof of success. Supposedly as a result of their antiproceeds drive, the cost of money laundering rose from about 6 percent in the mid-1980s to 25 percent by the mid-1990s. This claim is utterly baseless. There is no market per se. In one case an underworld entrepreneur might pay a certain percentage to wash money; in another, later case, a different underworld entrepreneur might pay a higher sum. It is impossible to claim on this basis that there is a general upward trend of laundering costs. Either fee might be for arranging to buy cashier's checks, for smuggling a suitcase of currency to the Cayman Islands, or for running a full-service operation in which a team of accountants, tax lawyers, and investment counselors set up a complex of offshore companies and secret bank accounts. This is not just a matter of comparing apples and oranges. Rather, it is more akin to comparing the price of a jar of applesauce to the cost of purchasing, maintaining, and harvesting a citrus grove.

Furthermore, even if rates are rising across the board, the claim that this hurts the criminal marketplace cannot stand unqualified. Raising the costs of money laundering through a concerted proceeds-of-crime crackdown will, in the first instance, redistribute criminal income from those committing the underlying crimes to those handling the money. This is precisely the kind of shift—from suppliers of goods and services to financial managers—observable in the legal economy, which no one suggests as a reason to expect legal GNP to fall. Similarly, redistributing profits will not, by itself, make a dent in the overall amount of criminal income or wealth being generated—which is the only ultimate test of the efficacy of the policy. In the case of drug money, and probably that from other vice offenses as well, it is by no means clear that the trafficker is the one to pay. To the extent that the demand for drugs is inelastic, any hike in laundering costs will be passed on to the consumer. The effect, on balance, will be to take more income from consumers and transfer it to criminal entrepreneurs. Just as anti–drug enforcement acts as a price support program to raise the incomes of successful dealers, anti-money-laundering measures may do the same for criminal money managers.

Finally, because all information comes either from those who were caught or from police stings, it is unclear what general inferences can be drawn from it. If the information comes from the former, the information will do less to provide data to law enforcement on what the prevailing market trends are than to send a message to the money-laundering industry to improve its techniques. If the information comes from the latter, there are other problems.

The police employ a particular technique not because it is most representative (something that can only be determined, if at all, after the fact) but because it is the one they best understand or have the resources and legal powers to deploy. They catch criminals and report success. Those reports become the evidence for claiming that the technique the police used represents money laundering in general. Which in turn becomes the basis for targeting more resources against a particular form of money laundering, with each success further confirming the original hypothesis, even if the actual trend in the money-laundering "market" is in some completely different direction. On the basis of what has shown up in hundreds of cases around the world over the last decade and a half, the most sensible working hypothesis would appear to be that money laundering is so decentralized and its technology so geared to mimicking a wide variety of innocent and ordinary financial management methods, that reported "trends" reveal more about the point on the learning curve reached by law enforcement rather than anything new in the pattern and pace of money laundering.[19]

Thus, there is no real proof that a proceeds-of-crime approach really succeeds in accomplishing its three major declared objectives. It cannot be proven to deter; it likely has little or no impact in preventing the corruption of legal markets; and there is no evidence it has been able to cripple any "organizations" by depriving them of capital. Still, there is a fourth rationalization for targeting proceeds of crime. It states simply that criminals should not be allowed to profit from their crimes. It is a moral principle with which few would disagree and which requires no empirical verification. However, on the subsidiary issue of how much "collateral damage" society should be willing to sustain to implement that principle, the amount of disagreement could be considerable.

Proceeds of Crime and the Seven Deadly Sins

Although police in other jurisdictions agitate, with increasing success, for improved powers to find, freeze, and forfeit, no country's record yet matches that of the United States, where the pursuit of the proceeds of crime has become less a means of controlling profit-driven crime than another form of it. This tendency manifests itself in seven particularly nasty ways.

The first is the very creation of the contrived offense called money laundering. Unlike the actions that generate the money, be they trafficking in endangered species, illegal dumping of toxic waste, contract killing, or telemarketing fraud, money laundering consists of acts that are innocent in and of themselves. For that reason it has proven difficult to explain to the layman (or, for that matter, to some experts) just what harm is done by it. Money launderers do not pull guns or con widows and orphans of their savings. Rather they make deposits, draw checks, purchase ordinary bank instruments, and wire payments from place to place. Because money laundering involves standard transactions through the legitimate financial system to disguise the origins and destination of illicitly derived money, laws that forbid handling the proceeds of crime have had to criminalize everything from making a series of deposits, each small enough to circumvent a reporting requirement, to rushing to board an international flight with a bearer bond tucked away, undeclared, in the traveler's attaché case. Setting up a shell company, sending a money order, or buying a cashier's check can all attract serious penalties. In the United States, even auto dealers, jewelers, and real estate agents who do nothing more than sell to someone later convicted of a criminal offense can be accused of helping to launder the proceeds.[20]

Indeed, with anti-money-laundering law, there is no need to make the charge, much less the punishment, fit the crime. Commercial frauds, currency counterfeiting, alien smuggling, and many other offenses have been prosecuted on the basis of violations of the money-laundering statutes. In that way the focus shifts from the underlying acts (which might invoke genuine public opprobrium) to the methods used by perpetrators to make off with the loot.[21] It makes about as much sense as creating a stand-alone offense called "driving the get-away car" for bank robbery cases. Such use of the law both trivializes the real offense and casts a chill over the entire criminal justice system by announcing that laws are there not to address crimes but to cater to the convenience of the prosecution. That is all the worse given that in the United States today, money-laundering charges can carry much heavier consequences than the underlying offense. Someone convicted of fraud, for example, typically does less time than someone who helped launder the resulting money, even if they had no idea that fraud had occurred.[22]

In addition, by criminalizing the handling of illicit funds, the state effectively forbids all business dealings with persons who might turn out to be criminals. Anyone who does so runs the risk of themselves facing criminal sanction; they are guilty not of a proscribed act but of association with tainted money. It has long been a criminal offense to receive stolen property and therefore to consciously become a conspirator in the act of theft. But now it is a criminal offense to engage in otherwise legitimate business transactions with someone later deemed a criminal, even if those transactions did nothing to assist that person with any further criminal acts.[23]

The second deadly sin committed by the proceeds frenzy has been to indiscriminately burden the U.S. and, increasingly, the global financial system with reporting requirements that are at best useless, at worst pernicious.[24]

Financial institutions are expected to provide information to law enforcement agencies on which those agencies can act. But this raises serious questions—about the efficacy of the reporting apparatus, about the competence of banking personnel to make the required judgments, and about the extent to which rights to privacy are necessarily violated on a routine basis to little or no apparent gain. The problem inheres not just in the information requirements and the way they have progressively escalated, but also in the very nature of the information and the banker's role in providing it.

These requirements began, first in the United States, then abroad, with the currency transaction report (CTR), with which financial institutions were to record large cash deposits (or withdrawals) and to detail information about the depositor and the origins of the money. Along with it came the currency and monetary instruments report (CMIR) for export and import of cash or monetary instruments greater than $5,000. To deal with the possibility that a criminal might prefer to use cash proceeds to buy high-valued consumer durables, Form 8300 followed; it requires that dealers in luxuries, collectables, and valuable durables demand information similar to that found on a CTR from any customer paying more than $10,000 cash.

As a second line of defense, banks not just in the United States but, increasingly, around the world are required to file suspicious transaction (or activity) reports. This report can be filed on top of a CTR. It can also be filed in instances in which the CTR requirement does not apply but the bank officer feels the transaction fits the "suspicious" bill.

Finally, a third layer—popular in the European community but thus far rejected in the United States—consists of know-your-client rules.[25] These involve not exogenously required forms but exogenously determined vetting procedures, which in turn could lead to additional information being passed on to law enforcement.

Although one type of information requirement seems to flow logically into the next, in fact each level represents a qualitative change in the relations between banker and client, and between financial institutions and the law enforcement apparatus.

A CTR is the least problematic. If a certain threshold is reached, then the institution is required by a clear, externally imposed rule to gather specific information and pass it on to the authorities. The institution's role is passive—it acts as a conduit for given types of data between client and government agency; the data is the same for all clients, and the client acts as a fully informed, conscious participant in the process. This is also true with respect to CMIRs and Form 8300s. Leaving aside the cottage industry that has grown up to circumvent these requirements, U.S. Treasury agents, for years, complained of being overwhelmed by paper; and Congress, for years, debated reducing the amount of paperwork by raising the reporting threshold and encouraging financial institutions to make more liberal use of their right to grant exemptions from the reporting requirements to certain categories of customers.[26] In effect, the efficacy of the system seemed, and still seems, threatened by the sheer volume of information it generates, which is precisely why some countries refuse to follow the United States's lead.

More importantly, however, even if the reports are filed correctly, it remains questionable just what they accomplish. Every major money-laundering case seems to start with exogenous information, usually informants' tips, that points the police in the direction of an individual, and the police then pull any forms that had been filed concerning that person. Far from being a source of breakthrough intelligence used to initiate investigations, the data reproduce information that could in most cases be obtained elsewhere.[27]

If the role of a financial institution in filing a CTR is passive, its role with regard to a suspicious activity report is reactive. The client or the client's transaction exhibits certain characteristics that trigger a response. The bank is not an automatic conduit but a police informant. Despite efforts by law enforcement to draw up lists of objective characteristics of suspicious transactions, the bank's decision is really based on subjective hunches. It may be rooted in stereotypes or mass media hyperbole. Meantime the client is not informed. On the contrary. The financial institution and its staff can themselves face criminal penalties for telling a client that a suspicious activity report is being filed.

With know-your-client rules, the financial institution notches up its role once again. It is no longer passive or even reactive, but proactive. It has, in effect, been deputized by the law enforcement apparatus. Nor is it clear where the financial institution's responsibilities stop. To really know a client's business, it is necessary to know the client's clients, and perhaps the client's client's clients. Indeed, to protect itself—ironically from the police rather than from the client—the institution may go overboard. Fear can degenerate into paranoia, which can impede efficiency, clutter operations, and compromise the bank's responsibilities to the client. And while all of this is happening, the client is left totally in the dark.

None of this is meant to suggest that banks should not be alert to signs of illicit activity. Rather the question is just how far they are expected to dig into their clients' affairs, and just how much of the job of police or revenue officers, trained for years in the detection of illicit transactions, banks can reasonably be expected to perform, particularly when the war on money laundering presents them with a conflict of interest between their role as profit-seeking institutions (which encourages them to roll out the welcome mat to depositors, and maybe throw in a box of cigars for those whose position is exceptionally liquid) and their new (involuntarily acquired) law enforcement obligations.

Furthermore, these rules fly squarely in the face of modern banking trends—where more and more transactions are initiated and conducted by the client, where tabulation of deposit records is centralized, and where as much business as possible is being impersonalized. Once again, the profit-seeking (cost-reducing) interests of the financial institution put it at loggerheads with any desire to draft the financial sector into the front lines.

This problem of detection is further exacerbated by the spread of cyber-banking, by the advent of electronic purses with peer-to-peer transfer capacity, and by the propensity of people to enter and leave countries not with cash or traveler's checks but with debit cards. All this threatens to make the reporting apparatus, now being carefully put in place, largely irrelevant. Yet to these trends, the police instinct will undoubtedly be to demand yet more regulations and more reports.

The third sin is the muddling of civil and criminal procedures, and the accompanying deterioration of a citizen's defenses against arbitrary acts by the state or its agents.

In strict theory, civil suits are supposed to involve (1) an action by one private citizen against another, (2) seeking damages that correspond to actual events, and (3) using procedures that require only a slim margin of proof (balance of probabilities). On the other hand, in strict theory, criminal prosecutions are supposed to involve (1) actions by the state or its agencies against a private citizen, (2) seeking punishment that can involve loss of life and liberty, and (3) using procedures that, because of the gross imbalance of resources and heavy consequences, require a high standard of proof (beyond a reasonable doubt).

This distinction logically suggests that there is something fundamentally at variance with natural justice when the state or its agencies can proceed against a private citizen in actions with punitive effects while being required to meet only a civil standard of proof. Yet that is the main thrust of asset-forfeiture practice as based on the legal fiction of guilty property. Once accused, property is presumed guilty unless its owner can find the financial and legal resources to prove otherwise. The use of paid informants in such cases is particularly offensive in both logic and justice. It requires relying on the worst motives of the worst people to make cases on the weakest of possible legal grounds.

Yet repeatedly the process is defended with the rationale that the purpose is remedial rather than punitive—a defense that is, quite frankly, absurd. It is impossible for seizure of property to be anything but punitive. It is impossible to declare a car or house or bank account to be the proceeds or the instrument of cocaine sales, for example, without simultaneously smearing its owner with the accusation of drug trafficking. But with no need for a criminal conviction prior to asset seizure, there is also no need for the state to enter into court proceedings a shred of evidence to substantiate the implicit accusation against the owner. Not only does punishment in the form of property forfeiture occur, but the owner has been to all intents and purposes found guilty not only in the eyes of the state but also in the eyes of his or her fellow citizens—and guilty without trial. Even worse, if the citizen has faced trial and been acquitted, yet the state proceeds successfully against the citizen's property in a civil action, the citizen is now de facto found guilty of the very offense for which he or she had previously been acquitted.

The fourth sin is the threat that follow-the-money mania poses to the integrity of the fiscal system. This is a threat that has deep, uniquely American historical roots. When the movement to ban alcohol and narcotics began in the United States during the late nineteenth century, it faced a constitutional problem. Regulating such matters seemed, at first glance, to be beyond the powers of the federal government. And state-by-state variations in prohibition laws would have rendered them unworkable. However, the U.S. Supreme Court ruled that the federal government had the right to regulate anything that it had the right to tax. Hence, the laws regulating alcohol as well as the early drug laws were written as revenue statutes. This meant that primary responsibility for enforcement went to Treasury agents.[28]

This melding of tax enforcement and crime control took another big step forward in the 1930s, when the U.S. government used charges of income tax evasion against Chicago kingpin Al Capone.[29] The objective in this and similar future cases was not to grab the assets of mobsters and so deter them from further sins or to cripple their "organizations." Rather it was simply to find something for which they could be tossed in jail. However, that put matters squarely in reverse. Instead of using the threat of criminal sanction to enforce tax regulations, law enforcement agencies were using tax law to enforce the criminal code in proceedings in which the real objective was to punish the individual rather than collect the overdue taxes. Simultaneously, by using tax law to prosecute criminals indirectly for other offenses, the agencies sent the public at large the message that it is all right to cheat on taxes provided the money originates from legitimate sources.[30]

Today the great majority of government revenues are derived from the direct taxation of income at progressive rates. The system is premised on self-assessment and voluntary compliance, that is, on trust backed up by the threat of criminal sanction. Central to the system's success is the guarantee of confidentiality, that tax information will not be leaked to competitors or creditors. Although revenue officials have long required the ability to use confidential tax information in criminal proceedings designed to enforce tax law, the process is now being put in reverse. Police are given permission to fish through tax files in pursuit of evidence for criminal investigations and forfeitures. The next step will come when the police are given the authority, which they are now seeking in the United States, to use tax files for purely civil forfeitures.

Fifth of the sins is that the proceeds approach has warped law enforcement priorities. When police pursue economically motivated crime, their logical targets for action should be first, predatory offenses that involve force or its threat; second, crimes associated with particularly blatant forms of fraud; and only third (if at all), market-based crimes involving willing participants in a free-market transaction. Today, thanks to the lethal combination of moral absolutism and asset seizure, these priorities have been reversed.

Pushed by the U.S. Justice Department, which repeatedly urges that more effort be put into forfeitures, the law enforcement apparatus has shifted attention from violent criminals who would be a genuine threat to society and toward wealthy ones. In the past, police were awarded performance bonuses and salary hikes based on how many arrests they made; now such bonuses are more likely based on how much money they can grab through forfeiture. As a result they prioritize actions according to the amount and type of seizable assets. They conduct pre-raid planning sessions to determine what should be taken. Cash, jewels, cars, boats, and commercial real estate that is easily liquidated have long been the favorites. Generally, the police avoid seizing entire businesses. They are hard to resell, especially if there are other partners who might not be charged. Furthermore, between the time of seizure and the time of the court-ordered forfeiture, the police have to operate the seized business. Police forces have found themselves in the intriguing position of running, at various points, a porn cinema, a gambling den, and a Nevada brothel.[31]

Simultaneously, there has been a reduction in the number of charges filed under laws that might lead to imposition of fines—which are paid to the public treasury—in favor of charges under laws in which assets can be seized and shared among police and prosecutors.

The result of all this is that some police forces and prosecutor's offices run at a profit, with budgets in excess of the amounts they were formerly voted when subject to civic control. Furthermore, the benefit from seizures can depend on an accident of geography—a well-heeled dealer nabbed driving through town—rather than on actual need. There are small-town forces so flush with drug cash that they now boast fully armed, state-of-the-art SWAT teams, although their previous experience with serious crime was an occasional Saturday night brawl in the local saloon.[32]

The chase for money also skews the choice of who gets prison time and who takes a walk, albeit somewhat lightened of cash and property. Wealthy persons can bargain their way out by offering the police part of their property, whereas the poor get hard time. The wealthier the accused, the greater the chance of this happening. This is a curious result indeed for a policy rationalized in public as the best way to make sure the king-pins of crime get their just desserts.[33]

Police corruption is the sixth sin. Deputies have been caught planting drugs and falsifying police reports to establish probable cause for seizure. In airports, Customs and police use drug courier profiles to target people and shake them down for their money, with ethnic minorities getting the overwhelming share of attention. This is supplemented by the use of drug-sniffing dogs, which pick up traces of cocaine on currency, thereby establishing probable cause—even though various tests have shown that the vast majority of U.S. currency carries enough drug residue (a miniscule amount) for dogs to detect. Indeed, some dogs have become so well trained that they now react to the smell of the money rather than the drug residue, producing the intriguing possibility that simply having cash in a wallet constitutes probable cause for it to be seized.[34]

The seventh and deadliest of all sins is a form of corruption that goes beyond the individual to the system. No better example exists than that of Operation Casablanca. In this sting operation, U.S. Customs turned a drug dealer, who was rewarded with a clean slate and a cut of whatever was seized, and put him to work to trap Latin American bankers. Without informing the Mexican police or government that an undercover operation was under way in their territory, U.S. Customs sent the dealer to approach bankers and request their assistance in laundering drug money. Some branch managers took the bait. The results were a series of arrests and convictions, massive forfeitures of money that had no relationship to actual drug trafficking, a nasty diplomatic incident, the collapse of the stock prices of the targeted banks, and the filling of the coffers of the drug dealer-turned-undercover operative with more than $7 million in booty.

While the Mexican drama was being played out, the same team turned to bankers from Venezuela, with considerably less success. When the undercover operative mentioned drug money to representatives of Venezuelan banks, he was shown the door. So the team decided on an alternate strategy: the dealer told a Miami-based bank officer that he wanted her to manage on his behalf millions in "hot money." Going further, the dealer presented himself as a Venezuelan businessman seeking to avoid the complication of dealing with the U.S. tax authorities. When the banker agreed, she was arrested and charged with drug money laundering. Although "hot money" is a standard banking term that refers simply to the propensity of funds to skip from place to place in response to everything from interest rate hikes to political instability, the banker was found guilty by a jury that apparently assumed it meant something similar to "hot goods." Fortunately the case was tossed out by an appeals judge who denounced government entrapment, expressed disgust at the use of an undercover operative with a big financial incentive to coax legitimate citizens into self-incrimination, and declared that no sane jury could have convicted the banker. Then the government threatened to appeal. Although the ultimate result was a plea bargain on one structuring charge, with no jail time, the case raised the critical question—How many languish in prison because they lack the financial means to fight through to the upper reaches of the court system, where something approximating justice might sometimes exist?

For several years Republican congressman Henry Hyde pressed for amendments that would have reduced some of the grosser abuses. Befitting his politics, Hyde's real concern was not the defense of the human rights of the class on whom most police abuse is heaped but of the property rights of middle-class suburban Americans. Initially the reform effort failed in the face of a law-enforcement counterattack. And for a time, Representative Hyde shifted his energies to more pressing matters, leading the abortive move to impeach Bill Clinton—not because Clinton had gutted the social welfare system, capitulated to the medical establishment on health care, or committed mass murder in Iraq but because of his idiosyncratic taste in custom-flavored cigars. Finally, in the spring of 2000, some modest reforms were introduced. They slightly strengthened innocent-owner protection, provided indigent owners with counsel, and obliged the government to pay compensation if the claimant prevailed. But they came at a high price. The police also won an expanded list of crimes for which civil forfeiture could apply, the unambiguous right to demand total instead of net proceeds of alleged crimes, and the ability to seize an entire bank account even if the funds were innocent, provided some supposedly criminal funds (no matter how small a sum) once ran through that account. Worse, there was a strong possibility that the reformers had shot their bolt, that the specter of forfeiture would haunt America and, increasingly, the world for ages to come.

Thus, a law enforcement strategy supposedly required to prevent huge sums of criminal liquidity from corrupting legal markets, undermining financial institutions, compromising the judicial system, threatening general prosperity, and subverting national security has itself become the threat—to innocent property owners, financial efficiency, civil rights, due process, fiscal balance, and the very integrity of law enforcement.[35] Even worse, it is being zealously exported around the world, even to countries in which neither the legal culture nor socioeconomic realities support it.

The Alternatives

On one level, chasing the so-called proceeds of crime is a luxury pursued with equanimity only in rich countries with high levels of savings—particularly the United States, whose accessible pool of savings includes those of much of the rest of the world. Many poorer countries, desperate to accumulate capital, have in the past chosen a different path. In those countries, actions that generate illegal funds might be prosecuted under criminal law, while the money itself is treated as a financial policy issue.[36] Whereas in the West the underground economy, including both its informal and criminal components, is usually small in relation to the legal economy, in many developing countries the underground economy can be substantial—although the informal component is always much larger than the criminal.[37] Here, far from blocking illegally earned money from behaving as if it were of legitimate origin and attempting to enter the legal economy, the main objective is precisely to encourage it to do so.

The problem is that illegally derived income, left to its own devices, behaves differently.[38] First, in an atmosphere of insecurity produced by the threat of detection and loss, it is much more prone than legal income to being quickly consumed rather than saved or invested. In the West that is a sociological oddity, manifesting itself in a here-today, gone-tomorrow lifestyle. In poor countries, already plagued by a shortage of savings, it may be an impediment to economic development. Furthermore, illegal income tends to be consumed in untraceable services, or blown on entertainment that promotes prestige among peers, or used for high-profile (readily liquidated items such as jewelry. Alternatively, if spent on basic goods, these tend to be acquired in clandestine form, stimulating the market for stolen or smuggled items.

To the extent that illegal incomes are saved, once again there are behavioral differences. A saver's immediate impulse may be to keep the money in stashes of high-denomination notes, preferably hard currencies such as U.S. dollars or deutsch marks or Swiss francs, provoking something of an internal capital flight away from the domestic currency. It may also be hidden away in gold (often smuggled) or invested in prestige items such as valuable works of art, which are liquid but whose value at time of purchase is difficult for regulators to establish. It will also have a higher propensity than legal money to hide abroad, promoting external capital flight.[39] In all these cases the savings are kept out of the formal financial system and therefore are unavailable to the legal economy.

If illegal income is put to work purchasing assets, the preferences are likely antidevelopmental. If it goes into property, it is far more likely to be spent on urban luxury real estate or on rural land employed for prestige purposes such as cattle ranching or horse breeding rather than food production. If the money is invested in actual operational businesses, the preferences are luxury services (which provide opportunities to skim and launder), professional sports (which are a source of prestige), or the entertainment sector—present-day Bombay is as beholden as was latter-day Hollywood to mob money for its huge film industry.

In general, when illegal money occurs in noteworthy concentrations, it seems to be focused on sectors from which it can be quickly liquidated in time of crisis or need, or on sectors that promise extra political and social influence. Not very high on the list are basic primary or secondary industries that are the sine qua non of economic development. Nor, unless there is extra encouragement or protection, is illegal money likely to be tempted to enter the formal capital market, where it can be put at the disposal of legitimate firms or the government.

If the sums of illicit money are small relative to the economy as a whole, as is the case in rich industrialized countries, the impact occurs purely at the enterprise level. But if the sums are relatively large, particularly in countries with low per capita income, perceived illegitimacy of government, or weak financial institutions, serious distortions can result. Faced with these difficulties, governments of countries so afflicted have in the past often chosen to attempt to make illegal income behave more like legal rather than to try to find, freeze, and forfeit.

The policies have been many and varied. Sometimes they take the form of passive accommodation. In many countries with banking systems that are weakly developed or widely distrusted, parallel loan markets—that is, everything from de facto pawn shops to sophisticated multibranch money-brokerage houses—are tolerated. In some countries, these parallel markets have played a role in agricultural and industrial lending that rivals that of the legitimate financial system. From the Andes to Southeast Asia, from sub-Saharan Africa to the Indian subcontinent, the examples are legion.

Some countries go further, seeking to actively draw the horded illegal cash into the formal economy via either banks or government securities. This, in fact, is precisely the role of bank secrecy laws in many jurisdictions. Although such laws have become notorious for their role in attracting criminal money, most infamously drug money, into a Caribbean or Pacific island haven for a quick wash job, some countries introduced bank secrecy laws to encourage the deposit of locally generated money, whether from the hoards of career criminals or the stashes of tax evaders, by offering protection from detection and seizure.

There are governments that have offered underground entrepreneurs the option of buying bearer securities. The objective, quite explicitly, is to attract illicit money to help government finances. For that service the entrepreneurs collect interest, courtesy of legitimate-sector taxpayers. Frequently in the past, Sri Lanka, India, and Pakistan have offered bearer bonds denominated variously in local currency, foreign exchange, and even gold, along with pledges that no questions would be asked about the origin of the funds and no impediments raised to the investors' ability to recover the principle plus interest.[40] Nor is the practice dead. A bearer bond issue in 1998 by Pakistan led to sharp clashes with the United States, which accused Pakistan of deliberately setting out to attract and launder the cash hordes of the world's drug kingpins—conveniently forgetting that the United States itself issued bearer treasury bills until a mere twenty years before.[41]

Such bearer securities do not really launder, much less amnesty, illicit money, even though they deliberately entice underground hordes by offering high interest. The bonds are bearer instruments. A laundry job logically requires for its completion that the owner of the funds be able to use them publicly and in his or her own name; amnesty, too, can occur only if the holder of funds is identified. Some countries have offered explicit amnesties. Some take the form of bank amnesties: underground money is deposited in designated bank accounts for a certain period, a laundry fee is paid to the state, and the registered depositor is then able to use the remaining funds without fear of seizure. Others take the form of state-issued whitener bonds. Unlike bearer bonds, whiteners require that the purchaser identify him or herself and typically bear a lower rate of interest. But once the bonds mature, the money is vested, free and clear, in the hands of the investor. All such amnesties are directed at the money, not at the individual, who can still be prosecuted for the acts that generated the funds.

A third variant of the amnesty offers some relief to the owner as well as a clean slate for the money. This variant is sometimes used to collect unpaid taxes. Although the institutional forms of tax amnesties differ widely, the basic principle is the same. The delinquents (including criminals who have compounded their initial felony by tax evasion) step forward to reveal how much income has been hidden from the tax collector, pay a certain amount in penalty that always works out to less than the normal tax load, and then are left with the rest of the money and with the previous (fiscal) offense forgiven. Much the same happens with capital flight amnesties, which are used to attract back money that has left in defiance of exchange controls. The money is placed in state banks, invested in public debt instruments, or merely declared on its return. The government clips a certain percentage and pronounces the rest clean and clear.

There are countless subvariants on these techniques, but they all have one thing in common—they fly squarely in the face of the current trend toward finding, freezing, and forfeiting criminal money. The fact that so many poor countries, desperately short of development capital, have for so long attempted to coax illegal earnings to behave more like legal in order to assure that the funds are available for the creation of agricultural, industrial, or public infrastructure explains, far better than the notion of some conspiracy by corrupt heads of state, why these countries have been so slow to follow the United States in anti-money-laundering and asset-forfeiture schemes.

To be sure there have been instances in which developing countries have decided to attack illegal hoards head-on, in order to neutralize rather than accommodate or legitimate them. The most common device is the mandatory currency conversion. There have been numerous examples— in India, Burma-Myanmar (at least three times), Nigeria (twice), Zaire, Iraq, the USSR, and more recently Russia, to name but a few. The logic is that by announcing a sudden de-monetization or mandatory exchange of some or all of the national currency, the government can catch, and negate, the hoards of cash held by black marketers and tax evaders. Sometimes the largest denomination bills are withdrawn from circulation, with or without compensation. Sometimes the entire currency is withdrawn, with the population permitted to exchange without question a certain limited quantity of old notes for new; the rest can either be annulled outright or exchanged if and only if the holders can adequately account for the notes' origins. The result is that space is cleared for the central monetary authority to issue more currency without risking inflation or depreciation; in effect, the purchasing power of the cash being destroyed is transferred to the central government.

Although superficially appealing, such demonetizations in practice have proven useless with respect to their nominal target and sometimes a disaster in terms of their impact on the population at large. Typically those black marketers who cannot simply bribe their way to an exemption or launder their cash through legitimate-looking businesses have already switched their savings to gold or foreign exchange or offshore bank accounts, leaving the petty traders and that sector of the population either unserved by or mistrustful of banks to take the fall. If the government is at all responsive to public pressure, as in the final days of the USSR, the political heat can force the authorities to raise the allowances and to signal to those scrutinizing excess holdings to go easy, therefore negating most of the impact.

Although extremely rare, there have been instances in which poorer, non-Western countries have used asset forfeiture as a tool to combat illicit enrichment. One of the most striking examples occurred in the Philippines after the overthrow of the Marcos dynasty. The new government created the Presidential Commission on Good Government (PCGG) and turned it loose to search out and sequester assets belonging to Ferdinand Marcos and his cronies. In short order the PCGG seized hundreds of millions of dollars worth of real estate, corporate shares, boats, cars, and bank accounts. This move was supposedly a prelude to court adjudication in which the assets either would be returned to their rightful owners or permanently ceded to the government to help it finance a program of land reform. Indeed, so enthusiastic was the commission in the early stages that it inspired entrepreneurial imitators: people would secure false credentials identifying themselves as officers of the commission and then go about the country extorting money from businessmen under the threat of being denounced as Marcos cronies.[42]

Not that the record of the PCGG itself was much better. Assets were seized out of pure vendetta; officers made off with jewels, aircraft, livestock, and other portables; corporations and land were grabbed from cronies of the old power elite and retransferred to cronies of the new power elite; the broadcasting system, seized almost en masse, was deployed to further the political objectives of the new rulers; all leads pointing to the extensive involvement of Japanese businesses in Marcos-era plundering were covered up to avoid offending the Philippines' largest foreign investor; assets were grabbed and then deals made for their release without any charges being filed against the owners; and, in the final analysis, the process ground to halt when the government, dominated by the sugar aristocracy, put the breaks on the land reform that the asset seizure was supposed to finance.[43] Just how much worse the record would have been when post-Mobutu Zaire created an Office of Ill-Gotten Gains to do likewise no one will know—the attempt to march across Africa's most resource-rich country, grabbing wealth from those identified, even if arbitrarily, as supporters of the old order, was aborted by the outbreak of a multisided war.

Perhaps all this collateral damage would be tolerable if there were no real alternative. Fortunately an alternative does exist, one with a long and proven history all over the world, which can easily solve the fundamental objective of taking away from criminals the proceeds of their crimes without the enormous threat to civil rights entailed by asset-forfeiture provisions. It will, however, be fought bitterly by a law enforcement apparatus desperate to keep control of the drug cash to which it has become addicted.[44]

Rendering unto Caesar?

Tax codes provide for fines and forfeitures, interest and penalties, and, interestingly enough, the means to seize wealth by using a reversed burden of proof. This reverse onus has been, legitimately, part of tax enforcement for centuries. In the days when most state revenues came from Customs duties, it was normal that merchants be required to prove that their cargoes had met all payments rightly due. Today, in the same spirit, a citizen with otherwise unaccounted for income must demonstrate that all outstanding tax obligations have been met. The origin of the income is irrelevant—what counts is the requirement that all citizens meet their fair share of the overall burden.

Although possible criminal charges provides the final line of offense, most tax procedures are civil, and most tax codes permit the revenue authorities to freeze and seize assets. With tax charges, there is no need to trace particular assets and impute them to any specific crime. All that is necessary is to demonstrate that someone's expenditures exceeded the reported income. When arrears, interest, and penalties are combined, the undeclared portion of the income will largely, and quite possibly, completely, vanish. Such tax procedures can move forward with no need for individuals to incriminate themselves with respect to the origins of the money. Unlike in civil forfeitures used as a means of crime control, tax actions do not attach to the person the stigma of a specific crime while denying that person the right to a trial to ascertain the truth or falsehood of the charges. Yet if the underlying theory of proceeds-of-crime is correct, the motive and the capital for further offenses will vanish.

The countercase is sometimes made that using the tax code cannot strip criminals of all their ill-gotten gains, because it can only be applied against their illegal income at the marginal tax rate. Furthermore, if tax law is used, criminals would be permitted to deduct expenses to determine the net amount due, leaving most of the proceeds still in their hands. But there are several obvious rebuttals.

In fact, once fines for failure to file or for filing false returns are added to interest charges on overdue balances, it is unlikely that any of the net income accruing to a profit-driven crime will be left for the criminal to enjoy or reinvest. Such a procedure might bite deeply into legally earned net income as well. If it does not, that suggests merely that the general tax rate structure is insufficiently progressive. Furthermore, even if all that disappears is actual profits or net income, that amount is sufficient—if the theory underlying the proceeds approach is correct—to remove the economic motive from crime. To the extent that money is the overwhelming factor in determining their behavior, criminals do not enjoy, nor are they motivated by, "proceeds"; what they do enjoy and what motivates them are profits. No one looks forward to laying out money to cover the costs of running a business.

Unlike the situation with proceeds-of-crime forfeitures, it is perfectly reasonable for fiscal purposes to start the process on the premise that net profits and proceeds are the same thing, unless and until the individual proves that costs were incurred. Although no one will countenance a burglar deducting the purchase price of his ladder, there is nothing morally objectionable about someone engaged in a market-based offense being permitted to write off costs—because the method used to commit the crime, a market transaction, is inherently legal, whereas force and fraud are not. Proper use of the penalty provisions of the tax code would then remove most, if not all, of the net income. And there are actual practical advantages. Allowing someone convicted of a market-based crime to deduct costs actually enhances rather than limits crime control. To claim deductions, the criminal must provide details about intermediate suppliers and employees, thus permitting police to roll up entire networks, rather than just isolated individuals, as well as giving police intelligence officers and independent researchers the hard data with which to map out networks and actually understand (for the first time) how criminal markets really operate.

Another objection is that using tax law legitimates criminal business by treating it like all other economic activity. This, too, is false. If the objective is to attack the motives and the capital of crime "cartels," then it makes no difference whether the money is carted off by using selective asset forfeiture or the tax code. Nor, for that matter, should it matter if the ultimate beneficiary is the state treasury, legitimate creditors of the criminal, family members in need, or even defense attorneys—the only person or institution that should be excluded from a division of the loot is the criminal and the law enforcement apparatus. And if the state chooses to proceed using the criminal rather than civil code, it is difficult to imagine why a person would feel better about a five-year sentence for tax evasion rather than five years for dealing cocaine—the fact of a jail sentence, a criminal record, and the loss of financial assets constitutes the punishment and, at least to some degree, the deterrent, no matter what the particular charge. Furthermore, attacking criminal profits through the tax code sends an important message: everyone must pay taxes, and if they are not paid voluntarily, the state has tough means at its disposal to collect what is due.

Not least of the advantages of prosecution via the tax law route is that there is no need for an artificial offense called money laundering. There is no need to criminalize a set of actions that are inherently legal and harmless. Even if those who handle the money for certain serious crimes are just as guilty as those who commit the underlying offense, that is an argument for redefining or clarifying the law forbidding the underlying offense to include the money managers firmly in its ambit. Because a market-based crime such as drugs, for example, requires (in addition to producers, exporters, importers, distributors, and retailers) personnel to handle the resulting money flows, laws can easily be rewritten to ensure that these personnel are added to the list of parties guilty of the predicate offense.

Eliminating the need to criminalize money laundering would also go far to return a sense of balance to public debate. So contrived is the crime of money laundering that for law enforcement agencies to win public acquiescence, the popular imagination had to be stoked by conjuring up images of great crime cartels dripping filthy lucre as they rapaciously eyed the commanding heights of the legitimate economy. It took a big lie to create a phony offense and set law enforcement off on a chase for money rather than criminal offenders.

Taken to the Cleaners?

Everyone agrees with the fundamental principle that criminals should not profit from their crimes. However, beyond that basic conviction, there is no real agreement about how large the problem of criminal money flows really is; about why society is actually worse off when criminals, rather than legitimate business people, consume, save, or invest; or about what level of collateral damage society should be called on to accept in the name of a war on criminal profits.

To be sure, it is possible to find the occasional criminal who is, in all senses, filthy rich. The big question—rarely posed and never answered— is how representative is that occasional underworld magnate in relation to the criminal economy as a whole? Is it really sensible to start rewriting laws on the basis of one or a few spectacular incidents, particularly when those laws potentially involve so much collateral damage? Is it not true that laws should be written to deal with a general antisocial trend rather than the occasional aberration? Such questions are particularly serious given that most of the spectacular proceeds-of-crime busts have been the result of stings, therefore making it impossible to determine a priori how much money would actually have been involved had law enforcement agencies not been egging on the process.

Despite the fact that so many key questions have remained not merely unanswered but usually unasked, police forces around the world are being turned loose to find, freeze, and forfeit the presumed proceeds of crime on the basis of little more than a vague assurance that this is the most resource-effective way to deal with economically motivated crime.

The bald fact remains that after fifteen years of progressive escalation of its use, no one has been able to determine with any remote degree of confidence whether the proceeds-of-crime approach to crime control has had any discernible impact on the operation of illegal markets or on the amount, distribution, and behavior of illegal income and wealth. The entire exercise rests on a series of inaccurate, or at least unprovable, assumptions and involves the commission of a series of sins against common decency and common sense. In the hands of law enforcement, the modern policy of attacking the proceeds of crime by finding, freezing, and forfeiting laundered money has been, to all intents and purposes, one great washout.

Satanic Purses
Osama bin Laden
and the Financing of Terror

Much contemporary crime-control policy is based on three interrelated assumptions: that the worst acts of crime are the work of large, hierarchically structured organizations; that those organizations are under the control of one or a few powerful individuals; and that the sums generated are enormous. From these assumptions, a major conclusion follows—that the best way to deal with the presumed epidemic of crime is to find, freeze, and forfeit the money.[1]

After the September 11, 2001, tragedy in the United States, when terrorists hijacked civilian airliners and used them as weapons of mass destruction in New York and Washington, those assumptions have become a part of national security rhetoric and action as well. The target of blame became a definable international organization headed by a powerful-but-bent individual flush with cash. And, in an effort to punish the perpetrators and prevent a repetition, the most important response, apart from unleashing the U.S. military against alleged command and training centers, took the form of tighter monetary regulations and deeper financial probes to help find and freeze terrorist assets before they could be used.

More specifically, it was presumed that:

1. The architect of the terrible crimes of September 11 was Osama bin Laden, a Muslim fundamentalist, who was responsible for previous outrages and who had issued a *fatwa* calling for the murder of Americans.
2. Drawing on his experiences fighting the Soviet Union in Afghanistan, bin Laden put together El-Qaʿida, a sophisticated transnational terrorist organization staffed with zealots he trained and financed and who stood at his command.[2]

3. Bin Laden and El-Qaʻida were able to commit atrocities because he possessed abundant financial resources.[3] These included $300 million from his share of a family construction empire and the returns from his own business enterprises, including a stake in the huge Afghan drug trade. He used networks of phony Islamic religious and charitable foundations, along with the *havala* underground banking system, to secretly move operating funds around the world. The estimate was that El-Qaʻida , through such means, disbursed $30–40 million per annum.[4]

4. Hence, to fight back, the United States is leading the world in deploying against the terrorists a new weapon, though one already well tested in more conventional forms of crime control, namely a concerted effort to search out and seize the money that constitutes the lifeblood of terrorist groups, to put the front organizations and pseudo-charities out of business, and to bring under regulatory scrutiny the underground banking system.[5]

At first glance, the force of this logic seems compelling. But on closer examination, the four presumptions seem laced with myth, confusion, and mass-media hyperbole, with perhaps a dash of deliberate disinformation.

First, as to Osama bin Laden's direct and criminal responsibility, it may be true. The case presented to the public, however, was based not merely on guilt by association, but on hearsay, rumor, and innuendo. Someone knew someone who was once, in those deliciously versatile phrases adopted from of "organized crime" jargon, "linked to" or "connected to" or "an associate of" bin Laden or one of his enterprises.[6] This would be a troublesome basis for criminal prosecution. It is far worse as a justification for unleashing the most awesome killing machine in history on one of the most wretched places on earth where a handful of people who seized power against the will of the population they rule harbored a fugitive from the justice system of another country whose spokespersons admitted that their "evidence" would not stand up in court.[7]

This is not to say that bin Laden is a nice guy. He is a dangerous megalomaniac who espouses a retrograde and violent ideology—although where anyone got the idea he had the right to issue a *fatwa* (something only senior religious scholars can do) remains a mystery. And although he was essentially trapped in Afghanistan for years before the tragedy of September 11, unable even to make phone calls (since U.S. intelligence routinely taps the Afghan phone system), there is a good chance he bears a moral, if not a legal, responsibility for at least some terrorist actions.

But certainly not all of the actions imputed to him. For example, claims repeated in a New York court indictment that he was the architect of the attack on U.S. forces in Somalia several years back were dismissed even by the former head of the State Department's office of counter-terrorism as "preposterous."[8] The result of such sweeping claims is to build up to mythic proportions the political and military status of someone who was, in fact, a civil engineer and part-time fundraiser for Islamic causes, some charitable, some developmental, some military in nature, who himself had no military background and whose battlefield exploits in Afghanistan during the anti-Soviet war appear to have been largely invented to coax money out of rich Saudis.

Other countries have found it expedient to follow the U.S. lead. The Kremlin insisted that bin Laden was responsible for the Moscow subway bombing, which was used to rationalize the second Chechnya war, even though the original leader of the breakaway republic was a senior and highly decorated Red Army veteran of the Afghan war. The Algerian government blamed him for the Islamist insurrection, which has been tearing the country apart for nearly a decade, an insurrection which began when that government blocked an election that would have given the Islamists power through a democratic vote. The Philippines insisted that bin Laden was behind the ongoing Moro rebellion which began decades before he was born.[9] Egypt fingered him for trying, with an assassination attempt on president-for-life Hosni Mubarak, to undermine that country's democratic institutions—only to be contradicted by Egypt's home-grown Gama'at el-Islamiya, which haughtily pointed out that it had planned for a full year the operation on its own.[10] And it would not be surprising if China eventually labels bin Laden responsible for the growing revolt among the Turkic Muslim minority in Xinjiang, a revolt originally stoked after World War II with money and arms from the CIA.[11]

Even if it turns out that bin Laden has a genuine legal responsibility for the September 11 crimes, instead of just a twisted propensity to indulge his ego after the fact, blowing him all out of proportion diverts attention from an array of political ills, the real reasons for which are much more complex and difficult to resolve.

The second presumption, that there is some coherent transnational terrorist organization called El-Qa'ida at bin Laden's beck and call, seems another serious oversimplification. Indeed, the origins of that view are themselves fascinating. Much the way Joseph Valachi's (selectively misread) testimony paved the way for a confirmation of the view of the American Mafia as a hierarchically structured body or the way Max Mermelstein supposedly dissected the innards of the "Medellín cartel," so a former El-Qaʿida "financial executive," Jamal el-Fadl, who broke with bin Laden after he was caught taking kickbacks and who later made a deal with American prosecutors, provided the information about a corporate body with bin Laden as CEO and a series of formal subdivisions dedicated to everything from raising money to sowing mayhem. This evidence seems to have been sufficiently persuasive for George W. Bush to claim that El-Qaʿida was to terrorism what the Mafia was to crime.

On one level the president may have been right. Just as law enforcement bodies insist on seeing hierarchically controlled institutions (the "Medellín cartel" and so forth) in place of informal networks and individuals engaged in arms-length commercial transactions, so the security services seem compelled to find great terrorist "cartels." In reality, El-Qaʿida seems less an organization than a loose association of independent cell-like entities that changes form and personnel ad hoc in response to threats and opportunities. Just as the Mafia is less a formal institution than a type of behavior, so too El-Qaʿida seems less an entity than a shared state of mind, less a political organization than a cult of personality that the United States seems committed to strengthening.[12]

The spiritual roots out of which El-Qaʿida grew date back to the Vietnam War when the CIA took over from a retreating French military intelligence, a special counterinsurgency apparatus based on the Hmong hill people of Laos and Vietnam.[13] Their social structure made them ideally suited to their role—the men were hired as anticommunist mercenaries, while the women, who did the farming, grew opium that first the French, then the Americans, assisted them to market. In turn, the income from opium helped to finance the anticommunist battles. That traffic continued even after opium gave way to heroin to serve a rich hard-currency market comprised of hundreds of thousands of American soldiers. And it followed the U.S. soldiers home.[14]

Similarly, after the Red Army rolled into Afghanistan, the CIA began to organize an insurgent army that at peak may have numbered 250,000. Much as in Southeast Asia, money was the key to the rise of the mujahideen. For in Afghanistan, regional chiefs and local warlords change sides regularly depending on who is paying the most. One of the main ways in which the mujahideen were paid was by their patrons' accommodating, at least by default, their smuggling rackets, including the flow of drugs. As in Southeast Asia, opium soon gave way to heroin and the local to the international market.

During the anti-Soviet struggle, the arms and drugs pipelines were inseparable. The CIA, backed by billions of dollars from the United States and Saudi Arabia, would secure arms, preferably of Soviet model, from

Egypt, China, and Israel, and from black market deals in East Bloc countries. From one end to another the pipeline leaked. Some weapons may have been skimmed at the outset by the CIA to equip other insurgencies where there was no authorization for U.S. intelligence involvement. Others seem to have been diverted by the brokers and arms dealers, with the theft covered by substituting inferior equipment or reporting the material lost at sea. On arrival at the port of Karachi, the Pakistani Inter-Services Intelligence (ISI) took charge. Some weapons were diverted to Pakistan army stockpiles or to other insurgencies, such as those in Kashmir and the Punjab. Some were sold on the black market for cash, using tribal leaders as intermediaries, because they could use their "underground" financial connections to guarantee payments from almost anywhere in the world. The rest would be moved north in sealed trucks and trains that Pakistani police and Customs were forbidden to inspect. The weapons were hauled to Peshawar, capital of Pakistan's North-West Frontier province and Afghan exile headquarters, or to the border city of Quetta in Baluchistan, to be turned over to the political chiefs of the Afghan resistance. At that point, more diversion occurred. The final stage, entrusted to "private" contractors who had business or family relationships with the Afghan exile leadership, required that weapons be hauled, often by mule train, into Afghanistan. The leaders of clans through whose territory the pipeline ran demanded tribute, payable in cash or in arms. Once in Afghanistan, arms were supplied to field commanders, some of whom exaggerated quantities used or lost in battle and sold off the difference.

In the meantime, there was return cargo. Afghanistan produces not only some of the world's finest hashish, but during its wars came to rival Burma as a source of opiates. It was often easier for one faction's drug caravans to get through government-controlled areas where a small bribe sufficed than through territory run by a rival mujahideen commander. Although there were some small refineries in Afghanistan, most heroin production took place across the border in the autonomous tribal region of Pakistan's North-West Frontier province in refineries jointly owned by Pakistani merchants and Afghan leaders.

From the North-West Frontier the drugs moved south, carried by the same ISI trucks that brought weapons north, still protected against Customs and police probes. Then some drugs were taken over by professional smugglers (some linked to Sikh guerrilla groups) who were already moving whiskey (banned under Islamic law) into Pakistan and arms back into India. Inside India, drugs would go to Bombay where underworld figures, rich on the gold traffic, arranged their export. Or they would head farther south where Tamil separatist guerrillas from Sri Lanka would move them out via their European courier system. Other shipments headed to Karachi where five families, each with a senior officer in its ranks, controlled exports. And some went westward by land. Baluchi tribesmen would carry drugs to Iran and transfer them to Kurdish groups to take across Turkey where the drugs entered a black-market complex of corrupt officials, political insurgents, career gangsters, and intelligence agents before taking the Balkan route into western Europe (where they later helped fuel the rise of the Kosovo Liberation Army). All of this traffic was well known to the United States which tolerated it because it kept the Afghan warlords on side, the drugs took a toll among Red Army soldiers, and very little Afghan heroin made it to the United States.[15]

The long-term costs, however, were enormous. They included the virtual destruction of Afghanistan—of a preconflict population of 23 million, 1.5 million died, hundreds of thousands were maimed, 5 million fled as refugees to neighboring countries, and the economic infrastructure, already weak, was largely destroyed. The only thing that flourished was opium. Costs included converting Pakistan's North-West Frontier province into the world's premier arms bazaar while unleashing on Pakistan a scourge of heavily armed religious and political dissident groups. And costs included producing thousands of highly motivated, well-trained insurgents ready to lend their talents to other causes once the anti-Soviet war ended.

To allow U.S. military personnel to keep a low profile during the anti-Soviet war, certain persons—drawn partly from the Pakistani military, partly from the Afghan refugee population, and partly from volunteers from Islamic countries—were picked for instruction as future trainers. To enhance deniability, the job of training the future trainers was often subcontracted to private American (and British) firms run by special-forces veterans. Then the trainers were sent to Pakistan to instruct the rank and file.

Recruitment was similarly privatized. Apart from campaigns across the Muslim world, within the United States recruitment centers were set up in the major American cities that hosted large Muslim or Arab populations. Along with manpower, the émigré communities were tapped as a source of money through the types of Islamic charities now being denounced as conduits for terrorist financing. To Muslims, giving to charity is more than just an act of generosity, it is a religious duty—one of the five pillars of Islam. At the same time, working through the front of charities and foundations, sometimes without their knowledge, is standard intelligence procedure. Thus, some Islamic charities were, if not created, then certainly encouraged and monitored by U.S. intelligence during the anti-Soviet campaign, if not beyond. Their function was twisted away from bona fide charitable work toward helping to support a military campaign that would eventually put a gang of cutthroats, bandits, and drug dealers into power in Kabul. Meanwhile, tens of thousands of volunteers from dozens of Islamic countries were being taught by the United States and Britain directly, or indirectly via Pakistan's ISI, techniques of strategic sabotage—how to improvise explosives from ordinary materials and take out key infrastructure. When Egyptian militants were caught in the United States mixing ammonia fertilizer with fuel oil, they were following a formula taught to Afghan resistance fighters by U.S. intelligence or its proxies.[16]

Osama bin Laden entered all of this as a small cog in an already well-oiled machine. Originally, his role was simply to tap rich Saudis for funds to aid the Afghan resistance. Later, he turned up with some construction equipment to build housing and training facilities along with a tunnel complex the CIA financed and the ISI used to store arms and train guerrillas. In fact, the term El-Qa'ida was originally applied to a rest house and barracks he built in Peshawar for recruits. Afterward, once bin Laden had moved to exile in the Sudan, El-Qa'ida was transformed into the name of a global terrorist conspiracy that supposedly operates on the basis of his legendary wealth.

The third presumption deals with bin Laden's fortune, reputedly derived from three main sources: the family construction firm; an independent business empire interfacing with El-Qa'ida; and the Afghan heroin trade, which has allegedly burgeoned under Taliban rule.

Bin Laden, so the legend goes, was the son of a Saudi construction tycoon and inherited the family empire on his father's death in the late 1960s. Young Osama must have been quite a chap—to take over the region's largest private construction conglomerate at age thirteen, even though he had nineteen brothers, nine of them older. In another version, he merely inherited $80 million from his father. Presuming the father made equal provision for his other sons (and ignoring anything he might have left to thirty-eight daughters), that would have meant the distribution at his death of $1.6 billion, several times the total assets of the company at that time, while still leaving the company with the financial wherewithal to continue to grow to its present $5 billion size. Obviously, the tales of his construction megamillions are grossly exaggerated. And any remaining connection between bin Laden and the mainstream of his family was severed in the early 1990s when he was denounced by Saudi Arabia and stripped of his citizenship. Despite recurrent rumors, it is extremely unlikely that the family would risk either their wealth, which depends on the good will of the Saudi regime, or their status of living in luxury in the United States, by maintaining clandestine financial links with their notorious sibling.[17]

Another reputed source of his funds is the enterprises he set up in the Sudan during the early 1990s. These also supposedly served as fronts for other operations. It is certainly true that bin Laden, with the agreement of the ruling National Islamic Front, invested in the Sudan both his resources plus what he could coax from other Saudis. The result was a series of undertakings in import-export, construction, land reclamation, refugee relief, and perhaps Islamic banking. Far from fronts, these projects were important to an impoverished country wracked by decades of civil war and crippled further by U.S. sanctions. Far from lucrative, almost all of the projects seem to have lost money. Their value depreciated further as the Sudanese currency plummeted. Any external assets associated with the bin Laden projects were frozen at American request after bombings of the U.S. embassies in Kenya and Tanzania, for which he was immediately blamed. And when the National Islamic Front was ousted by the military, most of the remaining bin Laden assets in the Sudan seem to have been stolen by the new strongmen. Thus, bin Laden may have been de facto bankrupt by the time he fled the Sudan and returned to Afghanistan, just in time for his old mujahideen colleagues to be ousted from power by the Taliban.[18]

Far from the Taliban being a creature of bin Laden (the often-repeated nonsense that El-Qaʿida "controls" the Afghan defense and foreign ministries), it was more of a joint venture of the Pakistani military and certain big U.S. petroleum companies. Pakistan saw the Taliban, whose cadres were indoctrinated while in exile in Pakistan, as a tool in its drive to control the trade of Central Asia after the disintegration of the Soviet Union, while the oil and gas companies, with the quiet endorsement of the U.S. government, were counting on the Taliban to stabilize the country prior to building through it a pipeline to draw Central Asian gas to Pakistan. That way the hydrocarbon resources of the area, the last untapped reserves on earth, could be freed from the control of either Russia or Iran. As to the story that the Taliban government survives in part on bin Laden's largesse, when he arrived in Afghanistan, he did pledge to undertake some public works, but the projects were abandoned after his funds were frozen.[19]

The final component of the bin Laden terrorist treasury supposedly derives from the fact that the Taliban regime cut in bin Laden for 10 percent in exchange for his aid in marketing Afghanistan's $8 billion per annum opium crop.[20] This is a story that must be taken, not with a grain of salt, not even with the whole shaker, but with an option on the output of the world's salt mines.

In 1917, when America entered World War I, the official line was that imperial Germany was responsible for narcotics entering the United States. In World War II, the culprit became Japan. In the 1950s, the head of the Bureau of Narcotics and Dangerous Drugs formally blamed the People's Republic of China. And in the early Reagan era the Soviet Union, Cuba, and even the PLO were at various points held responsible. Tales about Osama bin Laden's role in the world heroin trade must be understood in that context.[21]

Furthermore, the story fails to fit with the facts on the ground. In the 1980s and early 1990s, producing and trafficking in drugs were under the control of warlords and clan chiefs tied to the mujahideen fighters. That remained true after they overthrew the Communist government. When the feuding mujahideen, in turn, were ousted by the Taliban, one of the main complaints against the mujahideen was precisely the proliferation of drugs. The Taliban initially tried to move against opium, only to bump up against political and financial realities. Opium is not an official monopoly. Rather, it is an integral part of the structure of client-patron relations between peasants and local chiefs whom the Taliban could not afford to alienate. Where possible the Taliban did tax the production and trade of opiates, but the most important sources of its revenues were taxes on and contributions from the "trucking mafia" which runs general contraband from Karachi through Afghanistan to Central Asia, and secret subsidies from Pakistan. And because Afghan farmers collect about 1 percent of the international value of their opiates, even if the Taliban had briefly succeeded in imposing their 20-percent tax across the country, the total take could never have exceeded $20 million—which, if the rest of the far-fetched story were true, would give bin Laden a measly $2 million. Furthermore, shortly after the Taliban took power, a massive drought wiped out much of the crop. Finally, in 1999 the Taliban announced a total ban. The UN drug control office verified a dramatic drop in production from areas nominally under Taliban control. Indeed, the great bulk of the current crop originates in areas long controlled by the so-called Northern Alliance, with no obvious attempt by the United States to interfere.[22] Was the United States again turning a blind eye to the drug flow to buy the loyalty of the Northern Alliance bosses and provide them with the financial wherewithal to buy other clan chiefs and warlords?

With respect to financing, if bin Laden really had the megabillions imputed to him, why did he leave his supposed disciples so poorly funded? Those identified as the hijackers lived by low-wage jobs, petty scams, or begging money from their families.[23] Even if it is argued that security dictated minimal financial contacts with those about to pull off terrorist acts, that is certainly not true of those outside the target countries, in fact safe inside countries of refuge. Yet most information about bin Laden's operations seems to come from people who broke with him in squabbles about money, and those people present a view of a penny-pincher who allows those with detailed knowledge about his operations to just walk away.[24]

The truth is that the amount of money required even for crimes of the magnitude of September 11 is not especially large. This, in fact, is consistent with the operational pattern of urban insurgent groups all over the world. They form small, autonomous, and self-financing cells; if there is outside funding, it is minor; and any financial movements required tend to take the form of transfers of cash or other anonymous instruments. According to the official theory, Egypt's Gama'at el-Islamiya is the most important single component of the El-Qa'ida network. Yet to date it has had to finance itself by robbery and by counterfeiting Egyptian currency, remarkably risky endeavors for a group supposedly flooded with Osama bin Laden's cash.

Finally, it is necessary to look critically at the fourth presumption that concludes that the best way to prevent future terrorist outrages is to mimic recent fads in more orthodox law enforcement policy by following the money trail.

It is certainly important in many investigations to include a financial component. It can provide evidence to lead to guilty parties, and it can help locate the means to make restitution to victims. In short, it is useful *after* the event. But what the public is being told is that the money trail can function preemptively, to lead to those plotting the deeds or, at least, to lead to the money without which they would be unable to pull them off. This raises serious questions of logic and fact.

For the last several years, the Financial Crimes Enforcement Center run by the U.S. Treasury (FINCEN) and the CIA have been chasing the alleged bin Laden billions, and declaring freezes on institutions and individuals on the basis, it sometimes seems, of names drawn from a fez. Yet the earlier effort did nothing to stop the carnage on September 11, 2001. There is no reason to expect much better results in the future, no matter what new reporting regulations get passed.

In ordinary law enforcement, the rationale for a follow-the-money policy is that it takes away the motive (profit) and the means (working capital) to commit more crimes. Even if that argument is correct—in fact it is fatally flawed—it would not apply to terrorist financing. Here the motive is hardly profit—money is a resource, not an end in itself. And the notion that large sums are necessary to pull off big operations is simply false. Even in evidentiary terms, it is very difficult to follow a trail that involves fairly small sums and that may already be several years old. Much more sensible would be to put all available energy into directly tracking down those responsible. After all, the main asset possessed by the people who committed the September 11 crime was not money, which can always be readily obtained: it was commitment, and that cannot be frozen in a bank account.

Indeed, there is an opportunistic element to the emphasis on the financial trail. In the months prior to the September 11 attacks, the follow-the-money mania long whipped up by law enforcement had begun to meet increased resistance. It was pointed out that many new measures being demanded were redundant, and that the real problem was more the failure to use existing laws effectively than the absence of sufficient regulatory powers. In 2000, a bill introduced by the Clinton administration that would have given the U.S. Treasury broad power to bar banks and countries access to the U.S. financial system if they did not accede to U.S. demands for information was blocked by industry protests. And the enthusiasm of the Bush administration, both in terms of new domestic regulations and in terms of attempting to force the rest of the financial world to follow the American model, was on the wane.[25]

After September 11, there was a dramatic reversal. In short order came plans for granting to the Treasury the previously denied power to arbitrarily ban uncooperative foreign banks; instating previously rejected know-your-client rules that turn bankers into police informants; restricting transactions with offshore shell banks; instating the right to confiscate any cash sum greater than $10,000 crossing the U.S. border even if it were properly declared; and more.[26] Perhaps some of these measures are justified in their own right. But many (including a measure to deal with funds originating in foreign corruption) really have nothing to do with the control of terrorist financing. Rather, they represent a long-standing wish list of certain politicians and law enforcement officials drawn up for different reasons altogether.

Nonetheless, after September 11, there were two new points of attack: on the role of Islamic charities in raising and fronting for terrorist funds, and on the *havala* underground banking system in moving those funds to their place of deployment.

The notion of targeting Islamic charities and the groups they allegedly fund was originally a brainchild of the Israel lobby.[27] In a flip-flop that replicated in miniature the former U.S. strategy in Afghanistan, Israel, which had previously interfered with the flow of funds to the secular, nationalist PLO to assure that Islamic groups in Occupied Palestine were strengthened at its expense, suddenly discovered that groups like Hamas were more committed than the mainstream PLO to fighting occupation, and Lebanese groups like Hezbollah were much more serious about eject-ing the Israeli army from the South of Lebanon than the Lebanese gov-ernment. Hence, it pressured the U.S. government to close the Islamic charities and criminalize the act of sending money to Hamas and Hez-bollah. The United States has now acceded even though not a single Pales-tinian (and only one Lebanese with no known links to Hezbollah) took part in the hijackings, and even though the flow of funds from the United States through Jewish charities to fund illegal settlements in the West Bank surely dwarfs anything Islamic charities could possibly have sent to Hamas.[28] Indeed, an early chink in the antiterrorist "coalition" came when the Lebanese government refused to implement the freeze on Hezbollah, now an integral part of the legitimate Lebanese political scene and a group whose members are regarded as national heroes for their re-sistance activity.[29]

Perhaps most severely affected will be the networks of Islamic charities across the West. Not only is giving to charity a religious duty, but the char-ities are also essential to the well-being of the home countries of the donor population—sometimes remittances from the émigré population exceed foreign trade receipts. For across the Muslim world, massive unemploy-ment and drastic cutbacks in social services (often dictated by western financial institutions) coincide with fiscally strapped, corrupt, or incom-petent governments. This throws more of the burden of providing essen-tial social services onto the Islamic charities. Despite the fact that social and economic desperation is the most powerful incubator of violent po-litical dissent, in the wake of September 11, these charities were harassed and in some cases closed, and, even where left nominally intact, they were forced to operate under a cloud; those individuals who would normally give to them would be fearful of drawing official scrutiny and of being judged guilty by association. To be sure, an Islamic charity could, on oc-casion, be used in a scam or have its funds diverted to illicit purposes, in-cluding financing terrorism. But so too could the Salvation Army.[30]

The drive against "terrorist financing" also included efforts to regulate informal transfer systems, the type typical of much of Asia, particularly the *havala* system of the Indian subcontinent. The efforts result from the uncritical adoption by the national security apparatus of the stereotype long promoted by western police forces, namely that these informal trans-fer systems are a dangerous tool in the hands of evildoers. In fact, they came into being precisely because banking services, at least for ordinary people, were so poor. Various informal value-transfer systems remain to this day cheaper and more trustworthy and are used by everyone from émigré workers to international aid agencies.

Nor is there anything necessarily secretive about them. Just as the Chinese system of flying money was created by the emperor to assure the payment of taxes, one of the roots of the *havala* system was the shift around the turn of the twentieth century in India-Pakistan from taxes and rents paid in kind to taxes and rents that had to be paid in cash. As a result, the power of local money lenders over the peasantry increased, and with it their financial role, including that of making and receiving remittances in areas where banks were either nonexistent or open only to the Anglicized elite. A century later, particularly among the Pashtu tribes who straddle Pakistan and Afghanistan, the biggest parallel bankers are often government officials. And most are tribal chiefs who can make the guarantees and command the loyalty to ensure the system operates. Many of their transactions are done in the open, with witnesses and some sort of record keeping.[31] The same is true in other areas where the conventional banking system is weak, corrupt, indifferent to lower income groups, or simply nonexistent.

Ultimately, the only impact of a move against the informal value-transfer systems will be to scare off legitimate users and make the illegitimate ones deepen their cover. Thus, Somalia, for example, has (barely) survived on remittances from the Diaspora population through the informal banking system. In the wake of the new crackdown, those remittances dried up—people were afraid to trust their money to informal bankers for fear they would be branded supporters of terrorism or, at a minimum, have their funds confiscated by American or European authorities.[32]

Notes

Acknowledgments

1. However, there was a dissenting voice at the event. By chance a senior Mexican diplomat had phoned me for advice about how to deal with the fallout from Operation Casablanca, a U.S. law enforcement campaign that tarred the entire Mexican banking system (and government) as a hotbed of crime. Because he was en route to the UN unveiling, we hatched a scheme—if I was not invited to be present as co-author of the report under debate, I would join the Mexican delegation as a "technical advisor" to make my opinions known. The debate was reproduced in United Nations Office for Drug Control and Crime Prevention, Global Programme against Money-Laundering, *Attacking the Profits of Crime: Drugs, Money, and Laundering* (Vienna, 1998).

2. Incidentally, I recited this story at another UN conference, this one held by the International Scientific and Professional Advisory Council, a decade later, only to note that one member of the audience seemed to be squirming in his seat. Afterward, during the question period, he admitted that although he had not been part of the original research team that had produced the number, he had been part of a committee told a few years later that it was time to show some progress in the war on drugs. Hence they were asked to come up with some reasons why the number should be reduced to perhaps $400 billion. That number in turn enjoyed some currency, until they decided it was insufficiently media-genic, and the old $500 billion figure was restored.

Introduction

1. The most notorious example of this moral panic literature is from the late Claire Sterling, *Crime without Frontiers: The Worldwide Expansion of Organised Crime and the Pax Mafiosa* (London, 1994); this volume was published in the United States under the title *Thieves' World*. See also Brian Freemantle, *The Octopus: Europe in a Grip of Organised Crime* (London; 1995), for a book almost as hyperbolic and equally void of analytical merit.

2. This ad was distributed in the May 2001 issue of *Money Laundering Alert,* itself a pricey symptom of the war on money laundering.

3. The pioneering work was by Pierre Galante and Louis Sapin, translated and published in English as *The Marseilles Mafia* (London, 1979). See also Jean-Pierre Charbonneau, *The Canadian Connection* (Montreal, 1976); and Newsday, *The Heroin Trail* (New York, 1976).

4. None of this would have been possible without the assistance of another underworld, that of intelligence. The CIA had encouraged Corsican mobsters to take over the port of Marseilles and drive out the Communist Party–affiliated unions because the CIA wanted to secure Marseilles as a beachhead for moving Cold War–era military supplies into Europe.

The French intelligence services massively recruited Corsican mobsters to do heavy jobs, particularly against the insurgent organization d'armée secrète, made up of rebellious army officers and resentful former *colons* from Algeria. Half of those finally arrested had had tours of duty with one or more French intelligence services. This information, of course, was conspicuously absent from any of the two (three?) movies.

5. Even in a country so notoriously criminogenic as Colombia, this is true. Franciso Thoumi makes the crucial point that in much of Latin America, certainly in Colombia, legitimate businesses and the economic elite have long accumulated much of their wealth through what economists call rent-seeking behavior, which is at heart not much different from what "criminals" do. As criminal elements move from predatory to market-based crimes, this distinction becomes increasingly fuzzy. See Francisco Thoumi, *Political Economy and Illegal Drugs in Colombia* (Boulder, Colo., 1995).

6. For an excellent analysis of how supply-side controls in the form of increased border vigilance simply drive the problem underground and let the politicians proclaim success while doing nothing serious with respect to the fundamental problem, see Peter Andreas, *Border Games: Policing the U.S.–Mexico Divide* (Ithaca, N.Y., 2000).

7. For an interesting dissection of how the drug trade numbers are concocted and manipulated, see Peter Reuter, "The Mismeasurement of Illegal Drug Markets: The Implications of Its Irrelevance," in *Exploring the Underground Economy,* ed. Susan Pozo (Kalamazoo, Mich., 1996).

8. See, for example, the performance of Ramon Milian-Rodriguez, a former money launderer for Colombian narcos, who wowed the U.S. Senate with tales of running sums of $200 million a month in and out of the United States and of managing a drug-money–based investment portfolio of up to $10 billion (U.S. Senate, Committee on Governmental Affairs, Permanent Subcommittee on Investigation, *Drugs and Money Laundering in Panama* [Washington, D.C., 1988]).

9. My thanks to Francisco Thoumi, who explained this process in a seminar organized by the Ministry of Justice in Ottawa in September 2000. Thoumi refers to these numbers as "statistical pornography," designed to entice and mislead.

10. It is fascinating, and a little depressing, to observe that the number games not only remain just as egregious but have gotten progressively worse since the exposure, nearly thirty years ago, of their fraudulent nature in Max Singer, "The Vitality of Mythical Numbers," Singer demonstrated that the amount of property crime attributed to heroin addicts in New York was perhaps ten times as much as could properly be attributed to them.

11. See R. T. Naylor, "Corruption in the Modern Arms Business: Lessons from the Pentagon Scandals," in *The Economics of Corruption,* ed. Arvind Jain (Dordrecht, The Netherlands, 1998); or idem, *Patriots and Profiteers: On Economic Warfare, Embargo-Busting and State Sponsored Crime* (Toronto, 1999); or idem, *Economic Warfare: Sanctions, Embargo-Busting and the Human Cost* (Boston, 2001), chap. 4.

12. This is the main theme of R. T. Naylor, *Hot Money and the Politics of Debt* (New York, Toronto, and London, 1985–94).

13. See the excellent diagnosis by Joel Dyer, *The Perpetual Prisoner Machine: How America Profits from Crime* (Boulder, Colo., 2000).

Chapter 1. Mafias, Myths, and Markets

1. These are the words of the late Claire Sterling, a Cold War hack recycled into an international crime specialist. See Sterling, *Thieves' World* (New York, 1994); this volume was published in London as *Crime without Frontiers*. For a different opinion, see R. T. Naylor, "From Cold War to Crime War: The Search for a New 'National Security' Threat," *Transnational Organized Crime* 1, no. 4 (winter 1995).

2. Sterling, *Thieves' World,* is full of such hyperbolic assertions.

3. "Global Mafia," *Newsweek* 14/3/94; U.S. assistant secretary of state cited in L. P. Raine and F. J. Cilluffo, *Global Organized Crime: The New Empire of Evil* (Washington, D.C., 1994), 2.

4. See especially the survey in Joseph Albini, *The American Mafia: Genesis of a Legend* (New York, 1971). In their recent work, Herbert Edelhertz and Thomas Overcast (*The Business of Organized Crime* [Loomis, Calif., 1993]) simply accept as instances of organized crime any enterprise event that law enforcement agencies have chosen to prosecute under the rubric "organized crime." The mildest term to describe this procedure is "cop-out," no pun intended.

5. Alan Block, "The Organized Crime Control Act, 1970," *Public Historian* 2, no. 2 (winter 1980), 43.

6. Yet some are prepared to make that leap. See Michael Maltz, "On Defining 'Organized Crime,' " *Crime and Delinquency,* July 1976, 342: "A crime consists of a transaction proscribed by the criminal law between offender(s) and victim(s). . . . An organized crime is a crime committed by two or more offenders who are or intended to remain associated for the purpose of committing crimes."

7. This point was first forcibly raised by Thomas Schelling, one of the first economists to treat the problems of criminal enterprise seriously. His main works on the subject were collected and reprinted in his volume *Choice and Consequence* (Cambridge, Mass., 1984).

8. Mike Gray, *Drug Crazy: How We Got into This Mess and How We Can Get Out* (New York, 1998), 88.

9. For a general survey, see Jeff Atkinson, "Racketeer Influenced and Corrupt Organizations," *Journal of Criminal Law and Criminology* 69, no. 1 (1978). For purposes of the statute, "enterprise" was defined very widely in that it included virtually anything that made money. Nor did a criminal enterprise require any real corporate form; any individual could constitute an enterprise.

10. Peter Maas, *The Valachi Papers* (New York, 1968). The foreword by Rudolph Giuliani states, "Valachi exposed the Big Lie. He confirmed the existence of a secret organization of so-called Families engaged in a wide range of criminal activities" (p. x). He also comments that "The passage of the racketeering act commonly called the RICO statute was made possible largely because of Valachi's confessions" (p. xi).

11. In the 1980s, three of the more popular books dealing with the cocaine business were Paul Eddy, Hugo Sabofal, and Sara Walden, *The Cocaine Wars* (New York, 1988); Guy Gugliotta and Jeff Lean, *Kings of Cocaine* (New York, 1989); and Elaine Shannon, *Desperadoes: Latin Druglords, U.S. Lawmen, and the War America Can't Win* (New York, 1988).

12. See, for example, the testimony before the U.S. House of Representatives Foreign Affairs Committee, "International Drug Money Laundering: Issues and Options for Congress" (Washington, D.C., 1990), 6–7.

13. Some of the following points were first raised by Peter Reuter in *Disorganized Crime* (New York, 1983), and in *The Organization of Illegal Markets* (Washington, D.C., 1985).

14. Some of these issues were broached, in a very deductive though insightful way, in Schelling, *Choice and Consequence.*

15. See Mark Moore, "Organized Crime as a Business Enterprise," in *Major Issues in Organized Crime Control,* ed. H. Edelhertz (Washington, D.C., 1987), for a survey of the "models" of the criminal industrial association.

16. The pioneering view from within was conducted by Francis Ianni, in which he examined the interests and operations of the Lupollo Family. See Ianni, *A Family Business* (New York, 1972). The work was continued by Annelise Anderson, who studied an unnamed crime family in *The Business of Organized Crime* (Stanford, Calif., 1979). The conclusions that emerged from these investigations were confirmed and reinforced in Mark

Haller's careful dissection of the Bruno Family of south Philadelphia, *Life under Bruno: The Economics of an Organized Crime Family* (Harrisburg, Pa., 1991). Haller remarks, "The Family was not a business, nor did it operate businesses. . . . The Family, instead, was more like a fraternal organization."

17. Cited in *Forbes* 21/10/91.

18. Annelise Anderson, "Organized Crime, Mafia, and Governments," in *The Economics of Organized Crime*, ed. Gianluca Fiortenini and Sam Pelzman (Cambridge, Mass., 1995), 40.

19. Although they disagree about much else, on this point there is unanimity among Mafia scholars. See Albini, *American Mafia;* Pino Arlacchi, *Mafia Business: The Mafia Ethic and the Spirit of Capitalism* (Oxford, 1986), who states: "The mafia, as the term is commonly understood, does not exist" (p. 3); Judith Chubb, *The Mafia and Politics: The Italian State under Siege* (Ithaca, N.Y., 1989); and Diego Gambetta, *The Sicilian Mafia: The Business of Private Protection* (Cambridge, Mass., 1993).

20. Francis Ianni, "Formal and Social Organization in an Organized Crime Family: A Case Study," *University of Florida Law Review* 24 (1971).

21. This is well explained in Albini, *American Mafia,* 266.

22. This process is very well diagnosed in Peter Reuter, "The Decline of the American Mafia," *Public Interest,* no. 120 (summer 1995).

23. This is described in Haller, *Life under Bruno.*

24. It was not that Valachi deliberately misinformed. Much of his testimony was based on hearsay. He was too young to have witnessed many of the events he recounted, he held only the lowest of positions in the hierarchy he described, and he spent so long in jail before turning informant that most of his information was useless from the point of view of prosecution. (See Albini, *American Mafia,* 225.) Thanks to Alan Block, who has collected transcripts of the actual testimony.

25. Albini, *American Mafia,* 236.

26. Jay Albanese "What Lockheed and La Cosa Nostra Have in Common," *Crime and Delinquency,* April 1982, 227.

27. For a clear example of this kind of error, see Yves Lavigne, *Hell's Angels: Taking Care of Business* (Toronto, 1987). Like so many works on the Mafia, Lavigne's book lays out a simplistic membership structure that has existed since bikers were merely ex-pilots on wheels tearing up the roads for kicks on a Saturday afternoon; then Lavigne assumes the same structure has somehow transformed itself into a commercial operation. For example, the author states that "the chapter president is equivalent to the family boss," the secretary-treasurer is like the consiglieri, and so forth. Much the same organizational comparison could be made to the Boy Scouts of America.

28. Note, for example, the reality of the triads as it emerged during hearings of the U.S. Senate Judiciary Committee's Permanent Subcommittee on Investigations, *New International Criminal Organizations* (Washington, D.C., 1992).

29. There has been a sea change in understanding among some police specialists in recent years, a change that in part reflects the long-overdue recruitment of Chinese officers. This is especially noticeable in cities with large Chinese communities such as Toronto.

30. *New York Times* 19/11/86.

31. Gugliotta and Leen, *Kings of Cocaine,* 277.

32. Several books by journalists (such as Eddy, Sabofal, and Walden, *Cocaine Wars;* Gugliotta and Leen, *Kings of Cocaine;* and Shannon, *Desperadoes*) helped entrench the "Medellín cartel" mystique in the public consciousness. All consist of cops-and-robbers stories without definition of the term "cartel" or any examination of the actual structure of the industry. The worst of them, *Desperadoes* by Elaine Shannon, was made into an NBC miniseries in which the most elementary principle of journalistic ethics, the need to separate factual reporting from dramatization, was flagrantly violated.

33. The most analytical works in English on the structure and operation of the cocaine trade are Rensselaer Lee III, *The White Labyrinth: Cocaine and Political Power* (New Brunswick, N.J., 1989); and Francisco Thoumi, *Political Economy and Illegal Drugs in Colombia* (Boulder, Colo., 1995). Both authors strongly deny the notion of an operational cartel. Although Lee, in a more recent work with Patrick Clawson (*The Andean Cocaine Industry* [New York, 1996]), is more inclined to use the word "cartel," he also at many points demonstrates the falsity of the notion of a price-fixing, market-sharing agreement.

34. U.S. House of Representatives Committee on Banking, Finance, and Urban Affairs, Subcommittee on Financial Institution Supervision, *Hearings*, November 14–15, 1989, p. 35.

35. *Time* 1/7/91.

36. This is very well explained in Reuter, "Decline of the American Mafia."

37. Even Joseph Valachi insisted to his ever-growing fan club that he never used violence to collect in the loan-sharking operation that was his principal business venture.

38. For example, when a Canadian criminologist actually interviewed serious drug offenders who were behind bars to determine the amount of organization, extent of violence, links to other offenses, and so forth, he came up with precisely the opposite of the police stereotype: they were suburban-living minor executives who disliked violence, conducted business on trust, were not linked into any organizational hierarchy but merely worked though a handful of associates of the same background, and compared themselves with executives of the tobacco and liquor industries. The Royal Canadian Mounted Police's response to this finding was that it must represent a menacing "new breed" of drug dealer. As a Toronto cop said, "We still look at it as organized crime because they are organized" (*Globe and Mail* 30/4/01). So are the girl guides, and with a much more complex and durable structure.

39. Robert Lacey, *Little Man: Meyer Lansky and the Gangster Life* (Boston, 1991), 308ff. One reason that Lansky was far less well heeled than the legend suggests is that twice in his life he had to start over again virtually from zero: once after the expropriation of his Cuban properties by Fidel Castro, and again after the crash of his favorite savings bank in Geneva. But even so, the total could never have come close to $300 million.

40. James Cook, "But Where Are the Dons' Yachts?" *Forbes* 21/10/91; John Gotti actually became mob boss in part through campaigning that he would be more willing to share his wealth with other members of the family. He also shared far more than he wanted to with his lawyers. One revealing moment in the wiretap evidence introduced into his RICO trial had him railing against lawyers picking him clean (Ralph Blumenthal, *The Gotti Tapes* [New York, 1992], xxv). Defense lawyers for mob figures have a reputation for gouging, but it would be hard for them to make much of a dent in an annual revenue of $300 million.

41. Lacey, *Little Man,* 206. Peter Reuter and Jonathan Rubenstein have observed in a different context, with respect to the gambling data, that no one seems to really care how the calculations are performed, as long as they produce a large number ("Fact, Fancy and Organized Crime," *Public Interest* [1978], 62).

42. *Fortune* 20/6/88.

43. This is explained in more detail in the introduction to this volume.

44. These points are very aptly made in David Fried, "Rationalizing Criminal Forfeiture," *Journal of Criminal Law and Criminology,* 79, no. 2 (1988).

45. To be sure, the flow can go both ways. The Lupollo Family started out in legitimate street peddling, then branched into loan-sharking, gambling, and the entertainment business. As the crime family grew, members sometimes moved money from the legal into the illegal sector, but on balance the main flow was toward legitimacy (Ianni, *Family Business,* passim).

46. See, for example, Nikos Passas and David Nelken, "The Thin Line between Legitimate and Criminal Enterprises: Subsidy Frauds in the European Community," *Crime, Law, and Social Change* 19 (1993).

47. See Alan Block and Frank Scarpitti, *Poisoning For Profit: The Mafia and Toxic Waste in America* (New York, 1985); Andrew Szasz, "Corporations, Organized Crime, and the Disposal of Hazardous Waste," *Criminology* 24, no. 1 (1984); Donald Rebovich, *Dangerous Ground: The World of Hazardous Waste Crime* (New Brunswick, N.J., 1992); Timothy Carter, "Ascent of the Corporate Model in Environmental-Organized Crime," *Crime, Law, and Social Change* 31, no. 1 (1999).

48. This system of cigarette smuggling and the role of the tobacco companies are examined in Evert Clark and Nicholas Horrock, *Contrabandista* (New York, 1973). See also Phil Shepherd, "Transnational Corporations and the Denationalization of the Latin American Cigarette Industry," in *Historical Studies in International Corporate Business,* ed. Alice Teichova et al. (Cambridge, Mass., 1989); and Pierre Galante and Louis Sapin, *The Marseilles Mafia* (London, 1979).

49. For a general overview see R. T. Naylor, *Economic Warfare: Sanctions, Embargo-Busting, and the Human Cost* (Boston, 2001), chap. 6.

50. See the excellent treatment in Arkady Vaksberg, *The Soviet Mafia* (London, 1991), 75.

51. Gregory Gleason, "Nationalism or Organized Crime: The Case of the 'Cotton Scandal' in the USSR," *Corruption and Reform* 5 (1990).

52. These issues are discussed in a very lucid way in Thomas Packer, *The Limits of the Criminal Sanction* (Stanford, Calif., 1968).

Chapter 2. The Insurgent Economy

1. There is an excellent survey in François Jean and Jean-Christophe Rufin, *Economie des guerres civiles* (Paris, 1996).

2. See especially Joseph Hanlon, *Beggar Your Neighbour: Apartheid Power in Southern Africa* (London, 1986), 153ff., for an early analysis of the strategy. It has shifted but little since, although more recently the government has reclaimed extensive areas from UNITA control, leaving it with little more than the lucrative diamond-mining areas.

3. For a general overview of Sendero activities, see Gabriella Tarzona-Sevillano, *Sendero Luminoso and the Threat of Narco-Terrorism* (New York, 1990).

4. Attacking oil installations is in fact a popular tactic for guerrilla forces all over the world—from the Kurdish Workers' Party–PKK militias in Turkish Kurdistan to the Sudan People's Liberation Army to the United Liberation Front of Assam in India (*Middle East Reporter* 31/3/85; *Middle East International* 31/5/85; *Financial Times* 15/10/93; *Globe and Mail* 2/12/97).

5. *Financial Times* 6/12/96; www.stratfor.com, "Rebels Aiming at Colombian Economy," *Global Intelligence Update,* 5/03/01.

6. *Financial Times* 16/03/01.

7. *Far Eastern Economic Review* 19/9/75; *Wall Street Journal* 3/1/90.

8. *La Presse* 31/1/01.

9. *New York Times* 23/7/93.

10. Although the FMLN term "zones of control" is used throughout this chapter, there are equivalent terms used by other insurgent groups. The New People's Army in the Philippines refers to the same phenomena as "consolidated zones," and the Eritrean People's Liberation Front calls them "liberated zones." Interestingly, the Mozambique National Resistance (RENAMO), a group notorious for having no political program beyond destruction, used a slightly different but functionally equivalent classification: control areas, where it is sufficiently well entrenched to organize forced labor; tax areas, where it extorts supplies and money from the population; and destruction areas, where the objective is indiscriminate slaughter (*Globe and Mail* 26/5/88; Hanlon, *Beggar Your Neighbour,* 139).

11. The most outstanding work on the New People's Army is Gregg Jones, *Red Revolution: Inside the Philippines Guerrilla Movement* (Boulder, Colo., 1989).

12. *Christian Science Monitor* 20/7/94; *Sunday Star-Times* (Auckland) 13/7/97.

13. www.stratfor.com, "Nepal-Crisis," *Global Intelligence Update,* 4/01/01.

14. The literature on this phenomenon is vast. See, for example, the January-February 1990 issue of *Middle East Reports.* There is a summary in R. T. Naylor, *Economic Warfare: Embargoes, Sanctions, and Their Human Cost* (Boston, 2001), chap. 8.

15. For a summary of Contra fund-raising, see Naylor, *Economic Warfare,* chap. 14.

16. *Africa Confidential* 19/6/92.

17. A good source on the flow of aid from the United States is Jack Holland, *The American Connection: U.S. Guns, Money, and Influence in Northern Ireland* (New York, 1987).

18. *Sunday Times* 1/9/91; *L'Express* 11/9/92.

19. Robert Kaplan, "The Loneliest War," *Atlantic Monthly,* July 1988.

20. In Quebec in 1993, charges were brought against more than one hundred Somalis for welfare fraud, mainly for receiving checks simultaneously in Ontario and Quebec. In the previous two years, the dossiers of 731 Somali showed "anomalies," although just what that meant no one bothered to elaborate, leaving it to the public's overactive imagination (*La Presse* 30/10/93). None of the accusations of receiving welfare and spending it on arms was ever substantiated.

21. *Sunday Times* 28/6/96.

22. *The Times* 29/8/92; *Sunday Times* 30/8/92; *Guardian Weekly* 20/9/92.

23. *Globe and Mail* 17/7/89.

24. On the Tupamaros, see Robert Moss, *Urban Guerrillas* (London, 1972); and, more reliably, Alain Labrousse, *Les Tupamaros—Guerrilla urbaine en Uruguay* (Paris, 1971).

25. For an overview of the consequences farther afield, see John Cooley, *Unholy Wars: Afghanistan, America, and International Terrorism* (London, 1999).

26. *Far Eastern Economic Review* 5/3/89; *New York Times* 18/4/88; *Middle East,* October 1991. See also R. T. Naylor, *Patriots and Profiteers: On Economic Warfare, Embargo-Busting, and State Sponsored Crime* (Toronto, 1999), chap. 5.

27. The theoretical framework to follow is adopted from Peter Lupsha, "Organized Crime: Rational Choice Not Ethnic Group Behavior," *Law Enforcement Intelligence Digest,* winter 1988.

28. This typology is similar to but in some ways quite different from that of Edwin Stier and Peter Richards, and developed further by Peter Lupsha, "Organized Crime," in *Local Government Police Management,* 3d ed., ed. William Geller (Washington, D.C., 1991).

29. Alex McCoy, *The Politics of Heroin* (New York, 1991), 146–53.

30. One example is the experience of the Chinese People's Army. During their fight against the Japanese army of occupation and the subsequent civil war, the People's Army had substantial success recruiting social bandits and even opium traffickers to its ranks, some of whom became high-ranking officers.

31. Sometimes the links are even more arm's length. For example, urban guerrillas imprisoned in Brazil in the 1970s taught military tactics to members of a drug trafficking group that later adopted the name Comando Vermelho (Red Command), although it had not a shred of ideology to justify its name. The group supplemented its prison-acquired knowledge by encouraging members to join the army. Subsequently it not only was able to protect drug operations with military efficiency, but a group equipped with armor-piercing weapons once hit an armored car in São Paulo and walked off with $2.2 million (*New York Times* 31/8/93).

32. Jones, *Red Revolution,* 138.

33. Christopher Dobson and Ronald Payne, *The Weapons of Terror* (London, 1979), 19.

34. On the Huk rebellion in general see Benedict Kerkvliet, *The Huk Rebellion* (Berkeley, Calif., 1977); and Eduardo Lachica, *Huk: Philippines Agrarian Society in Revolt* (Manila, 1971).

35. A good survey of racketeering by the IRA is found in James Adams, *The Financing of Terror* (New York, 1986). The sections of the book dealing with other parts of the world are very poor and fairly unreliable. On the collapse of the UDA, see *New York Times* 14/3/88.

36. See Barbara Conway, *The Piracy Business* (London, 1982); and idem, *Maritime Fraud* (London, 1990); *L'evenement du Jeudi* 20/4/1989; *Middle East,* August 1988.

37. Duncan Perry, *The Politics of Terror: The Macedonian Revolutionary Movements, 1893–1912* (Durham, N.C., 1988).

38. See Murray Bloom, *Money of Their Own: The Great Counterfeiters* (New York, 1957), 18–33. For a pro-Church account of the insurrection, see Jean Meyer, *Apocalypse et revolution au Mexique: La guerre des Cristeros, 1926–1929* (Paris, 1974).

39. Andrew Tully, *Treasury Agent* (New York, 1958), 265.

40. *New York Times* 27/12/84, 12/2/88.

41. *Israeli Foreign Affairs* 8, no. 3 (March 25, 1992).

42. *Middle East,* October 1990.

43. *New York Times* 3/7/88, 29,30/3/96, 28/4/96; *Milwaukee Journal Sentinel* 14/11/96; *Village Voice* 9/5/95; *Los Angeles Times* 17/4/96; *Austin American-Statesman* 13/5/95; *Washington Post* 5/5/95; *Arizona Republic* 25/5/95; *Charleston Gazette* 25/10/96; Morris Dees, *Gathering Storm: America's Militia Threat* (New York, 1996).

44. Richard Clutterbuck, *Terrorism and Guerrilla Warfare* (London, 1987); Ovid Desmaris, *The Last Mafiosa* (New York, 1981), 32; Robert John and Sami Hadawi, *The Palestine Diary* (Beirut, 1985), 1:302 n., 2:86, 111, 340; *The Times* 24/1/46, 23/9/40, 25/9/45, 14 and 25/7/46, 29/11/46, 4,16/12/46, 27/6/47.

45. Edgar O'Ballance, *The Cyanide War: Tamil Insurrection in Sri Lanka* (London, 1989), 30.

46. Jonathan Randall, *Going All the Way* (New York, 1986), 98. This source misidentifies the robbers as belonging to the Democratic Front for the Liberation of Palestine.

47. *Far Eastern Economic Review* 14/4/88.

48. Cited in Jillian Becker, *Hitler's Children: The Story of the Baader-Meinhof Terrorist Gang* (New York, 1977), 180.

49. Moss, *Urban Guerrillas;* chapter 11 deals with the Tupamaros.

50. For details, see Lester Sobel, ed., *Political Terrorism* (New York, 1975). There is an excellent analysis by Susanne Purnell, in *Terrorism and Personal Protection,* ed. Brian Jenkins (Boston, 1985).

51. Richard Gillespie, *Soldiers of Peron: Argentina's Montoneros* (Oxford, 1982), 180–83.

52. *Canadian Business,* June 1983, examines the experiences of some kidnapped oil workers.

53. *Far Eastern Economic Review* 5/10/89; *India Today* 15/1/91.

54. *New York Times* 4/11/92; *India Today* 31/8/92; *Globe and Mail* 2/12/97.

55. See especially Adams, *Financing of Terror,* chap. 7, for a survey of IRA fund-raising activities. See also *Guardian Weekly* 2/10/88 and *Financial Times* 7/1/92.

56. Another parasitical technique the IRA is alleged to have employed to great advantage is (along with the Mafia) European Economic Community subsidy fraud. See *The Times* 8/2/89.

57. *Cambio16,* 15/1/90. The potential returns can lead to tax wars. Take, for example, the two main factions of the Kukis, a Christian tribal people divided between India and Burma. The Burma-based Kuki National Organization has called for an autonomous state in the Chin Hills, whereas the Kuki National Front in India demands the creation of an independent Kukiland made up of portions of Burma and Manipur. Both compete, sometimes at gunpoint, to impose "loyalty taxes" on the same population (*India Today* 30/6/93).

58. *Far Eastern Economic Review* 5/8/93.

59. Ibid., 11/3/74.

60. *New York Times* 29/10/90, 9/1/91, 10/11/92; *Latin America Weekly Report* 15/7/89; *Wall Street Journal* 9/1/91.

61. Steve Wienberg, *Armand Hammer: The Untold Story* (New York, 1989), 267–68.

62. *Latin America Special Report,* April 1992.

63. See especially Jones, *Red Revolution;* Lachica, *Huk: Philippines Agrarian Society in Revolt;* James Goodno, *The Philippines: Land of Broken Promises* (London, 1991).

64. *Middle East Times* 1/10/88.

65. Fouad Hamdan, "Waste Attack in the Mediterranean," *Greenpeace Mediterranean,* August 1996.

66. *Semana* 3/7/92; *Financial Times* 26/04/01.

67. *Financial Times* 22/3/01.

68. *New York Times* 12/8/92. For details, see Naylor, *Economic Warfare*, 324–27.

69. *Far Eastern Economic Review* 5/8/99.

70. See especially André Boucaud and Louis Boucaud, *Sur la piste des Seigneurs de la Guerre* (Paris, 1985).

71. *The Economist* 6/4/91; *Far Eastern Economic Review* 22/2/90; *Le Monde Diplomatique,* August 1989.

72. *Asiaweek* 11/10/91.

73. *Los Angeles Times* 18/11/90; *New York Times* 6/2/95; *FBIS-EAS* 23/1/95.

74. *Far Eastern Economic Review* 7/2/91; *FBIS-EAS* 12/5/94, 23/1/95; *New York Times* 30/7/97.

75. *The Manager,* January 1997.

76. McCoy, *Politics of Heroin,* 170–72, 351–52.

77. In general, see Bertil Linter, *The Rise and Fall of the Burmese Communist Party* (Ithaca, N.Y., 1990).

78. *The Economist* 6/4/91; *Far Eastern Economic Review* 28/6/90.

79. *Far Eastern Economic Review* 14/11/96.

80. See especially the excellent discussion in Rensselaer III, *White Labyrinth: Cocaine and Political Power* (New Brunswick, N.J., 1989).

81. The standard view of Sendero was challenged by research on the ground conducted by Edmundo Morales, *Cocaine—White Gold Rush in the Andes* (Tuscon, Az., 1989).

82. O'Ballance, *Cyanide War,* 71, 120.

83. These efforts by the Tigers to supplement their war chest by purchasing heroin in Bombay and reselling it in Europe date at least as far back as 1985, when an official of the organization was arrested in Rome with twenty-two kilos in his suitcase (*Sunday Times* 30/8/87; *India Today* 31/5/91).

84. *The Times* 26/11/88.

85. *Evening Standard* 8/11/93; *Montreal Gazette* 22/4/93; *Observer* 11/4/93; *Vancouver Sun* 22/4/93; *Calgary Herald* 30/4/93.

86. One of the more interesting sets of claims along these lines is made by DEA veteran Celerino Castillo III, in Celerino Castillo III and David Harmon, *Powderburns: Cocaine, Contras and the Drug War* (Oakville, Ontario, 1994).

87. *San Francisco Examiner* 16/3/86.

88. The literature dealing with the relationship of the Contras to drug trafficking is enormous. See, for example, Peter Dale Scott and Jonathan Marshall, *Cocaine Politics* (Berkeley, 1991); U.S. Senate Committee on Foreign Relations, Subcommittee on Terrorism, Narcotics, and International Operations, *Drugs, Law Enforcement, and Foreign Policy* (Washington, D.C., 1988). That the drug–Contra link was well known to U.S. intelligence was confirmed a decade later by internal CIA investigations (*New York Times* 17/7/98).

89. See, for example, Gary Webb, *Dark Alliance: The CIA, the Contras, and the Crack Cocaine Explosion* (New York, 1998); and Pete Brewton, *The Mafia, CIA, and George Bush: The Untold Story of America's Greatest Financial Debacle* (New York, 1992).

90. *New York Times* 8/4/87. For a general survey, see Naylor, *Economic Warfare,* chap. 16.

91. See the analysis of A. J. Singh in S. C. Tiwarc ed., *Terrorism in India* (New Delhi, 1990).

92. *The Times* 6/10/88.

93. *Mail and Guardian* 1/9/95, 15/12/97; De Wet Potgeiter, *Contraband: South Africa and the International Trade in Ivory and Rhino Horn* (Cape Town, 1995). Actually there is some doubt about whether any of the proceeds went to pay for arms from South Africa. Some contend that the arms were given for free and that the proceeds of wildlife poaching were pure gravy.

94. Jean Lesage, *L'Italie des enlèvements* (Paris, 1978), 164.

95. *Far Eastern Economic Review* 28/7/88, 19/5/88.

96. Ibid., 9/4/98.

97. The basic book on PLO finances is Cheryl Rubenberg, *The PLO: Its Institutional Infra-structure* (Belmont, Mass., 1982). There is fairly unreliable material in Adams, *Financing of Terror,* and material that verges on the preposterous in Neil Livingston and David Halevy, *Inside the PLO* (New York, 1990).

98. *Sunday Times* 24/2/85.

99. See Naylor, *Economic Warfare,* chaps. 8, 9, and 21.

100. *Latin America Weekly Report* 29/3/85.

101. *Barron's* 28/9/81.

102. Claire Sterling, *The Terror Network: The Secret War of International Terrorism* (New York, 1981), 175, 181.

103. Linter, *Rise and Fall of the Burmese Communist Party,* 35.

104. Exaggerated numbers played a similar role in the Philippines during the 1970s, where the public dismissed the Marcos government's claims about the size of the New People's Army, referring to them as "budgetary guerrillas."

105. An excellent overview of some of these trends in action is in Jean and Rufin, *Economie des guerres civiles.*

106. *Financial Times* 26/10/00. If the Royal Ulster Constabulary is right, drug trafficking in Ulster is now the preserve mainly of members of the loyalist paramilitaries—not of the UDA or the UVA itself but of individuals who might call on their comrades for backup to battle intruders or to collect from recalcitrant debtors.

107. *Far Eastern Economic Review* 5/8/93.

108. *India Today* 31/8/92.

109. *Financial Times* 3/11/98.

110. *Washington Post* 2/10/96; *New York Times* 6/5/96; *Los Angeles Times* 15/6/96; *Globe and Mail* 4/8/97.

111. *National Catholic Reporter* 2/10/95.

112. *FBIS-EAS* 18/11/94.

113. *The Economist* 23/8/97.

114. *Reuters* 2/7/98.

115. *Financial Times* 11/3/88. Access to arms was impeded with the collapse of the Burmese Communist Party, which used to control the border area and facilitate the movement of arms.

116. The theme of ecological causes of conflict has been treated by Thomas Homer-Dixon. See especially Homer-Dixon, "On the Threshold: Environmental Changes as Causes of Acute Conflict," *International Security* 16, no. 2 (fall 1991); and idem, "Environmental Scarcities and Violent Conflict: Evidence from Cases," *International Security* 19, no. 1 (1994).

117. See Tom Dale and Vernon Carter, *Topsoil and Civilization* (Norman, Okla., 1955). Dale and Carter point out that the sole important exceptions—and therefore the real birthplace of civilization—are the areas served by the Nile, Indus, and Tigris-Euphrates river systems, whose annual flooding replenished the soil. Also interesting in this regard is Clive Ponting, *A Green History of the World* (London, 1989).

118. Michael Renner, *Fighting For Survival: Environmental Decline, Social Conflict, and the New Age of Insecurity* (New York, 1999).

Chapter 3. Loose Cannons

1. *Financial Times* 19/1/87, 6/7/89; *New York Times* 8, 18/3/88.

2. On smuggling as the response to arms embargoes, see R. T. Naylor, *Economic Warfare: Sanctions, Embargo-Busting, and the Human Cost* (Boston, 2001).

3. The classic analysis is Helen Codere, *Fighting with Property: A Study of Kwakiutl Pot-laching and Warfare* (Seattle, 1950).

4. After the collapse of the Soviet Union, there was much self-congratulation in the West about the success of the strategy. See, for example, Peter Schweizer, *Victory: the Reagan*

Administration's Secret Strategy That Hastened the Collapse of the Soviet Union (New York, 1994). In fact, the arms race was an exacerbating factor but hardly the precipitating cause (Naylor, *Economic Warfare,* chap. 6).

5. On this transformation, see R. T. Naylor, "The Rise of the Modern Arms Black Market and the Fall of Supply Side Control," in *Society under Siege: Crime, Violence, and Illegal Weapons,* ed. Virginia Gamba (Halfway House, South Africa, 1998).

6. *Observer* 16/8/92; *World Press Review,* November 1993; Chris Smith, *Light Weapons and the International Arms Trade in UNDIR: Small Arms Management and Peacekeeping in Southern Africa* (Geneva, 1996), 9.

7. This process is described in R. T. Naylor, "Corruption in the Modern Arms Business: Lessons from the Pentagon Scandals," in *The Economics of Corruption,* ed. Arvind Jain (Dordrecht, The Netherlands, 1999).

8. There is nothing very new about arms industry corruption. See, for example, Gustavus Myers, *History of the Great American Fortunes* (New York, 1907); H. C. Engelbrecht and F. C. Hanighen, *Merchants of Death: A Study of the International Armaments Industry* (New York, 1934); Richard Lewisohn, *The Profits of War through the Ages* (New York, 1937); Donald McCormick, *Peddler of Death: The Life of Sir Basil Zaharoff* (London, 1965); and Richard Kaufman, *The War Profiteers* (New York, 1970).

9. See David Boulton, *The Lockheed Papers* (New York, 1978); and Anthony Sampson, *The Arms Bazaar* (London, 1977).

10. See, for example, the financial peregrinations in the Dotan affair involving Israeli agents and U.S. aircraft manufacturers (*Financial Times* 18/3/91; *New York Times* 19/3/91).

11. Quoted in *India Today* 15/5/87.

12. Recently it appeared that European arms makers were rebuilding offshore slush funds in anticipation of having their right to bribe, and then to deduct the bribes from their taxable income, taken away (*Financial Times* 2/9/00).

13. For a critique of the distinction, see Naylor, "Rise of the Modern Arms Black Market," 62–67.

14. *Far Eastern Economic Review* 2/7/92, 3/3/94, 6/10/94; *Wall Street Journal* 19/7/93; *The Economist* 29/1/94; *Globe and Mail* 8/12/95; *International Herald Tribune* 27/1/96.

15. *Far Eastern Economic Review* 3/2/94, 6/10/94.

16. *Wall Street Journal* 19/7/93; *The Economist* 29/1/94. South Korean firms are among the world's masters in handling bribe money. "There are a hundred ways to doctor corporate bookkeeping," remarked one accountant (*Far Eastern Economic Review* 30/11/95).

17. *Sunday Times* 23/1/94, 27/2/94; *Observer* 7/8/89; *The Ecologist* 24, no. 2 (March–April 1994); *The Economist* 5/2/94, 5/11/94.

18. *Observer* 13/11/94.

19. Once, when Israel ran short of U.S.-made 81-millimeter mortar ammunition and the United States had diverted its inventories to Vietnam, Israel sent agents to pick up ammunition off the nearby Cambodian black market (Timothy Green, *The Smugglers* [London, 1969], 133; James Hamilton-Paterson, *A Very Personal War* [London: 1971], 65).

20. Naylor, *Economic Warfare,* chaps. 7, 11, 16, and 18.

21. There are a number of works dealing with the secret Iraqi arms buildup, some of which degenerate into anti-Arab racism. They include Alan Friedman, *Spider's Web: The Secret History of How the White House Illegally Armed Iraq* (New York, 1993); Mark Phythian, *Arming Iraq: How the U.S. and Britain Secretly Built Saddam's War Machine* (Boston, 1997); and Kenneth Timmerman, *The Death Lobby: How the West Armed Iraq* (London, 1992).

22. Patrick Brogan and Albert Zarca, *Deadly Business: Sam Cummings, Interarms, and the Arms Trade* (New York, 1982).

23. Profiles of several prominent gunrunners of the immediate post–World War II decades are in George Thayer, *The War Business* (New York, 1969).

24. Adnan Khashoggi was only one particularly notorious example. Some aspects of his career are traced in Ronald Kessler, *The Richest Man in the World* (New York, 1986); and

David Holden, *The House of Saud: The Rise and Rule of the Most Powerful Dynasty in the Arab World* (New York, 1982).

25. See Martin Van Creveld, *The Transformation of War* (New York, 1991).

26. On the role of arms embargos in stimulating world weapons production and reducing international control, see Naylor, *Economic Warfare*, passim.

27. The financial impact of the debt crisis is analyzed in R. T. Naylor, *Hot Money and the Politics of Debt*, 2d ed. (Montreal, 1994).

28. In fact one reporter actually did so (*Wall Street Journal* 4/10/93; *New York Times* 6/6/94). To be fair, after a series of scandals, there was some tightening of the regulations—and the number of licensed dealers fell sharply from its previous total of nearly 300,000. See Tom Diaz, *Making a Killing: The Business of Guns in America* (New York, 1999).

29. See the account by Peter Furman in *Forbes* 10/5/93.

30. This is the price range suggested by former CIA and U.S. Naval Intelligence black market expert Edwin Wilson. See Peter Maas, *Manhunt: The Incredible Pursuit of a CIA Agent Turned Terrorist* (New York, 1986), 260. However, Chris Cowley (*Guns, Lies, and Spies* [London, 1992], 109–10) puts the figure at a minimum of 10 percent. His upper limit of 200 percent presumably should read 20 percent.

31. *Foreign Report* 19/12/91; *New York Times* 11/1/92; *World Press Review*, February 1992.

32. In 1994 it was estimated that although fewer than 64,000 New Yorkers had permits, there were about two million weapons in circulation in the city (*New York Times* 14/3/94).

33. *U.S. News and World Report* 2/6/98. The machine guns were made by upgrading semi-automatics with legally obtained materials.

34. *AsiaWeek* 10/3/93; *Far Eastern Economic Review* 23, 30/12/93; *World Press Review* 16/5/92.

35. *L'Express* 3/8/90; *Middle East Times* 13/11/90; *Middle East Reporter* 11/5/91, 8/6/91; *Sunday Times* 1/9/91.

36. *New York Times* 26/8/88.

37. *Middle East* October 1981; *Far Eastern Economic Review* 5/3/87; *New York Times* 18/4/88; *Jeune Afrique* 19/3/90; *Washington Post* 1, 6/5/87; Mohammed Yousaf, *The Bear Trap: Afghanistan's Untold Story* (London, 1992), denies most of the tales of corruption in the supply line—which the author ran.

38. *Wall Street Journal* 10/9/90; *AsiaWeek* 2/6/93.

39. *Financial Times* 24/1/92, 6/2/93; *Observer* 16/8/92, 28/2/93; *Sunday Times* 26/1/92; *Commersant* 9/6/92; *Moscow Times* 31/3/94.

40. *Washington Report on Middle East Affairs*, August–September 1992; Charles Petersen, "Moscow's New Arms Bazaar," *Orbis*, spring 1994; *Wall Street Journal* 2/9/94; *Sunday Times* 30/5/93; *Washington Post* 25/10/92, 29/8/93. For an up-to-date analysis, see John Berryman, "Russia and the Illicit Arms Trade," *Crime, Law, and Social Change* 38, nos. 1–2 (2000).

41. *L'Espresso* 30/8/87, 1/10/87; *Sunday Times* 13/9/87; *Business Week* 21/9/87; *Wall Street Journal* 8, 22/9/87; *Financial Times* 7, 9, 12/9/87; *The Economist* 12/9/87; *The Times* 6, 7/9/87; *Facts on File* 18/9/87; *Washington Post* 8/9/87; *L'Express* 25/9/87; *The Observer* 13/9/87; *Le Monde* 8/9/87.

42. *Jane's Intelligence Review*, September 1996.

43. Joseph Goulden, *The Death Merchant* (New York, 1984), 212.

44. One of the most detailed looks at this phenomenon is Jonathan Kwitny, *The Crimes of Patriots: A True Tale of Dope, Dirty Money, and the CIA* (New York, 1987).

45. *Washington Post* 3/9/89.

46. The literature on Israel's arms business is vast. As one example, see Andrew Cockburn and Leslie Cockburn, *Dangerous Liaison: The Inside Story of the U.S.–Israeli Covert Relationship* (Toronto, 1991).

47. *Far Eastern Economic Review* 8/9/88; *Sunday Times* 3/4/88; *Jerusalem Post* 4/5/88.

48. One of the most influential anti-covert-action works of the era was that of Victor Marchetti and John Marks, *The CIA and the Cult of Intelligence* (New York, 1974).

49. In state-to-state deals, there is really no need for brokers. Nonetheless, sometimes one or both sides insist. The seller might require the broker to kick back a certain percentage into a political slush fund, whereas the buyer might demand that the broker stuff some money into an offshore retirement fund (Thayer, *War Business,* 129).

50. William Hartung, *And Weapons for All* (New York, 1994), 255.

51. A superlative examination of this process in Saudi Arabia is provided in Said Aburish, *The Rise, Corruption, and Coming Fall of the House of Saud* (New York, 1994).

52. For summaries of some of the more notorious recent scandals, see Naylor, *Economic Warfare,* chaps. 16, 17, and 20.

53. Hartung, *Weapons for All,* 268.

54. There is an excellent treatment of the powder cartel and its activities in Walter de Bock and Jean-Charles Deniau, *Des armes pour l'Iran* (Paris, 1988).

55. *World Press Review,* February 1992.

56. Private communication.

57. *New York Times* 29/10/91; *Wall Street Journal* 29/10/92.

58. *Middle East Reporter* 8/6/91.

59. An excellent exposition that details some of these practices is Ragnar Benson, *Gunrunning for Fun and Profit* (Boulder, Colo., 1986).

60. *Pacific Islands Monthly,* July 1988.

61. *L'Express,* 13/2/87.

62. Green (*Smugglers,* 127) mentions this requirement in the 1960s, and, interestingly enough, the ships used by the Israeli gunrunner for the 1991 Croatian deal were so equipped (*Forbes* 10/5/93).

63. This is mentioned by Said Aburish (*Beirut Spy* [London, 1989], 50) with respect to the Iraqi regime. This was, of course, before the Gulf War, in whose aftermath the increasingly insecure regime engaged in a series of bloody purges of officers suspected of plotting against it.

64. Major Robert Turp reported the following exchange with a buyer for the secessionist forces of Katanga. Turp: "How much do you want out of it?" Buyer: "Major, I want you to know that I'm a patriot. . . . I want only a hundred percent myself" (Robert Turp, *Gunrunner: Confessions of an Arms Dealer* [London, 1972], 115).

65. Steven Emerson, *Secret Warriors: Inside the Covert Military Operations of the Reagan Era* (New York, 1988), 151–52, 198.

66. The literature on the Iran-Contra affair is enormous. The most comprehensive survey, which includes the financial mechanics, seems to be the U.S. congressional joint House and Senate investigation (*The Iran-Contra Affair* [Washington, D.C., 1987]).

67. *Far Eastern Economic Review* 14/12/95. Taiwan immediately followed suit, setting up the Islamic Oriental Establishment to give millions that could be used for arms to the Sudan.

68. *The Nation* 2/5/94.

69. *Wall Street Journal* 10/9/87, 5/1/89; Ronald Matthews, "Butter for Guns: The Growth of Under-the-Counter Trade," *World Today,* May 1992; Grant Hammond, *Countertrade, Offsets, and Barter in International Trade* (London, 1990).

70. *Observer* 19/3/89, 10/5/92; *Financial Times* 9/7/89.

71. *L'Express* 18/1/85; *Observer* 21, 28/4/85; *Middle East,* March 1986. Similar "Jews-for-arms" swaps occurred with Iran (*Observer* 13/9/87).

72. The payment mechanics are analyzed in *Euromoney,* October 1990.

73. Benson, *Gunrunning,* 20.

74. *The Independent* 16/10/94; *The Nation* 2/5/94; Paul Halloran and Mark Hollingsworth, *Thatcher's Gold: The Life and Times of Mark Thatcher* (London, 1995), 218.

75. There is a different account in U.S. Senate, Foreign Relations Committee, *The BCCI Affair* (Washington, D.C., 1992), 308–13.

76. Turp (*Gunrunner,* 7) recounts a sale to India in which he was offered—and refused—a letter of credit drawn on the State Bank of India. For the deal to be closed, the buyers had to find another, guaranteed neutral bank to guarantee the letter of credit.

77. Details are in Naylor, *Economic Warfare,* chap. 17.
78. *Globe and Mail* 1/5/84.
79. The best of several accounts is in Friedman, *Spider's Web,* but see also U.S. House of Representatives, Committee on Banking, Finance, and Urban Affairs, *Hearing,* April 9, 1991.
80. U.S. Senate, Foreign Relations Committee, *BCCI Affair,* 314.
81. On the general problem of maritime fraud, see Eric Ellen and Donald Campbell, *International Maritime Fraud* (London, 1981); Barbara Conway, *The Piracy Business* (London, 1981); and idem, *Maritime Fraud* (London, 1991).
82. Aburish, *Beirut Spy,* 8.
83. *Sunday Times* 28/10/84.
84. *Wall Street Journal* 30/1/87; De Bock and Deniau, *Armes pour l'Iran,* 36.
85. See, for example, Geoffrey Hodgson, *Lloyd's of London: A Reputation at Risk* (London, 1986), 175; Hermann Moll and Michael Leapman, *Broker of Death* (London, 1988), 30–31; and *Middle East,* December 1983.
86. See, for example, the story of George Perry in *New York Times* 10/3/83, 12/6/83, 2/12/86; *The Times* 10/3/83; *Facts on File* 14/1/83.
87. *Middle East International* 28/4/89; *Wall Street Journal* 4/4/89.
88. *Globe* 11/12/94.
89. See Mike Levi, "Regulating Money Laundering: The Death of Bank Secrecy in the U.K," *British Journal of Criminology* 31, no. 2 (1991).
90. For example, when France used arms and money sent to Iran to buy the freedom of some of its citizens kidnapped in Beirut (*Observer* 6/12/87, 8/5/88; *Guardian Weekly* 6/12/87, 15/5/88; *Jeune Afrique* 6/1/88; *Montreal Gazette* 8/5/88).
91. John De St. Jorre, *The Nigerian Civil War* (London, 1972), 241; Thayer, *War Business,* 167–68.
92. Thayer, *War Business,* 174.
93. Canadian Broadcasting Corporation, "Fifth Estate," December 3, 1991.
94. *Middle East International* 18/4/86.
95. *Globe* 11/12/96.
96. Private communication from an American gunrunner who operated on behalf of the FMLN for several years.
97. Benson, *Gunrunning,* 56.
98. On the earlier diamond-smuggling operations, see Green, *Smugglers,* 129. More recent details are traced in R. T. Naylor, "The Underworld of Diamonds," *Crime, Law, and Social Change* (forthcoming).
99. Alan Thornton and David Currey, *To Kill an Elephant: The Undercover Investigation into the Illegal Ivory Trade* (London, 1991); and De Wet Potgeiter, *Contraband: South Africa and the International Trade in Ivory and Rhino Horn* (Cape Town, 1995).
100. *Far Eastern Economic Review* 7/2/91, 14/10/93.
101. *Montreal Gazette* 2/9/90; *Times of London* 29/8/92; *Sunday Times* 30/8/92; *New Republic* 23/11/92; *New York Times* 14/12/94; *U.S. News and World Report* 21/12/92.
102. *Sunday Telegram* 9/7/89.
103. *Guardian* 9/1/88.
104. Some of these weapons, it must be noted, leaked from criminals into the hands of tribal militias and anti-Indonesia guerrillas across the frontier in Irian Jaya.
105. See the opinion of the managing director of Sam Cummings's Interarmsco in *Business Week* 29/12/86.
106. In the United States, in the early 1990s, of approximately 20,000 employees of the Customs service, some 500 (that is, 2.5 percent) examined outbound cargoes. The result was that in 1992, for example, Customs managed 500 convictions for smuggling narcotics in and 21 for illegally moving weapons out (Deborah Lutterbeck, "License to Deal," *Common Cause Magazine,* summer 1994).

107. *Security Intelligence Report* 31/10/94.
108. *Globe and Mail* 31/8/94.
109. *Montreal Gazette* 9/11/96.

Chapter 4. Treasure Island

1. *The Banker,* October 1996.
2. *Money Laundering Alert,* July and August 2000.
3. The classic analyses are Richard Tawney, *Religion and the Rise of Capitalism* (London, 1926); and Max Weber, *The Protestant Ethic and the Spirit Of Capitalism* (New York, 1930). See also John Thomas Noonan, *Scholastic Analysis of Usury* (Cambridge, U.K., 1957).
4. See especially C. M. Senior, *A Nation of Pirates* (London, 1976).
5. This is examined at length in R. T. Naylor, *Hot Money and the Politics of Debt* (New York, 1986; reprint, Montreal, 1994).
6. This definition is slightly different from that of the Financial Action Task Force, which divided the three steps of money laundering into placement (the fusion of cash into the legal economy or the smuggling of it out of the country), layering (separation from source by creating complex covering structures), and integration (placing laundered funds back into the economy). The problem with this definition is that instead of three distinct stages, it refers to an action, an intention, and a perception, all of which may be true but do not give a really accurate picture of a process.
7. On the interface of intelligence and money laundering, see Naylor, *Hot Money,* chap. 20; and R. T. Naylor, *Economic Warfare: Sanctions, Embargo-Busting, and the Human Cost* (Boston, 2001), passim.
8. Berkeley Rice, *Trafficking: The Boom and Bust of the Air America Cocaine Ring* (New York, 1989), 69. The airline was deliberately named after the notorious CIA air arm. There were even Customs officers willing to believe they were one and the same, and to be appropriately accommodating.
9. *New York Times* 24/1/90; *New York Law Journal* 4/3/91.
10. Sam Giancana and Chuck Giancana, *Double Cross* (New York, 1992), 399. The same was true for John Gotti, boss of the so-called Gambino Family (*Forbes* 21/10/91). The generality of this practice was also attested to by the informant Jimmy "the Weasel" Frattionna (*New York Times* 25/3/84).
11. *Boston Globe* Spotlight Team, *Money Laundering* (Boston, 1986). One of Montreal's leading cigarette smugglers, at least until the year 2000, used the Blue Bonnets racetrack for precisely this purpose (private communication).
12. A lottery-laundry through Liechtenstein seemed to be the core service offered by something calling itself "the first internet money laundering service" (http://www2.s-gimb.lj.edus.si/natan/money/launder.html).
13. *Money Laundering Alert,* August 1995. On the basis of the number of familiar faces appearing in newspaper announcements of the latest lucky winners of Canadian government lotteries, Montreal police suspected that lottery corporation insiders fed the names of winners to local mobsters to give them a chance to make the holder of the ticket an offer the holder could not refuse.
14. In the 1980s in Puerto Rico, specialist dealers would buy winning tickets at a slight premium on behalf of clients, cash the tickets at the disbursement office, and collect a check made out in the name of their client or anyone else the client wanted to designate as payee. Because no records were kept of the sale of tickets, it was virtually impossible to prove that the holder was not the bona fide winner. The scheme was so widely known that bankers would recommend it to clients (U.S. Senate, Judiciary Committee, Permanent Subcommittee on Investigations, *Money Laundering in Puerto Rico* [Washington, D.C., 1985], 11, 29).

15. Margaret Beare and Stephen Schneider, *Tracing of Illicit Funds: Money Laundering in Canada* (Ottawa, 1990), 162–63; K. "Hawkeye" Gross, *Drug Smuggling: The Forbidden Book* (Boulder, Colo., 1991), 100.
16. The saga is recounted in the *Boston Globe* 17/4/85.
17. See, for example, Phillip Curtin, *Cross-Cultural Trade in World History* (Cambridge, U.K., 1984). On the modern spread, see Joel Kotkin, *Tribes: How Race, Religion, and Identity Determine Success in the New Global Economy* (New York, 1993).
18. I am indebted to Rafy Kourouian for observations on trade diasporas among Armenians, Sikhs, Chiau-chou Chinese, and Hasidic Jews.
19. See Richard J. Mangan, "The Southeast Asian Banking System," *DEA Quarterly,* winter 1984, for a law enforcement perspective. This "study" is ostensibly classified, although copies circulate freely throughout the research community. It is unclear if it was classified because the Drug Enforcement Agency (DEA) thought it contained significant information or because its contents are so foolish. For an insightful survey, see William L. Cassidy, "Fei-Ch'ien Flying Money: A Study of Chinese Underground Banking," address given to the 12th Annual International Asian Organized Crime Conference, June 26, 1990.
20. A sketch of the rise of the Chinese entrepreneurial diaspora is in Sterling Seagrave, *Lords of the Rim* (New York, 1995).
21. FinCEN [U.S. Financial Crimes Center], *Colombian Black Market Peso Exchange,* advisory issue no. 9 (November 1997). Similar sentiments were expressed in National Drug Intelligence Center, *Conference Report—Money Laundering: U.S. Vulnerabilities* (Johnston, Pa., 1998).
22. One of the pioneers was Isaac Kattan-Kassin, a member of a family of Syrian Jews whose father had been a money changer in Aleppo. See Robert Powis, *The Money Launderers* (Chicago, 1992), 32–49. So notorious did his handiwork become that it was deliberately imitated in a federal sting called Operation Swordfish. See David McClintick, *Swordfish: A True Story of Ambition, Savagery, and Betrayal* (New York, 1993).
23. *New York Times* 27/9/91.
24. "This finding suggests that a large percentage of the U.S. currency stock was held for purposes not directly related to measured domestic activity" (*Federal Reserve Bulletin,* March 1987). See also *Wall Street Journal* 5/2/87, 4/10/90; *Financial Times* 12/4/95; Case Sprinkle, "The Case of the Missing Money," *Journal of Economic Perspectives* 7, no. 4 (fall 1993).
25. See, for example, U.S. General Accounting Office, *Money Laundering: U.S. Efforts to Fight It Are Threatened by Currency Smuggling* (Washington, D.C., 1994).
26. A good example is the $7 million skimmed from the "Crazy Eddie" retailing empire and flown to Israel (*New York Times* 19/7/92).
27. Paul Eddy and Sara Walden, *Hunting Marco Polo* (New York, 1991), 136.
28. Air America, for example, made so much money transporting drugs that it did not bother to charge its Colombian clients for the cash leg of the trip (Rice, *Trafficking,* 85).
29. Beare and Schneider, *Tracing of Illicit Funds,* 250.
30. W. G. Hill, *PT2—The Practice: Freedom and Privacy Tactics, A Reference Handbook* (Hunts, U.K., 1994), 55.
31. Testimony of Max Mermelstein before the U.S. House of Representatives, Committee on Banking, Finance, and Urban Affairs, Subcommittee on Financial Institution Supervision, *Hearings,* November 14–15 (Washington, D.C., 1989), 8–10. *Money Laundering Alert,* March 1992.
32. Hill, *PT2,* 32.
33. The quotation is from Milian-Rodriguez's testimony before the U.S. Senate, Committee on Foreign Relations, Subcommittee on Terrorism, Narcotics, and International Operations, of February 11, 1988. The sums cited were preposterous. Virtually every "revelation" by Milian-Rodriguez was reported slavishly in the press. Yet his testimony on several matters was considered so unreliable that the U.S. attorney general's office issued a public affidavit to that effect (John Dingues, *Our Man in Panama* [New York, 1991], xxx).

34. See U.S. General Accounting Office, *Money Laundering*, 19, for one that did not get through.
35. Giancana and Giancana, *Double Cross*, 263.
36. Paul Murphy, *La Popessa* (New York, 1983), 252.
37. Giancana and Giancana, *Double Cross*, 444.
38. *Los Angeles Times* 1/12/94.
39. See Ambassador "X," *Above the Law: The Complete Guide to Diplomatic Immunity* (Lexington, Ky., 1991); and Chuck Ashman and Pamela Truscott, *Diplomatic Crime* (Washington, D.C., 1987).
40. In 1989 a senior official of the Peruvian foreign ministry was arrested in Britain, where he had no accreditation, carrying twenty kilos of cocaine (*Globe and Mail* 27/3/89).
41. For a general survey, see Roger Molander, David Mussington, and Peter Wilson, *Cyberpayments and Money Laundering: Problems and Promise* (Santa Monica, Calif., 1998).
42. See the excellent treatment in Tom Sandage, *The Victorian Internet* (New York, 1999).
43. See Stephen Kobrin, "Electronic Cash and the End of National Markets" *Foreign Policy* 107 (summer 1997).
44. This is well described in Kevin Kelly, *Out of Control: The New Biology of Machines, Social Systems, and the Economic World* (New York, 1994).
45. See *The O—A Private Newsletter* 17 (2000).
46. U.S. Senate, Committee on Governmental Affairs, Permanent Subcommittee on Investigations, *Current Trends in Money Laundering* (Washington, D.C., 1992), 12.
47. In the actual jargon, breaking down deposits below the reporting threshold is called structuring, whereas buying cashier's checks in small denominations is smurfing, after the comic book characters. In fact the two terms are often used interchangeably. The second suitably reflects the cartoonish nature of most reporting on money laundering.
48. According to the *New York Times* (5/5/83), the ring was busted after a tip-off from the bank to the IRS. But the U.S. Financial Crimes Center (FinCEN) claims that bank employees were bribed to cooperate (*Trends,* July 1992).
49. Works on the topic of fake IDs go out of date quickly. But the most recent information is usually available through Loompanics Unlimited, which prides itself on being a publisher of rare and unusual books, or from such "financial planning" services as Scope International. The classic is M. L. Shannon, *The Paper Trip,* which has been undated several times, most recently in 1993 (San Francisco).
50. Gerald Posner, *Warlords of Crime* (New York, 1988), 225.
51. See Robert Powis, *Bank Secrecy Act Compliance,* 3d ed. (Rolling Meadows, Ill., 1989).
52. Max Mermelstein, the highest ranking "officer" of the so-called Medellín cartel to turn informant, told a U.S. congressional committee in 1989 that "Everybody would brag that the bank they were doing business with was never filing the paperwork, and that whoever they were dealing with at the bank was getting a percentage" (U.S. House of Representatives, Committee on Banking, Finance, and Urban Affairs, Subcommittee on Financial Institution Regulations, *Hearings,* November 14–15, 1989, 26).
53. For those with unique combinations of courage and imagination, there is another technique that plays on the weakness of the system for stopping the export of bulk cash. Cash is smuggled out of the United States, then brought back quite openly and declared at the border, particularly the Mexican border, as the means for or product of a legitimate business deal. At most the Customs officer is likely to suspect that it represents flight capital, something more than welcome in the United States. A CMIR form is issued and presented to the bank as proof of the legitimate character of the money. Once the money is deposited in a U.S. bank, it can be wired abroad to the haven of choice.
54. John Gregg, *How to Launder Money* (Port Townsend, Wisc., 1982), advised that the easiest solution was simply to rely on reverse psychology: if someone were willing to fill out the forms, the bank would assume they had nothing to hide.
55. Back in 1989, Terence Burke, the deputy administrator of the DEA, stated before a Senate hearing that "the volume of paperwork is such that we are receiving virtually no leads

from that documentation, from those CTRs, because the analysts are overwhelmed by the volume of it" (U.S. Senate, Foreign Relations Committee, Subcommittee on Terrorism, Narcotics, and International Operations, *International Money Laundering: Law Enforcement and Foreign Policy* [Washington, D.C., 1989], 14). However, in the same hearing before the same committee, Brian Bruh, head of FinCEN, disagreed (106).

56. When the scandal broke, the "crown prince" of the Hasidic sect involved fled to Israel, along with several of the principals, and only later returned to the United States with an injunction from his sect's highest religious court that he say nothing about the affair. See *Washington Jewish Week* 31/3/88; *North California Jewish Bulletin* 13/1/89; *Jerusalem Post* 7/4/88, 12/5/88; *Israeli Foreign Affairs*, May 1988, and February, April, and November 1989.

57. *Kol Ha'ir* 14/4/89.

58. *Yediot Ahronot* 17/7/92.

59. Ibid.; *Inside Israel*, November 1992.

60. There is excellent coverage of this and several related instances in *Israeli Foreign Affairs*, May 1993.

61. *Los Angeles Times* 12, 13, 28/1/93; *Forward* 29/1/93; *The Independent* 13/1/93; *Star Tribune* 13/1/93; *Observer* 21/2/93.

62. *New York Times* 17, 18/6/97; *Daily Telegraph* 18, 19/6/97; *Newsday* 23/6/97; *Los Angeles Times* 17–19/6/97.

63. This is a strange term. All bank accounts are numbered. The issue here is that the account is coded so that no one except top management can find out who the beneficial owner is. See Nicholas Faith, *Safety in Numbers: The Mysterious World of Swiss Banking* (New York, 1982). This book details much fascinating history, but its denunciations of Swiss banking practices are now out of date.

64. *The Economist* 20/8/88.

65. Technically a new national currency, the balboa, was created to replace the Colombian peso. In fact the balboa was fixed at parity to the dollar; the U.S. gold dollar was to circulate freely; Panama was only permitted to issue gold and silver coins, no bills; and the silver coins had to be secured by U.S. gold (Mario Hernandez, "Financial System of Panama," in *Emerging Financial Centers: Legal and Institutional Framework*, ed. Robert Effros [Washington, D.C., 1982]).

66. A good survey of the "service" economy is Stan Duncan, "The Spoils of War," *Dollars and Sense*, December 1990, although some of its assertions about Noriega and drug trafficking should be discounted.

67. There is a survey of the relevant laws in James Lorenzetti, "The Offshore Trust: A Contemporary Asset Protection Scheme," *Journal of Commercial Law Review* 102, no. 2 (1997). For a more popular exposition, see Arnold Goldstein, *How to Protect Your Money Offshore* (Deerfield Park, Fla., 1996).

68. A useful overview is Reinhard Stern, *The Austria and Liechtenstein Report* (Waterlooville, United Kingdom, 1994).

69. These are outlined in Gerhard Kurtz, *How to Profit and Avoid Taxes by Setting up Your Own Private International Bank* (Hong Kong, 1994); and Jerome Schneider, *Complete Guide to Offshore Financial Havens* (Beverly Hills, Calif., 1990).

70. The story is told in Jonathan Kwitney, *The Fountain Pen Conspiracy* (New York, 1973).

71. *Business Week* 23/9/91; *National Mortgage News* 30/12/91.

72. *Wall Street Journal* 8/2/83.

73. Schneider used his background to impress his clients with his big-league connections, telling them he had made off with $1 million in equipment; the company put the figure at $65,000 (*Los Angeles Times* 24/6/85, 16/4/89; *San Diego Union-Tribune* 29/2/84; *U.S. News and World Report* 1/8/83).

74. U.S. Senate, Committee on Governmental Affairs, Permanent Subcommittee on Investigations, *Crime and Secrecy* (Washington, D.C., 1983), 11–13.

75. *Washington Post* 23/4/89.
76. These banks were actually chartered in other locations but managed by a Bahamian off-shore company. The "Bahamas" label was a marketing device because the country had a much better reputation in banking circles than, say, Montserrat.
77. *The Economist* 16/3/91.
78. As a source of revenue, the banks were really not such a big deal. The license fees amounted to only 5 percent of government revenues. The real profits went to the promoters who sold the banks and a few local lawyers who handled the mechanics (*The Economist* 9/12/89).
79. *Latin America Regional Report—Caribbean* 28/9/89; *The Times* 8/1/90.
80. *U.S. News and World Report* 1/8/83.
81. *Wall Street Journal* 21/3/84, 20,30/4/84, 24/8/84; *San Diego Union-Tribune* 5/2/86.
82. *The Times* 3/2/90; *New York Times* 27/7/89; Michael Levi, "Pecunia Non Olet: Cleansing the Money-Launderers from the Temple," *Crime, Law, and Social Change* 16 (1991), 221. *Financial Post* 30/9/88.
83. *Latin America Regional Report—Caribbean* 5/4/90, 27/8/92; Economist Intelligence Unit, *Windward and Leeward Islands* (London, 1989), 23.
84. Robert Sherrill, *Oil Follies* (Garden City, N.Y., 1983), 512ff.; *Wall Street Journal* 23/3/87, 17, 26/6/87; *New York Times* 23/3/87, 16, 26/6/87; *Miami Herald* 26/6/87.
85. *American Banker* 2/11/81. *Prushinowski v. Samples*, U.S. Court of Appeals, Fourth Circuit, 24/5/84; *United Press International* 25/5/84.
86. *Observer* 20/12/92, 3/1/93, 21/2/93; *Calgary Herald* 3/1/93.
87. Richard Blum, *Offshore Haven Banks, Trusts, and Companies: The Business of Crime in the Euromarket* (New York, 1984), 98; *Pacific Islands Monthly*, September 1978, January 1979; *Wall Street Journal* 17/11/78; *Vancouver Sun* 25/8/79.
88. United Press International 10/2/86, 7/3/88.
89. U.S Senate, Permanent Subcommittee on Investigations, *Crime and Secrecy*, 31.
90. *Pacific Islands Monthly*, April 1987; *Wall Street Journal* 29/1/86, 1/8/86. Yet another of the area's finest was the First Bank of Saipan, purchased by an Ontario businessman with a criminal record for mail fraud, who used the bank to peddle worthless letters of credit (*Globe and Mail* 3/3/84).
91. *Los Angeles Times* 4/12/91.
92. *The Times* 3/2/90.
93. Kurtz, *How to Profit and Avoid Taxes*, 8–9.
94. *Money Laundering Alert*, April 2001; *International Enforcement Law Reporter* 17, no. 5 (May 2001).
95. A survey of early attempts is in Erwin Strauss, *How to Start Your Own Country*, 2d ed. (Port Townsend, Wisc., 1984).
96. *Bismarck Tribune* 21/5/89; *Cleveland Scene* 25/11/99; *American Banker* 5/2/88.
97. James Cocoran, *Bitter Harvest: Gordon Kahl and the Posse Comitatus* (New York, 1990), 25; *The Economist* 13/10/84, 2/11/85.
98. Phillip Finch, *God, Guts, and Guns* (New York, 1983), 105; *New York Times* 12/3/84.
99. *Time* 28/2/84; *Washington Post* 16/2/83.
100. *U.S News and World Report* 8/8/83.
101. According to law enforcement officers, the Posse-linked barter system served more than 20,000 people and laundered up to $500,000 per day. In fact, Posse itself never had more than 10,000 "members," and when barter houses across several states were raided, the police seized precious metals that were worth no more than $2 million. The raid was not exactly a brilliant success. The federal agents ran into trouble with a judge, who found that the warrants were too broadly written and thus impinged on freedom of association; he ordered the return of all seized bullion and documents (Cocoran, *Bitter Harvest*, 163; *New York Times* 11, 12/4/85).
102. Although groups from the fundamentalist Right attracted the most attention, the United States witnessed many other declarations of sovereignty, including those from Indian reser-

vations that hosted gambling and free-trade zones. Some reservations branched out into financial services. For example, two schemers set up a sovereign state called the Cherokee Sovereign Indian Nations and used it, along with a host of British Virgin Islands shell companies, to sell worthless insurance across the United States, mainly to people who could not get real coverage, such as cancer victims.

103. Russell Miller, *Bare-Faced Messiah* (London, 1987), chaps. 17 and 18.

104. There are a number of outstanding works that detail the LSD story. See in particular Stewart Tendler and David May, *The Brotherhood of Eternal Love* (London, 1983); and Martin Lee and Bruce Schlain, *Acid Dreams: The CIA, LSD, and the Sixties Rebellion* (New York, 1985). The CIA involvement is specifically treated in John Marks, *The Search for the Manchurian Candidate: The CIA and Mind Control* (reprint; New York, 1991). There is an excellent short overview by Mary Jo Worth, "The Story of the Acid Profiteers," *Village Voice*, August 22, 1974.

105. The Castle Bank story is recounted in Alan Block, *Masters of Paradise: Organized Crime and the Internal Revenue Service in the Bahamas* (New Brunswick, N.J., 1991).

106. His career is discussed in Robert A. Hutchison, *Vesco* (New York, 1974); and Arthur Herzog, *Vesco* (New York, 1987).

107. *Montreal Gazette* 8/7/89.

108. *Pacific Islands Monthly,* August and September 1972.

109. Strauss, *How to Start Your Own Country,* 113–20; Jerome Tuccille, *The Underground Economy* (New York, 1982), 29–43; Jim Hougan, *Spooks: The Haunting of America—The Private Use of Secret Agents* (New York, 1879), 98–99; *Wall Street Journal* 10/1/86; *Pacific Islands Monthly,* June and July 1980; *Far Eastern Economic Review* 12,20/6/80, 30/10/81; *Globe and Mail* 5/4/84. Actually, Vanuatu's offshore banking legislation dated from 1971, but little use was made of it until other legislative measures were added in the 1980s.

110. *Latin America Political Report* 1/6/79; *Latin America Regional Reports: Caribbean* 27/3/81; *New York Times* 7/6/81; Julian Sher, *White Hoods: Canada's Ku Klux Klan* (Vancouver, 1984), 166–79; James Dubro, *Mob Rule: Inside the Canadian Mafia* (Toronto, 1986), 291–94.

111. All this is recounted, in a somewhat one-sided way, in James Marcham's memoirs, *Paradise Raped: Life, Love, an Power in the Seychelles* (London, 1983).

112. *Africa Confidential* 17/3/78.

113. *Observer* 26/4/87.

114. *Time* 14/12/81; *Facts on File* 11/12/81; *Africa Confidential* 1/10/86, 4/11/87. Although the plot had apparently been worked out by representatives of the old regime and financed by selling future shares in a luxury casino they planned to build, it had the quiet backing of the South African intelligence services.

115. *Financial Times* 2/2/96; FinCEN Advisory, *Enhanced Scrutiny for Transactions Involving the Seychelles* 1, no. 2 (March 1996); Organisation for Economic Co-operation and Development (OECD), "Financial Action Task Force Condemns New Investment Law in Seychelles," OECD press release, Paris, 1/2/96.

116. *Dallas Observer* 2/5/96; *Washington Post* 5/11/95.

117. *Euromoney,* April 1991; *Forbes* 7/1/91.

118. The pioneering banks were in Portugal. By the middle of the 1990s, anonymously issued Portuguese cards were usable at no less than 2,250 cash dispensers in that country, along with most stores and restaurants, and its acceptability spread across the rest of Europe. Even prostitutes started to take it in payment (W. G. Hill, *Banking in Silence: The Complete Manual on How to Protect Your Money* [Rowlands Castle, United Kingdom, 1994], 139–41). Now banks in several countries issue the cards, on a selective basis, sometimes through the medium of brokerage companies.

119. Ibid., 131.

120. These have been recently offered to subscribers by Quester Press in Britain.

121. Hill, *Banking in Silence,* 155.
122. Some of the biggest money-laundering scandals of recent years in the United States have revolved around apparent abuse of the correspondent account (*Money Laundering Alert,* March and April 2001).
123. Gerhard Kurtz, *How to Become a Legal Holder of a Second Passport and Why You Should* (Hong Kong, 1994).
124. This is how, for example, one of the people involved in the Brinks-Mat gold heist in Britain brought money back from Panama—he sold a piece of property to his own Panama corporation for ten times the purchase price (*The Economist* 20/8/88).
125. In fact with an obliging broker, it is not necessary to work through offshore companies. The scam can operate just like a strictly onshore equivalent. One of the best examples was run between Hong Kong and the United States. In conjunction with a Hong Kong bank that set up dummy companies for clients, the U.S. firm would buy gold futures from and then sell them back to its clients. The deals were potentially very lucrative—the leverage involved meant that a $1 million investment could produce $30–40 million. Whichever way the market moved, the firm would tear up the losing ticket and send the money to the client in the United States disguised as a capital gain, less its own fee of 2–6 percent (Posner, *Warlords of Crime,* 233). For a thorough explanation of the use of international options, told by a master, Michele Sindona, see Nick Tosches, *Power on Earth: Michele Sindona's Explosive Story* (New York, 1986), 97.
126. Hill, *Banking in Silence,* 147–48; Global Consulting Group, *Client Loan Program: Confidential Information* (San José, Costa Rica, 1992).
127. Stern, *Austria and Liechtenstein Report,* 73.
128. *Wall Street Journal* 29/9/94.
129. See Marcel Cassard, "The Role of Offshore Centres in International Financial Intermediation," *International Monetary Fund Working Paper,* September 1994.

Chapter 5. The Underworld of Gold

Anyone wanting to understand gold today must start with the works of Timothy Green. I have also benefited greatly from the work and comments of several colleagues (Willard Myers notably among them) and students. This chapter has been greatly improved by the critical suggestions of industry insiders, who must remain anonymous.

1. There is a variety of fine old works on the role of gold and silver in the Spanish conquest of the Americas and its consequences. The classics are Alex Del Mar, *History of Monetary Systems* (New York, 1895); idem, *History of Money in America* (New York, 1899); and idem, *History of the Precious Metals* (New York, 1902). A more modern and drabber account is in Pierre Vilar, *History of Gold and Money* (London, 1976).
2. For the earlier role of bullion, see Eli Heckscher, *Mercantilism* (London, 1962).
3. See Arthur L. Smith, *Hitler's Gold* (Oxford, 1989). There has been recently a flood of attention to the phenomenon of Nazi gold and the role of Swiss banks, although it does little to change the overall picture. See, for example, William Slany, "U.S. and Allied Efforts to Recover and Restore Gold and Other Assets Stolen or Hidden by Germany during World War II," U.S. State Department, May 1997. The revival of the issue sparked a rash of books, including James Pool, *Hitler and His Secret Partners* (New York, 1997); Tom Bower, *Nazi Gold* (New York, 1997); Adam Lebor, *Hitler's Secret Bankers* (Secaucus, N.J., 1997); and Isabel Vincent, *Hitler's Secret Partners* (Toronto, 1997).
4. This story is told by Ian Sayer and Douglas Botting, *Nazi Gold* (New York, 1984).
5. Sterling Seagrave, *The Marcos Dynasty* (New York, 1988).
6. Timothy Green, *The Prospects for Gold* (London, 1987), 124; idem, *The World of Gold* (London, 1993), 2; *The Independent* 1/11/90; *Sacramento Bee* 2/5/93.
7. *The Economist* 16/1/88. Originally the Central Bank denied that there was any gold missing (*Financial Times* 15/3/86), perhaps in an effort to reassure nervous international creditors.

8. *Financial Times* 31/1/87.
9. Ibid., 12/9/74.
10. Ibid., 13/12/97.
11. *New York Times* 11/4/85, 3/7/88.
12. *South China Morning Post* 25/7/88.
13. Part of their story is related in James Hepburn, *The Black Flag* (London, 1994), 175–88.
14. U.S. Senate, Committee on Governmental Affairs, Permanent Subcommittee on Investigations, *Emerging Criminal Groups* (Washington, D.C., 1986), 70, 154.
15. *Los Angeles Times* 12/4/90.
16. *Financial Times* 10/12/84 contains a slightly different and rather puzzling account of the operation.
17. See, among other sources, Pierre Auchlin and Frank Garbely, *Contre-Enquête* (Lausanne, 1990); Jean Ziegler, *La suisse lave plus blanc* (Paris, 1990); Peter Furhman, "The Bulgarian Connection," *Forbes* 17/4/89; Daniel Zuberbuhler, *Enquête de la Commission fédérale des banques sur le comportement des grandes banques dans l'affaire Magharian/ blanchissage d'argent "Libanon-Connection"* (Bern, 1989); and *Le Hebdo* 15/8/88, 11/11/88, 15, 29/12/88, 9, 16/2/89, 2/3/89, 18/5/89.
18. For an overview of the operation of precious metals swindles at this time, see U.S. Senate, Committee on Governmental Affairs, Permanent Subcommittee on Investigations, *Commodity Investment Fraud* (Washington, D.C., 1984).
19. *Wall Street Journal* 20/3/84; *Financial Times* 18/11/83.
20. *Wall Street Journal* 12/10/83.
21. *New York Times* 7/9/88; *Wall Street Journal* 7/9/88.
22. *Barron's* 22/2/88; *Investor's Daily* 5/7/90; *Washington Post* 31/12/91.
23. *Financial Post* (Toronto) 29/10/94; *Sun-Sentinel* (Fort-Lauderdale) 5/11/94.
24. *Guardian* 19/10/94.
25. *Far Eastern Economic Review* 27/9/84.
26. *Middle East Times* 10/3/92.
27. *The Independent* 1/11/90; *Middle East Times* 30/7/91; *Sacramento Bee* 2/5/93.
28. *AIM*, April 1994.
29. *Mining Annual Review*, June 1992.
30. *Financial Times* 24, 25/3/01.
31. *Financial Times* 17/12/88; *Financial Post* 3/7/89; *New York Times* 23/8/93. The rush also bolstered Brazil's output of diamonds, and even of tin, sufficiently for it to challenge Malaysia's position as the number one world producer. See the excellent survey of the Amazon alluvial gold boom in Laura Jarnagin Pang and Eul-Soo Pang, "The Seamier Side of El Dorado," *Hemisfile* 7, no. 1 (January-February 1996); and idem, "Golden Rules," *Hemisfile* 7, no. 2 (March-April 1996). On the flesh trade, see *Sunday Times* 26/4/92.
32. *Globe and Mail* 30/8/93. One gold and diamond miner stated: "The opening of the Brazilian frontier is just like the American pioneers, with covered wagons fighting Indians. We don't have horses, we have airplanes" (*New York Times* 30/11/89). One explanation for some of the massacres was that Yanomani Indians were working as guides for the Venezuelan National Guard, who extort gold from the miners (*New York Times* 23/8/93).
33. *Time* 10/1/94; Jed Greer, "The Price of Gold," *The Ecologist*, May-June 1993.
34. Greenpeace, *The Real Face of the Kangaroo*, 2000).
35. These structures are examined in David Cleary, *Anatomy of the Amazon Gold Rush* (London, 1990).
36. *Latin America Weekly Report* 8/6/84.
37. At peak they accounted for 85 percent of gold production, although more recently the proportions have fallen drastically now that the easy pickings are gone. Industry sources have suggested the rate has dropped to only a bit above half.
38. *International Herald Tribune* 21/2/84; *Latin American Regional Report—Andean Region* 22/6/84; *Financial Times* 19/1/84; *New York Times* 30/11/89.

39. *Latin American Commodities Report* 15/6/84; *Financial Times* 25/3/88; *Globe and Mail* 17/5/90.

40. Private communication, December 1993.

41. *Latin American Commodities Report* 28/10/83, 22/6/84.

42. *Latin America Weekly Report* 26/3/87.

43. *Africa Confidential* 5/2/88; Green, *Prospects for Gold; Montreal Gazette* 4/1/97.

44. *Far Eastern Economic Review* 16/12/99.

45. *Canadian Business,* September 1986.

46. Diane Francis, *Contre-preneurs* (Toronto, 1988), 35–42.

47. *Panorama* 11/10/77; *The Times* 23/9/77, 21/12/77, 1/6/78, 15/9/78, 23/3/80; *Sunday Times* 22/5/77, 22/1/78, 17/9/78; *Vancouver Sun* 22,23/9/77, 15/9/78; *Globe and Mail* 23,24/9/77.

48. *Financial Post* 21, 30/5/97; *Barron's* 26/5/97.

49. *Financial Post* 26/4/97.

50. *Globe and Mail* 15/6/96.

51. Of several works on the Bre-X scandal, the best is Douglas Goold and Andrew Willis, *The Bre-X Fraud* (Toronto, 1997).

52. I am indebted to a former student for much of the information that follows. The actual numbers involved in the affair are difficult to pin down, so tangled were the maneuvers. The initial charges claimed a defalcation of $250 million (*Financial Times* 3/6/94). The International Monetary Fund calculated that several interrelated operations may have cost the government $430 million (*Financial Times* 10/6/94).

53. *Weekly Review* (Nairobi) 16, 23/4/93.

54. Ibid., 4/6/93.

55. *Daily Nation* 3/8/93.

56. Ibid., 3/5/93, 12/9/93, 2, 4, 12, 19/4/95, 20, 25/9/5, 8/9/95; *East African Standard* 4/4/95; *Financial Times* 10/6/94; *Weekly Review* 30/7/93, 6/8/93. There was also some suspicion that the Goldenberg operation was really a front for high-ranking members of the ruling party (*Africa Confidential* 19/3/93).

57. In Tanzania in 1988, the official data recorded gold output at forty-one kilograms, whereas the unofficial count put gold output at nine metric tons (*Financial Times* 11/9/90).

58. Ibid., 13/6/94.

59. Ibid., 11/12/85, 13/6/86, 19/2/94, 13/6/94; *New York Times* 17/7/95; *Chicago Tribune* 5/2/91; *Reuters* 20, 7/9/93.

60. David Kempton and Richard Levine, "Soviet and Russian Relations with Foreign Corporations: The Case of Gold and Diamonds," *Slavic Review* 54, no. 1 (spring 1995).

61. Green, *World of Gold,* 197.

62. Peter Furhman, "The Man with the Golden Headache," *Forbes* 18/9/89.

63. *Commersant* 2/6/93.

64. There are a number of unsubstantiated stories of thefts of gold reserves starting in 1990. By some accounts, the amount of looted gold by the end of 1991 had reached two thousand tons. There is a rather hysterical account in Claire Sterling, *Crime without Frontiers* (London, 1994), 169–70. See also Roland Jacquard, *La fin de l'empire rouge* (Paris, 1992), chap. 10.

65. This process is described well in *Financial Times* 22/6/92.

66. See Ragnar Benson, *Gunrunning for Fun and Profit* (Boulder, Colo., 1986), 2. Reputedly, Israeli arms dealers and Mossad agents also carry gold in their survival kits (Claire Hoy and Victor Ostrovsky, *By Way of Deception* [Toronto, 1990], 67).

67. *The Times* 18/6/83.

68. *New York Times* 8/2/90.

69. *Financial Times* 14/3/91.

70. The story is told in detail by Andrew Hogg, Jim McDougall, and Robin Morgan, *Bullion* (London, 1988); it is updated with much detail about the money flow in Jeffrey Robinson, *The Laundrymen* (London, 1994), chap. 9.

71. *Independent* 15/4/94; *The Times* 26/3/95, 2/8/95.

72. The story is told in Mihir Bose and Cathy Gunn, *Fraud: The Growth Industry of the Eighties* (London, 1989), chaps. 3 and 4.

73. Green, *Prospects for Gold,* 149, 193, 247.

74. *Le Hebdo* 2/3/89.

75. Ibid., 11/11/88.

76. There is an account of the bank's rise and fall in Nicholas Faith, *Safety in Numbers: The Mysterious World of Swiss Banking* (New York, 1982), 182.

77. U.S. Department of State, Bureau for International Narcotics and Law Enforcement Affairs, *International Narcotics Control Strategy Report* (Washington, D.C., 1995); *Guardian* 22/1/94.

78. This is a process well described in Timothy Green, *The World of Gold Today* (London, 1973).

79. *Financial Times* 23/2/87.

80. *Jerusalem Post* 5/7/90, 19/10/94, 13/3/96.

81. *Daily Telegraph* 8/1/93; *The Times* 8/1/93; *South China Morning Post* 9/1/93.

82. For a participant's account of the Tangier black market during the war, see the memoirs of a former British intelligence operative, Edward Wharton-Tigar, *Burning Bright* (London, 1987).

83. Jacques Delarue, *Trafics et crimes sous l'Occupation* (Paris, 1968), 42; René Sedillot, *Histoire du franc* (Paris, 1979), 194.

84. There is an excellent account in Alain Vernay, *Les paradis fiscaux* (Paris, 1968), chap. 2.

85. Alfred McCoy, *The Politics of Heroin* (New York, 1991), 292-93.

86. The Safra story is told in selective detail in Bryan Burroughs, *Vendetta: American Express and the Smearing of Edmund Safra* (New York, 1992).

87. *Financial Times* 23/2/87.

88. Green, *World of Gold,* 255.

89. See Petrus van Duyne, "Organized Crime and Business-Crime Enterprises in The Netherlands," *Crime, Law, and Social Change* 19 (1995).

90. *The Times* 19/10/92, 18/11/92; *Financial Times* 19/10/92; *Guardian* 21/10/92; *The Herald* (Glasgow) 19/10/92.

91. For a full explanation of the military pay certificate system, see R. T. Naylor, *Economic Warfare: Embargoes, Sanctions and Their Human Cost* (Boston, 2001), 63-65.

92. For a detailed examination of the Vietnam currency black market, see U.S. Senate, Judiciary Committee, Permanent Subcommittee on Investigations, *Illegal Currency Manipulations Affecting South Vietnam,* part 3 (Washington, D.C., 1969).

93. *Singapore Business Times* 21/9/95.

94. This information was relayed to me privately by a student who interviewed Mr. X about his business methods.

95. *Far Eastern Economic Review* 4/10/74, 24/5/90.

96. *Illustrated Weekly of India* 27/3/93; *India Today* 30/4/93.

97. Suraj Gupta, *Black Income in India* (Delhi, 1992), 87.

98. *Illustrated Weekly of India* 14/8/93.

99. For a partial inventory, see *AsiaWeek* 25/5/90, and *India Today* 31/10/86.

100. *Chicago Tribune* (4/2/91) reports on a group of Somali women caught by Bangladesh customers en route from Hong Kong to India with $170,000 worth of gold. The president's son was caught attempting to take twelve kilos of Sierra Leone gold into India just as his father had banned the private export of gold (*Observer* 14/6/87). In 1998, police in Sri Lanka arrested a postal official's son as part of a network in the Central Mail Exchange that was running a mail order gold-smuggling operation (*Shanghai Daily* 26/3/98).

101. An excellent overview of the role of the dhow is in Norman Miller, *The Indian Ocean: Traditional Trade on a Smuggler's Sea,* American Universities Field Staff, Africa/Asia 1980, no. 7 (Hanover, N.H., 1980).

102. An interesting perspective on the emergence of modern rackets in the Bombay area is found in Benedict Costa, *Bombay: The Twilight Zone* (Delhi, 1972).

103. Green, *World of Gold,* 296.

104. See variously Green, *World of Gold Today,* chap. 12; idem, *The Smugglers* (London, 1967), 208; *Illustrated Weekly of India* 10/11/74; M. A. Sujan and V. C. Trivadi, *Smuggling: The Inside Story* (Bombay, 1976), 30 and passim.

105. *Far Eastern Economic Review* 16/4/82.

106. *Saudi Gazette* 25/4/95.

107. See Timothy Green, *The World of Diamonds* (London, 1981), for interesting information on the emergence of the Indian cutting industry and its role in contraband movements.

108. *The Economist* 22/12/79.

109. *Far Eastern Economic Review* 29/12/88; *India Today* 31/10/88.

110. For an overview of the traditional traffic, before guns and drugs became so important, see Sujan and Trivadi, *Smuggling.*

111. There is a brief, partial overview in Angelina Malhotra, "India's Underground Bankers," *Asia, Inc.,* August 1995. This article incorrectly imputes to the Vietnam War the origins of India's havala banking system. In fact the system can be traced at least as far back as World War II.

112. See, for example, C. P. S. Nayyar, "Can a Traditional Financial Technology Co-Exist with Modern Financial Technologies: The Indian Experience," *Savings and Development* 10, no. 1 (1986); and Thomas Timberg and C. V. Aiyar, "Informal Credit Markets in India," *Economic Development and Cultural Change* (1984).

113. *Times of India* 22/6/86.

114. Two excellent works on the Indo-Pakistani underground banking system are Malhotra, "India's Underground Bankers"; and B. V. Kumar, "Capital Flight Operations and the Developing World," in *Money Laundering, Asset Forfeiture, and International Financial Crimes,* vol. 1, ed. Fletcher Baldwin and Robert Monro (New York, 1993).

115. *Illustrated Weekly of India* 10/11/74.

116. *Times of India* 22/6/86.

117. On this phenomenon, see, for example, Kamal Nayan Kubra, *The Black Economy in India* (Delhi, 1982); idem, *Black Money* (Delhi, 1985); and idem, *India's Black Economy and Maldevelopment* (Delhi, 1986).

118. *New York Times* 18/1/88; *The Economist* 11/5/91; *Illustrated Weekly of India* 15/3/93.

119. *India Today* 31/2/92; *AsiaWeek* 19/5/93; *Asia, Inc.,* August 1995.

120. *Economic and Political Weekly* 28/3/92; *India Today* 15/3/93; *Illustrated Weekly of India* 8/3/93.

121. *New York Times* 8/1/98.

122. *Institutional Investor,* January 1999.

123. *The Economist* 16/1/99.

124. Private communication.

125. *New York Times* 13/9/95.

126. *Time* 16/12/91; *Washington Times* 27/11/91; *Money Laundering Alert,* January 1993.

127. *Boston Globe* 21/10/84. This account is rather confused.

128. See Anne Woolner, *Washed in Gold* (New York, 1994); and Robert Powis, *The Money Launderers* (Chicago, 1992), chap. 5. Woolner's account gives much more detail surrounding the events and the investigation; that of Powis is considerably more analytical of the actual money movements. See also *Los Angeles Times* 27/12/90; *New York Times* 30/3/89, 14/8/89; *Wall Street Journal* 1/3/90; *Barron's* 26/6/89; *U.S. News and World Report* 21/8/89; *Time* 18/12/89.

129. For specific reasons, see R. T. Naylor, "From Underworld to Underground," *Crime, Law, and Social Change* 24 (1996).

130. *Los Angeles Times* 1/12/90, 27/2/91, 7/3/91.

131. Christopher Columbus, letter from Jamaica, 1503.

Chapter 6. Washout

1. See, for example, United Nations, Commission on Narcotic Drugs, *Countering Money Laundering* (Vienna, 1997).

2. In 1984, that opinion was concurred in by no less prestigious a body than the President's Commission on Organized Crime. "Without the ability to freely utilize its ill-gotten gains, the underworld will have been delivered a crippling blow" (President's Commission on Organized Crime, *The Cash Connection: Organized Crime, Financial Institutions, and Money Laundering* [Washington, D.C., 1984], 1n.).

3. Steven Kessler, *Civil and Criminal Forfeiture: Federal and State Practice* (New York, 1994) 140.

4. "We can strip the entrepreneurs of their illegal profits," not just current but past, claimed the chairman of the U.S. House of Representatives Foreign Affairs Committee in 1990 (*International Drug Money Laundering: Issues and Options for Congress* [Washington, D.C., 1990], 6). In Italy, too, the minister of the interior declared two years later, "We must hit them where it hurts most—in the pocket" (*Financial Times* 1/12/92).

5. *Washington Post* 18/9/89. For a dissection of the myth of the Medellín cartel, see Rensselaer Lee III, *The White Labyrinth: Cocaine and Political Power* (New Brunswick, N.J., 1989); and Francisco Thoumi, *Political Economy and Illegal Drugs in Colombia* (Boulder, Colo., 1995).

6. Testimony of Deputy Associate Attorney General Jeffrey Harris before the U.S. Senate, Judiciary Committee, Subcommittee on Security and Terrorism, "Drug Enforcement Administration Oversight and Authorization," 1982, as cited in David Fried, "Rationalizing Criminal Forfeiture," *Journal of Criminal Law and Criminology* 19, no. 2 (1988), 363n.

7. See Michael Brake and Chris Hale, *Public Order and Private Lives* (London, 1992).

8. On the forces behind Prohibition, see Mark Thornton, *The Economics of Prohibition* (Salt Lake City, Utah, 1991). See also the excellent treatment in Mike Gray, *Drug Crazy: How We Got into This Mess and How We Can Get Out* (New York, 1998).

9. This is well analyzed in Stephen Fox, *Blood and Power: Organized Crime in Twentieth Century America* (New York, 1989).

10. U.S. Senate, Committee on Banking, Housing, and Urban Affairs, Subcommittee on Consumer and Regulatory Affairs, *Drug Money Laundering Control Efforts* (Washington, D.C., 1990), 3.

11. *Money Laundering Alert,* June 2001.

12. This kind of legal imperialism was of course one of the main targets of the Leninist attack on capitalism in the early twentieth century. But even more moderate critics railed against it. See in particular John Hobson, *Imperialism: A Study* (London, 1907). A diagnosis of its effects also figured prominently in Karl Polanyi's post-mortem on the age of liberalism, *The Great Transformation* (Boston, 1947).

13. See especially Viviana Zelizer, *The Social Meaning of Money* (New York, 1994).

14. See the analysis of Anilise Anderson, *The Business of Organized Crime* (Stanford, Calif., 1979) and Peter Reuter, *The Organization Of Illegal Markets* (Washington, D.C., 1985).

15. For a survey of some of the worst excesses, see Rep. Henry Hyde, *Forfeiting Our Property Rights: Is Your Property Safe from Seizure?* (Washington, D.C., 1995). Forfeiture Endangers American Rights (FEAR) does an excellent job monitoring the abuses undertaken by the organization. See their web site at www.fear.org.

16. See, for example, Pino Arlacchi, "The Need for a Global Attack on Money-Laundering," in United Nations Office for Drug Control and Crime Prevention, *Attacking the Proceeds of Crime: Drugs, Money, and Laundering* (Vienna, 1998), 5–6.

17. Nicholas de Feir, "Asset Forfeiture: How Far Can U.S. Courts Go?" *International Financial Law Review,* March 1992.

18. *Business Week* 4/5/90.

19. Financial Action Task Force, *Report on Money-Laundering Techniques, 1996–97* (Paris, 1997), noted that members reported no new techniques for laundering money. That, of course, simply means police forces were unable to uncover any cases using new and presumably better techniques.

20. Charles Intriago, *International Money Laundering* (London, 1991), 55.

21. *Money Laundering Alert,* January and July 1999.

22. Allan Levine and Cindi Brandt, "Dirty Money," *Criminal Justice,* winter 1998. Yet the response of the U.S. Department of Justice to revelations of the gap between the sentencing guidelines for fraud and those for money laundering was to call for increased penalties for fraud to bring them up to the level of those for money laundering.

23. John K. Villa, "A Critical View of Bank Secrecy Act Enforcement and the Money Laundering Statutes," *Catholic University Law Review* 37 (1988), 497–500.

24. See especially Berta Esperanza Hernandez, "RIP to IRP—Money Laundering and Drug Trafficking Score a Knockout Victory over Bank Secrecy," *North Carolina Journal of International Law and Commercial Regulation* 18 (1993); and Mike Levi, "Regulating Money Laundering: The Death of Bank Secrecy in the U.K," *British Journal of Criminology* 31, no. 2 (spring 1991).

25. On the imbroglio over know-your-client rules, see *Money Laundering Alert,* March and April 1999.

26. Ibid., May and November 1994.

27. See, for example, the position of Chairman Frank Annunzio in a hearing before the House Banking Committee, of November 14–15, 1989: "The DEA has never developed a case based on the CTRs. . . . Just about every single money-laundering case starts with a tip." Noting that since 1984, 23 million CTRs had been filed yet the bureaucrats were asking for even tighter reporting regulations, he noted correctly that "we need not more reporting but better reporting" (2–3).

28. See the excellent discussion in Gray, *Drug Crazy,* 45, 78, 88.

29. Two decades later, former bootlegger and labor racketeer Frank Costello got the same treatment (Andrew Tully, *Treasury Agent* [New York, 1958], 9).

30. Former IRS Commissioner Fred Goldberg claimed that the lack of resources devoted to tax crimes from money of legal origin was a major contributing factor to the decline in voluntary compliance in the United States (*Money Laundering Alert,* February 1992).

31. Bureau of Justice Assistance, *Asset Forfeiture—The Management and Disposition of Seized Assets* (Washington, D.C., 1988), 3; Royal Canadian Mounted Police, *National Drug Intelligence Estimate* (Ottawa, 1988–89), 110.

32. See *Sunday Times* 2/8/92 for how the police force of Little Hampton, Rhode Island, became the richest force per capita in the United States, with all the latest gadgetry and fancy buildings, even though it was a village effectively without crime.

33. Leonard Levy, *License to Steal: The Forfeiture of Property* (Chapel Hill, 1996), 128–29.

34. *Globe and Mail* 15/11/94.

35. Many of these outrages were documented in 1991 by a series of articles on forfeiture in the *Pittsburgh Press;* they continue to be documented by Forfeiture Endangers American Rights (FEAR).

36. See R. T. Naylor, "From Underworld to Underground: Enterprise Crime, 'Informal Sector' Business, and the Public Policy Response," *Crime, Law, and Social Change* 24 (1996) for details.

37. For a time there was a concerted effort to prove that in Western countries the underground economy was enormous. See, for example, Bruno Frey and Werner Pommerehne, "Measuring the Hidden Economy: Though This Be Madness, There Is Method in It," in *The Underground Economy in the United States and Abroad,* ed. Vito Tanzi (Lexington, Ky., 1982). Their subtitle is half true. Today most of the research has been seriously questioned if not discredited outright. One of the finest critiques of the most popular method-

ology used to generate large numbers is Richard Porter and Amanda Bayer, "Monetary Perspectives on Underground Activity in the United States," in *The Underground Economies: Tax Evasion and Information Distortion*, ed. Edgar Feige (New York, 1989). See the recent symposium on measuring the underground economy in *Economic Journal* 109, no. 456 (June 1999); and Phillip Smith, "Assessing the Size of the Underground Economy in Canada: The Statistics Canada Perspective," *Canadian Economic Observer*, May 1994.

38. Apart from Naylor, "Underworld to Underground," there have been remarkably few systematic efforts to dissect the behavioral differences, and consequences of those differences, between legal and illegal money flows. For one exception, see Thoumi, *Political Economy and Illegal Drugs in Colombia*.

39. On the impact of capital flight, see Donald Lessard and John Williamson, *Capital Flight and Third World Debt* (Washington, D.C., 1987).

40. The best analysis is in Mushtaq Khan, *Potential Use of the Black Economy: The Case of Bearer Bond Schemes in Pakistan* (Islamabad, 1989).

41. On the latest in a series of such efforts, see Raja Asghar, "Pakistan Offers No-Questions Dollar, Pound Bonds," Reuters 2/10/98.

42. On the process of acquiring wealth by Marcos and his associates, see Sterling Seagrave, *The Marcos Dynasty* (New York, 1988); and Belinda Aquino, *The Politics Of Plunder* (Quezon City, The Philippines, 1987). Both should be read with a certain degree of skepticism.

43. *Far Eastern Economic Review* 17/10/87, 4/8/87; *New York Times* 17/10/88; *The Economist* 15/8/88.

44. When some states began using controlled substance taxes to add further charges against drug traffickers, law enforcement fought against the principle, seeing in it the first step to the state resurrecting its prior claim to illegal profits. The Boston police superintendent, for example, insisted that "We would fight all the way any attempt by the state to take a cut of that money" ("Bulletin of Justice Assistance," *Asset Forfeiture Bulletin*, December 1989, 4).

Afterword: Satanic Purses

1. My thanks to George Archer, Jack Blum, Asif Hasnain, Homa Hoodfar, Mike Levi, Azfar Khan, and Sam Noumoff for comments and criticisms on early drafts of this afterword.

2. Two of the best works on the issue are John Cooley, *Unholy Wars: Afghanistan, America and International Terrorism*, 2d ed. (London, 2000); and Ahmed Rashid, *Taliban: Militant Islam, Oil, and Fundamentalism in Central Asia* (New Haven, 2001).

3. Bin Laden's money is the key to his power, U.S. officials and CIA analysts have long insisted. (*Washington Post* 28/8/98.)

4. See, for example, *The Express* 1/10/01.

5. "Havala" is the most common rendering for the underground banking system and is used in India. But, tracing it back to its Arabic roots, it should be spelled "hawalah," while in Pakistan it is more commonly called the "hundi" system.

6. *The Independent* 19/9/01. For an excellent example of this process of assigning guilt by association with an "associate" see *Boston Herald* 14/10/01.

7. The British government's recent public statement of the "case" was also prefaced with such a disclaimer. It was posted to the UK government's website on Oct. 5, 2001 under the title "Responsibility for the Terrorist Atrocities in the United States, 11 September 2001."

8. Mary Anne Weaver, "The Real bin Laden" *New Yorker*, 24/01/00.

9. Here there may be an element of fact. Osama bin Laden's brother-in-law operates charities in the Moro areas using Saudi money. Whether the charities are "fronts" or "scams" for funding the Abu Sayyaf rebel group is another matter. (*Newsweek* 22/10/01.) In any event the group was one of the beneficiaries of extensive U.S. official aid in Afghanistan

and simply transferred personnel to the Philippines afterward. Hence, the CIA can be seen as just as guilty of running scams and fronts and of training rebel cadres for the Philippines as bin Laden, likely more so.

10. Weaver, "Real bin Laden."
11. John Prados, *President's Secret Wars: CIA and Pentagon Covert Operations since World War II* (New York, 1986), 64.
12. *New York Times* 11/11/2001.
13. Cooley, *Unholy Wars*, 22–23
14. The best overview is in Alfred McCoy, *The Politics of Heroin in Southeast Asia* (New York, 1972) and *The Politics of Heroin: CIA Complicity in the Global Drug Trade* (New York, 1991).
15. For a summary, see R. T. Naylor, *Economic Warfare: Sanctions, Embargoes, and Their Human Cost* (Boston, 2001), Chap. 5, or *Patriots and Profiteers: On Economic Warfare, Embargo-Busting, and State-Sponsored Crime* (Toronto, 1999), Chap. 5.
16. Cooley, *Unholy Wars*, 81–97, 223, 243
17. *New York Times* 28/10/01; Weaver, "Real bin Laden."
18. Cooley, *Unholy Wars*, 121; *Financial Times* 24/9/01; *The Independent* 16/9/01.
19. *Financial Times* 28/9/01; Rashid, *Taliban*, 27, 139.
20. *The Scotsman* 20/9/01.
21. On black propaganda involving drugs, see Edward Jay Epstein, *Agency of Fear: Opiates and Political Power in America* (New York, 1990).
22. *New York Times* 22/10/01; *Financial Times* 14/10/01; *The Scotsman* 4/10/01; Rashid, *Taliban*, 100–24.
23. *Wall Street Journal* 20/9/01; *Financial Times* 24/9/01.
24. *New York Times* 11/11/2001.
25. *New York Times* 20/9/01.
26. *New York Times* 5/10/01; *Money Laundering Alert* Oct. 2001.
27. Dr. James Zogby in *Moneyclips* 4/2/95.
28. *New York Times* 3/11/01.
29. *New York Times* 9/11/01.
30. In the only comprehensive look at the phenomenon, Nikos Passas noted that informal value-transfer systems of this type do not represent any money-laundering threat different from that of ordinary banking, that the overwhelming share of their transactions are either totally legitimate or represent things like minor tax- or exchange–control evasion schemes, and that much of the fuss in the press is based on a few sensationalized instances. (Nikos Passas, *Informal Value Transfer Systems and Criminal Organizations*, study done for the Dutch Ministry of Justice, 1999.)
31. Thanks to Azfar Khan and his fieldwork among the Pathan (Pashtu) peoples of Pakistan's North-West Frontier province. Private communication.
32. *Financial Times* 25/10/01. On the other hand, in Pakistan, so much money has been rushed home for fear it will be confiscated in this western numismatic jihad that the Central Bank has had to intervene to support the dollar against a rapidly climbing rupee. (*Financial Times* 5/10/01.)

Index